HOLT McDOUGAL LITE

Interactive Reader

GRADE 6

Printed in the U.S.A.

ISBN-13 978-0-547-27139-2

ISBN-10 0-547-27139-5

9 10 0982 18 17 16 15 14

4500507897

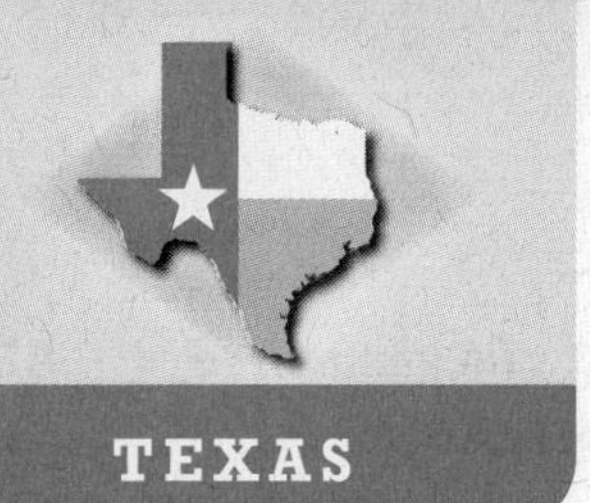

TABLE OF CONTENTS

TEXAS SKILLS

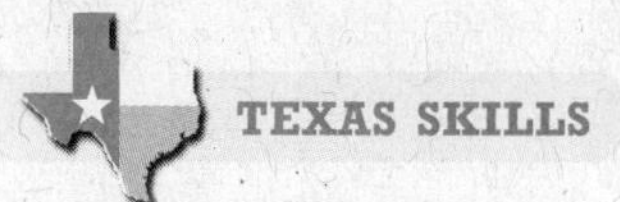
TEXAS SKILLS

TEXAS SKILLS

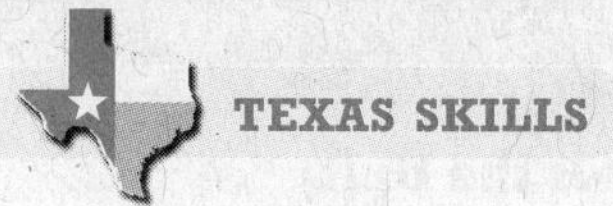

RESOURCES

Academic Vocabulary for Unit 1

Academic Vocabulary is the language you use to discuss literary and informational texts. Preview the following Academic Vocabulary words. You will use these words as you write and talk about the selections in this unit.

affect (ə-fekt') *v.* to produce a response or reaction
*How does the main character's fear **affect** his behavior?*

analyze (an'ə-līz') *v.* to separate, or break into parts and examine
***Analyze** the story's plot and decide if you find it realistic.*

evidence (ev'ə-dəns) *n.* specific information that supports a claim
*What **evidence** does the author use to support her claim?*

impact (im-pakt') *v.* to have a direct effect on
*How does this action **impact** the resolution of the plot?*

provide (prə-vīd') *v.* to supply; make something available
***Provide** examples from the story to support your opinion.*

Think of a movie or TV show that you've seen and enjoyed lately. Briefly describe your experience, using at least two Academic Vocabulary words in your response. **Analyze** how the movie or TV show **affected** you.

ACADEMIC VOCABULARY 3

Academic Vocabulary for the Unit

Academic vocabulary is the language you use to talk and write about the subjects you are studying, including math, science, social studies, and language arts. It is the language you use in your classroom and the language you find in books, tests, and formal writing. Understanding and using academic vocabulary correctly will help you succeed in school and on assessments.

You will find five academic vocabulary words, defined for ready reference and use at the beginning of each unit. You will have the opportunity to practice using these words after each selection.

Before Reading

All Summer in a Day

Short Story by Ray Bradbury

READING 6A Summarize elements of plot development (e.g., rising action, turning point, climax, falling action, denouement) in various works of fiction.

What if your whole WORLD changed?

People often become comfortable in the familiar world of their family, friends, and daily routines. However, people move and traditions change. When your world changes, whether by a little or a lot, it can have an impact on your life. In "All Summer in a Day," a young girl feels lost in a new place.

LIST IT List the people, places, events and ideas in your world that are most precious to you. How would you feel if any of these things disappeared?

My World

People

Places

Events

Ideas

Literary Analysis: Plot and Setting

The **plot** is the series of events that make up a story, including the conflict and its resolution. **Setting** is *where* and *when* a story takes place. In science fiction stories, the setting is often the distant future. This setting usually causes the events of the plot to unfold in an unexpected way. As you read "All Summer in a Day," look for clues that tell you when and where the story takes place. Record setting details in the chart below. Use these details to think about the setting's influence on the story's conflict and resolution, or denouement.

Setting Details	Influence on the Conflict and Resolution
"It had been raining for seven years."	*Students are anxious to see the sun.*

18 INTERACTIVE READER / UNIT 1: PLOT, CONFLICT, AND SETTING

Before Reading

Before Reading pages introduce you to the literary and reading skills you will practice as you read. Vocabulary words for the selection are introduced here as well.

Big Question

Each selection or group of selections begins with an activity that gets you thinking about the real-life questions that literature addresses. Sometimes you'll work in a group or with a partner to complete this activity. After reading, you'll return to this activity. Don't be surprised if you have a different perspective.

Literary Analysis

This section presents a brief, easy-to-understand lesson that introduces an important literary element and explains what to look for in the selection you are about to read.

Reading Skill: Make Inferences

As a reader you are a detective. Details, events, and dialogue in a story are your clues. You put the clues together with your own knowledge to **make inferences,** or guesses.

As you read "All Summer in a Day," use an equation like the one shown to record the inferences you make about the characters' feelings and their actions.

RC-6(D) Make inferences about text.

Clues from the Story		My Knowledge		Inference
Margot is not part of the group.	+	*Not being part of a group can make you feel sad.*	=	*Margot feels sad.*

Vocabulary in Context

Note: Words are listed in the order in which they appear in the story.

slacken (slăk'ən) *v.* to slow down or lessen
They hope the sun will come out when the rain ***slackens.***

apparatus (ăp'ə-răt'əs) *n.* a device or set of equipment used for a specific purpose
The ***apparatus*** *used to open the hatch was broken.*

immense (ĭ-mĕns') *adj.* extremely big; huge
The ***immense*** *planet offered many areas to explore.*

tumultuously (tōō-mŭl'chōō-əs'lē) *adv.* in a wild or disorderly way
Branches and leaves shook ***tumultuously*** *during the storm.*

resilient (rĭ-zĭl'yənt) *adj.* flexible and springy
The sturdy shelters are built to be ***resilient*** *to high winds.*

savor (sā'vər) *v.* to take great pleasure in
The traveler sat quietly to ***savor*** *the unusual landscape.*

Vocabulary Practice

Review the vocabulary words. Ray Bradbury uses these words to create a world that is very different from our own. Use at least two of these words in a description of the world you inhabit.

ALL SUMMER IN A DAY 19

Reading Skill or Strategy

This lesson presents a reading skill or strategy that will help your reading comprehension, such as making inferences, making connections, or paraphrasing. You will have opportunities to practice these skills as you read the selection.

Vocabulary in Context

Vocabulary words for the selection are introduced before reading. Each entry gives the pronunciation and definition of the word as well as a context sentence. **Vocabulary Practice** activities give you an opportunity to use selection vocabulary.

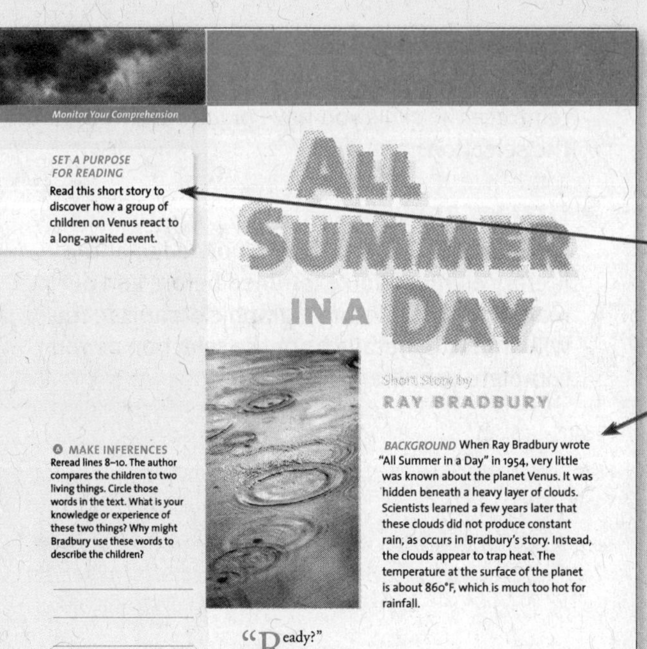

Monitor Your Comprehension

SET A PURPOSE FOR READING
Read this short story to discover how a group of children on Venus react to a long-awaited event.

ALL SUMMER IN A DAY

Short Story by
RAY BRADBURY

BACKGROUND When Ray Bradbury wrote "All Summer in a Day" in 1954, very little was known about the planet Venus. It was hidden beneath a heavy layer of clouds. Scientists learned a few years later that these clouds did not produce constant rain, as occurs in Bradbury's story. Instead, the clouds appear to trap heat. The temperature at the surface of the planet is about 860°F, which is much too hot for rainfall.

"Ready?"
"Ready."
"Now?"
"Soon."
"Do the scientists really know? Will it happen today, will it?"
"Look, look; see for yourself!"
The children pressed to each other like so many roses, so many weeds, intermixed, peering out for a look at the hidden sun.

MAKE INFERENCES
Reread lines 8–10. The author compares the children to two living things. Circle those words in the text. What is your knowledge or experience of these two things? Why might Bradbury use these words to describe the children?

20 INTERACTIVE READER / UNIT 1: PLOT, CONFLICT, AND SETTING

Reading the Selection

Notes in the side columns guide your interaction with the selection. Many notes ask you to underline or circle in the text itself. Others provide lines on which you can write your responses.

Set a Purpose for Reading

This feature gives you a reason for reading the selection.

Background

This paragraph provides important information about the selection you are about to read. It helps you understand the context of the literature through additional information about the author, the subject, or the time period during which the selection was written.

Monitor Your Comprehension

apparatus, thus muffling and finally cutting off all noise, all of the blasts and repercussions and thunders, and then, secondly, ripped the film from the projector and inserted in its place a peaceful tropical slide which did not move or tremor. The world ground to a standstill. The silence was so immense and unbelievable that you felt that your ears had been stuffed or you had lost your hearing altogether. The children put their hands to their ears. They stood apart. The door slid back and the smell of the silent, waiting world came in to them.

The sun came out. ⓒ

It was the color of flaming bronze and it was very large. And the sky around it was a blazing blue tile color. And the jungle burned with sunlight as the children, released from their spell, rushed out, yelling, into the summer-time.

"Now, don't go too far," called the teacher after them. "You've only one hour, you know. You wouldn't want to get caught out!"

But they were running and turning their faces up to the sky and feeling the sun on their cheeks like a warm iron; they were taking off their jackets and letting the sun burn their arms.

"Oh, it's better than the sun-lamps, isn't it?"

"Much, much better!"

They stopped running and stood in the great jungle that covered Venus, that grew and never stopped growing, tumultuously, even as you watched it. It was a nest of octopuses, clustering up great arms of flesh-like weed, wavering, flowering in this brief spring. It was the color of rubber and ash, this jungle, from the many years without sun. It was the color of stones and white cheeses and ink. ⓓ

The children lay out, laughing, on the jungle mattress, and heard it sigh and squeak under them, resilient and alive. They ran among the trees, they slipped and fell, they

apparatus (ăp'ə-răt'əs) *n.* a device or set of equipment used for a specific purpose

immense (ĭ-mĕns') *adj.* extremely big; huge

ⓒ SETTING
Reread lines 134–148. What changes do the children notice when the rain stops?

tumultuously (tōō-mŭl'chōō-əs'lē) *adv.* in a wild or disorderly way

ⓓ SETTING
Underline words and phrases that describe what is unusual about the plants on Venus.

resilient (rĭ-zĭl'yənt) *adj.* flexible and springy

ALL SUMMER IN A DAY 25

Side notes provide a variety of activities for you to complete as you read the selection.

Literary Analysis or **Reading Skill** or **Strategy**

These notes help you identify and analyze the literary element or reading skill you learned about on the **Before Reading** pages.

Vocabulary words

Vocabulary words introduced on the **Before Reading** page are defined in the side column and appear underlined in blue within the selection, allowing you to see them in context.

Additional Side Notes

Pause & Reflect notes give you a chance to stop reading and take time to think about what you have just read.

Visual Vocabulary provides photographs in addition to definitions, to illustrate the meaning of words when it helps to picture a word's meaning.

After Reading

Literary Analysis: Plot and Setting

The setting of "All Summer in a Day" is a key influence on the plot. In the Setting Circle below, fill in the middle circle with details about the setting. The fill in the outer circle with plot important plot events from the story. Finally, use your completed chart to answer the question that follows.

READING 6A Summarize elements of plot development (e.g., rising action, turning point, climax, falling action, denouement).

Story Event
The children are waiting for the rain to stop

Story Event

Setting

Story Event

Story Event

Think about how the setting of this story influences the plot, including the conflict and resolution. Would there still be a story if Bradbury's Venus had less extreme weather? Explain.

ALL SUMMER IN A DAY 29

After Reading

After Reading pages feature graphic organizers to reinforce the skills you have practiced throughout the selection.

Literary Analysis

Here you demonstrate your knowledge of the literary element you examined before and during reading by completing a graphic organizer. You will often cite details from the selection as you complete your literary analysis.

After Reading

Reading Skill: Make Inferences

Make an inference about each character based on details from the story.

RC-6(D) Make inferences about text.

MARGOT	**Detail:** will not play games or participate in class activities with other children (lines 68–75)
My Inference:	
WILLIAM	**Detail:** pushes and shoves Margot as they wait to see the sun (lines 102–111)
My Inference:	
THE CHILDREN	**Detail:** look at each other and then away (lines 214–219)
My Inference:	

What if your whole WORLD changed?

How might the children in the story change now that they have seen the sun?

Vocabulary Practice

For each numbered item below, choose the word that differs most in meaning from the other words.

1. (a) prepare, (b) appreciate, (c) enjoy, (d) savor
2. (a) appliance, (b) device, (c) apparatus, (d) operator
3. (a) slacken, (b) enlarge, (c) decrease, (d) lessen
4. (a) enormous, (b) immense, (c) distant, (d) gigantic
5. (a) tumultuously, (b) carefully, (c) thoughtfully, (d) cautiously
6. (a) elastic, (b) nervous, (c) flexible, (d) resilient

30 INTERACTIVE READER / UNIT 1: PLOT, CONFLICT, AND SETTING

Reading Skill or Strategy

The Reading Skill or Strategy activity follows up on the skill you used to help you understand the text.

Big Question

Here's a chance to think again about the Big Question you examined before reading. It offers an opportunity to consider whether your viewpoint has changed now that you have read the selection.

Vocabulary Practice

This activity helps you assess your understanding of the selection vocabulary words.

Academic Vocabulary in Speaking

affect	analyze	evidence	impact	provide

TURN AND TALK With a partner, discuss the possible **impact** on Margot of being shut in the closet. Record **evidence** from the text in the lines below to support your response. Use at least two Academic Vocabulary words in your discussion. Definitions of the words are on page 3.

READING 6A Summarize elements of plot development (e.g., rising action, turning point, climax, falling action, denouement).

Texas Assessment Practice

DIRECTIONS Use "All Summer in a Day" to answers questions 1–6.

1 The setting of the story is —
  - (A) a space station
  - (B) a remote area on Earth
  - (C) the planet Venus
  - (D) a planet in a distant galaxy

2 You can infer that when Margot is locked inside the closet she feels —
  - (F) embarrassed
  - (G) jealous
  - (H) content
  - (J) miserable

3 The most important aspect of the story's setting is —
  - (A) weather conditions on Venus
  - (B) the tunnels in the school
  - (C) the time of day
  - (D) the season of the year.

4 From William's words and actions you can infer that he —
  - (F) is impressed by Margot
  - (G) is helpful to newcomers in his class
  - (H) resents Margot's presence in the school
  - (J) wants to be liked by classmates

5 You can infer that Margot's parents are worried about her because they —
  - (A) brought her to live on Venus
  - (B) spoke to the teacher about her behavior
  - (C) read her poem about the sun
  - (D) are considering moving back to Earth

6 Which setting detail moves the plot to its resolution?
  - (F) An hour passes.
  - (G) It starts raining again.
  - (H) The children go back inside.
  - (J) The children let Margot out of the closet.

ALL SUMMER IN A DAY 31

Academic Vocabulary

In this activity, you use the academic vocabulary words for the unit in a speaking or writing activity about the selection.

Texas Assessment Practice

Finally, after each selection, multiple-choice questions assess your knowledge of the selection and the skill taught with it.

Included in this unit: TEKS 5, 6A, 10D, 12B, RC-6(C), RC-6(D), RC-6(E), RC-6(F)

UNIT 1 What's Happening?

PLOT, CONFLICT, AND SETTING

Be sure to read the Reader's Workshop on pp. 28–33 in *Holt McDougal Literature*.

Academic Vocabulary for Unit 1

Academic Vocabulary is the language you use to discuss literary and informational texts. Preview the following Academic Vocabulary words. You will use these words as you write and talk about the selections in this unit.

affect (a-fekt') *v.* to produce a response or reaction
*How does the main character's fear **affect** his behavior?*

•

analyze (an'ə-līz') *v.* to separate, or break into parts and examine
***Analyze** the story's plot and decide if you find it realistic.*

•

evidence (ev'ə-dəns) *n.* specific information that supports a claim
*What **evidence** does the author use to support her claim?*

•

impact (im-pakt') *v.* to have a direct effect on
*How does this action **impact** the resolution of the plot?*

•

provide (prə-vīd') *v.* to supply; make something available
***Provide** examples from the story to support your opinion.*

Think of a movie or TV show that you've seen and enjoyed lately. Briefly describe your experience, using at least two Academic Vocabulary words in your response. **Analyze** how the movie or TV show **affected** you.

READING 6A Summarize elements of plot development (e.g., rising action, turning point, climax, falling action, denouement).

The School Play

Short Story by **Gary Soto**

What do you FEAR most?

Have you ever jumped at the sight of a harmless bug? Or, maybe you have waited a long time to ride a roller coaster only to change your mind when it was your turn. Things that frighten people range from big to small, from living to nonliving, from the seen to the unseen. In "The School Play," a student struggles to overcome a fear many people face.

SURVEY What are you most afraid of? Some of the most common fears people have are listed in the survey in the side column. Rank the fears from one to ten, with one being the thing you are most afraid of. Then survey the class to find out what is the most common fear in your classroom.

Face Your Fears!

Rank the following fears 1–10 to see what scares you the most:

_____ *Heights*

_____ *Spiders and Insects*

_____ *Being in the Dark*

_____ *Dentists*

_____ *Thunder and Lightning*

_____ *Failing a Test*

_____ *Being Bullied*

_____ *Airplane Rides*

_____ *Public Speaking*

_____ *Being in a Crowd*

Literary Analysis: Plot Elements

Everything in a story happens for a reason. The series of events is the story's **plot**. The plot usually follows a pattern, as shown in this graphic.

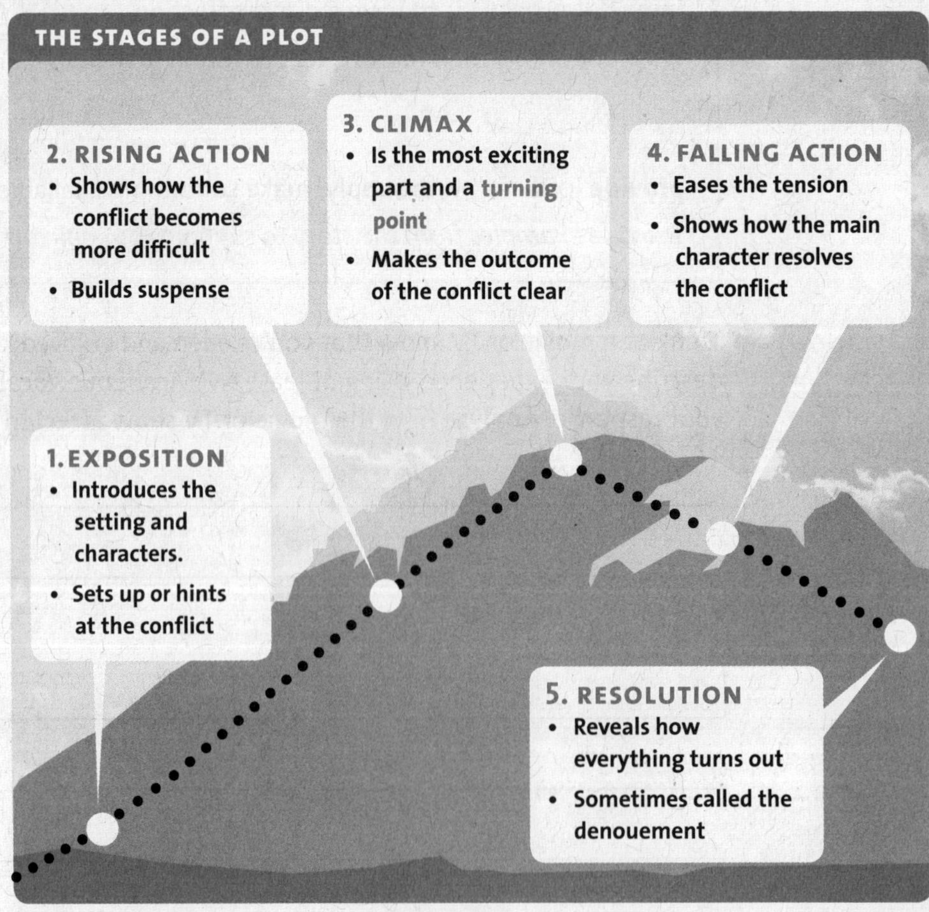

THE STAGES OF A PLOT
1. EXPOSITION
• Introduces the setting and characters.
• Sets up or hints at the conflict
2. RISING ACTION
• Shows how the conflict becomes more difficult
• Builds suspense
3. CLIMAX
• Is the most exciting part and a turning point
• Makes the outcome of the conflict clear
4. FALLING ACTION
• Eases the tension
• Shows how the main character resolves the conflict
5. RESOLUTION
• Reveals how everything turns out
• Sometimes called the denouement

As you read "The School Play," notice the events that occur in each stage of the story's plot.

Reading Strategy: Monitor

RC-6(C) Monitor and adjust comprehension (rereading a portion aloud; generating questions).

Have you ever forgotten what you just read? To avoid this problem, **monitor** your reading by pausing occasionally to check your understanding. One way to monitor is to ask yourself questions about what you are reading. Sometimes you'll need to reread to find the answer. Other times you'll find the answer later on in the story.

As you read "The School Play," record questions about what is happening in the story in a chart like the one shown.

My Questions	Answers
What is inside the cardboard box?	

Vocabulary in Context

Note: Words are listed in the order in which they appear in the story.

prop (prŏp) *n.* an object an actor uses in a play
*The main **prop** in the play is a map of the West.*

smirk (smûrk) *v.* to smile in an insulting way
*Belinda wanted to **smirk** when the actor forgot his lines.*

relentless (rĭ-lĕnt′lĭs) *adj.* refusing to stop or give up
*The audience's **relentless** talking distracts the actors.*

narrative (năr′ə-tĭv) *n.* a story
*Robert's friend delivers the **narrative** about the background of the play.*

Vocabulary Practice

Review the vocabulary words and think about their meanings. Then write a prediction about the conflict you think the main character of "The School Play" will face.

SET A PURPOSE FOR READING

Read this short story to discover how one young actor deals with his stage fright.

THE SCHOOL PLAY

Short Story by

GARY SOTO

BACKGROUND In this story, sixth-grade students perform a play about a group of settlers known as the Donner Party. While trying to cross the Sierra Nevada Mountains in eastern California, the Donner Party was trapped in a snowstorm. The travelers ran out of food and some died of starvation. In desperation, some group members ate the bodies of the dead.

A PLOT: EXPOSITION
Pause at line 10. What background information have you learned about Robert? Circle what you learn about Belinda.

In the school play at the end of his sixth-grade year, all Robert Suarez had to remember to say was, "Nothing's wrong. I can see," to a pioneer woman, who was really Belinda Lopez. Instead of a pioneer woman, Belinda was one of the toughest girls since the beginning of the world. She was known to slap boys and grind their faces into the grass so that they bit into chunks of wormy earth. More than once Robert had witnessed Belinda staring down the janitor's pit bull, who licked his frothing chops but didn't dare mess with her. A

The class rehearsed for three weeks, at first without costumes. Early one morning Mrs. Bunnin wobbled into the classroom lugging a large cardboard box. She wiped her brow and said, "Thanks for the help, Robert."

Robert was at his desk scribbling a ballpoint tattoo that spelled DUDE on the tops of his knuckles. He looked up and stared, blinking at his teacher. "Oh, did you need some help?" he asked.

She rolled her eyes at him and told him to stop writing on his skin. "You'll look like a criminal," she scolded.

Robert stuffed his hands into his pockets as he rose from his seat. "What's in the box?" he asked.

She muttered under her breath. She popped open the taped top and brought out skirts, hats, snowshoes, scarves, and vests. She tossed Robert a red beard, which he held up to his face, thinking it made him look handsome.

"I like it," Robert said. He sneezed and ran his hand across his moist nose.

His classmates were coming into the classroom and looked at Robert in awe. "That's bad," Ruben said. "What do I get?"

Mrs. Bunnin threw him a wrinkled shirt. Ruben raised it to his chest and said, "My dad could wear this. Can I give it to him after the play is done?"

Mrs. Bunnin turned away in silence. **PAUSE & REFLECT**

Most of the actors didn't have speaking parts. They just got cutout crepe-paper snowflakes to pin to their shirts or crepe-paper leaves to wear.

During the blizzard in which Robert delivered his line, Belinda asked, "Is there something wrong with your eyes?" Robert looked at the audience, which at the moment was a classroom of empty chairs, a dented world globe that had been dropped by almost everyone, one limp flag, one

Monitor Your Comprehension

PAUSE & REFLECT

Reread lines 19–35. Underline words and phrases that tell what Mrs. Bunnin is like. What kind of relationship does Mrs. Bunnin have with her students? Use words that you've underlined in your response.

Monitor Your Comprehension

prop (prŏp) *n.* an object an actor uses in a play

B PLOT: RISING ACTION
Reread lines 50–66. What **conflict**, or struggle, is developing?

smirk (smûrk) *v.* to smile in an insulting way

Why does Belinda smirk?

C MONITOR
What is the actual line Belinda is supposed to say?

wastebasket, and a picture of George Washington, whose eyes followed you around the room when you got up to sharpen your pencil. Robert answered, "Nothing's wrong. I can see."

Mrs. Bunnin, biting on the end of her pencil, said, "Louder, both of you."

Belinda stepped up, nostrils flaring so that the shadows on her nose quivered, and said louder, "Sucka, is there something wrong with your eye-balls?"

"Nothing's wrong. I can see."

"Louder! Make sure the audience can hear you," Mrs. Bunnin directed. She tapped her pencil hard against the desk. She scolded, "Robert, I'm not going to tell you again to quit fooling with the beard."

"It's itchy."

"We can't do anything about that. Actors need **props**. You're an actor. Now try again."

Robert and Belinda stood center stage as they waited for Mrs. Bunnin to call "Action!" When she did, Belinda approached Robert slowly. "Sucka face, is there anything wrong with your mug?" Belinda asked. Her eyes were squinted in anger. For a moment Robert saw his head grinding into the playground grass. **B**

"Nothing's wrong. I can see."

Robert giggled behind his red beard. Belinda popped her gum and **smirked**. She stood with her hands on her hips.

"What? What did you say?" Mrs. Bunnin asked, pulling off her glasses. "Are you chewing gum, Belinda?"

"No, Mrs. Bunnin," Belinda lied. "I just forgot my lines." **C**

Belinda turned to face the snowflake boys clumped together in the back. She rolled out her tongue, on which rested a ball of gray gum, depleted of sweetness under her

<u>**relentless**</u> chomp. She whispered "sucka" and giggled so that her nose quivered dark shadows.

The play, *The Last Stand,* was about the Donner party just before they got hungry and started eating each other. Everyone who scored at least twelve out of fifteen on their spelling tests got to say at least one line. Everyone else had to stand and be trees or snowflakes.

Mrs. Bunnin wanted the play to be a success. She couldn't risk having kids with bad memories on stage. The nonspeaking trees and snowflakes stood humming snow flurries, blistering wind, and hail, which they produced by clacking their teeth.

Robert's mother was proud of him because he was living up to the legend of Robert De Niro, for whom he was named. Over dinner he said, "Nothing's wrong. I can see," when his brother asked him to pass the dishtowel, their communal napkin. His sister said, "It's your turn to do dishes," and he said, "Nothing's wrong. I can see." His dog, Queenie, begged him for more than water and a dog biscuit. He touched his dog's own hairy beard and said, "Nothing's wrong. I can see."

One warm spring night, Robert lay on his back in the backyard, counting shooting stars. He was up to three when David, a friend who was really his brother's friend, hopped the fence and asked, "What's the matter with you?"

"Nothing's wrong. I can see," Robert answered. He sat up, feeling good because the line came naturally, without much thought. He leaned back on his elbow and asked David what he wanted to be when he grew up. **D**

"I don't know yet," David said, plucking at the grass. "Maybe a fighter pilot. What do you want to be?"

relentless (rĭ-lĕnt'lĭs) *adj.* refusing to stop or give up

D MONITOR
Reread lines 89–106. Why does Robert respond with his line when anyone speaks to him at home? Think of a second question to add to the chart below. Look for answers to your questions as you read.

My Questions

1. Why is this line so important to Robert?
2. ______

↓

Answers

1. ______
2. ______

E **MONITOR**
Reread lines 119–137. Underline words and phrases that reveal how Robert feels the day before the play. List questions that you have about his behavior. You may need to read ahead to find your answers.

"I want to guard the president. I could wrestle the assassins and be on television. But I'd pin those dudes, and people would say, 'That's him, our hero.'" David plucked at a stalk of grass and thought deeply.

Robert thought of telling David that he really wanted to be someone with a supergreat memory, who could recall facts that most people thought were unimportant. He didn't know if there was such a job, but he thought it would be great to sit at home by the telephone waiting for scientists to call him and ask hard questions.

The three weeks passed quickly. The day before the play, Robert felt happy as he walked home from school with no homework. As he turned onto his street, he found a dollar floating over the currents of wind.

"A buck," he screamed to himself. He snapped it up and looked for others. But he didn't find any more. It was his lucky day, though. At recess he had hit a home run on a fluke bunt—a fluke because the catcher had kicked the ball, another player had thrown it into center field, and the pitcher wasn't looking when Robert slowed down at third, then burst home with dust flying behind him.

That night, it was his sister's turn to do the dishes. They had eaten enchiladas with the works, so she slaved with suds up to her elbows. Robert bathed in bubble bath, the suds peaked high like the Donner Pass. He thought about how full he was and how those poor people had had nothing to eat but snow. I can live on nothing, he thought and whistled like wind through a mountain pass, raking flat the suds with his palm. E

The next day, after lunch, he was ready for the play, red beard in hand and his one line trembling on his lips. Classes herded into the auditorium. As the actors dressed

Monitor Your Comprehension

and argued about stepping on each other's feet, Robert stood near a cardboard barrel full of toys, whispering over and over to himself, "Nothing's wrong. I can see." He was hot, itchy, and confused when he tied on the beard. He sneezed when a strand of the beard entered his nostril. He said louder, "Nothing's wrong. I can see," but the words seemed to get caught in the beard. "Nothing, no, no. I can see great," he said louder, then under his breath because the words seemed wrong. "Nothing's wrong, can't you see? Nothing's wrong. I can see you." Worried, he approached Belinda and asked if she remembered his line. Balling her hand into a fist, Belinda warned, "Sucka, I'm gonna bury your ugly face in the ground if you mess up." F

"I won't," Robert said as he walked away. He bit a nail and looked into the barrel of toys. A clown's mask stared back at him. He prayed that his line would come back to him. He would hate to disappoint his teacher and didn't like the thought of his face being rubbed into spiky grass.

The curtain parted slightly, and the principal came out smiling onto the stage. She said some words about pioneer history and then, stern faced, warned the audience not to scrape the chairs on the just-waxed floor. The principal then introduced Mrs. Bunnin, who told the audience about how they had rehearsed for weeks.

Meanwhile, the class stood quietly in place with lunchtime spaghetti on their breath. They were ready. Belinda had swallowed her gum because she knew this was for real. The snowflakes clumped together and began howling.

Robert retied his beard. Belinda, smoothing her skirt, looked at him and said, "If you know what's good for you, you'd better do it right." Robert grew nervous when the curtain parted and his classmates who were assigned to do snow, wind, and hail broke into song.

F PLOT: RISING ACTION
Reread lines 138–153. Underline words and phrases that show that the tension is increasing. Explain why the tension is greater now.

narrative (năr'ə-tĭv) *n.* a story

Alfonso stepped forward with his **narrative** about a blot on American history that would live with us forever. He looked at the audience, lost for a minute. He continued by saying that if the Donner party could come back, hungry from not eating for over a hundred years, they would be sorry for what they had done.

The play began with some boys in snowshoes shuffling around the stage, muttering that the blizzard would cut them off from civilization. They looked up, held out their hands, and said in unison,[1] "Snow." One stepped center stage and said, "I wish I had never left the prairie." Another one said, "California is just over there." He pointed, and some of the first graders looked in the direction of the piano.

"What are we going to do?" one kid asked, brushing pretend snow off his vest.

"I'm getting pretty hungry," another said, rubbing her stomach.

The audience seemed to be following the play. A ribbon of sweat ran down Robert's face. When his scene came up, he staggered to center stage and dropped to the floor, just as Mrs. Bunnin had said, just as he had seen Robert De Niro do in that movie about a boxer. Belinda, bending over with an "Oh, my," yanked him up so hard that something clicked in his elbow. She boomed, "Is there anything wrong with your eyes?"

Robert rubbed his elbow, then his eyes, and said, "I can see nothing wrong. Wrong is nothing, I can see." G

"How are we going to get through?" she boomed, wringing her hands together at the audience, some of whom had their mouths taped shut because they were known talkers. "My husband needs a doctor." The drama

G PLOT: TURNING POINT/CLIMAX

The **climax** is the story's most exciting moment, when you find out how the problem or conflict will be resolved. Underline the line that Robert delivers during the performance. How is his delivery of the line a turning point in the story?

1. **in unison** (yo͞o'nĭ-sən): at the same time.

advanced through snow, wind, and hail that sounded like chattering teeth.

Belinda turned to Robert and muttered, "You mess-up. You're gonna hate life."

But Robert thought he'd done okay. At least, he reasoned to himself, I got the words right. Just not in the right order.

With his part of the play done, he joined the snowflakes and trees, chattering his teeth the loudest. He howled wind like a baying hound and snapped his fingers furiously in a snow flurry. He trembled from the cold.

The play ended with Alfonso saying that if they came back to life, the Donner party would be sorry for eating each other. "It's just not right," he argued. "You gotta suck it up in bad times." (H)

Robert figured that Alfonso was right. He remembered how one day his sister had locked him in the closet and he didn't eat or drink for five hours. When he got out, he hit his sister, but not so hard as to leave a bruise. He then ate three sandwiches and felt a whole lot better.

The cast then paraded up the aisle into the audience. Belinda pinched Robert hard, but only once because she was thinking that it could have been worse. As he passed a smiling and relieved Mrs. Bunnin, she patted Robert's shoulder and said, "Almost perfect."

(H) PLOT: FALLING ACTION
Pause at line 221. What effect does Robert's delivery of his lines have on the end of the play?

Robert was happy. He'd made it through without passing out from fear. Now the first and second graders were looking at him and clapping. He was sure everyone wondered who the actor was behind that smooth voice and red, red beard. ❶

❶ **PLOT: RESOLUTION / DENOUEMENT**
How do Robert, Belinda, and Mrs. Bunnin each feel about Robert's performance?

ROBERT

BELINDA

MRS. BUNNIN

Literary Analysis: Plot Elements

The plot of "The School Play" centers on Robert's fear of forgetting his line. In each box of the chart below, write down the important event or events that happen at each stage of the plot.

READING 6A Summarize elements of plot development (e.g., rising action, turning point, climax, falling action, denouement).

PLOT STRUCTURE OF "THE SCHOOL PLAY"

2. RISING ACTION

3. CLIMAX

4. FALLING ACTION

1. EXPOSITION

5. RESOLUTION

Review your side-column responses and your completed plot diagram. Do you think the plot of this story is realistic? Why or why not?

RC-6(C) Monitor and adjust comprehension (rereading a portion aloud; generating questions).

Reading Strategy: Monitor

Think about how you monitored your reading of "The School Play." Evaluate your reading strategy by circling the most accurate response for each statement: N = Never, S = Sometimes, O = Often

I paused to check my understanding. N S O

I wrote questions on my chart about what I was reading. N S O

I answered my questions. N S O

I reread passages silently. N S O

I reread passages aloud. N S O

I looked for answers as I continued reading. N S O

Which aspect of the strategy was most helpful to you? Explain.

What do you FEAR most?

What advice would you give Robert to help him overcome his fear in the future?

Vocabulary Practice

READING 6A Summarize elements of plot development (e.g., rising action, turning point, climax, falling action, denouement).

Circle the letter of the word or phrase that has the same, or nearly the same, meaning as the boldfaced word.

1. a thrilling **narrative:** **(a)** argument, **(b)** story, **(c)** debate, **(d)** notice
2. **prop** for a play: **(a)** script, **(b)** costume, **(c)** object, **(d)** director
3. **relentless** noise: **(a)** constant, **(b)** deafening, **(c)** frightening, **(d)** occasional
4. to **smirk** at someone: **(a)** stare rudely, **(b)** laugh quietly, **(c)** yell loudly, **(d)** smile defiantly

Academic Vocabulary in Speaking

affect	analyze	evidence	impact	provide

TURN AND TALK With a partner, discuss the resolution of "The School Play." How would the story be **affected** if Robert acted upset as he came offstage? Use at least two Academic Vocabulary words in your response. Definitions for these words are on page 3.

Texas Assessment Practice

DIRECTIONS Use "The School Play" to answers questions 1–6.

1 In the exposition of "The School Play" readers learn that Robert is —

- (A) willing to practice his line over and over
- (B) distracted by his itchy beard
- (C) intimidated by his scene partner Belinda
- (D) interested in U. S. history

2 What does Robert do to try to remember his line?

- (F) He writes it on his hand.
- (G) He draws a picture of it.
- (H) He recites it over and over.
- (J) He dreams about it over and over.

3 When you monitor your reading you —

- (A) check your reading speed
- (B) pause occasionally to check your understanding
- (C) visualize the characters and plot
- (D) predict what will happen next

4 The conflict, or problem begins when —

- (F) Robert does not help Mrs. Bunnin with the props
- (G) Belinda pops her gum
- (H) Belinda threatens to hurt Robert if he misspeaks his line
- (J) Robert forgets his line

5 Robert's conflict is resolved when he —

- (A) finds a dollar
- (B) practices his lines with family and friends
- (C) tries on the red beard
- (D) says his line without upsetting Belinda or Mrs. Bunnin

6 How has Robert changed by the end of the story?

- (F) He is more critical of himself.
- (G) He is more critical of Belinda.
- (H) He is more accepting of himself.
- (J) He is more accepting of Belinda.

All Summer in a Day

Short Story by Ray Bradbury

READING 6A Summarize elements of plot development (e.g., rising action, turning point, climax, falling action, denouement) in various works of fiction.

What if your whole WORLD changed?

People often become comfortable in the familiar world of their family, friends, and daily routines. However, people move and traditions change. When your world changes, whether by a little or a lot, it can have an impact on your life. In "All Summer in a Day," a young girl feels lost in a new place.

LIST IT List the people, places, events and ideas in your world that are most precious to you. How would you feel if any of these things disappeared?

My World

People

Places

Events

Ideas

Literary Analysis: Plot and Setting

The **plot** is the series of events that make up a story, including the conflict and its resolution. **Setting** is *where* and *when* a story takes place. In science fiction stories, the setting is often the distant future. This setting usually causes the events of the plot to unfold in an unexpected way. As you read "All Summer in a Day," look for clues that tell you when and where the story takes place. Record setting details in the chart below. Use these details to think about the setting's influence on the story's conflict and resolution, or denouement.

Setting Details	Influence on the Conflict and Resolution
"It had been raining for seven years."	Students are anxious to see the sun.

Reading Skill: Make Inferences

RC-6(D) Make inferences about text.

As a reader you are a detective. Details, events, and dialogue in a story are your clues. You put the clues together with your own knowledge to **make inferences,** or guesses.

As you read "All Summer in a Day," use an equation like the one shown to record the inferences you make about the characters' feelings and their actions.

Clues from the Story		My Knowledge		Inference
Margot is not part of the group.	+	*Not being part of a group can make you feel sad.*	=	*Margot feels sad.*

Vocabulary in Context

Note: Words are listed in the order in which they appear in the story.

slacken (slăk'ən) *v.* to slow down or lessen
*They hope the sun will come out when the rain **slackens.***

apparatus (ăp'ə-răt'əs) *n.* a device or set of equipment used for a specific purpose
*The **apparatus** used to open the hatch was broken.*

immense (ĭ-mĕns') *adj.* extremely big; huge
*The **immense** planet offered many areas to explore.*

tumultuously (to͝o-mŭl'cho͞o-əs'lē) *adv.* in a wild or disorderly way
*Branches and leaves shook **tumultuously** during the storm.*

resilient (rĭ-zĭl'yənt) *adj.* flexible and springy
*The sturdy shelters are built to be **resilient** to high winds.*

savor (sā'vər) *v.* to take great pleasure in
*The traveler sat quietly to **savor** the unusual landscape.*

Vocabulary Practice

Review the vocabulary words. Ray Bradbury uses these words to create a world that is very different from our own. Use at least two of these words in a description of the world you inhabit.

____

____

Monitor Your Comprehension

SET A PURPOSE FOR READING

Read this short story to discover how a group of children on Venus react to a long-awaited event.

Short Story by

RAY BRADBURY

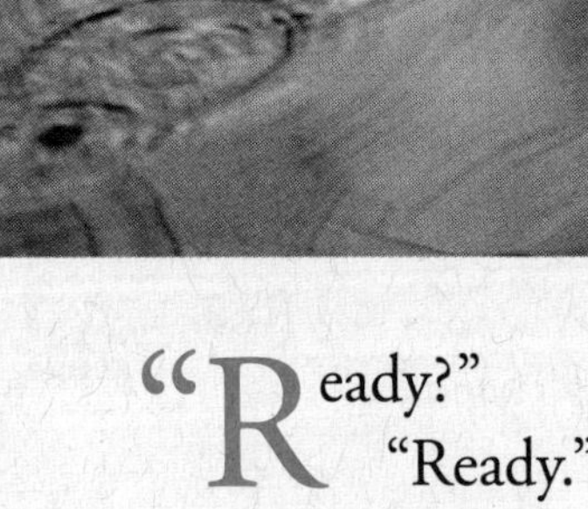

BACKGROUND When Ray Bradbury wrote "All Summer in a Day" in 1954, very little was known about the planet Venus. It was hidden beneath a heavy layer of clouds. Scientists learned a few years later that these clouds did not produce constant rain, as occurs in Bradbury's story. Instead, the clouds appear to trap heat. The temperature at the surface of the planet is about 860°F, which is much too hot for rainfall.

"Ready?"

"Ready."

"Now?"

"Soon."

"Do the scientists really know? Will it happen today, will it?"

"Look, look; see for yourself!"

The children pressed to each other like so many roses, so many weeds, intermixed, peering out for a look at the hidden sun. (A)

(A) MAKE INFERENCES
Reread lines 8–10. The author compares the children to two living things. Circle those words in the text. What is your knowledge or experience of these two things? Why might Bradbury use these words to describe the children?

It had been raining for seven years; thousands upon thousands of days compounded and filled from one end to the other with rain, with the drum and gush of water, with the sweet crystal fall of showers and the concussion[1] of storms so heavy they were tidal waves come over the islands. A thousand forests had been crushed under the rain and grown up a thousand times to be crushed again. And this was the way life was forever on the planet Venus, and this was the school room of the children of the rocket men and women who had come to a raining world to set up civilization and live out their lives. B

"It's stopping, it's stopping!"

"Yes, yes!"

Margot stood apart from them, from these children who could never remember a time when there wasn't rain and rain and rain. They were all nine years old, and if there had been a day, seven years ago, when the sun came out for an hour and showed its face to the stunned world, they could not recall. Sometimes, at night, she heard them stir, in remembrance, and she knew they were dreaming and remembering gold or a yellow crayon or a coin large enough to buy the world with. She knew that they thought they remembered a warmness, like a blushing in the face, in the body, in the arms and legs and trembling hands. But then they always awoke to the tatting drum,[2] the endless shaking down of clear bead necklaces upon the roof, the walk, the gardens, the forest, and their dreams were gone.

PAUSE & REFLECT

All day yesterday they had read in class, about the sun. About how like a lemon it was, and how hot. And they had written small stories or essays or poems about it:

1. **concussion** (kən-kŭsh'ən): pounding.
2. **tatting drum:** a continuous, soft, beating sound.

Monitor Your Comprehension

B SETTING

Reread lines 11–21. Underline words and phrases that reveal information about the setting. What do the **details** suggest about where and when the story takes place?

PAUSE & REFLECT

Reread lines 24–37. How does Margot feel about her classmates?

"I think the sun is a flower,
That blooms for just one hour."

That was Margot's poem, read in a quiet voice in the still classroom while the rain was falling outside.

"Aw, you didn't write that!" protested one of the boys.

"I did," said Margot. "I *did*."

"William!" said the teacher.

But that was yesterday. Now, the rain was **slackening**, and the children were crushed to the great thick windows.

"Where's teacher?"

"She'll be back."

"She'd better hurry, we'll miss it!"

They turned on themselves, like a feverish wheel, all tumbling spokes.

Margot stood alone. She was a very frail girl who looked as if she had been lost in the rain for years and the rain had washed out the blue from her eyes and the red from her mouth and the yellow from her hair. She was an old photograph dusted from an album, whitened away, and if she spoke at all her voice would be a ghost. Now she stood, separate, staring at the rain and the loud wet world beyond the huge glass. C

"What're *you* looking at?" said William.

Margot said nothing.

"Speak when you're spoken to." He gave her a shove. But she did not move; rather, she let herself be moved only by him and nothing else.

They edged away from her, they would not look at her. She felt them go away. And this was because she would play no games with them in the echoing tunnels of the underground city. If they tagged her and ran, she stood blinking after them and did not follow. When the class sang

slacken (slăk′ən) *v.* to slow down or lessen

What effect is the **slackening** rain likely to have on the children?

____

____

____

____

____

C SETTING

Reread lines 55–62. Underline words and phrases that describe Margot. What effect has the constant rain had on Margot? Explain, using details from the text.

songs about happiness and life and games, her lips barely moved. Only when they sang about the sun and the summer did her lips move, as she watched the drenched windows.

And then, of course, the biggest crime of all was that she had come here only five years ago from Earth, and she remembered the sun and the way the sun was and the sky was, when she was four, in Ohio. And they, they had been on Venus all their lives, and they had been only two years old when last the sun came out, and had long since forgotten the color and heat of it and the way that it really was. But Margot remembered. **D**

"It's like a penny," she said once, eyes closed.

"No it's not!" the children cried.

"It's like a fire," she said, "in the stove."

"You're lying; you don't remember!" cried the children.

But she remembered and stood quietly apart from all of them and watched the patterning windows. And once, a month ago, she had refused to shower in the school shower-rooms, had clutched her hands to her ears and over her head, screaming the water mustn't touch her head. So after that, dimly, dimly, she sensed it, she was different and they knew her difference and kept away. **E**

There was talk that her father and mother were taking her back to Earth next year; it seemed vital to her that they do so, though it would mean the loss of thousands of dollars to her family. And so, the children hated her for all these reasons, of big and little consequence. They hated her pale, snow face, her waiting silence, her thinness and her possible future.

"Get away!" The boy gave her another push. "What're you waiting for?"

Monitor Your Comprehension

D SETTING
What is the conflict between Margot and her classmates? How has the setting affected the conflict?

E MAKE INFERENCES
Reread lines 88–94. Use the chart to infer why Margot refuses to take a shower.

Story Clues

+

My Knowledge

=

Inference

Monitor Your Comprehension

F SETTING
Reread lines 102–113. If Venus had a climate like Earth's, would Margot have a problem with the boy? Explain how a change in setting would affect the conflict.

Then, for the first time, she turned and looked at him. And what she was waiting for was in her eyes.

"Well, don't wait around here!" cried the boy, savagely. "You won't see nothing!"

Her lips moved.

"Nothing!" he cried. "It was all a joke, wasn't it?" He turned to the other children. "Nothing's happening today. *Is* it?"

They all blinked at him and then, understanding, laughed and shook their heads. "Nothing, nothing!" F

"Oh, but," Margot whispered, her eyes helpless. "But, this is the day, the scientists predict, they say, they *know,* the sun . . ."

"All a joke!" said the boy, and seized her roughly. "Hey, everyone, let's put her in a closet before teacher comes!"

"No," said Margot, falling back.

They surged about her, caught her up, and bore her, protesting, and then pleading, and then crying, back into a tunnel, a room, a closet, where they slammed and locked the door. They stood looking at the door and saw it tremble from her beating and throwing herself against it. They heard her muffled cries. Then, smiling, they turned and went out and back down the tunnel, just as the teacher arrived.

"Ready, children?" She glanced at her watch.

"Yes!" said everyone.

"Are we all here?"

"Yes!"

The rain slackened still more.

They crowded to the huge door.

The rain stopped.

It was as if, in the midst of a film concerning an avalanche, a tornado, a hurricane, a volcanic eruption, something had, first, gone wrong with the sound

apparatus, thus muffling and finally cutting off all noise, all of the blasts and repercussions and thunders, and then, secondly, ripped the film from the projector and inserted in its place a peaceful tropical slide which did not move or tremor. The world ground to a standstill. The silence was so **immense** and unbelievable that you felt that your ears had been stuffed or you had lost your hearing altogether. The children put their hands to their ears. They stood apart. The door slid back and the smell of the silent, waiting world came in to them.

The sun came out. Ⓖ

It was the color of flaming bronze and it was very large. And the sky around it was a blazing blue tile color. And the jungle burned with sunlight as the children, released from their spell, rushed out, yelling, into the summer-time.

"Now, don't go too far," called the teacher after them. "You've only one hour, you know. You wouldn't want to get caught out!"

But they were running and turning their faces up to the sky and feeling the sun on their cheeks like a warm iron; they were taking off their jackets and letting the sun burn their arms.

"Oh, it's better than the sun-lamps, isn't it?"

"Much, much better!"

They stopped running and stood in the great jungle that covered Venus, that grew and never stopped growing, **tumultuously**, even as you watched it. It was a nest of octopuses, clustering up great arms of flesh-like weed, wavering, flowering in this brief spring. It was the color of rubber and ash, this jungle, from the many years without sun. It was the color of stones and white cheeses and ink. Ⓗ

The children lay out, laughing, on the jungle mattress, and heard it sigh and squeak under them, **resilient** and alive. They ran among the trees, they slipped and fell, they

Monitor Your Comprehension

apparatus (ăp′ə-răt′əs) *n.* a device or set of equipment used for a specific purpose

immense (ĭ-mĕns′) *adj.* extremely big; huge

Ⓖ SETTING
Reread lines 134–148. What changes do the children notice when the rain stops?

____

____

____

____

____

____

____

____

tumultuously (to͞o-mŭl′cho͞o-əs′lē) *adv.* in a wild or disorderly way

Ⓗ SETTING
Underline words and phrases that describe what is unusual about the plants on Venus.

resilient (rĭ-zĭl′yənt) *adj.* flexible and springy

pushed each other, they played hide-and-seek and tag, but most of all they squinted at the sun until tears ran down their faces, they put their hands up at that yellowness and that amazing blueness, and they breathed of the fresh fresh air and listened and listened to the silence which suspended them in a blessed sea of no sound and no motion. They looked at everything and **savored** everything. Then, wildly, like animals escaped from their caves, they ran and ran in shouting circles. They ran for an hour and did not stop running. PAUSE & REFLECT

savor (sā'vər) *v.* to take great pleasure in

PAUSE & REFLECT
Reread lines 170–182. Circle words that show the children's actions. How do the children react to the change in the weather?

And then—

In the midst of their running, one of the girls wailed.

Everyone stopped.

The girl, standing in the open, held out her hand.

"Oh, look, look," she said, trembling.

They came slowly to look at her opened palm.

In the center of it, cupped and huge, was a single raindrop.

She began to cry, looking at it.

They glanced quickly at the sky.

"Oh. Oh."

A few cold drops fell on their noses and their cheeks and their mouths. The sun faded behind a stir of mist. A wind blew cool around them. They turned and started to walk back toward the underground house, their hands at their sides, their smiles vanishing away.

A boom of thunder startled them and like leaves before a new hurricane, they tumbled upon each other and ran. Lightning struck ten miles away, five miles away, a mile, a half-mile. The sky darkened into midnight in a flash.

They stood in the doorway of the underground for a moment until it was raining hard. Then they closed the door and heard the gigantic sound of the rain falling in tons and avalanches everywhere and forever. ❶

"Will it be seven more years?"

"Yes. Seven."

Then one of them gave a little cry.

"Margot!"

"What?"

"She's still in the closet where we locked her."

"Margot."

They stood as if someone had driven them, like so many stakes, into the floor. They looked at each other and then looked away. They glanced out at the world that was raining now and raining and raining steadily. They could not meet each other's glances. Their faces were solemn and pale. They looked at their hands and feet, their faces down.

"Margot."

One of the girls said, "Well . . . ?"

No one moved.

"Go on," whispered the girl.

Monitor Your Comprehension

❶ SETTING

Other than on the day when the sun comes out, do you think the children ever get to go outside? Cite evidence to support your answer.

Monitor Your Comprehension

J MAKE INFERENCES
Use the chart to make an inference about how the children might feel toward Margot now that they, too, have seen the sun.

Story Clues

+

My Knowledge

=

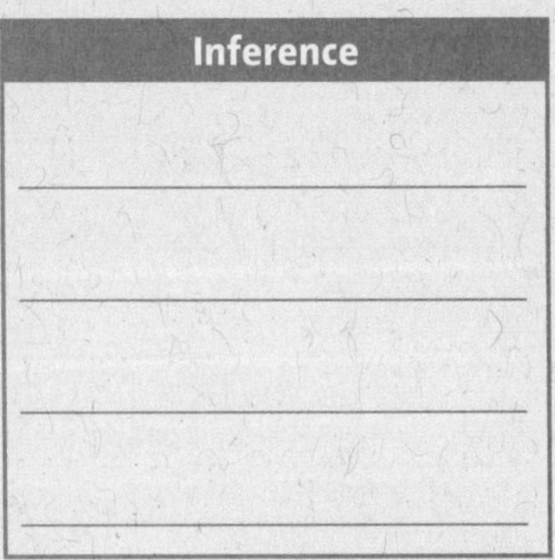

They walked slowly down the hall in the sound of cold rain. They turned through the doorway to the room, in the sound of the storm and thunder, lightning on their faces, blue and terrible. They walked over to the closet door slowly and stood by it.

Behind the closet door was only silence.

They unlocked the door, even more slowly, and let Margot out. J

Literary Analysis: Plot and Setting

The setting of "All Summer in a Day" is a key influence on the plot. In the Setting Circle below, fill in the middle circle with details about the setting. The fill in the outer circle with plot important plot events from the story. Finally, use your completed chart to answer the question that follows.

READING 6A Summarize elements of plot development (e.g., rising action, turning point, climax, falling action, denouement).

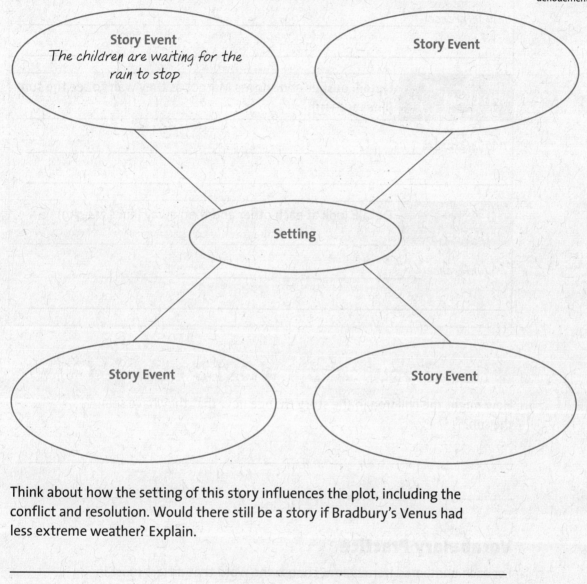

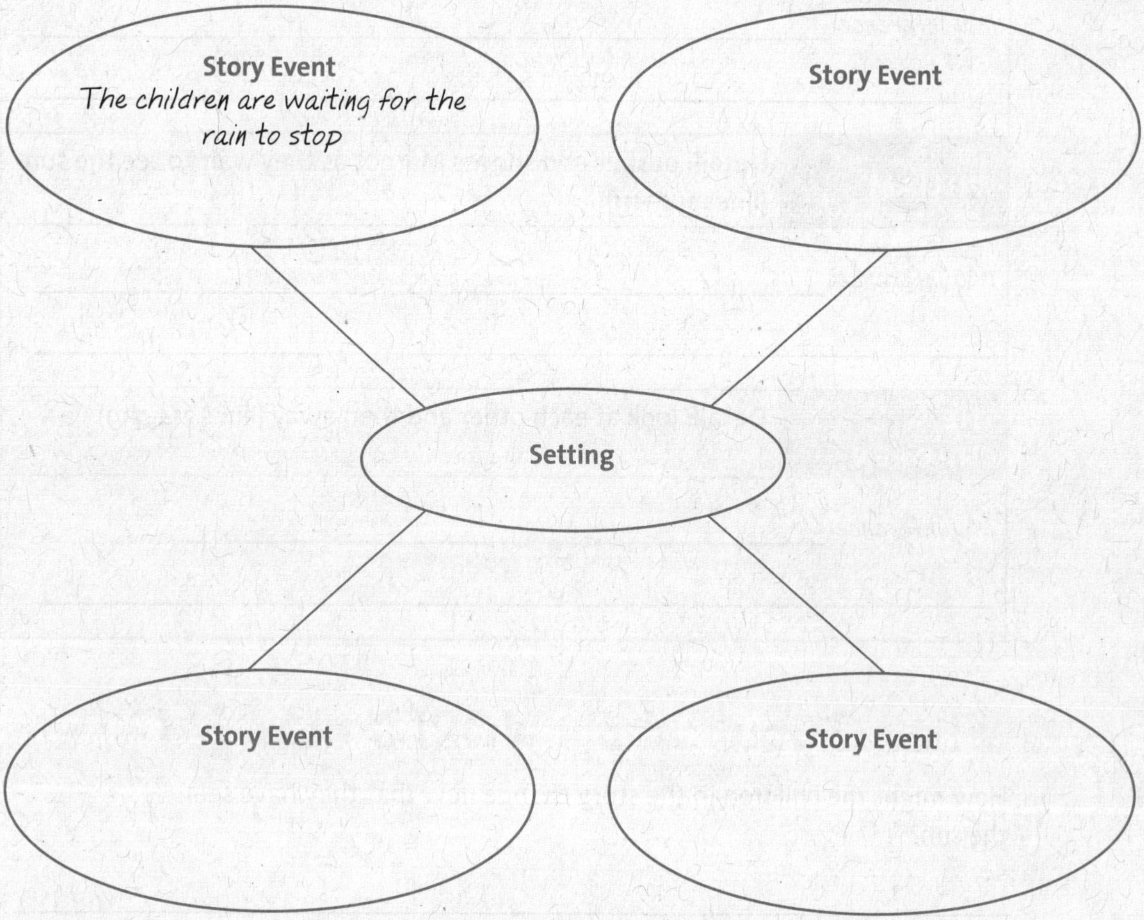

Story Event
The children are waiting for the rain to stop

Story Event

Setting

Story Event

Story Event

Think about how the setting of this story influences the plot, including the conflict and resolution. Would there still be a story if Bradbury's Venus had less extreme weather? Explain.

____

____

____

____

____

____

After Reading

RC-6(D) Make inferences about text.

Reading Skill: Make Inferences

Make an inference about each character based on details from the story.

MARGOT	**Detail:** will not play games or participate in class activities with other children (lines 68–75)
My Inference: ______	
WILLIAM	**Detail:** pushes and shoves Margot as they wait to see the sun (lines 102–111)
My Inference: ______	
THE CHILDREN	**Detail:** look at each other and then away (lines 214–219)
My Inference: ______	

What if your whole WORLD changed?

How might the children in the story change now that they have seen the sun?

______

______

Vocabulary Practice

For each numbered item below, choose the word that differs most in meaning from the other words.

1. **(a)** prepare, **(b)** appreciate, **(c)** enjoy, **(d)** savor
2. **(a)** appliance, **(b)** device, **(c)** apparatus, **(d)** operator
3. **(a)** slacken, **(b)** enlarge, **(c)** decrease, **(d)** lessen
4. **(a)** enormous, **(b)** immense, **(c)** distant, **(d)** gigantic
5. **(a)** tumultuously, **(b)** carefully, **(c)** thoughtfully, **(d)** cautiously
6. **(a)** elastic, **(b)** nervous, **(c)** flexible, **(d)** resilient

Academic Vocabulary in Speaking

affect	analyze	evidence	impact	provide

READING 6A Summarize elements of plot development (e.g., rising action, turning point, climax, falling action, denouement).

TURN AND TALK With a partner, discuss the possible **impact** on Margot of being shut in the closet. Record **evidence** from the text in the lines below to support your response. Use at least two Academic Vocabulary words in your discussion. Definitions of the words are on page 3.

____

____

____

____

Texas Assessment Practice

DIRECTIONS Use "All Summer in a Day" to answers questions 1–6.

1 The setting of the story is —

- (A) a space station
- (B) a remote area on Earth
- (C) the planet Venus
- (D) a planet in a distant galaxy

2 You can infer that when Margot is locked inside the closet she feels —

- (F) embarrassed
- (G) sleepy
- (H) content
- (J) miserable

3 The most important aspect of the story's setting is —

- (A) weather conditions on Venus
- (B) the tunnels in the school
- (C) the time of day
- (D) the season of the year.

4 From William's words and actions you can infer that he —

- (F) is impressed by Margot
- (G) is helpful to newcomers in his class
- (H) resents Margot's presence in the school
- (J) wants to be liked by classmates

5 You can infer that Margot's parents are worried about her because they —

- (A) brought her to live on Venus
- (B) spoke to the teacher about her behavior
- (C) read her poem about the sun
- (D) are considering moving back to Earth

6 Which setting detail moves the plot to its resolution?

- (F) An hour passes.
- (G) It starts raining again.
- (H) The children go back inside.
- (J) The children let Margot out of the closet.

READING 10D Synthesize and make logical connections across three texts representing different genres. **12B** Interpret factual, quantitative, and technical information presented in illustrations. **RC-6(E)** Synthesize texts in ways that maintain meaning and logical order across texts.

Settling in Space

- Magazine Article, page 33
- Online Article, page 35
- Illustration, page 39

Background

In "All Summer in a Day," you read about people living on Venus. What is Venus *really* like? What would it be like to live in a space colony? Study the articles and images on the next few pages to get the science facts about Bradbury's science fiction setting.

Skill Focus: Synthesize Ideas Across Texts

When you read several texts on the same topic, you naturally connect the ideas you find in each piece. You can then synthesize this information by putting it all together. Follow these steps to synthesize the ideas in the selections that follow:

1. **Find the Main Idea** The **main idea** is the most important point the writer makes about a topic. To find the main idea of a piece of nonfiction, ask, "What's the subject?" The title may help you decide. Then ask, "What about it?" Your answer is the main idea. Remember that a text may have more than one main idea.
2. **Make Connections** Consider the relationships among the main ideas of all of the texts. How are they connected? How are they different? How does one idea relate to or expand on another?
3. **Synthesize Ideas** To **synthesize** information means to take individual pieces of information and combine them in order to gain a better understanding of a topic.

As you read the following selections, organize your ideas about each article in the chart below.

Selection	Main Ideas	Supporting
"Weather That's Out of This World"	• *Venus's weather is much worse than Earth's weather.*	• *The temperature on Venus can melt lead.* • *Acid rain constantly falls on Venus.*
"Space Settlements"		
"Artists' View of a Space Colony"		

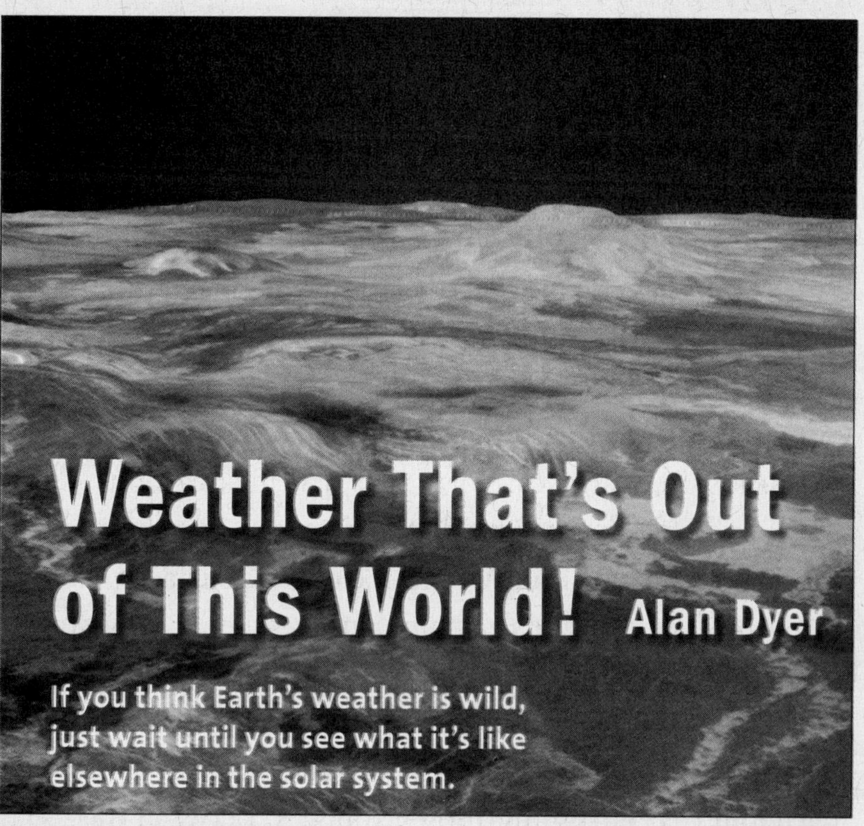

Weather That's Out of This World!
Alan Dyer
If you think Earth's weather is wild, just wait until you see what it's like elsewhere in the solar system.

Hot, Sizzling Venus

"This is VTN—the Venus Television Network—with the latest forecast for the second planet from the Sun: hot today, hot tomorrow, and hot the following day. It will also be cloudy, with no sign of any sunshine. Take your glass umbrella—we're in for more acid rain."

If there were meteorologists on Venus, that's the kind of forecast they would have to give. Venus is a nasty place to live. Think of the hottest day you can remember. Then imagine what it would be like if it were 10 times hotter—that's what it's like on Venus.

Venus is the hottest planet in the solar system. The temperature at its surface is a searing 860 degrees Fahrenheit, day and night. The superhigh temperature surprised many astronomers, who once thought

SET A PURPOSE FOR READING

Read the following selections to discover what life might be like if humans lived in space.

FOCUS ON FORM

A **science article** is a short piece of nonfiction about a scientific subject. The author's purpose for writing a science article is usually to inform or explain. Science articles often use **text features**—headings, different type, illustrations, captions, bulleted lists—to help present information more clearly.

Ⓐ FIND THE MAIN IDEA
Pause at line 32. State the main idea of this article. Then, find three details that support the main idea. Add this information to your chart.

Main Idea

Supporting Details

Mercury would be hotter, since it is closer to the Sun. But Venus has something very important that Mercury lacks—an atmosphere. Unlike Earth's atmosphere, which is made of oxygen and nitrogen, the air on Venus is mostly carbon dioxide gas, one of the so-called greenhouse gases. Like the glass in a greenhouse, carbon dioxide in the air traps heat coming from the Sun. With no place to go, the heat builds up. In the case of Venus, its thick carbon dioxide blanket has made the planet so hot that some metals, such as lead, would melt on its surface.

Adding to Venus's unpleasant weather is a constant drizzle from the thick clouds that surround the planet. But it's not water that falls from the sky there. Instead, the rain is made of droplets of sulfuric acid, a corrosive liquid that burns anything it touches. Between the blistering heat and the sizzling acid rain, Venus's weather is much worse than anything we could find on Earth. Ⓐ

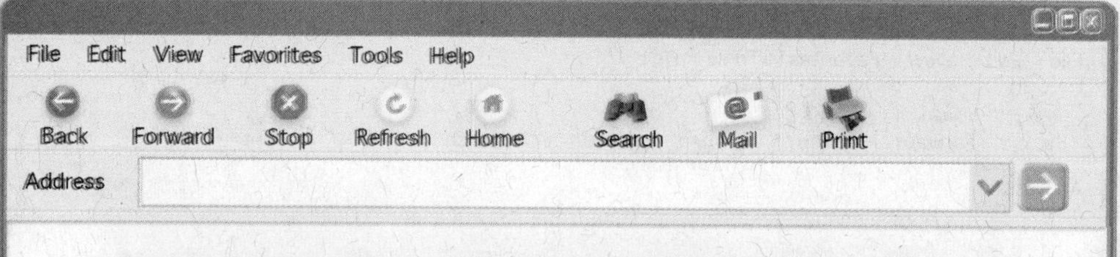

What Is an Orbital Space Colony?

An orbital space colony is a giant spacecraft big enough to live in. Orbital colonies will travel endlessly through space while the folks inside play, work, and socialize.

What Will Life Be Like?

Living inside a space colony will, in many ways, be like living on Earth. People will have houses or apartments. They will go to work and to school. There will be shops, sports teams, concerts, and movies. People will go to parties with their friends, just like on Earth. However, there will also be many differences. Ⓑ

Today we live on the outside of a planet. Earth is thousands of kilometers across, so big that it looks

Internet

Ⓑ SYNTHESIZE IDEAS ACROSS TEXTS

Reread lines 1–9. Underline the statement that reveals the topic of this online article. How might space colonies enable people to study Venus?

C SYNTHESIZE IDEAS ACROSS TEXTS

Reread lines 21–26. Underline information about air and water quality on a space colony. How does the quality of life in a space colony compare to the quality of life on Venus as described in the previous article?

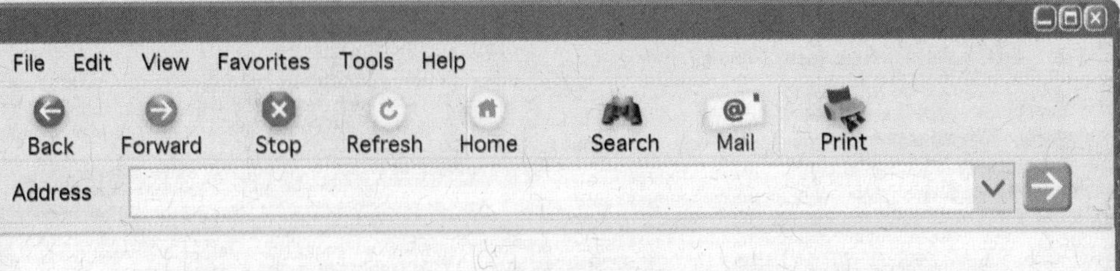

like we are living on a flat surface. Instead of living on the outside of a huge planet, space settlers will live inside very large spacecraft. The spacecraft will be large enough for people to take a good walk, but not so big that it will look like you live on a flat surface. People will live on the inside of spheres, cylinders, and toruses (or donut shapes). These shapes are ideal for space colonies because colonies must rotate to produce pseudo-gravity, or false gravity.

The air and water we need to live is produced naturally here on Earth. On a space colony millions of times smaller than Earth, we will need to constantly monitor the air and water and take quick action if anything begins to go wrong. Otherwise, the entire population would be endangered within a matter of hours. C

Here on Earth, many people feel they can use things and throw them away. There are plenty of materials all around us. On a space colony, every atom will be precious, so recycling will be a way of life. Nothing, except perhaps the most toxic wastes, will be thrown away. Everything will be endlessly recycled, especially water. Waste water will run to the outside of the spacecraft, where sunlight will sterilize the waste, after which everything will be used again.

Agriculture will be different too. On Earth, huge farms take advantage of soil and water conditions to

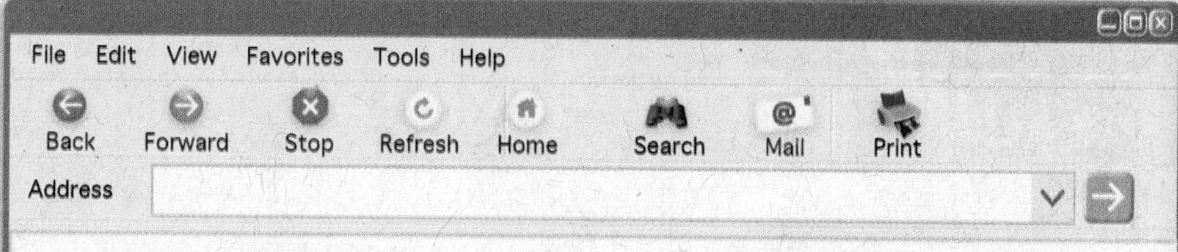

grow the food we need to live. On a space colony, food will be grown in small, carefully controlled rooms where conditions are kept perfect for the crops being grown. This will lead to abundant crops, so the area needed for agriculture will be far smaller than on Earth. D

How Will We Build One?

No one has ever built a space colony, and it will be very difficult to do. Building cities in space will require materials, energy, transportation, communications, life support, and radiation protection. E

- **Materials** Launching materials from Earth is very expensive, so bulk materials will have to come from the Moon or asteroids and comets near Earth.
- **Energy** Solar energy is abundant and reliable. Massive structures will be needed to change sunlight into large amounts of electrical power for settlement use.
- **Transportation** Present launch costs are very high, ranging from $2,000 to $14,000 per pound. To settle space, much better launch vehicles would be needed to avoid serious damage to Earth's atmosphere from the thousands, perhaps millions, of launches required.
- **Communications** Compared to the other requirements, communication is relatively easy. Much

Internet

D SYNTHESIZE IDEAS ACROSS TEXTS
Reread lines 36–42. How will the conditions for growing food enable people to survive in space?

E SYNTHESIZE IDEAS ACROSS TEXTS
Reread lines 43–46. What is the main idea in these lines? Skim the bulleted items that follow. How does each support the main idea?

F SYNTHESIZE IDEAS ACROSS TEXTS
Recall what you learned about Venus's weather in the first article. How does that information add to your understanding of the necessity of the life support described in lines 63–66?

PAUSE & REFLECT
How did the information from this online article improve your understanding of living in space?

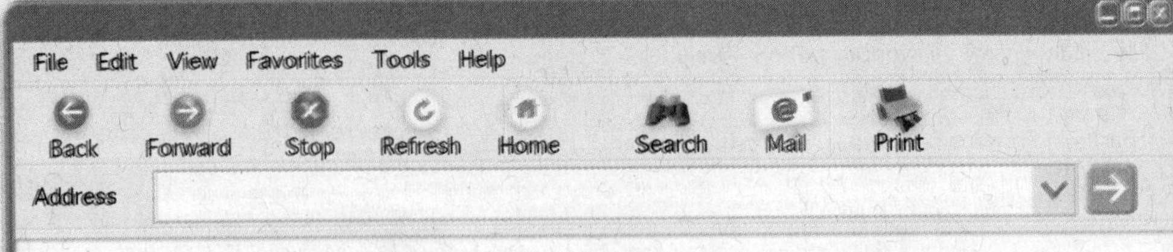

of our current communications—cell phone signals, for example—already pass through satellites.

- **Life Support** People will need air, water, food, and reasonable temperatures to survive. In space settlements, a relatively small, closed system must provide all of these to support life. F
- **Radiation Protection** Cosmic rays and solar flares create deadly radiation in space. To protect life, settlements must be shielded from most incoming radiation.

How Big Will the Colonies Be?

Since space colonies are for permanent living, not just a few months' work, they are expected to be about 100 times larger than today's space stations. Currently available materials could be used to build colonies that would be home to a population of ten or twenty thousand people. Designs even exist for colonies that would fit millions of people, but the first colonies will almost certainly be smaller.

Right now, space colonies are just an idea, but someday space colonies may crisscross the solar system, providing homes for a trillion people. What an achievement that will be. PAUSE & REFLECT

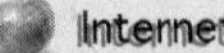

ARTIST'S VIEW OF A

SPACE COLONY

As scientists explore the possibilities of how to colonize space, many of the concepts they present to the public can be difficult to visualize. For that reason, artists often work with scientists to help convey their ideas. Here, artists have illustrated the inside view of a possible space colony. G

G SCIENCE ARTICLE
In scientific articles, an artist's illustrations provide supporting and clarifying information. How does this illustration add to your understanding of living in a space colony?

Practicing Your Skills

READING 10D Synthesize and make logical connections across three texts representing different genres. **12B** Interpret factual, quantitative, and technical information presented in illustrations. **RC-6(E)** Synthesize texts in ways that maintain meaning and logical order across texts.

The three texts you just read provide several ideas about living in space. Review the chart you created as you read each selection. Make sure the information in your chart represents the main ideas in each selection and includes details that support each selection's main idea. Then use the chart below to show to identify the two most important pieces of information in each article.

Selection	Most Important Information
"Weather That's Out of This World!"	1) ___ ___ ___ 2) ___ ___ ___
"Space Settlements"	1) ___ ___ ___ 2) ___ ___ ___
"Artist's View of a Space Colony"	1) ___ ___ ___ 2) ___ ___ ___

Synthesize Ideas Across Texts

Write a paragraph in which you sum up what you've learned about living in space. Synthesize, or combine, what you learned.

READING 10D Synthesize and make logical connections across three texts representing different genres. **12B** Interpret factual, quantitative, and technical information presented in illustrations.

____

____

____

Academic Vocabulary in Speaking

affect	analyze	evidence	impact	provide

TURN AND TALK With a partner, discuss how the illustration of an orbital space colony **impacts** your understanding of living in space. Include at least two Academic Vocabulary words in your response. Definitions of these words are on page 3.

Texas Assessment Practice

DIRECTIONS Use the selections in "Settling in Space" to answer questions 1–4.

1 Which detail from "Weather That's Out of This World" supports the main idea that Venus's weather is worse than Earth's?

- (A) Venus has an atmosphere.
- (B) Mercury is closer to the Sun.
- (C) The surface temperature of Venus is 860°F
- (D) The air on Venus is carbon dioxide gas.

2 Which of the following statements is a main idea of "Space Settlements"?

- (F) Like Earth, a space colony would revolve around the Sun.
- (G) A space colony could exactly match the conditions on Earth.
- (H) An orbiting space colony would allow people to visit every planet in our solar system.
- (J) There will be similarities and differences between Earth and the space colony.

3 How does "Artist's View of a Space Colony" differ from "Space Settlements"?

- (A) It uses illustrations to explain space colonies.
- (B) It provides first-hand accounts of life in a space colony.
- (C) It uses text features like headings and bulleted lists.
- (D) It describes how life in a space colony will be like life on Earth.

4 From reading all three selections you can tell that —

- (F) people will be able to live on a space colony within five years
- (G) materials for building a space colony are readily available on Venus
- (H) it is difficult to recreate the living conditions found on Earth
- (J) communication will be one of the greatest challenges to living in space colonies

READING 5 Understand, make inferences, and draw conclusions about the structure and elements of drama.

The Prince and the Pauper

Novel by Mark Twain
Dramatized by Joellen Bland

Who would you BE if you could?

Interview 1

Questions

Responses

Interview 2

Questions

Responses

Most of us can name at least one person who has a life we sometimes envy. This person may be an actor, an athlete, a singer, or even a friend. However, you might not envy him or her if you knew what his or her life was really like. In *The Prince and the Pauper,* two characters learn unexpected lessons about themselves and each other when they trade places.

ROLE-PLAY With a classmate, choose two famous people whose lives you admire. In the side column, list questions you would want to ask them. Jot down answers you think they might give. Be sure to include the struggles or challenges they face in their lives.

Literary Analysis: Conflict in Drama

In drama, as in short stories, the plot revolves around a central **conflict.** Since drama is meant to be performed by actors, a drama's conflict usually unfolds through the action and dialogue (conversation between characters).

Unlike a book, which has chapters, a play is divided into acts and scenes. This play takes place in eight scenes that revolve around two boys who switch identities. As you read, use the chart below to note how the plot develops and the conflict becomes more complicated in each scene.

Scene	Plot Details	Conflict
One	Tom and the prince exchange clothes.	The guards mistake the prince for Tom, and the king thinks that Tom is the prince.

Reading Strategy: Reading a Play

READING 5 Understand, make inferences, draw conclusions about the structure and elements of drama.

In a drama, **stage directions** provide key information that readers would normally see or hear in a performance, such as

- setting, scenery, and props (*Westminster Palace, England,* Scene 1, line 2)
- music, sound effects, and lighting (*fanfare of trumpets is heard,* Scene 3, lines 231–232)
- Characters' movements, behavior, or ways of speaking (*surprised, standing up quickly,* Scene 4, lines 285)

As you read the play, think about the stage directions and what they help you to understand.

Stage Direction	Type of Direction	What It Tells Me
Fanfare of trumpets is heard. (Scene 3, lines 231–232)	Sound effects	Someone is entering.

Vocabulary in Context

Note: Words are listed in the order in which they appear in the play.

pauper (pô′pər) *n.* someone who is extremely poor

Tom looked like a prince, but he was a ***pauper****.*

sane (sān) *adj.* mentally healthy; reasonable

The king began to doubt that his son was ***sane****.*

affliction (ə-flĭk′shən) *n.* a cause of pain, suffering, or worry

An ***affliction*** *seemed to make the prince forgetful.*

imposter (ĭm-pŏs′tər) *n.* a person who uses a false name or identity

Was he the real prince or an ***imposter****?*

successor (sək-sĕs′ər) *n.* a person who follows another, taking on his or her rights or duties

The king expected his son to be his ***successor****.*

recollection (rək′ə-lĕk′shən) *n.* something remembered

The boy had no ***recollection*** *of where he put the Seal of England.*

Vocabulary Practice

Review the vocabulary words and think about their meanings. Then, with a partner discuss what the play's main conflict might be.

SET A PURPOSE FOR READING

Read this play to discover how two boys learn the leadership qualities needed to govern effectively.

The Prince and the Pauper

Novel by

MARK TWAIN

Dramatized by

JOELLEN BLAND

BACKGROUND Mark Twain set some of his novels, including *The Prince and the Pauper,* in England, where he was greatly admired. The prince in Twain's story is based on Edward, son of King Henry VIII of England. After Henry's death in 1547, the nine-year-old Edward took the throne, becoming King Edward VI. Joellen Bland later adapted Twain's novel as a play.

CHARACTERS

Edward, Prince of Wales
Tom Canty, the Pauper
Lord Hertford
Lord St. John
King Henry VIII
Herald
Miles Hendon
John Canty, Tom's father
Hugo, a young thief
Two Women
Justice
Constable
Jailer
Sir Hugh Hendon
Two Prisoners
Two Guards
Three Pages
Lords and Ladies
Villagers

SCENE ONE

Time: *1547.*

Setting: *Westminster Palace, England. Gates leading to courtyard are at right. Slightly to the left, off courtyard and inside gates, interior of palace anteroom*[1] *is visible. There is a couch with a rich robe draped on it, screen at rear, bellcord, mirror, chairs, and a table with bowl of nuts, and a large golden seal on it. Piece of armor hangs on one wall. Exits are rear and downstage.* Ⓐ

At Curtain Rise: Two Guards—*one at right, one at left—stand in front of gates, and several Villagers hover nearby, straining to see into courtyard where Prince may be seen through fence, playing.* Two Women *enter right.*

1st Woman. I have walked all morning just to have a glimpse of Westminster Palace.

2nd Woman. Maybe if we can get near enough to the gates, we can have a glimpse of the young Prince. (Tom Canty, *dirty and ragged, comes out of crowd and steps close to gates.*)

Tom. I have always dreamed of seeing a real Prince! (*Excited, he presses his nose against gates.*)

1st Guard. Mind your manners, you young beggar! (*Seizes Tom by collar and sends him sprawling into crowd.* Villagers *laugh, as* Tom *slowly gets to his feet.*)

Prince (*rushing to gates*). How dare you treat a poor subject of the King in such a manner! Open the gates and let him in! (*As* Villagers *see* Prince, *they take off their hats and bow low.*)

Villagers (*shouting together*). Long live the Prince of Wales! (Guards *open gates and* Tom *slowly passes through, as if in a dream.*) Ⓑ

---

1. **anteroom** (ăn′tē-ro͞om′): an outer room that leads to another room and is often used as a waiting room.

Monitor Your Comprehension

Ⓐ READING A PLAY
In a play, each scene begins with a description of its setting. Reread lines 1–8. Circle the words in the stage directions that tell when and where the first scene will take place.

Ⓑ READING A PLAY
Reread lines 15–28. Look carefully at the stage directions. What do they reveal about the each boy?

Tom Canty: ____________

____

____

____

Prince Edward: ____________

____

____

____

____

____

____

Monitor Your Comprehension

Prince (*to Tom*). You look tired, and you have been treated cruelly. I am Edward, Prince of Wales. What is your name?

Tom (*looking around in awe*). Tom Canty, Your Highness.

Prince. Come into the palace with me, Tom. (Prince *leads* Tom *into anteroom.* Villagers *pantomime conversation, and all but a few exit.*) Where do you live, Tom?

Tom. In the city, Your Highness, in Offal Court.

Prince. Offal Court? That is an odd name. Do you have parents?

Tom. Yes, Your Highness.

Prince. How does your father treat you?

Tom. If it please you, Your Highness, when I am not able to beg a penny for our supper, he treats me to beatings.

Prince (*shocked*). What! Beatings? My father is not a calm man, but he does not beat me. (*looks at* Tom *thoughtfully*) You speak well and have an easy grace. Have you been schooled?

Tom. Very little, Your Highness. A good priest who shares our house in Offal Court has taught me from his books.

Prince. Do you have a pleasant life in Offal Court?

Tom. Pleasant enough, Your Highness, save when I am hungry. We have Punch and Judy shows, and sometimes we lads have fights in the street.

Prince (*eagerly*). I should like that. Tell me more.

Tom. In summer, we run races and swim in the river, and we love to wallow in the mud.

Prince (*sighing, wistfully*). If I could wear your clothes and play in the mud just once, with no one to forbid me, I think I could give up the crown! C

C CONFLICT IN DRAMA
Reread lines 40–57. Underline words and phrases that give you a clear picture of Tom's life. What does the Prince of Wales find appealing about Tom's life?

Tom (*shaking his head*). And if I could wear your fine clothes just once, Your Highness . . .

Prince. Would you like that? Come, then. We shall change places. You can take off your rags and put on my clothes—and I will put on yours. (*He leads* Tom *behind screen, and they return shortly, each wearing the other's clothes.*) Let's look at ourselves in this mirror. (*leads* Tom *to mirror*)

Tom. Oh, Your Highness, it is not proper for me to wear such clothes.

Prince (*excitedly, as he looks in mirror*). Heavens, do you not see it? We look like brothers! We have the same features and bearing.[2] If we went about together, dressed alike, there is no one who could say which is the Prince of Wales and which is Tom Canty! **D**

Tom (*drawing back and rubbing his hand*). Your Highness, I am frightened. . . .

Prince. Do not worry. (*seeing Tom rub his hand*) Is that a bruise on your hand?

Tom. Yes, but it is a slight thing, Your Highness.

Prince (*angrily*). It was shameful and cruel of that guard to strike you. Do not stir a step until I come back. I command you! (*He picks up golden Seal of England*[3] *and carefully puts it into piece of armor. He then dashes out to gates.*) Open! Unbar the gates at once! (2nd Guard *opens gates, and as* Prince *runs out, in rags,* 1st Guard *seizes him, boxes him on the ear, and knocks him to the ground.*)

1st Guard. Take that, you little beggar, for the trouble you have made for me with the Prince. (Villagers *roar with laughter.*)

Prince (*picking himself up, turning on* Guard *furiously*). I am Prince of Wales! You shall hang for laying your hand on me!

2. **features and bearing:** facial appearance and way of standing or walking.
3. **Seal of England:** a device used to stamp a special design, usually a picture of the ruler, onto a document, thus indicating that it has royal approval.

D CONFLICT IN DRAMA
A **conflict** is a problem or struggle that a character faces in a story. What major conflict is introduced in this conversation between Tom and the prince?

Monitor Your Comprehension

E READING A PLAY
Reread the stage directions in lines 89–92 and 99–102. How do the guards treat each boy? What do their reactions show?

Lines 89–92 ______________

Lines 99–102 ______________

1st Guard (*presenting arms; mockingly*). I salute Your Gracious Highness! (*Then, angrily,* 1st Guard *shoves* Prince *roughly aside.*) Be off, you mad bag of rags! (Prince *is surrounded by* Villagers, *who hustle him off.*)

Villagers (*ad lib,*[4] *as they exit, shouting*). Make way for His Royal Highness! Make way for the Prince of Wales! Hail to the Prince! (*etc.*)

Tom (*admiring himself in mirror*). If only the boys in Offal Court could see me! They will not believe me when I tell them about this. (*looks around anxiously*) But where is the Prince? (*Looks cautiously into courtyard.* Two Guards *immediately snap to attention and salute. He quickly ducks back into anteroom as* Lords Hertford *and* St. John *enter at rear.*) E

Hertford (*going toward* Tom, *then stopping and bowing low*). My Lord, you look distressed. What is wrong?

Tom (*trembling*). Oh, I beg of you, be merciful. I am no Prince, but poor Tom Canty of Offal Court. Please let me see the Prince, and he will give my rags back to me and let me go unhurt. (*kneeling*) Please, be merciful and spare me!

Hertford (*puzzled and disturbed*). Your Highness, on your knees? To me? (*bows quickly, then, aside to* St. John) The Prince has gone mad! We must inform the King. (*to Tom*) A moment, your Highness. (*Hertford and* St. John *exit rear.*)

Tom. Oh, there is no hope for me now. They will hang me for certain! (Hertford *and* St. John *re-enter, supporting* King. Tom *watches in awe as they help him to couch, where he sinks down wearily.*)

King (*beckoning* Tom *close to him*). Now, my son, Edward, my prince. What is this? Do you mean to deceive me, the King, your father, who loves you and treats you so kindly?

4. **ad lib:** talk together about what is going on, but without an actual script.

Monitor Your Comprehension

Tom (*dropping to his knees*). You are the King? Then I have no hope!

King (*stunned*). My child, you are not well. Do not break your father's old heart. Say you know me.

Tom. Yes, you are my lord the King, whom God preserve.

King. True, that is right. Now, you will not deny that you are Prince of Wales, as they say you did just a while ago?

Tom. I beg you, Your Grace, believe me. I am the lowest of your subjects, being born a **pauper**, and it is by a great mistake that I am here. I am too young to die. Oh, please, spare me, sire!

pauper (pô′pər) *n.* someone who is extremely poor

King (*amazed*). Die? Do not talk so, my child. You shall not die. **PAUSE & REFLECT**

PAUSE & REFLECT
Pause at line 132. Why is Tom afraid? Why does the King reassure him?

Tom (*gratefully*). God save you, my king! And now, may I go?

King. Go? Where would you go?

Tom. Back to the alley where I was born and bred to misery.

King. My poor child, rest your head here. (*He holds* Tom's *head and pats his shoulder, then turns to* Hertford *and* St. John.) Alas, I am old and ill, and my son is mad. But this shall pass. Mad or **sane**, he is my heir and shall rule England. Tomorrow he shall be installed and confirmed in his princely dignity! Bring the Great Seal!

Hertford (*bowing low*). Please, Your Majesty, you took the Great Seal from the Chancellor two days ago to give to His Highness the Prince.

King. So I did. (*to* Tom) My child, tell me, where is the Great Seal?

Tom (*trembling*). Indeed, my lord, I do not know.

sane (sān) *adj.* mentally healthy; reasonable

Monitor Your Comprehension

affliction (ə-flĭk'shən) *n.* a cause of pain, suffering, or worry

F CONFLICT IN DRAMA
How does Tom's interaction with the king make the conflict more complicated?

G READING A PLAY
Reread 162–173. How do the actions of the characters create humor in this part of the play?

King. Ah, your **affliction** hangs heavily upon you. 'Tis no matter. You will remember later. Listen, carefully! (*gently, but firmly*) I command you to hide your affliction in all ways that be within your power. You shall deny to no one that you are the true prince, and if your memory should fail you upon any occasion of state, you shall be advised by your uncle, the Lord Hertford.

Tom (*resigned*). The King has spoken. The King shall be obeyed.

King. And now, my child, I go to rest. (*He stands weakly, and* Hertford *leads him off, rear.*) F

Tom (*wearily, to* St. John). May it please your lordship to let me rest now?

St. John. So it please Your Highness, it is for you to command and us to obey. But it is wise that you rest, for this evening you must attend the Lord Mayor's banquet in your honor. (*He pulls bellcord, and* Three Pages *enter and kneel before* Tom.)

Tom. Banquet? (*Terrified, he sits on couch and reaches for cup of water, but* 1st Page *instantly seizes cup, drops on one knee, and serves it to him.* Tom *starts to take off his boots, but* 2nd Page *stops him and does it for him. He tries to remove his cape and gloves, and* 3rd Page *does it for him.*) I wonder that you do not try to breathe for me also! (*Lies down cautiously. Pages cover him with robe, then back away and exit.*) G

St. John (*to* Hertford, *as he enters*). Plainly, what do you think?

Hertford. Plainly, this. The King is near death, my nephew the Prince of Wales is clearly mad and will mount the throne mad. God protect England, for she will need it!

St. John. Does it not seem strange that madness could so change his manner from what it used to be? It troubles me, his saying he is not the Prince.

Hertford. Peace, my lord! If he were an **imposter** and called himself Prince, that would be natural. But was there ever an impostor, who being called Prince by the King and court, denied it? Never! This is the true Prince gone mad. And tonight all London shall honor him. (Hertford *and* St. John *exit.* Tom *sits up, looks around helplessly, then gets up.*)

Tom. I should have thought to order something to eat. (*sees bowl of nuts on table*) Ah! Here are some nuts! (*looks around, sees Great Seal in armor, takes it out, looks at it curiously*) This will make a good nutcracker. (*He takes bowl of nuts, sits on couch and begins to crack nuts with Great Seal and eat them, as curtain falls.*)

SCENE TWO

Time: *Later that night.*

Setting: *A street in London, near Offal Court. Played before the curtain.*

At Curtain Rise: Prince *limps in, dirty and tousled. He looks around wearily. Several* Villagers *pass by, pushing against him.* (H)

Prince. I have never seen this poor section of London. I must be near Offal Court. If I can only find it before I drop! (John Canty *steps out of crowd, seizes* Prince *roughly.*)

Canty. Out at this time of night, and I warrant you haven't brought a farthing[5] home! If that is the case and I do not break all the bones in your miserable body, then I am not John Canty!

Prince (*eagerly*). Oh, are you his father?

Canty. His father? I am *your* father, and—

Prince. Take me to the palace at once, and your son will be returned to you. The King, my father, will make you rich

5. **farthing:** a former British coin worth one-fourth of a British penny.

Monitor Your Comprehension

imposter (ĭm-pŏs′tər) *n.* a person who uses a false name or identity

Why don't the king's men think that Tom is an **imposter**?

(H) **READING A PLAY**

Reread lines 193–197. Circle the stage directions that give information about the setting. Underline the stage directions that describe character movements and behavior. What do these stage directions tell you about what's happening?

Monitor Your Comprehension

CONFLICT IN DRAMA
Reread lines 201–218. What happens when the prince meets Tom's father? Add these details to the chart on page 42.

CONFLICT IN DRAMA
Reread lines 230–235. What does the death of the king mean for Tom? How might this event affect the conflict? Add details about the conflict in Scene Three to the chart on page 42.

beyond your wildest dreams. Oh, save me, for I am indeed the Prince of Wales.

Canty (*staring in amazement*). Gone stark mad! But mad or not, I'll soon find where the soft places lie in your bones. Come home! (*starts to drag* Prince off)

Prince (*struggling*). Let me go! I am the Prince of Wales, and the King shall have your life for this!

Canty (*angrily*). I'll take no more of your madness! (*raises stick to strike, but* Prince *struggles free and runs off, and* Canty *runs after him*)

SCENE THREE

Setting: *Same as Scene 1, with addition of dining table, set with dishes and goblets, on raised platform. Throne-like chair is at head of table.*

At Curtain Rise: *A banquet is in progress.* Tom, *in royal robes, sits at head of table, with* Hertford *at his right and* St. John *at his left.* Lords *and* Ladies *sit around table eating and talking softly.*

Tom (*to* Hertford). What is this, my Lord? (*holds up a plate*)

Hertford. Lettuce and turnips, Your Highness.

Tom. Lettuce and turnips? I have never seen them before. Am I to eat them?

Hertford (*discreetly*). Yes, Your Highness, if you so desire. (Tom *begins to eat food with his fingers. Fanfare of trumpets*[6] *is heard, and* Herald)

Herald (*reading from scroll*). His Majesty, King Henry VIII, is dead! The King is dead! (*All rise and turn to* Tom, *who sits, stunned.*)

---

6. **fanfare of trumpets:** a short tune or call, usually indicating that something important is about to occur.

All (*together*). The King is dead. Long live the King! Long live Edward, King of England! (*All bow to* Tom. Herald *bows and exits.*)

Hertford (*to* Tom). Your Majesty, we must call the council. Come, St. John. (Hertford *and* St. John *lead* Tom *off at rear.* Lords *and* Ladies *follow, talking among themselves. At gates, down right,* Villagers *enter and mill about.* Prince *enters right, pounds on gates and shouts.*)

Prince. Open the gates! I am the Prince of Wales! Open, I say! And though I am friendless with no one to help me, I will not be driven from my ground.

Miles Hendon (*entering through crowd*). Though you be Prince or not, you are indeed a gallant lad and not friendless. Here I stand to prove it, and you might have a worse friend than Miles Hendon.

1st Villager. 'Tis another prince in disguise. Take the lad and dunk him in the pond! (*He seizes* Prince, *but* Miles *strikes him with flat of his sword. Crowd, now angry, presses forward threateningly, when fanfare of trumpets is heard offstage. Herald, carrying scroll, enters up left at gates.*) K

Herald. Make way for the King's messenger! (*reading from scroll*) His Majesty, King Henry VIII, is dead! The King is dead! (*He exits right, repeating message, and* Villagers *stand in stunned silence.*)

Prince (*stunned*). The King is dead!

1st Villager (*shouting*). Long live Edward, King of England!

Villagers (*together*). Long live the King! (*shouting, ad lib*) Long live King Edward! Heaven protect Edward, King of England! (*etc.*)

Miles (*taking* Prince *by the arm*). Come, lad, before the crowd remembers us. I have a room at the inn, and you can

K READING A PLAY

Reread lines 244–255. Underline the stage directions concerning Miles Hendon. What do they tell you about this new character?

Monitor Your Comprehension

L READING A PLAY
Reread lines 261–268. What happens just as the prince leaves the courtyard with Miles?

PAUSE & REFLECT
What role might Miles play in future events? Provide details from the text that support your response.

stay there. (*He hurries off with stunned* Prince. Tom, *led by* Hertford, *enters courtyard up rear.* Villagers *see them.*) L

Villagers (*together*). Long live the King! (*They fall to their knees as curtains close.*)

SCENE FOUR

Setting: *Miles' room at the inn. At right is table set with dishes and bowls of food, a chair at each side. At left is bed, with table and chair next to it, and a window. Candle is on table.*

At Curtain Rise: Miles *and* Prince *approach table.*

Miles. I have had a hot supper prepared. I'll bet you're hungry, lad.

Prince. Yes, I am. It's kind of you to let me stay with you, Miles. I am truly Edward, King of England, and you shall not go unrewarded. (*sits at table*)

Miles (*to himself*). First he called himself Prince, and now he is King. Well, I will humor him. (*starts to sit*)

Prince (*angrily*). Stop! Would you sit in the presence of the King?

Miles (*surprised, standing up quickly*). I beg your pardon, Your Majesty. I was not thinking. (*Stares uncertainly at* Prince, *who sits at table, expectantly. Miles starts to uncover dishes of food, serves* Prince *and fills glasses.*) **PAUSE & REFLECT**

Prince. Miles, you have a gallant way about you. Are you nobly born?

Miles. My father is a baronet,[7] Your Majesty.

Prince. Then you must also be a baronet.

Miles (*shaking his head*). My father banished me from home seven years ago, so I fought in the wars. I was taken prisoner, and I have spent the past seven years in prison. Now I am free, and I am returning home.

7. **baronet:** a rank of honor in Britain, below a baron and above a knight.

Monitor Your Comprehension

Prince. You have been shamefully wronged! But I will make things right for you. You have saved me from injury and possible death. Name your reward and if it be within the compass of my royal power, it is yours.

Miles (*pausing briefly, then dropping to his knee*). Since Your Majesty is pleased to hold my simple duty worthy of reward, I ask that I and my **successors** may hold the privilege of sitting in the presence of the King.

successor (sək-sĕs′ər) *n.* a person who follows another, taking on his or her rights or duties

Prince (*taking* Miles' *sword, tapping him lightly on each shoulder*). Rise and seat yourself. (*returns sword to* Miles, *then rises and goes over to bed*)

Miles (*rising*). He should have been born a king. He plays the part to a marvel! If I had not thought of this favor, I might have had to stand for weeks. (*sits down and begins to eat*)

Prince. Sir Miles, you will stand guard while I sleep? (*lies down and instantly falls asleep*)

Miles. Yes, Your Majesty. (*With a rueful look at his uneaten supper, he stands up.*) Poor little chap. I suppose his mind has been disordered with ill usage. (*covers* Prince *with his cape*) Well, I will be his friend and watch over him. (*Blows out candle, then yawns, sits on chair next to bed, and falls asleep.* John Canty *and* Hugo *appear at window, peer around room, then enter cautiously through window. They lift the sleeping* Prince, *staring nervously at* Miles.)

Canty (*in loud whisper*). I swore the day he was born he would be a thief and a beggar, and I won't lose him now. Lead the way to the camp Hugo! (Canty *and* Hugo *carry* Prince *off right, as* Miles *sleeps on and curtain falls.*) Ⓜ

Ⓜ CONFLICT IN DRAMA
Reread lines 311–323. Why is John Canty so anxious to recover his son? How will this event affect the prince's chance of regaining his throne? Add details about the conflict in Scene Four to the chart on page 42.

SCENE FIVE

Time: *Two weeks later.*

Setting: *Country village street.*

Before Curtain Rise: Villagers *walk about.* Canty, Hugo, *and* Prince *enter.*

Canty. I will go in this direction. Hugo, keep my mad son with you, and see that he doesn't escape again! (*exits*)

Hugo (*seizing* Prince *by the arm*). He won't escape! I'll see that he earns his bread today, or else!

Prince (*pulling away*). I will not beg with you, and I will not steal! I have suffered enough in this miserable company of thieves!

Hugo. You shall suffer more if you do not do as I tell you! (*raises clenched fist at* Prince) Refuse if you dare! (Woman *enters, carrying wrapped bundle in a basket on her arm.*) Wait here until I come back. (Hugo *sneaks along after* Woman, *then snatches her bundle, runs back to* Prince, *and thrusts it into his arms.*) Run after me and call, "Stop, thief!" But be sure you lead her astray! (*Runs off.* Prince *throws down bundle in disgust.*) Ⓝ

Ⓝ **READING A PLAY**
Reread lines 330–342. How is the prince treated by Canty and Hugo?

Woman. Help! Thief! Stop, thief! (*rushes at* Prince *and seizes him, just as several* Villagers *enter*) You little thief! What do you mean by robbing a poor woman? Somebody bring the constable! (Miles *enters and watches.*)

1st Villager (*grabbing* Prince). I'll teach him a lesson, the little villain!

Prince (*struggling*). Take your hands off me! I did not rob this woman!

Miles (*stepping out of crowd and pushing man back with the flat of his sword*). Let us proceed gently, my friends. This is a matter for the law.

Prince (*springing to* Miles' *side*). You have come just in time, Sir Miles. Carve this rabble to rags!

Miles. Speak softly. Trust in me and all shall go well.

Constable (*entering and reaching for* Prince). Come along, young rascal!

Monitor Your Comprehension

Miles. Gently, good friend. He shall go peaceably to the Justice.

Prince. I will not go before a Justice! I did not do this thing!

Miles (*taking him aside*). Sire, will you reject the laws of the realm, yet demand that your subjects respect them?

Prince (*calmer*). You are right, Sir Miles. Whatever the King requires a subject to suffer under the law, he will suffer himself while he holds the station of a subject. (Constable *leads them off right. Villagers follow. Curtain.*) PAUSE & REFLECT

PAUSE & REFLECT
Reread lines 362–367. What has the prince learned so far about trading places? Add details about the conflict in Scene Five to the chart on page 42.

SCENE SIX

Setting: *Office of the Justice. A high bench is at center.*

At Curtain Rise: Justice *sits behind bench.* Constable *enters with* Miles *and* Prince, *followed by* Villagers. Woman *carries wrapped bundle.*

Constable (*to* Justice). A young thief, your worship, is accused of stealing a dressed pig from this poor woman.

Justice (*looking down at* Prince, *then* Woman). My good woman, are you absolutely certain this lad stole your pig?

Woman. It was none other than he, your worship.

Justice. Are there no witnesses to the contrary? (*All shake their heads.*) Then the lad stands convicted. (*to* Woman) What do you hold this property to be worth?

Woman. Three shillings and eight pence, your worship.

Justice (*leaning down to* Woman). Good woman, do you know that when one steals a thing above the value of thirteen pence, the law says he shall hang for it?

Woman (*upset*). Oh, what have I done? I would not hang the poor boy for the whole world! Save me from this, your worship. What can I do?

Justice (*gravely*). You may revise the value, since it is not yet written in the record.

Woman. Then call the pig eight pence, your worship.

Justice. So be it. You may take your property and go. (Woman *starts off, and is followed by* Constable. Miles *follows them cautiously down right.*)

Constable (*stopping* Woman). Good woman, I will buy your pig from you. (*takes coins from pocket*) Here is eight pence.

Woman. Eight pence! It cost me three shillings and eight pence!

Constable. Indeed! Then come back before his worship and answer for this. The lad must hang!

Woman. No! No! Say no more. Give me the eight pence and hold your peace. (Constable *hands her coins and takes pig.* Woman *exits, angrily.* Miles *returns to bench.*)

Justice. The boy is sentenced to a fortnight[8] in the common jail. Take him away, Constable! (Justice *exits.* Prince *gives* Miles *a nervous glance.*)

Miles (*following* Constable). Good sir, turn your back a moment and let the poor lad escape. He is innocent.

Constable (*outraged*). What? You say this to me? Sir, I arrest you in—

Miles. Do not be so hasty! (*slyly*) The pig you have purchased for eight pence may cost you your neck, man.

Constable (*laughing nervously*). Ah, but I was merely jesting with the woman, sir.

Miles. Would the Justice think it a jest?

Constable. Good sir! The Justice has no more sympathy with a jest than a dead corpse! (*perplexed*) Very well, I will turn my back and see nothing! But go quickly! (*exits*) ⊙

⊙ **CONFLICT IN DRAMA**
As the play progresses, Miles' role expands. Reread lines 399–416. What is Miles trying to accomplish in this scene?

---

8. **fortnight:** 14 days.

Miles (*to* Prince). Come, my liege.[9] We are free to go. And that band of thieves shall not set hands on you again, I swear it!

Prince (*wearily*). Can you believe, Sir Miles, that in the last fortnight, I, the King of England, have escaped from thieves and begged for food on the road? I have slept in a barn with a calf! I have washed dishes in a peasant's kitchen, and narrowly escaped death. And not once in all my wanderings did I see a courier[10] searching for me! Is it no matter for commotion and distress that the head of state is gone?

Miles (*sadly, aside*). Still busy with his pathetic dream. (*to* Prince) It is strange indeed, my liege. But come, I will take you to my father's home in Kent. We are not far away. There you may rest in a house with seventy rooms! Come, I am all impatience to be home again! (*They exit,* Miles *in cheerful spirits,* Prince *looking puzzled, as curtains close.*) Ⓟ

PAUSE & REFLECT

SCENE SEVEN

Setting: *Village jail. Bare stage, with barred window on one wall.*

At Curtain Rise: Two Prisoners, *in chains, are onstage.* Jailer *shoves* Miles *and* Prince, *in chains, onstage. They struggle and protest.*

Miles. But I tell you, I am Miles Hendon! My brother, Sir Hugh, has stolen my bride and my estate!

Jailer. Be silent! Impostor! Sir Hugh will see that you pay well for claiming to be his dead brother and for assaulting him in his own house! (*exits*)

---

9. **my liege** (lēj): my lord.
10. **courier** (ko͝or'ē-ər): messenger.

Monitor Your Comprehension

Ⓟ CONFLICT IN DRAMA
Reread lines 420–433. Note that the prince is surprised that no one is looking for him. Should he be surprised? Why or why not?

PAUSE & REFLECT
Why does the prince look puzzled as the scene closes? Add details about the conflict in Scene Six to the chart on page 42.

Monitor Your Comprehension

Q CONFLICT IN DRAMA
Reread lines 457–458. What does this information, revealed by the prisoner, mean for the prince? Add details about the conflict in Scene Seven to the chart on page 42.

Miles (*sitting, with head in hands*). Oh, my dear Edith . . . now wife to my brother Hugh, against her will, and my poor father . . . dead!

1st Prisoner. At least you have your life, sir. I am sentenced to be hanged for killing a deer in the King's park.

2nd Prisoner. And I must hang for stealing a yard of cloth to dress my children.

Prince (*moved; to* Prisoners). When I mount my throne, you shall all be free. And the laws that have dishonored you shall be swept from the books. (*turning away*) Kings should go to school to learn their own laws and be merciful.

1st Prisoner. What does the lad mean? I have heard that the King is mad, but merciful.

2nd Prisoner. He is to be crowned at Westminster tomorrow. Q

Prince (*violently*). King? What King, good sir?

1st Prisoner. Why, we have only one, his most sacred majesty, King Edward the Sixth.

2nd Prisoner. And whether he be mad or not, his praises are on all men's lips. He has saved many innocent lives, and now he means to destroy the cruelest laws that oppress the people.

Prince (*turning away, shaking his head*). How can this be? Surely it is not that little beggar boy! (Sir Hugh *enters with* Jailer.)

Sir Hugh. Seize the impostor!

Miles (*as* Jailer *pulls him to his feet*). Hugh, this has gone far enough!

Sir Hugh. You will sit in the public stocks for two hours, and the boy would join you if he were not so young. See to it, jailer, and after two hours, you may release them.

Monitor Your Comprehension

Meanwhile, I ride to London for the coronation![11] (Sir Hugh *exits* and Miles *is hustled out by* Jailer.)

Prince. Coronation! What does he mean? There can be no coronation without me! (*curtain falls.*)

SCENE EIGHT

Time: *Coronation Day.*

Setting: *Outside gates of Westminster Abbey, played before curtain. Painted screen or flat at rear represents Abbey. Throne is in center. Bench is near it.*

At Curtain Rise: Lords *and* Ladies *crowd Abbey. Outside gates,* Guards *drive back cheering* Villagers, *among them* Miles.

Miles (*distraught*). I've lost him! Poor little chap! He has been swallowed up in the crowd! (*Fanfare of trumpets is heard, then silence.* Hertford, St. John, Lords *and* Ladies *enter slowly, in a procession, followed by* Pages, *one of whom carries crown on a small cushion.* Tom *follows procession, looking about nervously. Suddenly,* Prince, *in rags, steps out from crowd, his hand raised.*) Ⓡ

Ⓡ **READING A PLAY**
Reread lines 484–490. How do the stage directions in this part of the play contribute to tension in the drama?

11. **coronation:** the act of crowning someone king or queen. In England coronations usually take place at a large church in London called Westminster Abbey.

S CONFLICT IN DRAMA
Reread lines 491–497. What does the meeting between Tom and the prince suggest about how the prince's problem might be resolved?

Prince. I forbid you to set the crown of England upon that head. I am the King!

Hertford. Seize the little vagabond!

Tom. I forbid it! He is the King! (*kneels before* Prince) Oh, my lord the King, let poor Tom Canty be the first to say, "Put on your crown and enter into your own right again." (Hertford *and several* Lords *look closely at both boys.*) S

Hertford. This is strange indeed. (*to* Tom) By your favor, sir, I wish to ask certain questions of this lad.

Prince. I will answer truly whatever you may ask, my lord.

Hertford. But if you have been well trained, you may answer my questions as well as our lord the King. I need a definite proof. (*thinks a moment*) Ah! Where lies the Great Seal of England? It has been missing for weeks, and only the true Prince of Wales can say where it lies.

Tom. Wait! Was the seal round and thick, with letters engraved on it? (Hertford *nods.*) I know where it is, but it was not I who put it there. The rightful King shall tell you. (*to* Prince) Think, my King, it was the very last thing you did that day before you rushed out of the palace wearing my rags.

recollection (rək′ə-lĕk′shən) *n.* something remembered

Why might the prince have no **recollection** of where he put the Great Seal?

Prince (*pausing*). I recall how we exchanged clothes, but have no **recollection** of hiding the Great Seal.

Tom (*eagerly*). Remember when you saw the bruise on my hand, you ran to the door, but first you hid this thing you call the Seal.

Prince (*suddenly*). Ah! I remember! (*to* St. John) Go, my good St. John, and you shall find the Great Seal in the armor that hangs on the wall in my chamber. (St. John *hesitates, but at a nod from* Tom, *hurries off.*)

Tom (*pleased*). Right, my King! Now the scepter[12] of England is yours again. (St. John *returns in a moment with Great Seal.*)

All (*shouting*). Long live Edward, King of England! (Tom *takes off his cape and throws it over* Prince's *rags. Trumpet fanfare is heard.* St. John *takes crown and places it on* Prince. *All kneel.*) T

Hertford. Let the small impostor be flung into the Tower!

Prince (*firmly*). I will not have it so. But for him, I would not have my crown. (*to* Tom) My poor boy, how was it that you could remember where I hid the Seal, when I could not?

Tom (*embarrassed*). I did not know what it was, my King, and I used it to . . . to crack nuts. (*All laugh, and* Tom *steps back.* Miles *steps forward, staring in amazement.*)

Miles. Is he really the King? Is he indeed the sovereign of England, and not the poor and friendless Tom o' Bedlam[13] I thought he was? (*He sinks down on bench.*) I wish I had a bag to hide my head in!

1st Guard (*rushing up to him*). Stand up, you mannerless clown! How dare you sit in the presence of the King!

Prince. Do not touch him! He is my trusty servant, Miles Hendon, who saved me from shame and possible death. For his service, he owns the right to sit in my presence.

Miles (*bowing, then kneeling*). Your Majesty!

Prince. Rise, Sir Miles. I command that Sir Hugh Hendon, who sits within this hall, be seized and put under lock and key until I have need of him. (*beckons to* Tom) From what I have heard, Tom Canty, you have governed the realm with royal gentleness and mercy in my absence. Henceforth, you shall hold the honorable title of King's Ward! (Tom *kneels*

12. **scepter** (sĕp′tər): a baton or other emblem of royal authority.
13. **Tom o' Bedlam:** an insane person, such as someone hospitalized at St. Mary of Bethlehem Hospital, or Bedlam Hospital, in London.

Monitor Your Comprehension

T CONFLICT IN DRAMA
Reread lines 517–527. How is the major conflict resolved? Add details about the conflict to the chart on page 42.

Monitor Your Comprehension

PAUSE & REFLECT
Consider how Tom appears to be able to rule without any preparation, while the prince learns how to rule through his experiences as a pauper. What message does this play convey about good leadership qualities?

and kisses Prince's *hand.*) And because I have suffered with the poorest of my subjects and felt the cruel force of unjust laws, I pledge myself to a reign of mercy for all! (*All bow low, then rise.*)

All (*shouting*). Long live the King! Long live Edward, King of England! (*curtain*) **PAUSE & REFLECT**

Literary Analysis: Conflict in Drama

The main conflict in the drama *The Prince and the Pauper* revolves around a change of identities. In the chart below, write down the main event of each scene. Then, circle the scene in which the resolution takes place.

READING 5 Understand, make inferences, and draw conclusions about the structure and elements of drama.

Scene 1:	*The guards mistake the prince for Tom, and the king thinks that Tom is the prince.*
Scene 2:	
Scene 3:	
Scene 4:	
Scene 5:	
Scene 6:	
Scene 7:	
Scene 8:	

Review your notes for *The Prince and the Pauper* and your completed charts. What lessons did the boys learn about themselves and each other by trading places?

____

____

____

After Reading

READING 5 Understand, make inferences, and draw conclusions about the structure and elements of drama.

Reading Strategy: Reading a Play

Review your "Reading a Play" notes on stage directions. Pick one example from the play of each type of stage direction, and explain how it helped you understand the play.

Type of Direction	Example	How It Helps
Setting, Scenery, Props		
Music, Sound Effects, Lighting		
Characters' Movements, Behavior, or Ways of Speaking		

Who would you BE if you could?

What does *The Prince and the Pauper* teach readers about wanting to be someone else?

___

___

Vocabulary Practice

Choose the letter of the word or phrase that best completes each sentence below.

1. A **sane** person is **(a)** reasonable, **(b)** foolish, **(c)** gifted.
2. Someone who can treat a physical **affliction** is a **(a)** judge, **(b)** teacher, **(c)** doctor.
3. A **recollection** is a **(a)** debt, **(b)** memory, **(c)** dream.
4. The coach's **successor** will **(a)** assist at games, **(b)** keep score, **(c)** coach the team next.
5. A **pauper** is a **(a)** robber, **(b)** poor person, **(c)** ruler.
6. An **imposter** is a **(a)** designer, **(b)** fake, **(c)** helper.

Academic Vocabulary in Speaking

READING 5 Understand, make inferences, and draw conclusions about the structure and elements of drama.

affect	analyze	evidence	impact	provide

TURN AND TALK With a partner, **analyze** the stage directions used to describe Tom Canty in the play. How do the stage directions **affect** the way you imagine him? Does Tom seem more lifelike or worthy of your sympathy because of these directions? Try to use at least two Academic Vocabulary words in your response. Definitions of these words are on page 3.

Texas Assessment Practice

DIRECTIONS Use *The Prince and the Pauper* to answer questions 1–6.

1 The prince and Tom realize that they look like brothers when they —

- (A) first meet
- (B) reunite at the end
- (C) are each struck by a guard
- (D) look in the mirror after trading clothes

2 What element of drama provides key information to readers that normally they would see or hear during a performance?

- (F) characters
- (G) plot
- (H) stage directions
- (J) conflict

3 The main conflict of this play is about —

- (A) giving up an identity and not being able to reclaim it
- (B) giving up a rich lifestyle and wanting it back
- (C) learning the truth about how people with little or no money are treated
- (D) learning the truth about how a royal court operates

4 What does the Prince of Wales find appealing about Tom's life?

- (F) the beatings
- (G) the clothing
- (H) the freedom
- (J) the poverty

5 The play's main conflict is resolved when —

- (A) Tom finds the Great Seal
- (B) the prince tells St. John where to find the Great Seal
- (C) Miles returns the prince to the royal court
- (D) Tom returns to Offal Court

6 Why does Miles help the prince?

- (F) He feels sorry for a boy he believes is mad.
- (G) He hopes to get a position in the royal court.
- (H) He thinks the prince will pay him a large sum of money.
- (J) He wants to locate Tom.

READING 5 Explain the similarities and differences between the setting, characters, and plot of a play and those in a film based upon the same story line. **RC-6(F)** Make connections across multiple texts of various genres.

Twain's Tale Transplanted to Today

Film Review

Background

The play version of *The Prince and the Pauper* keeps the same basic setting, characters, and plot as Mark Twain's novel. A recent movie adaptation of *The Prince and the Pauper* brings the story to America and modern times. In this film review, you'll read about the similarities and differences between the movie and Twain's classic story.

Skill Focus: Compare and Contrast Versions of a Story

Some stories are so popular and timeless that they exist in different forms, or versions. A well-known tale such as "Snow White," for example, has been adapted many times. Stories can even be retold in a different genre, or type, of literature. A novel might become a play, which is made into a movie, then adapted into a musical, and then turned into a graphic novel.

When you compare and contrast different versions of a story:

- Think about the characters, setting, and plot, or story line, of each story. Ask yourself: *Are the characters and setting the same or different? How similar are the story lines?*
- Look for clue words and phrases. A similarity can be signaled by words and phrases such as *alike, the same as, similar to, faithful to, as in*. A difference can be signaled by *unlike, differ, instead of, different*.

As you read the film review, use this chart to note the main similarities and differences between Twain's classic tale and the movie version.

The Prince and the Pauper

Story Parts	Play	Film
Setting	sixteenth-century England	
Characters	Tom Canty, a pauper	
Plot		

Twain's Tale
TRANSPLANTED TO TODAY

Sprouse twins on the red carpet

Does the world really need another version of Mark Twain's classic story *The Prince and the Pauper*? The creators of the 2007 film *The Prince and the Pauper: A Modern Twain Story* thought so—probably because they were counting on large numbers of young viewers jumping at the chance to see "twin sensations" Cole and Dylan Sprouse in a story seemingly tailor-made for these twin brothers.

The Prince and the Pauper: A Modern Twain Story transplants the often-told tale to today's world. In fact, certain details in this update are more faithful to Twain's original story than one might expect. For example, Dylan Sprouse's character is named Tom Canty, the same as the pauper character in Twain's story, and Cole Sprouse plays Eddie Tudor, a clever updating of the name of Edward, the Tudor prince. There's also a helpful adult friend named Miles. The basic outline of the plot remains essentially the same: two boys from "opposite sides of the track" meet accidentally. One is rich and famous and the other is

SET A PURPOSE FOR READING

Read "Twain's Tale Transplanted to Today" to understand the similarities and differences between Mark Twain's classic story, *The Prince and the Pauper,* and a movie version of it.

FOCUS ON FORM

A **film review** is a short essay about a movie that the writer has seen. The author's main purpose for writing a film review is to express an opinion. A film review also includes details that describe the major events in the film.

not, but they are the spitting image of each other. Each boy is unhappy with his own life and thinks the other boy's life has certain advantages. The boys suddenly decide to switch identities in order to see whether the grass really is greener on the other side. When the boys are unexpectedly separated after trading places, each boy gets trapped in a life that's not his own. As in Twain's story, each boy is surrounded by adults who fear he is going insane—or worse. The boys have to overcome various obstacles in order to return to their rightful places, and no one believes that the boys are who they say they are until a final reunion reveals the truth to all. Ⓐ

The updates to Twain's story are cleverly handled. Instead of sixteenth-century England, the setting is Palm Beach and Miami Beach in the present day. Instead of events revolving around a royal court, they revolve around the world of movies and acting. The "prince" is what might be considered royalty today—a teen actor with millions of fans. The "pauper" is a kid from a difficult background who has to work for his grandfather's landscaping business. In this version of the story, however, the two boys are united by more than physical appearance: they both feel lonely, and they both feel misunderstood by the adults in their lives. Acting is what they have in common, though in different ways: Tom, who idolizes Eddie, wants more than anything to be an actor. Eddie, who is an actor, resents the time his career takes up and would rather be playing with other kids. Ⓑ

As in Twain's story, when the boys change places, each gets the opportunity to learn something

Ⓐ COMPARE AND CONTRAST VERSIONS
Reread lines 9–33. Underline clue words and phrases that signal similarities. Circle the similarities in the characters and plot that the reviewer notes.

Ⓑ COMPARE AND CONTRAST VERSIONS
Reread lines 34–50. Underline words and phrases that signal differences. What differences in character and setting does the reviewer mention? Add them to the chart.

Setting
Play:
Film:

Character
Play:
Film:

important about life. Eddie Tudor, the "prince" in this film, is not the thoughtful observer of life that the prince in Twain's novel is, and he has a long way to go in becoming a wiser person. Tom Canty is, from the beginning, a better person than his idol Eddie in every way—even, as it turns out, as an actor. Like his pauper namesake in the Twain novel, Tom makes a great substitute for the real "prince." **C**

When Eddie finally makes it back to the movie set, he just wants to beat the stuffing out of Tom for impersonating him. Only after a slapstick chase scene and a final winding-down of events does Eddie show signs that he has become a better person from living Tom's life: he hugs his mother (his film producer) and tells her he understands that she is hard on him because she loves him.

Tom benefits the most directly from the switch, for he learns that his dreams of being an actor are not idle fantasies. He really *can* act. Eddie's transformation is less direct and comes through a plot twist involving Tom's adult friend Miles, a washed-up actor who had attempted to teach Eddie (thinking he was Tom) the importance of treating other people with kindness and respect.

In a nice touch, the film ends with Tom and Eddie acting together in a traditional film version of *The Prince and the Pauper*, reminding us of the timelessness of this story. Although this direct-to-video film is unlikely to win any awards or become a classic, it is a pleasant family film with plenty of humor and a few gentle messages that kids should hear and adults shouldn't forget. **PAUSE & REFLECT**

C COMPARE AND CONTRAST VERSIONS
Reread lines 51–60. How is the prince in the play different from the "prince" in the movie?

PAUSE & REFLECT
Explain whether a viewer of the film version of *The Prince and the Pauper* could enjoy the story without reading the play version.

READING 5 Explain the similarities and differences between the setting, characters, and plot of a play and those in a film based upon the same story line. RC-6(F) Make connections across multiple texts of various genres.

Practicing Your Skills

Review your notes for *The Prince and the Pauper* and "Twain's Tale Transplanted to Today." Complete the chart to compare the main characters in the play and the film. Then answer the question that follows.

Characters	Play	Film
Tom Canty		
Prince Edward/ Eddie Tudor		

Compare and Contrast Versions of a Story

Compare and contrast the "prince" character and the "pauper" character in the film with the prince and the pauper of the play. Which character in the film version seems closer to his counterpart in the play version? Explain.

Academic Vocabulary in Speaking

affect	analyze	evidence	impact	provide

TURN AND TALK Discuss with a partner how the setting and characters of the film appeal to audiences today. What other settings and characters might work well for an updated version of this story? **Provide** at least two examples in your discussion. Include at least two Academic Vocabulary words in your response. Definitions of these words are on page 3.

READING 5 Explain the similarities and differences between the setting, characters, and plot of a play and those in a film based upon the same story line. **RC-6(F)** Make connections across multiple texts of various genres.

Texas Assessment Practice

DIRECTIONS Use "Twain's Tale Transplanted to Today" to answer questions 1–6.

1 The author's main purpose for writing a film review is to —

- (A) explain what happens in the film
- (B) express an opinion about the film
- (C) inform the reader about where and when the film takes place
- (D) persuade the reader to read the novel

2 According to the reviewer, the main difference between the film and Twain's original story lies mostly in the —

- (F) time and place
- (G) series of events
- (H) character Miles
- (J) stage directions

3 The main similarity between the film and the play lies mostly in the —

- (A) characters
- (B) setting
- (C) plot or story line
- (D) title

4 One way in which the two boys in the film are similar is that both have —

- (F) an interest in the royal court
- (G) an interest in acting
- (H) a network of close friends
- (J) previously acted in school plays

5 How is the story line of the play version and film version similar?

- (A) Both the play and the film involve a royal court.
- (B) Both conclude with a modern-day version of Twain's story.
- (C) The pauper character is disloyal to the prince in both versions.
- (D) There is a case of mistaken identify in both versions.

6 How is the character of Eddie Tudor in the film version different from the prince in the play version?

- (F) He is not as likable in the film.
- (G) He makes better decisions in the film.
- (H) He is more willing to change in the film.
- (J) He works hard in the film.

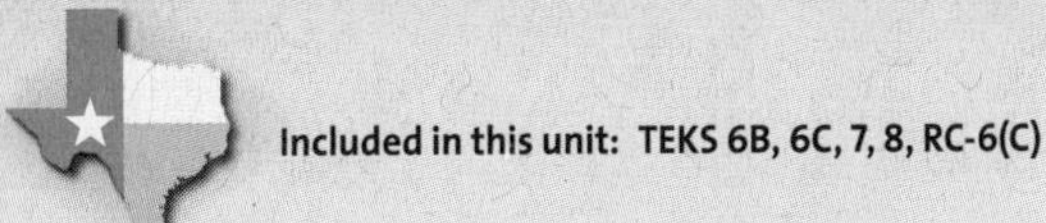

Included in this unit: TEKS 6B, 6C, 7, 8, RC-6(C)

UNIT 2 Person to Person

ANALYZING CHARACTER AND POINT OF VIEW

Be sure to read the Reader's Workshop on pp. 192–197 in *Holt McDougal Literature*.

Academic Vocabulary for Unit 2

Academic Vocabulary is the language you use to discuss literary and informational texts. Preview the following Academic Vocabulary words. You will use these words as you write and talk about the selections in this unit.

convey (kən-vā′) *v.* to make known, express
*What does the main character say to **convey** his feelings?*

•

create (krē-āt′) *v.* to produce something; to use imagination to invent things
*The writer includes realistic details to **create** a believable setting.*

•

influence (in-flo͞o′əns) *n.* ability or power to affect thought, behavior, or development
*Which character had the greatest **influence** on the main character?*

•

interact (in′tər-akt′) *v.* to talk to and deal with others
*What surprises you most about the way the characters **interact**?*

•

qualities (kwôl′ə-tēz) *n.* traits; distinguishing characteristics
*Describe one of the main character's admirable **qualities**.*

Think of a character from a book you've read or a movie you've seen. Write a brief paragraph to describe the **qualities** that made the character memorable, using at least two Academic Vocabulary words in your response.

___

___

___

___

___

Before Reading

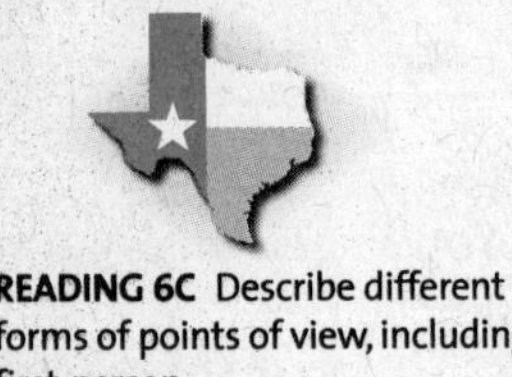

READING 6C Describe different forms of points of view, including first-person.

Eleven

Short Story by Sandra Cisneros

Is AGE more than a number?

For some people, a birthday is an exciting event. With each increase in age, they feel more mature. For others, a birthday is just the day they were born. Inside, they may not feel any different than they did the day before. In "Eleven," a young girl struggles with what it means to grow older.

DISCUSS Think about what your age means to you. List the things that matter to you now. Then, consider how you might feel about the things that matter to you when you are a year older. Share your ideas with the class.

What matters to me

1) Now: ______________________

____

____

One year from now: ______________________

____

____

2) Now: ______________________

____

____

One year from now: ______________________

____

____

3) Now: ______________________

____

____

One year from now: ______________________

____

____

Literary Analysis: First-Person Point of View

This story lets you into the mind of its main character, Rachel, who is also the narrator. Rachel uses the **first-person point of view,** speaking as "I." The chart below explains first-person point of view.

- reveals qualities through words, thoughts, and feelings
- is a character in the story using the pronouns *I, me,* and *my*
- STORY
- does not know what other characters are thinking and feeling

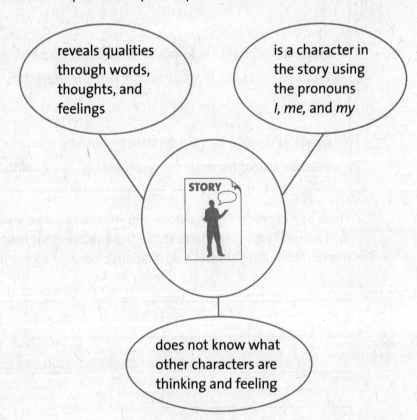

As you read, consider what you learn from the first-person narrator. Also, think about the information that Rachel cannot share with you, such as what other characters are thinking.

Reading Strategy: Connect

READING 8 Understand how an author's sensory language creates imagery. **RC-6(C)** Monitor and adjust comprehension (creating sensory images).

Authors often express an idea or feeling with **imagery,** words and phrases that appeal to the senses of sight, taste, touch, smell, and hearing. The imagery in a story may remind you of your own feelings, experiences, and imagination. When you connect sensory imagery to your own ideas, it will help you to better understand what you are reading.

As you read "Eleven," notes in the side column will ask you to record imagery and your own connections in a chart like the one below.

Imagery	My Connections
"Underneath the year that makes you eleven"	Remember still feeling 10 on my 11th birthday.

Vocabulary in Context

Note: Words are listed in the order in which they appear in the story.

raggedy (răg'ĭ-dē) *adj.* tattered or worn out
*Her old, **raggedy** clothes embarrassed her.*

alley (ăl'ē) *n.* a narrow street behind or between buildings
*After school, she ran home through the back **alley**.*

except (ĭk-sĕpt') *prep.* but; however
***Except** for math, the girl did well in school.*

invisible (ĭn-vĭz'ə-bəl) *adj.* not able to be seen
*She felt **invisible** among the crowds of students.*

Vocabulary Practice

Review the vocabulary words and think about their meanings. Then use one or more of the words to write a short description of a memory from when you were younger.

____

____

____

____

____

SET A PURPOSE FOR READING

Read "Eleven" to find out what Rachel thinks about turning eleven.

ELEVEN

Short Story by

SANDRA CISNEROS

BACKGROUND Sandra Cisneros was born in Chicago and grew up speaking Spanish and English. In much of her writing, Cisneros explores the feeling of being shy and out of place. Her childhood experiences, her family, and her Mexican American heritage all find a place in her writing.

What they don't understand about birthdays and what they never tell you is that when you're eleven, you're also ten, and nine, and eight, and seven, and six, and five, and four, and three, and two, and one. And when you wake up on your eleventh birthday you expect to feel eleven, but you don't. You open your eyes and everything's just like yesterday, only it's today. And you don't feel eleven at all. You feel like you're still ten. And you are—underneath the year that makes you eleven. Ⓐ

Like some days you might say something stupid, and that's the part of you that's still ten. Or maybe some days you might need to sit on your mama's lap because you're scared, and that's the part of you that's five. And maybe one day when you're all grown up maybe you will need to cry like if you're three, and that's okay. That's what

Ⓐ **FIRST-PERSON POINT OF VIEW**

What thoughts and feelings does the narrator reveal about herself in lines 1–9?

Monitor Your Comprehension

I tell Mama when she's sad and needs to cry. Maybe she's feeling three.

Because the way you grow old is kind of like an onion or like the rings inside a tree trunk or like my little wooden dolls that fit one inside the other, each year inside the next one. That's how being eleven years old is.

You don't feel eleven. Not right away. It takes a few days, weeks even, sometimes even months before you say Eleven when they ask you. And you don't feel smart eleven, not until you're almost twelve. That's the way it is.

Only today I wish I didn't have only eleven years rattling inside me like pennies in a tin Band-Aid box. Today I wish I was one hundred and two instead of eleven because if I was one hundred and two I'd have known what to say when Mrs. Price put the red sweater on my desk. I would've known how to tell her it wasn't mine instead of just sitting there with that look on my face and nothing coming out of my mouth.

"Whose is this?" Mrs. Price says, and she holds the red sweater up in the air for all the class to see. "Whose? It's been sitting in the coatroom for a month."

"Not mine," says everybody. "Not me."

"It has to belong to somebody," Mrs. Price keeps saying, but nobody can remember. It's an ugly sweater with red plastic buttons and a collar and sleeves all stretched out like you could use it for a jump rope. It's maybe a thousand years old and even if it belonged to me I wouldn't say so. **B**

Maybe because I'm skinny, maybe because she doesn't like me, that stupid Sylvia Saldívar says, "I think it belongs to Rachel." An ugly sweater like that, all **raggedy** and old, but Mrs. Price believes her. Mrs. Price takes the sweater and puts it right on my desk, but when I open my mouth nothing comes out.

"That's not, I don't, you're not . . . Not mine," I finally say in a little voice that was maybe me when I was four.

B CONNECT
Reread lines 38–42. How does the imagery describing the sweater help you understand how Rachel feels?

____
____
____
____
____
____

raggedy (răg'ĭ-dē) *adj.* tattered or worn out

Monitor Your Comprehension

C FIRST-PERSON POINT OF VIEW
In stories using first-person point of view, the narrator's words reveal his or her own personality. In lines 52–53, Rachel thinks, "Because she's older and the teacher, she's right and I'm not." What does this tell you about Rachel?

alley (ăl′ē) *n.* a narrow street behind or between buildings

except (ĭk-sĕpt′) *prep.* but; however

D FIRST-PERSON POINT OF VIEW
Reread lines 78–82. What impression of Mrs. Price does Rachel give the reader?

"Of course it's yours," Mrs. Price says. "I remember you wearing it once." Because she's older and the teacher, she's right and I'm not. C

Not mine, not mine, not mine, but Mrs. Price is already turning to page thirty-two, and math problem number four. I don't know why but all of a sudden I'm feeling sick inside, like the part of me that's three wants to come out of my eyes, only I squeeze them shut tight and bite down on my teeth real hard and try to remember today I am eleven, eleven. Mama is making a cake for me for tonight, and when Papa comes home everybody will sing Happy birthday, happy birthday to you.

But when the sick feeling goes away and I open my eyes, the red sweater's still sitting there like a big red mountain. I move the red sweater to the corner of my desk with my ruler. I move my pencil and books and eraser as far from it as possible. I even move my chair a little to the right. Not mine, not mine, not mine.

In my head I'm thinking how long till lunchtime, how long till I can take the red sweater and throw it over the schoolyard fence, or leave it hanging on a parking meter, or bunch it up into a little ball and toss it in the **alley**. **Except** when math period ends Mrs. Price says loud and in front of everybody, "Now, Rachel, that's enough," because she sees I've shoved the red sweater to the tippy-tip corner of my desk and it's hanging all over the edge like a waterfall, but I don't care.

"Rachel," Mrs. Price says. She says it like she's getting mad. "You put that sweater on right now and no more nonsense."

"But it's not—"

"Now!" Mrs. Price says. D

This is when I wish I wasn't eleven, because all the years inside of me—ten, nine, eight, seven, six, five, four, three, two, and one—are pushing at the back of my eyes when I put one arm through one sleeve of the sweater that smells like cottage cheese, and then the other arm through the other and stand there with my arms apart like if the sweater hurts me and it does, all itchy and full of germs that aren't even mine.

That's when everything I've been holding in since this morning, since when Mrs. Price put the sweater on my desk, finally lets go, and all of a sudden I'm crying in front of everybody. I wish I was **invisible** but I'm not. I'm eleven and it's my birthday today and I'm crying like I'm three in front of everybody. I put my head down on the desk and bury my face in my stupid clown-sweater arms. My face all hot and spit coming out of my mouth because I can't stop the little animal noises from coming out of me, until there aren't any more tears left in my eyes, and it's just my body shaking like when you have the hiccups, and my whole head hurts like when you drink milk too fast. Ⓔ

But the worst part is right before the bell rings for lunch. That stupid Phyllis Lopez, who is even dumber than Sylvia Saldívar, says she remembers the red sweater is hers! I take it off right away and give it to her, only Mrs. Price pretends like everything's okay. Ⓕ

Today I'm eleven. There's a cake Mama's making for tonight, and when Papa comes home from work we'll eat it. There'll be candles and presents and everybody will sing Happy birthday, happy birthday to you, Rachel, only it's too late.

I'm eleven today. I'm eleven, ten, nine, eight, seven, six, five, four, three, two, and one, but I wish I was one

Monitor Your Comprehension

invisible (ĭn-vĭz'ə-bəl) *adj.* not able to be seen

Ⓔ CONNECT
Reread lines 83–103. Which images help you understand Rachel's feelings? Add them to your chart.

Imagery

↓

My Connections

Ⓕ FIRST-PERSON POINT OF VIEW
Reread lines 104–108. How does the first-person point of view affect what you know about Sylvia and Phyllis?

Monitor Your Comprehension

PAUSE & REFLECT
Explain whether you think Rachel overreacts to the incident with the sweater. How else could she have responded?

hundred and two. I wish I was anything but eleven, because I want today to be far away already, far away like a runaway balloon, like a tiny *o* in the sky, so tiny-tiny you have to close your eyes to see it. **PAUSE & REFLECT**

Literary Analysis: First-Person Point of View

In "Eleven," Rachel tells the story using first-person point of view. As the narrator of the story, Rachel shares many of her thoughts and feelings. However, she is not able to tell us the thoughts and feelings of the other characters. Complete the chart below by recording what you learned about characters and what you would still like to know.

READING 6C Describe different forms of points of view, including first-person.

	What I Learned from Rachel	What I Would Like to Know
Rachel		
Mrs. Price		
Sylvia and Phyllis		

Review your notes for "Eleven." What might Mrs. Price have been thinking when she put the sweater on Rachel's desk? How do you think Mrs. Price would describe the incident from her point of view?

After Reading

READING 8 Understand how an author's sensory language creates imagery. **RC-6(C)** Monitor and adjust comprehension (creating sensory images).

Reading Strategy: Connect

Near the end of "Eleven" (lines 83–119), Rachel focuses on three different images. In the first column, record the connections Rachel makes with these images. In the second column, describe two or more feelings you might normally associate with these images

Image	Connections for Rachel	My Connections
a red sweater		
a birthday party		
a runaway balloon		

Explain whether your connections are similar or different to Rachel's.

____

____

____

Is AGE more than a number?

Revisit the list you wrote about what your age means to you on page 76. Think about the list Rachel might have written. Use details from the story to complete a list of what Rachel's age means to her.

____

____

____

Vocabulary Practice

Choose the letter of the word or phrase that is most closely related to the boldfaced word.

1. **except:** **(a)** not including, **(b)** with, **(c)** as well as, **(d)** plus
2. **invisible:** **(a)** impossible, **(b)** white, **(c)** unseen, **(d)** unwell
3. **alley:** **(a)** highway, **(b)** narrow path, **(c)** parking lot, **(d)** freeway
4. **raggedy:** **(a)** shabby, **(b)** tidy, **(c)** elegant, **(d)** beautiful

Academic Vocabulary in Writing

READING 8 Understand how an author's sensory language creates imagery. RC-6(C) Monitor and adjust comprehension (creating sensory images).

convey	create	influence	interact	qualities

What surprised you most about the way Mrs. Price and Rachel **interacted?** What does each character say to **convey** her feelings? Write a paragraph about what you think. Include at least two Academic Vocabulary words in your response. Definitions of the words are on page 75.

Texas Assessment Practice

DIRECTIONS Use "Eleven" to answer questions 1–6.

1 You can tell that this story is told from the first-person point of view because the narrator —

- (A) does not take part in the story's action
- (B) does not reveal her own feelings
- (C) uses the pronoun "I"
- (D) knows what other characters are feeling

2 Which image from the story helps show what Rachel feels growing older is like?

- (F) *the rings inside a tree trunk*
- (G) *a runaway balloon*
- (H) *the sweater that smells like cottage cheese*
- (J) *a big red mountain*

3 How does Rachel respond when she puts on the sweater?

- (A) She buries her head in her arms and cries.
- (B) She yells at Mrs. Price and her classmates.
- (C) She laughs at how ugly it is.
- (D) She runs from the room.

4 What might change if this story were told from the third-person point of view?

- (F) The characters would show more emotion.
- (G) Readers would know who owned the sweater sooner.
- (H) We would know the thoughts and feelings of every character.
- (J) Mrs. Price would be meaner.

5 Which statement best describes how Rachel feels about her birthday celebration?

- (A) It won't make her enjoy parties.
- (B) It won't make her feel better.
- (C) It will make her feel embarrassed.
- (D) It will make her feel happier.

6 Which statement best describes Rachel?

- (F) She is quick to tell people what she thinks.
- (G) She is positive and hopeful.
- (H) She is angry and unfriendly.
- (J) She is thoughtful but not very confident.

READING 6B Recognize dialect and conversational voice and explain how authors use dialogue to convey characters.

Jeremiah's Song

Short Story by **Walter Dean Myers**

When is a story a TREASURE?

Why do some stories get passed along from one generation to the next? Think about why a story might be a treasure—a story worth remembering and sharing with others. Is the story funny, sad, and even scary? Does it teach you something? In "Jeremiah's Song," the young characters consider the value of an older man's stories.

QUICKWRITE In a journal entry, briefly describe a story that is meaningful to you. The story can be one you have heard, read, or seen. Explain why this story is important to you.

Journal Entry

Description of story: ______

Why it's important to me: ______

Literary Analysis: Dialect and Conversational Voice

You can learn a lot about a character by paying attention to the way he or she speaks. If a story's narrator uses a **conversational voice,** readers feel like the narrator is speaking directly to them. When writers use **dialect,** characters speak in a way that is common to a particular region and community. As you read, examine conversational voice and dialect by asking yourself questions like the ones that follow.

Conversational Voice	• In what ways is the narrator's voice unique? • What words and phrases make the narrator's voice sound like everyday speech? • What does the conversational voice tell me about how the narrator feels?
Dialect	• What are some clues, such as words, phrases, grammar, or spelling, that help me identify the region or community? • How can I restate the dialect in my own words? • What does this dialect tell me about the narrator?

Reading Strategy: Monitor

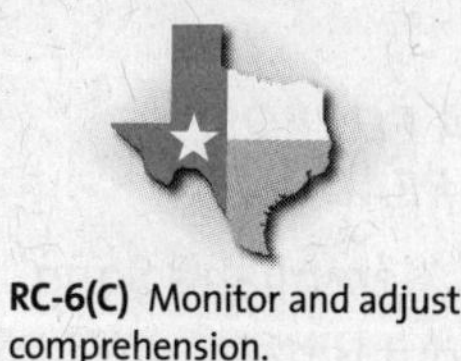

RC-6(C) Monitor and adjust comprehension.

As you read, it is helpful to occasionally **monitor,** or check, your understanding. One way to monitor is to **clarify** what you've read. This means you stop and make sure that you can clearly explain what is going on in the story. If not, reread and look for clues to help you restate the information in your own words. As you read "Jeremiah's Song," you will monitor and clarify meaning as shown in the chart below.

This Confuses Me	My Own Words
I'm not sure how the characters are related to each other.	*Ellie is the narrator's cousin.*

Vocabulary in Context

Note: Words are listed in the order in which they appear in the story.

stroke (strōk) *n.* a sudden, severe attack; a sudden loss of blood flow to the brain, often leading to physical or mental damage

*He couldn't move his arm after he had a **stroke**.*

diagnosis (dī'əg-nō'sĭs) *n.* the identification of a disease through examination of a patient.

*The doctor made a **diagnosis** about what was wrong.*

condition (kən-dĭsh'ən) *n.* a disease or state of health

*Grandpa has a serious **condition**, but it can be treated.*

setback (sĕt'băk') *n.* an unexpected stop in progress; a change from better to worse

*Getting a cold was only a small **setback** in his recovery.*

Vocabulary Practice

Review the vocabulary words and think about their meanings. Then, brainstorm with a partner what you think "Jeremiah's Song" could be about based on the list above. Write down your prediction.

____

____

____

____

SET A PURPOSE FOR READING

Read "Jeremiah's Song" to find out what Jeremiah's stories have to teach.

Jeremiah's SONG

Short Story by

WALTER DEAN MYERS

BACKGROUND Storytelling has a long history in the African-American Community. Stories of family ties, folklore, and struggles for civil rights create strong bonds from one generation to the next. In "Jeremiah's Song," Grandpa Jeremiah shares the stories of his ancestors with the young people in his life.

I knowed my cousin Ellie was gonna be mad when Macon Smith come around to the house. She didn't have no use for Macon even when things was going right, and when Grandpa Jeremiah was fixing to die I just knowed she wasn't gonna be liking him hanging around. Grandpa Jeremiah raised Ellie after her folks died and they used to be real close. Then she got to go on to college and when she come back the first year she was different. She didn't want to hear all them stories he used to tell her anymore. Ellie said the stories wasn't true, and that's why she didn't want to hear them. Ⓐ

I didn't know if they was true or not. Tell the truth I didn't think much on it either way, but I liked to hear them stories. Grandpa Jeremiah said they wasn't stories anyway, they was songs.

Ⓐ MONITOR

Clarify what you've learned so far. Which characters have been introduced? What conflicts seem to be developing?

"They the songs of my people," he used to say.

I didn't see how they was songs, not regular songs anyway. Every little thing we did down in Curry seemed to matter to Ellie that first summer she come home from college. You couldn't do nothin' that was gonna please her. She didn't even come to church much. 'Course she come on Sunday or everybody would have had a regular fit, but she didn't come on Thursday nights and she didn't come on Saturday even though she used to sing in the gospel choir.

"I guess they teachin' her somethin' worthwhile up there at Greensboro," Grandpa Jeremiah said to Sister Todd. "I sure don't see what it is, though."

"You ain't never had no book learning, Jeremiah," Sister Todd shot back. She wiped at where a trickle of sweat made a little path through the white dusting powder she put on her chest to keep cool. "Them old ways you got ain't got nothing for these young folks." B

"I guess you right," Grandpa Jeremiah said.

He said it but I could see he didn't like it none. He was a big man with a big head and had most all his hair even if it was white. All that summer, instead of sitting on the porch telling stories like he used to when I was real little, he would sit out there by himself while Ellie stayed in the house and watched the television or read a book. Sometimes I would think about asking him to tell me one of them stories he used to tell but they was too scary now that I didn't have nobody to sleep with but myself. I asked Ellie to sleep with me but she wouldn't.

"You're nine years old," she said, sounding real proper. "You're old enough to sleep alone."

I *knew* that. I just wanted her to sleep with me because I liked sleeping with her. Before she went off to college she used to put cocoa butter on her arms and face and it would smell real nice. When she come back from college she put something else on, but that smelled nice too.

Monitor Your Comprehension

B DIALECT
The dialect the narrator uses reflects speech patterns common to some African-American communities in the southern United States. It reflects a style of speaking that is informal and includes nonstandard grammar. To help comprehend dialect, try restating a sentence or thought in your own words.

Dialect: "You ain't never had no book learning, Jeremiah." (line 28)

Restatement:

Restate the sentence in lines 31–32:

Monitor Your Comprehension

stroke (strōk) *n.* a sudden, severe attack; a sudden loss of blood flow to the brain, often leading to physical or mental damage

C CONVERSATIONAL VOICE
Reread lines 51–68. Notice the language the narrator uses to talk about Macon. How would you describe the narrator's characterization of Macon? How does the narrator feel about him?

D MONITOR
Reread lines 72–75. What does the narrator mean when he says that the stories "would be past my mind by the time I had to go to bed"?

It was right after Ellie went back to school that Grandpa Jeremiah had him a **stroke** and Macon started coming around. I think his mama probably made him come at first, but you could see he liked it. Macon had always been around, sitting over near the stuck window at church or going on the blueberry truck when we went picking down at Mister Gregory's place. For a long time he was just another kid, even though he was older'n me, but then, all of a sudden, he growed something fierce. I used to be up to his shoulder one time and then, before I could turn around good, I was only up to his shirt pocket. He changed too. When he used to just hang around with the other boys and play ball or shoot at birds he would laugh a lot. He didn't laugh so much anymore and I figured he was just about grown. When Grandpa got sick he used to come around and help out with things around the house that was too hard for me to do. I mean, I could have done all the chores, but it would just take me longer. **C**

When the work for the day was finished and the sows[1] fed, Grandpa would kind of ease into one of his stories and Macon, he would sit and listen to them and be real interested. I didn't mind listening to the stories when Grandpa told them to Macon because he would be telling them in the middle of the afternoon and they would be past my mind by the time I had to go to bed. **D**

Macon had an old guitar he used to mess with, too. He wasn't too bad on it, and sometimes Grandpa would tell him to play us a tune. He could play something he called "the Delta Blues" real good, but when Sister Todd or somebody from the church come around he'd play "Precious Lord" or "Just a Closer Walk With Thee."

Grandpa Jeremiah had been feeling poorly from that stroke, and one of his legs got a little drag to it. Just about

1. **sows:** adult female hogs.

the time Ellie come from school the next summer he was real sick. He was breathing loud so you could hear it even in the next room, and he would stay in bed a lot even when there was something that needed doing or fixing.

"I don't think he's going to make it much longer," Dr. Crawford said. "The only thing I can do is to give him something for the pain."

"Are you sure of your **diagnosis**?" Ellie asked. She was sitting around the table with Sister Todd, Deacon[2] Turner, and his little skinny wife.

Dr. Crawford looked at Ellie like he was surprised to hear her talking. "Yes, I'm sure," he said. "He had tests a few weeks ago and his **condition** was bad then."

"How much time he got?" Sister Todd asked.

"Maybe a week or two at best," Dr. Crawford said.

When he said that, Deacon Turner's wife started crying and goin' on and I give her a hard look but she just went on. I was the one who loved Grandpa Jeremiah the most and she didn't hardly even know him so I didn't see why she was crying. E

Everybody started tiptoeing around the house after that. They would go in and ask Grandpa Jeremiah if he was comfortable and stuff like that or take him some food or a cold glass of lemonade.

Sister Todd come over and stayed with us. Mostly what she did is make supper and do a lot of praying, which was good because I figured that maybe God would do something to make Grandpa Jeremiah well. When she wasn't doing that she was piecing on[3] a fancy quilt she was making for some white people in Wilmington.

Ellie, she went around asking everybody how they felt about Dr. Crawford and then she went into town and

---

2. **Deacon:** a term used for church members who assist their church's priest or minister.

3. **piecing on:** mending or adding blocks of fabric.

Monitor Your Comprehension

diagnosis (dī'əg-nō'sĭs) *n.* the identification of a disease through examination of a patient

Why might Ellie have questioned the doctor's diagnosis?

condition (kən-dĭsh'ən) *n.* a disease or state of health

E DIALECT

What does the narrator mean when he says in lines 100–101, "I give her a hard look but she just went on"?

asked about the tests and things. Sister Jenkins asked her if she thought she knowed more than Dr. Crawford, and Ellie rolled her eyes at her, but Sister Jenkins was reading out her Bible and didn't make no notice of it.

Then Macon come over.

He had been away on what he called "a little piece of a job" and hadn't heard how bad off Grandpa Jeremiah was. When he come over he talked to Ellie and she told him what was going on and then he got him a soft drink from the refrigerator and sat out on the porch and before you know it he was crying.

You could look at his face and tell the difference between him sweating and the tears. The sweat was close against his skin and shiny and the tears come down fatter and more sparkly. (F)

(F) CONVERSATIONAL VOICE
Reread lines 127–130 and think about the words the narrator uses to describe Macon sitting on the porch. How do you think the narrator feels?

Macon sat on the porch, without saying a word, until the sun went down and the crickets started chirping and carrying on. Then he went in to where Grandpa Jeremiah was and stayed in there for a long time.

Sister Todd was saying that Grandpa Jeremiah needed his rest and Ellie went in to see what Macon was doing. Then she come out real mad.

"He got Grandpa telling those old stories again," Ellie said. "I told him Grandpa needed his rest and for him not to be staying all night."

He did leave soon, but bright and early the next morning Macon was back again. This time he brought his guitar with him and he went on in to Grandpa Jeremiah's room. I went in, too.

Grandpa Jeremiah's room smelled terrible. It was all closed up so no drafts could get on him and the whole room was smelled down with disinfect[4] and medicine. Grandpa Jeremiah lay propped up on the bed and he was

4. **disinfect**: short for *disinfectant*, a chemical that destroys germs and bacteria.

so gray he looked scary. His hair wasn't combed down and his head on the pillow with his white hair sticking out was enough to send me flying if Macon hadn't been there. He was skinny, too. He looked like his skin got loose on his bones, and when he lifted his arms, it hung down like he was just wearing it instead of it being a part of him. G

Macon sat slant shouldered with his guitar across his lap. He was messin' with the guitar, not making any music, but just going over the strings as Grandpa talked.

"Old Carrie went around out back to where they kept the pigs penned up and she felt a cold wind across her face. . . ." Grandpa Jeremiah was telling the story about how a old woman out tricked the Devil and got her son back. I had heard the story before, and I knew it was pretty scary. "When she felt the cold breeze she didn't blink nary[5] an eye, but looked straight ahead. . . ."

All the time Grandpa Jeremiah was talking I could see Macon fingering his guitar. I tried to imagine what it would be like if he was actually plucking the strings. I tried to fix my mind on that because I didn't like the way the story went with the old woman wrestling with the Devil.

We sat there for nearly all the afternoon until Ellie and Sister Todd come in and said that supper was ready. Me and Macon went out and ate some collard greens, ham hocks, and rice. Then Macon he went back in and listened to some more of Grandpa's stories until it was time for him to go home. I wasn't about to go in there and listen to no stories at night.

Dr. Crawford come around a few days later and said that Grandpa Jeremiah was doing a little better.

"You think the Good Lord gonna pull him through?" Sister Todd asked.

"I don't tell the Good Lord what He should or should not be doing," Dr. Crawford said, looking over at Sister

---

5. **nary:** not one; not any.

Monitor Your Comprehension

G CONVERSATIONAL VOICE

Reread lines 151–154. Underline words and phrases that the narrator uses to describe how skinny Grandpa Jeremiah is. How does the narrator feel about seeing Grandpa Jeremiah in this condition?

Todd and at Ellie. "I just said that *my* patient seems to be doing okay for his condition."

"He been telling Macon all his stories," I said.

"Macon doesn't seem to understand that Grandpa Jeremiah needs his strength," Ellie said. "Now that he's improving, we don't want him to have a **setback**."

setback (sĕt'băk') *n.* an unexpected stop in progress; a change from better to worse

"No use in stopping him from telling his stories," Dr. Crawford said. "If it makes him feel good it's as good as any medicine I can give him."

I saw that this didn't set with Ellie, and when Dr. Crawford had left I asked her why.

"Dr. Crawford means well," she said, "but we have to get away from the kind of life that keeps us in the past." Ⓗ

Ⓗ MONITOR
Reread lines 191–194. What does Ellie mean when she says "we have to get away from the kind of life that keeps us in the past"?

She didn't say why we should be trying to get away from the stories and I really didn't care too much. All I knew was that when Macon was sitting in the room with Grandpa Jeremiah I wasn't nearly as scared as I used to be when it was just me and Ellie listening. I told that to Macon.

"You getting to be a big man, that's all," he said.

That was true. Me and Macon was getting to be good friends, too. I didn't even mind so much when he started being friends with Ellie later. It seemed kind of natural, almost like Macon was supposed to be there with us instead of just visiting.

Grandpa wasn't getting no better, but he wasn't getting no worse, either.

"You liking Macon now?" I asked Ellie when we got to the middle of July. She was dishing out a plate of smothered chops[6] for him and I hadn't even heard him ask for anything to eat.

"Macon's funny," Ellie said, not answering my question. "He's in there listening to all of those old stories like he's

6. **smothered chops:** pork chops thickly covered with a sauce or gravy.

really interested in them. It's almost as if he and Grandpa Jeremiah are talking about something more than the stories, a secret language."

I didn't think I was supposed to say anything about that to Macon, but once, when Ellie, Sister Todd, and Macon were out on the porch shelling butter beans after Grandpa got tired and was resting, I went into his room and told him what Ellie had said.

"She said that?" Grandpa Jeremiah's face was skinny and old looking but his eyes looked like a baby's, they was so bright.

"Right there in the kitchen is where she said it," I said. "And I don't know what it mean but I was wondering about it."

"I didn't think she had any feeling for them stories," Grandpa Jeremiah said. "If she think we talking secrets, maybe she don't."

"I think she getting a feeling for Macon," I said.

"That's okay, too," Grandpa Jeremiah said. "They both young."

"Yeah, but them stories you be telling, Grandpa, they about old people who lived a long time ago," I said.

"Well, those the folks you got to know about," Grandpa Jeremiah said. "You think on what those folks been through, and what they was feeling, and you add it up with what you been through and what you been feeling, then you got you something."

"What you got Grandpa?"

"You got you a bridge," Grandpa said. "And a meaning. Then when things get so hard you about to break, you can sneak across that bridge and see some folks who went before you and see how they didn't break. ❶

Monitor Your Comprehension

❶ MONITOR
Reread lines 234–245. Why are the stories important to Grandpa Jeremiah? Clarify this information to the chart below.

This Confuses me
Why stories are important to Jeremiah

↓

My Words

Monitor Your Comprehension

Some got bent and some got twisted and a few fell along the way, but they didn't break."

"Am I going to break, Grandpa?"

"You? As strong as you is?" Grandpa Jeremiah pushed himself up on his elbow and give me a look. "No way you going to break, boy. You gonna be strong as they come. One day you gonna tell all them stories I told you to your young'uns and they'll be as strong as you."

"Suppose I ain't got no stories, can I make some up?"

"Sure you can, boy. You make 'em up and twist 'em around. Don't make no mind. Long as you got 'em."

"Is that what Macon is doing?" I asked. "Making up stories to play on his guitar?"

"He'll do with 'em what he see fit, I suppose," Grandpa Jeremiah said. "Can't ask more than that from a man." J

It rained the first three days of August. It wasn't a hard rain but it rained anyway. The mailman said it was good for the crops over East but I didn't care about that so I didn't pay him no mind. What I did mind was when it rain like that the field mice come in and get in things like the flour bin and I always got the blame for leaving it open.

When the rain stopped I was pretty glad. Macon come over and sat with Grandpa and had something to eat with us. Sister Todd come over, too.

"How Grandpa doing?" Sister Todd asked. "They been asking about him in the church."

"He's doing all right," Ellie said.

"He's kind of quiet today," Macon said. "He was just talking about how the hogs needed breeding."

"He must have run out of stories to tell," Sister Todd said. "He'll be repeating on himself like my father used to do. That's the way I *hear* old folks get."

J DIALECT
You can learn about characters by paying attention to the way they speak with each other. What can you tell about the relationship between the narrator and Grandpa Jeremiah from their dialogue in lines 241–260?

Everybody laughed at that because Sister Todd was pretty old, too. Maybe we was all happy because the sun was out after so much rain. When Sister Todd went in to take Grandpa Jeremiah a plate of potato salad with no mayonnaise like he liked it, she told him about how people was asking for him and he told her to tell them he was doing okay and to remember him in their prayers.

Sister Todd came over the next afternoon, too, with some rhubarb pie with cheese on it, which is my favorite pie. When she took a piece into Grandpa Jeremiah's room she come right out again and told Ellie to go fetch the Bible.

It was a hot day when they had the funeral. Mostly everybody was there. The church was hot as anything, even though they had the window open. Some yellowjacks flew in and buzzed around Sister Todd's niece and then around Deacon Turner's wife and settled right on her hat and stayed there until we all stood and sang "Soon a Will Be Done."

At the graveyard Macon played "Precious Lord" and I cried hard even though I told myself that I wasn't going to cry the way Ellie and Sister Todd was, but it was such a sad thing when we left and Grandpa Jeremiah was still out to the grave that I couldn't help it.

During the funeral and all, Macon kind of told everybody where to go and where to sit and which of the three cars to ride in. After it was over he come by the house and sat on the front porch and played on his guitar. Ellie was standing leaning against the rail and she was crying but it wasn't a hard crying. It was a soft crying, the kind that last inside of you for a long time. K

Macon was playing a tune I hadn't heard before. I thought it might have been what he was working at when Grandpa Jeremiah was telling him those stories and I

K CONVERSATIONAL VOICE

Reread lines 289–306. Underline examples of the observations the young narrator makes about the funeral. How does the use of a young narrator affect the way the story is told?

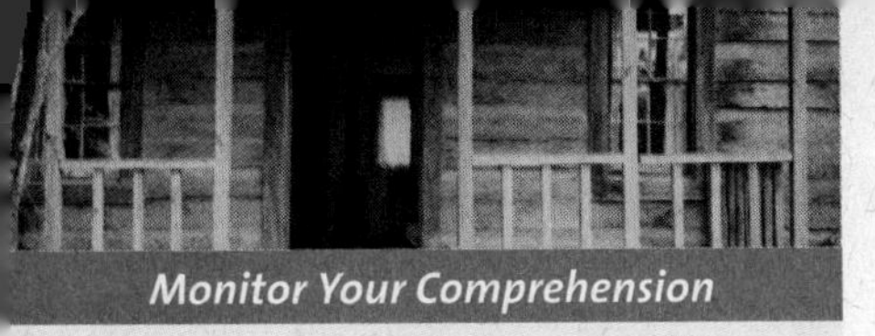

Monitor Your Comprehension

PAUSE & REFLECT
Do you think the narrator learned more from Grandpa Jeremiah or from Macon? Explain.

watched his fingers but I couldn't tell if it was or not. It wasn't nothing special, that tune Macon was playing, maybe halfway between them Delta Blues he would do when Sister Todd wasn't around and something you would play at church. It was something different and something the same at the same time. I watched his fingers go over that guitar and figured I could learn that tune one day if I had a mind to. **PAUSE & REFLECT**

Literary Analysis: Dialect and Conversational Voice

The nine-year-old narrator of "Jeremiah's Song" speaks with a conversational voice. Find three examples of narration that seem especially typical of how a child might tell a story and record them in the chart below. Then explain the effect that child narrator and voice have on the story.

READING 6B Recognize dialect and conversational voice and explain how authors use dialogue to convey characters.

Example:	Effect on the Story:
"I was the one who loved Grandpa Jeremiah the most and she didn't hardly even know him so I didn't see why she was crying." (lines 101–103)	
Example:	
Example:	

What does the author's use of dialect add to the story? How would the story be different if Myers had not used dialect?

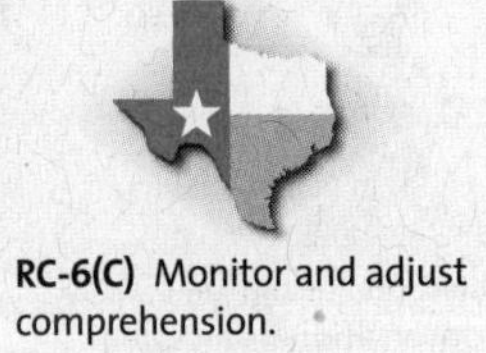

RC-6(C) Monitor and adjust comprehension.

Reading Strategy: Monitor

As you read, it helps to stop occasionally to clarify what is happening. After you read, it is also important to clarify your understanding of the story as a whole. Complete the chart to clarify your understanding of the story and its title.

"Macon was playing a tune...It was something different and something the same at the same time. I watched his fingers go over that guitar and figured I could learn that tune one day if I had a mind to." (lines 307–317)	
My Own Words:	
Why Music Is Important to the Story:	**Why the Title Fits the Story:**

When is a story a TREASURE?

In your opinion, which characters treasure Grandpa Jeremiah's stories the most? Explain your ideas.

Vocabulary Practice

Tell whether each statement is true or false.

1. You usually get a **diagnosis** from a doctor. ________
2. A **setback** during a long project is very exciting. ________
3. Having a heart **condition** means that you have strong feelings. ________
4. After having a **stroke,** you might not be able to speak as clearly. ________

Academic Vocabulary in Writing

READING 6B Recognize dialect and conversational voice and explain how authors use dialogue to convey characters.

convey	create	influence	interact	qualities

Has anyone **influenced** your life the way that Grandpa Jeremiah touched the lives of those around him? Use at least one Academic Vocabulary word in your response. Definitions of these words are on page 75.

____

____

Texas Assessment Practice

DIRECTIONS Use "Jeremiah's Song" to answer questions 1–6.

1 You can tell that the narrator of the story —

(A) is too young to understand his grandfather's stories
(B) doesn't trust Macon
(C) pays attention to the people in his life and the events taking place
(D) doesn't want to know that his grandfather is at the end of his life

2 Ellie became unhappy with things at home —

(F) when the narrator became friends with Macon
(G) after she moved away to work in the city
(H) after hearing the doctor's diagnosis
(J) when she first came home from college

3 In which example of the narrator's speech are his words most conversational?

(A) *He said it but I could see he didn't like it none.*
(B) *She was dishing out a plate of smothered chops for him.*
(C) *When the rain stopped I was pretty glad.*
(D) *"I think she getting a feeling for Mason," I said.*

4 Macon tells the narrator, "You getting to be a big man, that's all." By this, he means that —

(F) the narrator is too old to be afraid of scary stories
(G) the narrator is growing up
(H) he's worried that the narrator is becoming conceited
(J) the narrator is well known in town

5 When Grandpa Jeremiah describes his stories as a bridge he means that the stories —

(A) are best told while traveling
(B) protect against dangers
(C) can be difficult to cross
(D) connect with the past

6 Which statement suggests ideas that the narrator is beginning to understand?

(F) *I could learn that tune one day if I had a mind to.*
(G) *It was a hot day when they had the funeral.*
(H) *Maybe we was all happy because the sun was out after so much rain.*
(J) *At the graveyard Macon played "Precious Lord."*

READING 7 Identify the literary language and devices used in personal narratives and compare their characteristics with those of an autobiography.

Role-Playing and Discovery

Personal Essay by **Jerry Pinkney**

The Life and Adventures of Nat Love

Autobiography by **Nat Love**

What makes a MEMORY last?

Favorite memories can come from weekend activities, family outings, or adventures. When you look back on your life, what events will you remember most clearly, and why? Read "Role-Playing and Discovery" and the excerpt from *The Life and Adventures of Nat Love* to see how two different authors write about their lives.

LIST IT List some favorite activities. Then share your list with a group of classmates, explaining why each activity is important to you and why you might include it in your own life story.

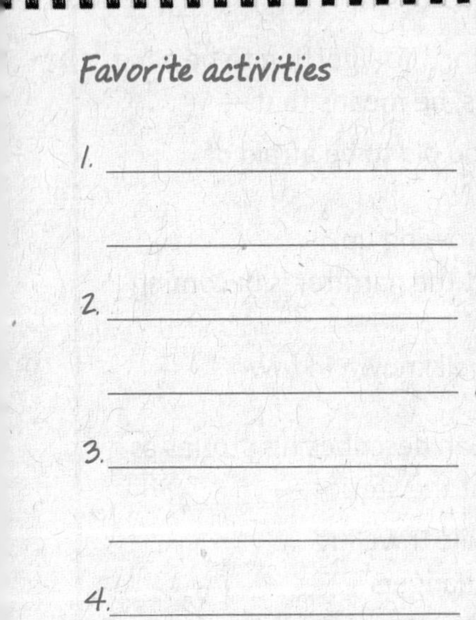

Literary Analysis: Narrative Nonfiction

Like fiction, narrative nonfiction tells a story. However, in nonfiction, characters, plots, and settings are real, not imaginary. **Autobiographies** and **personal narratives** are two types of nonfiction. The graphic shows how they are different and alike.

Autobiography	Personal Narrative
An **autobiography** is a book-length story of the writer's own life. It focuses on the most important people and events in the writer's life over time	A **personal narrative** is an essay about single subject or moment in the writer's life. It usually reflects a writer's, experiences, feelings, and personality.

Both

- are written in first-person point of view.
- include events, characters, and settings that are real, not imagined.

Reading Skill: Identify Language and Tone

READING 7 Identify the literary language and devices used in personal narratives and compare their characteristics with those of an autobiography.

Nonfiction writers may use **descriptive language** to help readers imagine something, usually by appealing to the senses of sight, hearing, smell, touch, or taste. Descriptive language often conveys tone. **Tone** refers to the writer's attitude—the way the writer feels about his or her topic. As you read, record examples of descriptive language that convey imagery and tone similar to the one shown in this chart.

Title:	Descriptive Language:	Tone:
"Role-Playing and Discovery"	"Off we would rush," "dreamed of exploring the early frontier" (lines 1–5)	excited, happy

Vocabulary in Context

Note: Words are listed in the order in which they appear in the personal essay.

intensity (ĭn-tĕn′sĭ-tē) *n.* extreme amount of energy or feeling
Pinkney and his friends played games with surprising ***intensity****.*

resounding (rĭ-zound′ĭng) *adj.* unmistakable; loud
He answered the question with a ***resounding*** *"No!"*

profound (prə-found′) *adj.* very deep or great
The movie had a ***profound*** *effect on me.*

impressionable (ĭm-prĕsh′ə-nə-bəl) *adj.* easily influenced
The ***impressionable*** *child was easily convinced.*

Vocabulary Practice

Review the vocabulary words and think about their meanings. Then use the vocabulary words to write sentences that would make viewers want to see a thrilling new action movie.

____

____

____

____

____

____

Monitor Your Comprehension

SET A PURPOSE FOR READING

Read "Role-Playing and Discovery" to learn how Pinkney's childhood experiences lead him to important questions and connections.

Role-Playing and Discovery

Personal Essay by

JERRY PINKNEY

BACKGROUND The westerns Jerry Pinkney watched when he was a boy were a popular type of movie in the 1930s and 1940s. Westerns feature brave cowboys and present an idealized view of the American West. The typical plot of a western centers on the theme of good and evil, with the cowboy battling wicked villains.

On Saturdays, after household chores were finished, I would meet up with my best friends. Off we would rush to the movies. Tickets were ten cents, and there was always a double feature. I was most excited when there were westerns. As a young boy growing up in Philadelphia, Pennsylvania, I dreamed of exploring the early frontier.

My friends and I played at being cowboys and explorers. With much enthusiasm and **intensity**, we inhabited the characters portrayed on the silver screen. We fashioned our costumes and gear from what we could find at home or purchase from the local five-and-dime store. I would whittle out of wood a bowie knife modeled after the one Jim Bowie had at his side while defending the Alamo. I would then take my turn at being Roy Rogers, the cowboy,

intensity (ĭn-tĕn'sĭ-tē) *n.* extreme amount of energy or feeling

Jim Beckwourth

or Daniel Boone,[1] the famous pioneer, journeying through the rugged wilderness. Ⓐ

Jean Baptiste du Sable

If anyone had asked at that time if my excitement was due to an early interest in history, my answer would have been a **resounding**, "No!" However, looking back, I realize that answer would not have been entirely true. Yes, we did have fun, and yes, our flights into the past seemed to be more about action than about learning history, but that role-playing seeded my interest in discovery. When I learned as an adult that one out of three cowboys was black or Mexican, that discovery was moving and **profound**.

Nat Love

I do wonder, though, how we would have been affected as young boys if, at that **impressionable** time, we had known about Nat Love, a cowboy; Bill Pickett, a rodeo cowboy; Jim Beckwourth, a fur trader; or Jean Baptiste Du Sable, the explorer—all persons of African descent. Ⓑ

1. **Jim Bowie . . . Roy Rogers . . . Daniel Boone:** Bowie (1796–1836) and Boone (1734–1820) were famous historical figures of the American West. Roy Rogers (1911–1998) was a movie and television cowboy from the 1930s through the 1960s.

Monitor Your Comprehension

Ⓐ IDENTIFY LANGUAGE AND TONE

Reread lines 1–21 and underline details that convey a picture of the author and his friends. How would you describe the tone in these lines?

resounding (rĭ-zound'ĭng) *adj.* unmistakable; loud

profound (prə-found') *adj.* very deep or great

Why do you think Pinkney's discovery had such a **profound** effect on him?

impressionable (ĭm-prĕsh'ə-nə-bəl) *adj.* easily influenced

Ⓑ PERSONAL NARRATIVE

Reread lines 35–46. Why does Pinkney save such a strong statement for his closing paragraph?

SET A PURPOSE FOR READING

Read *The Life and Adventures of Nat Love* to discover the tasks, skills, and challenges involved in the life of a cowboy that Pinkney probably would have admired.

The Life and Adventures of Nat Love

Autobiography by

NAT LOVE

BACKGROUND Nat Love was born into slavery in 1854. By age fifteen, he left his family in Tennessee to search for adventure. He became a champion cowboy, earning the nickname "Deadwood Dick" after winning a shooting contest in Deadwood, South Dakota.

Having now fairly begun my life as a cowboy, I was fast learning the many ins and outs of the business, while my many roamings over the range country gave me a knowledge of it not possessed by many at that time. Being of a naturally observant disposition, I noticed many things to which others attached no significance. This quality of observance proved of incalculable benefit to me in many ways during my life as a range rider in the western country. My employment with the Pete Gallinger company took me all over the Pan Handle country, Texas, Arizona, and New Mexico with herds of horses and cattle for market and to be delivered to other ranch owners and large cattle breeders. Naturally I became very well acquainted with all the many different trails and grazing ranges located in the stretch of country between the north of Montana and the Gulf of Mexico, and between the Missouri state line and the Pacific Ocean. This whole territory I have covered many times in the saddle, sometimes at the rate of eighty or one hundred miles a day. These long rides and much traveling over the country were of great benefit to me, as it enabled me to meet so many different people connected with the cattle business and also to learn the different trails and the lay of the country generally. C

Among the other things that I picked up on my wanderings, was a knowledge of the Spanish language, which I learned to speak like a native. I also became very well acquainted with the many different brands[1] scattered over this stretch of country, consequently it was not long before the cattle men began to recognize my worth and the Gallinger Company made me their chief brand reader, which duties I performed for several years with honor to myself and satisfaction to my employers. In the cattle country, all the large cattle raisers had their squad of brand readers whose duty it was to attend all the big round-ups[2] and cuttings throughout the country, and to pick out their own brands and to see that the different brands were not altered or counterfeited. They also had to look to the branding of the young stock. D

During the big round-ups it was our duty to pick out our brand, and then send them home under the charge of our cowboys, likewise the newly branded stock. After each brand was cut out and started homeward, we had to stay with the round up to see that strays from the different herds from the surrounding country did not again get mixed up, until the different home ranges were reached. This work employed a large number of cowboys, who lived, ate and often slept in the saddle, as they covered many hundreds of miles in a very short space of time . . . After the general round up was over, cowboy sports and a good time generally was in order for those engaged in it. The interest of nearly all of us centered in the riding of what was known as the 7 Y-L steer. A big long horn wild steer, generally the worst in the herd, was cut out and turned loose on the open prairie. The cowboy who could

1. **brands:** marks indicating ownership put on animals with a hot iron. Each ranch had a specific brand to identify its animals.
2. **round-ups:** gatherings of livestock.

Monitor Your Comprehension

C IDENTIFY LANGUAGE
Underline the duties that Love describes in lines 1–23. How are these details different from the details Pinkney's essay?

D IDENTIFY TONE
Love uses words like *honor, satisfaction,* and *duty* in this paragraph. What word or phrase would you use to describe the tone of this autobiography? Explain your choice.

Monitor Your Comprehension

PAUSE & REFLECT
Reread lines 49–69. Circle vivid verbs, adjectives, and phrases Love uses that help you picture this scene. Do you think this scene portrays something Jerry Pinkney and his friends might have role-played? Explain.

E AUTOBIOGRAPHY
Reread lines 81–88. Underline an insight Love shares about cowboys. How do his examples of the life of a cowboy support his conclusion?

rope and ride him would get the steer as his reward, and let me assure you, dear reader, that it was not so easy as it sounds. The steer separated from its fellows would become extremely ferocious and wild, and the man who attempted to rope and ride him would be in momentary danger of losing his life if he relaxed in the least his vigilance and caution, because a wild steer is naturally ferocious. Even in cutting them out of the round up I have known them to get mad and attack the cowboys who only saved themselves by the quickness of their horses, or the friendly intervention of a comrade who happened to be near enough to rope the maddened long horn, and thus divert his attention to other things. But in the case of the 7 Y-L steer such intervention is against the rules, and the cowboy who attempts to rope and ride the steer must at all times look out for himself. . . . **PAUSE & REFLECT**

The cowboy who is successful in roping the steer must then mount and ride him. If he does that successfully the steer becomes his personal property to do with as he will—only a slight reward for the risking of his life and the trouble of accomplishing the feat. But it is done more for sport's sake than anything else, and the love of showing off, a weakness of all cowboys more or less. But really it takes a high class of horsemanship to ride a long horn, to get on his back and stay there as he runs, jumps, pitches side ways, backwards, forward, up and down, then over the prairie like a streak of lightning. I have had the experience and I can assure you it is no child's play. More than one 7 Y-L steer has fallen to my lot, but I had to work for it, and work hard. After all it was only part of the general routine of the cowboy's life, in which danger plays so important a part. . . . Above all things, the test of a cowboy's worth is his gameness and his nerve. He is not supposed to know what fear means, and I assure you there are very few who know the meaning of that word. **E**

After Reading

Literary Analysis: Narrative Nonfiction

How are *Role-Playing and Discovery* and *The Life and Adventures of Nat Love* alike and different? In the chart below, answer the questions to analyze the characteristics of these two forms of narrative nonfiction.

READING 7 Identify the literary language and devices used in personal narratives and compare their characteristics with those of an autobiography.

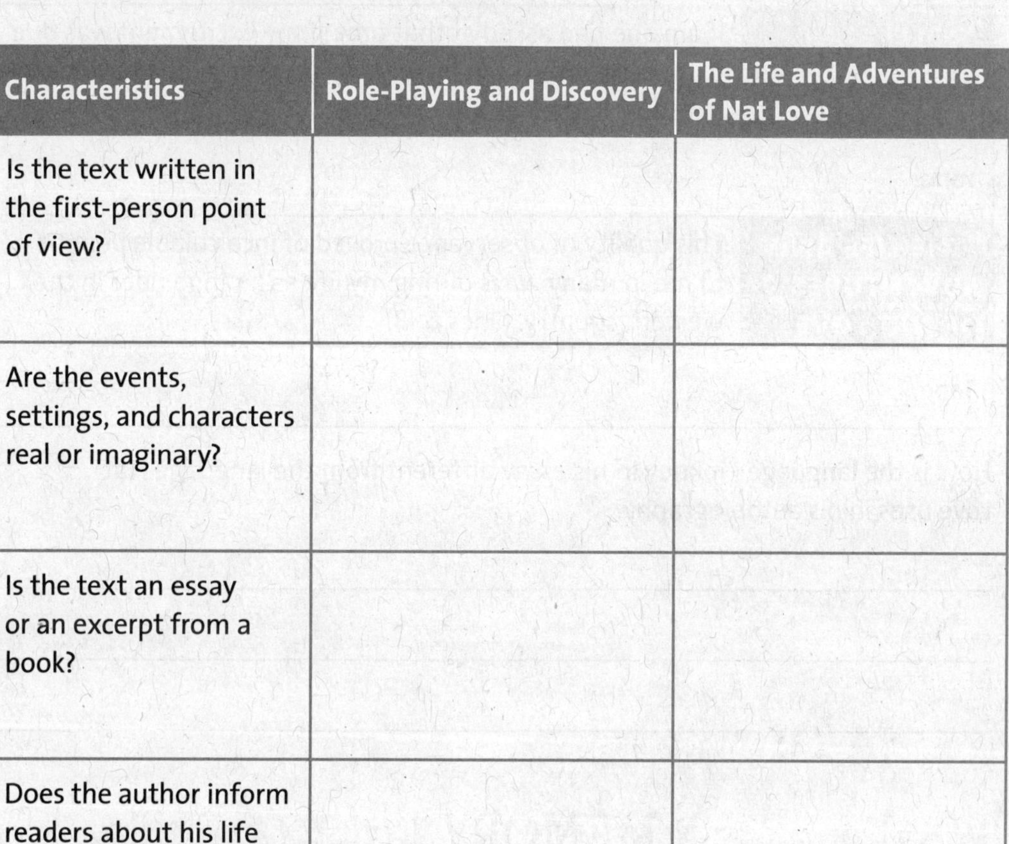

Characteristics	Role-Playing and Discovery	The Life and Adventures of Nat Love
Is the text written in the first-person point of view?		
Are the events, settings, and characters real or imaginary?		
Is the text an essay or an excerpt from a book?		
Does the author inform readers about his life or express his thoughts and feelings?		

Explain how a personal narrative is different from an autobiography. Use specific examples from both selections in your explanation.

READING 7 Identify the literary language and devices used in personal narratives and compare their characteristics with those of an autobiography.

Reading Skill: Identify Language and Tone

Read the statements from each selection. Write two words that describe the tone of each statement.

"ROLE-PLAYING AND DISCOVERY"	If anyone had asked at that time if my excitement was due to an early interest in history, my answer would have been a resounding, "No!" (lines 17–19)
Tone:	
"THE LIFE AND ADVENTURES OF NAT LOVE"	This quality of observance proved of incalculable benefit to me in many ways during my life as a range rider in the western country. (lines 6–8)
Tone:	

How is the language Pinkney in his essay different from the language Nat Love uses in his autobiography?

____

____

____

What makes a MEMORY last?

Review your notes from the activity on page 102. After reading the selections, which of your favorite activities do you think would be most important to include in your life story? Why?

____

____

____

Vocabulary Practice

Write the letter of the phrase next to the vocabulary word that illustrates its meaning.

______ **1. impressionable**	**a.** a severe thunderstorm
______ **2. intensity**	**b.** a loud cheer
______ **3. profound**	**c.** an eager young student
______ **4. resounding**	**d.** a very moving story

Academic Vocabulary in Writing

READING 7 Identify the literary language and devices used in personal narratives and compare their characteristics with those of an autobiography.

convey	create	influence	interact	qualities

What **qualities** of Nat Love's life as a cowboy might Jerry Pinkney have admired? How might reading Love's autobiography have **influenced** Jerry Pinkney? Write a few sentences to answer these questions. Include at least one Academic Vocabulary word in your response. Definitions of these words are on page 75.

____

____

____

____

Texas Assessment Practice

DIRECTIONS Use the two selections you have read to answer questions 1–4.

1 The tone in the closing paragraph of Pinkney's essay can best be described as —

- (A) questioning
- (B) argumentative
- (C) boastful
- (D) apologetic

2 Love's main duty as a cowboy was to —

- (F) learn the brands used in round ups
- (G) herd horses and cattle across the range for market and delivery
- (H) rope wild steer
- (J) communicate fluently in Spanish and English

3 The descriptive language in lines 76–80 of Love's autobiography appeals primarily to the sense of —

- (A) sound
- (B) touch
- (C) sight
- (D) hearing

4 Which statement does not accurately describe both of these nonfiction narratives?

- (F) The texts are written in first person.
- (G) The texts are essays.
- (H) The authors discuss events in their lives.
- (J) The events in the texts are real, not imagined.

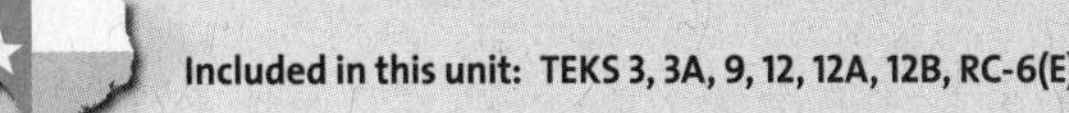

Included in this unit: TEKS 3, 3A, 9, 12, 12A, 12B, RC-6(E)

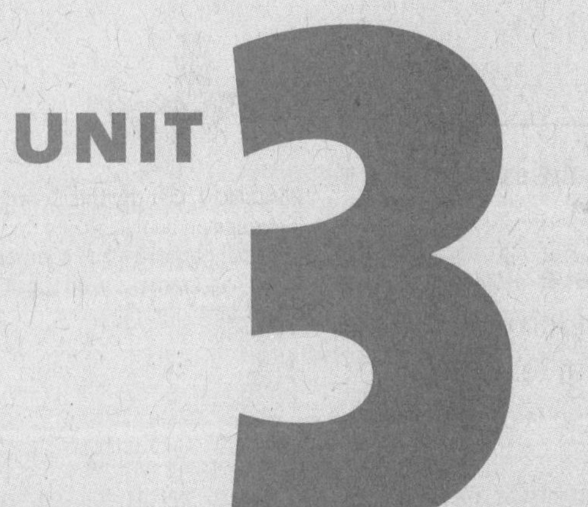

UNIT 3

The Big Idea

UNDERSTANDING THEME

Be sure to read the Reader's Workshop on pp. 318–323 in *Holt McDougal Literature*.

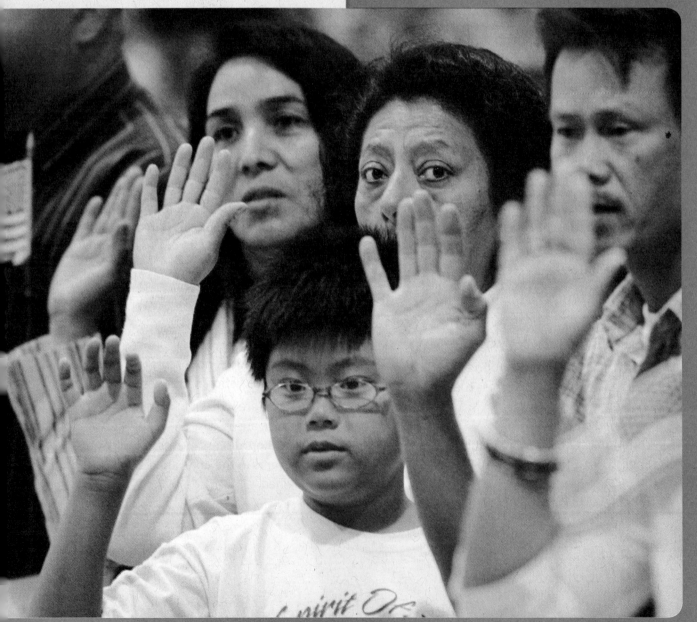

Academic Vocabulary for Unit 3

Academic Vocabulary is the language you use to discuss literary and informational texts. Preview the following Academic Vocabulary words. You will use these words as you write and talk about the selections in this unit.

attitude (at'ə-to͞od') *n.* a state of mind or feeling

*What is the main character's **attitude** toward his parents?*

•

communicate (kə-myo͞o'ni-kāt') *v.* to express thoughts or feelings clearly so that other people can understand them

*Which details from the poem **communicate** the poet's view of nature?*

•

context (kän'tekst') *n.* words and phrases that come before and after a word in a passage that help explain its meaning

*Explain how **context** helps you to understand the unfamiliar word.*

•

illustrate (il'ə-strāt') *v.* to explain or make something clear

*The writer **illustrates** the theme through the characters actions.*

•

implicit (im-plis' it) *adj.* not stated directly, but understood in what is expressed

*What is the **implicit** theme of the story?*

Think of a book you've read or a movie you've seen recently. Briefly describe its message or theme, using at least two Academic Vocabulary words in your response. How did the author or director **communicate** this theme?

READING 3A Infer the implicit theme of a work of fiction, distinguishing theme from topic.

The Dog of Pompeii

Short Story by **Louis Untermeyer**

What would you RISK for someone else?

Some people take risks for the excitement of it, whether they are trying a new skateboarding trick or auditioning for a play. Others, such as a student entering a spelling bee, take risks hoping to gain a reward. In "The Dog of Pompeii," one character risks his life simply to help someone.

Risks I'd be Willing to Take

- *Climb a tree to help my little sister get down*

LIST IT Brainstorm a list of situations in which you would be willing to take a risk for another person. Then compare your list with a classmate's. Place a checkmark next to any risks you have in common and a star next to those found only on your list. Discuss what would motivate you to take each risk.

Literary Analysis: Theme Versus Topic

Most stories center around a **theme,** or a message about life that the writer shares with readers. A story's theme is different from its **topic,** or what the story is about.

	Length	Example
Topic	can usually be stated in a word or two	love
Theme	more complex than a topic; usually described in a sentence	Love can help people solve their differences.

One topic of "The Dog of Pompeii" is friendship. As you read, look for the larger message the author wants to share. Remember a theme is **implicit**, or not stated directly. The following elements can all be clues to the theme:

- The **title** may hint at the theme by highlighting an important idea, setting, or character.
- A story's **plot** may focus on a conflict that is central to its theme.
- **Characters** can reflect theme through their actions, thoughts, and words.
- The **setting** and **images** can suggest a theme.

Reading Strategy: Reading Historical Fiction

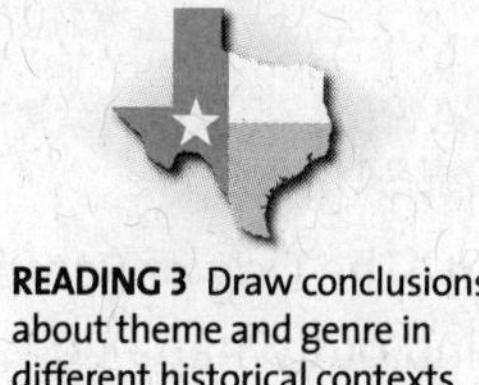

READING 3 Draw conclusions about theme and genre in different historical contexts.

Writers of **historical fiction** use both real and made-up settings, events, and characters from the past. "The Dog of Pompeii" is set in a real place and describes a real event. As you read, notes in the side column will ask you to list details that make the story's setting and main events come alive. Then you will draw conclusions about how the historical and cultural context helps build the story's theme.

Setting	Details
the town of Pompeii	*open-air theaters* *athletic stadiums* *fireworks*
Event	**Details**
a volcanic eruption	*fire* *unnatural darkness* *falling ashes*

Vocabulary in Context

Note: Words are listed in the order in which they appear in the story.

corrupt (kə-rŭpt′) *v.* to cause something to change from good to bad
The lava from the volcano began to ***corrupt*** *the soil.*

ponder (pŏn′dər) *v.* to think seriously about; reflect on
Tito ***pondered*** *his dog's strange behavior.*

dislodge (dĭs-lŏj′) *v.* to move from a settled position
The volcano's blast ***dislodged*** *heavy stones from the mountain.*

agonize (ăg′ə-nīz′) *v.* to suffer extreme physical or mental pain
The shrieking of the ***agonized*** *people frightened Tito.*

emerge (ĭ-mûrj′) *v.* to come into view
At last Tito ***emerged*** *from the marine gate and ran to the sea.*

Vocabulary Practice

Review the vocabulary words and think about their meanings. Then, use at least two of the words to describe a natural disaster.

___

___

___

SET A PURPOSE FOR READING

Read "The Dog of Pompeii" to find out what a dog risks to help his friend.

The DOG *of* POMPEII

Short Story by

LOUIS UNTERMEYER

BACKGROUND This story takes place in Pompeii (pŏm-pā'), a real Roman city that was buried by a volcanic eruption in A.D. 79. Of Pompeii's estimated population of 20,000, at least 2,000 were killed. After the eruption, Pompeii lay undisturbed until its ruins were discovered in the late 1500s. The remains of the city, preserved by volcanic ash, present a picture of life in the Roman Empire.

Tito and his dog Bimbo lived (if you could call it living) under the wall where it joined the inner gate. They really didn't live there; they just slept there. They lived anywhere. Pompeii was one of the gayest of the old Latin towns, but although Tito was never an unhappy boy, he was not exactly a merry one. The streets were always lively with shining chariots and bright red trappings;[1] the open-air theaters rocked with laughing crowds; sham battles and athletic sports were free for the asking in the great stadium. Once a year the Caesar[2] visited the pleasure city, and the fireworks lasted for days; the sacrifices in the forum[3] were better than a show. But Tito saw none of these

1. **trappings:** ornamental coverings or decorations.
2. **the Caesar:** the Roman emperor.
3. **forum:** the public square or marketplace of an ancient Roman city.

things. He was blind—had been blind from birth. He was known to everyone in the poorer quarters. But no one could say how old he was, no one remembered his parents, no one could tell where he came from. Bimbo was another mystery. As long as people could remember seeing Tito—about twelve or thirteen years—they had seen Bimbo. Bimbo had never left his side. He was not only dog but nurse, pillow, playmate, mother, and father to Tito. Ⓐ

Did I say Bimbo never left his master? (Perhaps I had better say comrade, for if anyone was the master, it was Bimbo.) I was wrong. Bimbo did trust Tito alone exactly three times a day. It was a fixed routine, a custom understood between boy and dog since the beginning of their friendship, and the way it worked was this: Early in the morning, shortly after dawn, while Tito was still dreaming, Bimbo would disappear. When Tito woke, Bimbo would be sitting quietly at his side, his ears cocked, his stump of a tail tapping the ground, and a fresh-baked bread—more like a large round roll—at his feet. Tito would stretch himself; Bimbo would yawn; then they would breakfast. At noon, no matter where they happened to be, Bimbo would put his paw on Tito's knee, and the two of them would return to the inner gate. Tito would curl up in the corner (almost like a dog) and go to sleep, while Bimbo, looking quite important (almost like a boy), would disappear again. In half an hour he'd be back with their lunch. Sometimes it would be a piece of fruit or a scrap of meat; often it was nothing but a dry crust. But sometimes there would be one of those flat, rich cakes, sprinkled with raisins and sugar, that Tito liked so much. At suppertime the same thing happened, although there was a little less of everything, for things were hard to snatch in the evening with the streets full of people. Besides, Bimbo didn't approve of too much food before

Monitor Your Comprehension

Ⓐ HISTORICAL FICTION
Reread lines 4–20. Underline details in the passage that tell you that this story is set in the past. Add them to your chart.

Setting
the town of Pompeii

↓

Details

Monitor Your Comprehension

B THEME VERSUS TOPIC
Reread lines 21–49. How does Bimbo show his loyalty to Tito?

C HISTORICAL FICTION
Reread lines 71–76. What details about food help bring the ancient setting to life? Add them to the chart.

Setting
the town of Pompeii

↓

Details

going to sleep. A heavy supper made boys too restless and dogs too stodgy—and it was the business of a dog to sleep lightly with one ear open and muscles ready for action. B

But whether there was much or little, hot or cold, fresh or dry, food was always there. Tito never asked where it came from and Bimbo never told him. There was plenty of rainwater in the hollows of soft stones; the old egg-woman at the corner sometimes gave him a cupful of strong goat's milk; in the grape season the fat winemaker let him have drippings of the mild juice. So there was no danger of going hungry or thirsty. There was plenty of everything in Pompeii if you knew where to find it—and if you had a dog like Bimbo.

As I said before, Tito was not the merriest boy in Pompeii. He could not romp with the other youngsters and play hare and hounds and I spy and follow-your-master and ball-against-the-building and jackstones and kings and robbers with them. But that did not make him sorry for himself. If he could not see the sights that delighted the lads of Pompeii, he could hear and smell things they never noticed. He could really see more with his ears and nose than they could with their eyes. When he and Bimbo went out walking, he knew just where they were going and exactly what was happening.

"Ah," he'd sniff and say as they passed a handsome villa, "Glaucus Pansa is giving a grand dinner tonight. They're going to have three kinds of bread, and roast pigling, and stuffed goose, and a great stew—I think bear stew—and a fig pie." And Bimbo would note that this would be a good place to visit tomorrow. C

Or, "H'm," Tito would murmur, half through his lips, half through his nostrils. "The wife of Marcus Lucretius is expecting her mother. She's shaking out every piece of goods in the house; she's going to use the best clothes—the ones she's been keeping in pine needles and camphor[4]—and there's an extra girl in the kitchen. Come, Bimbo, let's get out of the dust!"

Or, as they passed a small but elegant dwelling opposite the public baths,[5] "Too bad! The tragic poet is ill again. It must be a bad fever this time, for they're trying smoke fumes instead of medicine. Whew! I'm glad I'm not a tragic poet!"

Or, as they neared the forum, "Mm-m! What good things they have in the macellum today!" (It really was a sort of butcher-grocer-marketplace, but Tito didn't know any better. He called it the macellum.) "Dates from Africa, and salt oysters from sea caves, and cuttlefish, and new honey, and sweet onions, and—ugh!—water-buffalo steaks. Come, let's see what's what in the forum." And Bimbo, just as curious as his comrade, hurried on. Being a dog, he trusted his ears and nose (like Tito) more than his eyes. And so the two of them entered the center of Pompeii. **D**

The forum was the part of the town to which everybody came at least once during each day. It was the central square, and everything happened here. There were no private houses; all was public—the chief temples, the gold and red bazaars, the silk shops, the town hall, the booths belonging to the weavers and jewel merchants, the wealthy woolen market, the shrine of the household gods. Everything glittered here. The buildings looked as if they were new—which, in a sense, they were. The earthquake of twelve years ago had brought down all the old structures, and since the citizens of Pompeii were ambitious to rival Naples and even Rome, they had seized the opportunity to rebuild the whole town. And they

4. **camphor** (kăm′fər): a strong-smelling substance used to keep moths away.

5. **public baths:** large public complexes with locker rooms, steam rooms, and bathing pools kept at different temperatures. In many parts of the Roman Empire, a trip to the public baths was a daily ritual for many people.

Monitor Your Comprehension

D THEME VERSUS TOPIC
What details help you infer that Bimbo is important to Tito?

Monitor Your Comprehension

corrupt (kə-rŭpt') *v.* to cause something to change from good to bad

PAUSE & REFLECT
Why do you think the people of Pompeii had so many explanations for what caused the earthquakes?

had done it all within a dozen years. There was scarcely a building that was older than Tito.

Tito had heard a great deal about the earthquake, though being about a year old at the time, he could scarcely remember it. This particular quake had been a light one—as earthquakes go. The weaker houses had been shaken down; parts of the outworn wall had been wrecked; but there was little loss of life, and the brilliant new Pompeii had taken the place of the old. No one knew what caused these earthquakes. Records showed they had happened in the neighborhood since the beginning of time. Sailors said that it was to teach the lazy city folk a lesson and make them appreciate those who risked the dangers of the sea to bring them luxuries and protect their town from invaders. The priests said that the gods took this way of showing their anger to those who refused to worship properly and who failed to bring enough sacrifices to the altars and (though they didn't say it in so many words) presents to the priests. The tradesmen said that the foreign merchants had **corrupted** the ground and it was no longer safe to traffic in imported goods that came from strange places and carried a curse with them. Everyone had a different explanation—and everyone's explanation was louder and sillier than his neighbor's. **PAUSE & REFLECT**

They were talking about it this afternoon as Tito and Bimbo came out of the side street into the public square. The forum was the favorite promenade[6] for rich and poor. What with the priests arguing with the politicians, servants doing the day's shopping, tradesmen crying their wares, women displaying the latest fashions from Greece

6. **promenade** (prŏm'ə-nād'): a public place for walking and socializing.

and Egypt, children playing hide-and-seek among the marble columns, knots of soldiers, sailors, peasants from the provinces—to say nothing of those who merely came to lounge and look on—the square was crowded to its last inch. His ears even more than his nose guided Tito to the place where the talk was loudest. It was in front of the shrine of the household gods that, naturally enough, the householders were arguing. E

"I tell you," rumbled a voice which Tito recognized as bath master Rufus's, "there won't be another earthquake in my lifetime or yours. There may be a tremble or two, but earthquakes, like lightnings, never strike twice in the same place."

"Do they not?" asked a thin voice Tito had never heard. It had a high, sharp ring to it, and Tito knew it as the accent of a stranger. "How about the two towns of Sicily that have been ruined three times within fifteen years by the eruptions of Mount Etna? And were they not warned? And does that column of smoke above Vesuvius mean nothing?"

"That?" Tito could hear the grunt with which one question answered another. "That's always there. We use it for our weather guide. When the smoke stands up straight, we know we'll have fair weather; when it flattens out, it's sure to be foggy; when it drifts to the east—"

"Yes, yes," cut in the edged voice. "I've heard about your mountain barometer.[7] But the column of smoke seems hundreds of feet higher than usual, and it's thickening and spreading like a shadowy tree. They say in Naples—"

"Oh, Naples!" Tito knew this voice by the little squeak that went with it. It was Attilio, the cameo[8] cutter. "*They* talk while we suffer. Little help we got from them last time. Naples commits the crimes, and Pompeii pays the price.

7. **mountain barometer:** A barometer is an instrument for measuring the pressure of air and predicting weather changes. The people of Pompeii used the smoke from the volcano as a sort of barometer.

8. **cameo:** a shell or gem with a picture carved on it.

Monitor Your Comprehension

E HISTORICAL FICTION
Reread lines 135–148. Underline important details that describe the activity at forum.

What does the description tell you about life in Pompeii?

Monitor Your Comprehension

F HISTORICAL FICTION
Reread lines 154–175. Underline the locations outside of Pompeii that are mentioned. What does the reaction to the mention of these other places tell you about life in Pompeii at the time?

ponder (pŏn′dər) *v.* to think seriously about; reflect on

G THEME VERSUS TOPIC
Why is Tito thankful for Bimbo?

It's become a proverb with us. Let them mind their own business." F

"Yes," grumbled Rufus, "and others, too."

"Very well, my confident friends," responded the thin voice, which now sounded curiously flat. "We also have a proverb—and it is this: Those who will not listen to men must be taught by the gods. I say no more. But I leave a last warning. Remember the holy ones. Look to your temples. And when the smoke tree above Vesuvius grows to the shape of an umbrella pine, look to your lives."

Tito could hear the air whistle as the speaker drew his toga about him, and the quick shuffle of feet told him the stranger had gone.

"Now what," said the cameo cutter, "did he mean by that?"

"I wonder," grunted Rufus. "I wonder."

Tito wondered, too. And Bimbo, his head at a thoughtful angle, looked as if he had been doing a heavy piece of **pondering**. By nightfall the argument had been forgotten. If the smoke had increased, no one saw it in the dark. Besides, it was Caesar's birthday, and the town was in holiday mood. Tito and Bimbo were among the merrymakers, dodging the charioteers who shouted at them. A dozen times they almost upset baskets of sweets and jars of Vesuvian wine, said to be as fiery as the streams inside the volcano, and a dozen times they were cursed and cuffed. But Tito never missed his footing. He was thankful for his keen ears and quick instinct—most thankful of all for Bimbo. G

They visited the uncovered theater, and though Tito could not see the faces of the actors, he could follow the

play better than most of the audience, for their attention wandered—they were distracted by the scenery, the costumes, the by-play, even by themselves—while Tito's whole attention was centered in what he heard. Then to the city walls, where the people of Pompeii watched a mock naval battle in which the city was attacked by the sea and saved after thousands of flaming arrows had been exchanged and countless colored torches had been burned. Though the thrill of flaring ships and lighted skies was lost to Tito, the shouts and cheers excited him as much as any, and he cried out with the loudest of them.

The next morning there were *two* of the beloved raisin and sugar cakes for his breakfast. Bimbo was unusually active and thumped his bit of a tail until Tito was afraid he would wear it out. The boy could not imagine whether Bimbo was urging him to some sort of game or was trying to tell him something. After a while, he ceased to notice Bimbo. He felt drowsy. Last night's late hours had tired him. Besides, there was a heavy mist in the air—no, a thick fog rather than a mist—a fog that got into his throat and scraped it and made him cough. He walked as far as the marine gate to get a breath of the sea. But the blanket of haze had spread all over the bay, and even the salt air seemed smoky. (H)

He went to bed before dusk and slept. But he did not sleep well. He had too many dreams—dreams of ships lurching in the forum, of losing his way in a screaming crowd, of armies marching across his chest, of being pulled over every rough pavement of Pompeii.

He woke early. Or, rather, he was pulled awake. Bimbo was doing the pulling. The dog had dragged Tito to his

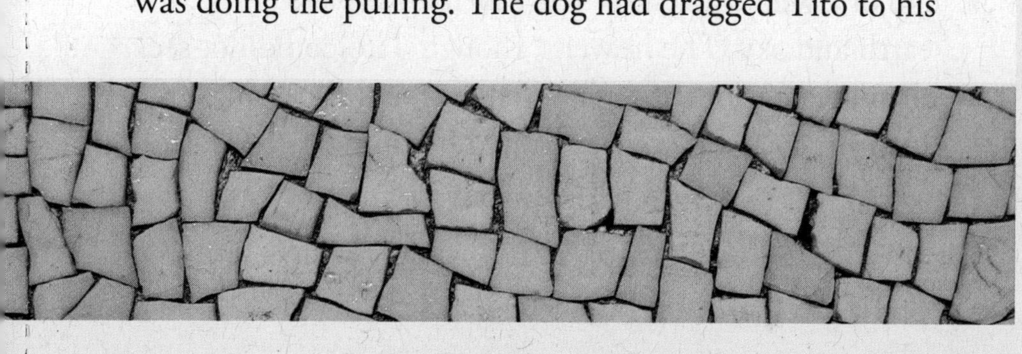

Monitor Your Comprehension

(H) THEME VERSUS TOPIC
Reread lines 216–228. Underline the sentence that describes Bimbo's unusual behavior. In what way does Tito's reaction to Bimbo's behavior suggest that something has changed?

Monitor Your Comprehension

feet and was urging the boy along. Somewhere. Where, Tito did not know. His feet stumbled uncertainly; he was still half asleep. For a while he noticed nothing except the fact that it was hard to breathe. The air was hot. And heavy. So heavy that he could taste it. The air, it seemed, had turned to powder, a warm powder that stung his nostrils and burned his sightless eyes.

Then he began to hear sounds. Peculiar sounds. Like animals under the earth. Hissings and groanings and muffled cries that a dying creature might make **dislodging** the stones of his underground cave. There was no doubt of it now. The noises came from underneath. He not only heard them—he could feel them. The earth twitched; the twitching changed to an uneven shrugging of the soil. Then, as Bimbo half pulled, half coaxed him across, the ground jerked away from his feet and he was thrown against a stone fountain.

dislodge (dĭs-lŏj') *v.* to move from a settled position

What might be causing the land under Pompeii to dislodge?

The water—hot water—splashing in his face revived him. He got to his feet, Bimbo steadying him, helping him on again. The noises grew louder; they came closer. The cries were even more animal-like than before, but now they came from human throats. A few people, quicker of foot and more hurried by fear, began to rush by. A family or two—then a section—then, it seemed, an army broken out of bounds. Tito, bewildered though he was, could recognize Rufus as he bellowed past him, like a water buffalo gone mad. Time was lost in a nightmare.

It was then the crashing began. First a sharp crackling, like a monstrous snapping of twigs; then a roar like the fall of a whole forest of trees; then an explosion that tore earth and sky. The heavens, though Tito could not see them, were shot through with continual flickerings of fire. Lightnings above were answered by thunders beneath. A house fell. Then another. By a miracle the two companions had escaped the dangerous side streets and were in a more open space. It was the forum. They rested here awhile—how long he did not know.

Tito had no idea of the time of day. He could *feel* it was black—an unnatural blackness. Something inside—perhaps the lack of breakfast and lunch—told him it was past noon. But it didn't matter. Nothing seemed to matter. He was getting drowsy, too drowsy to walk. But walk he must. He knew it. And Bimbo knew it; the sharp tugs told him so. Nor was it a moment too soon. The sacred ground of the forum was safe no longer. It was beginning to rock, then to pitch, then to split. As they stumbled out of the square, the earth wriggled like a caught snake, and all the columns of the temple of Jupiter came down. It was the end of the world—or so it seemed.

To walk was not enough now. They must run. Tito was too frightened to know what to do or where to go. He had lost all sense of direction. He started to go back to the inner gate; but Bimbo, straining his back to the last inch, almost pulled his clothes from him. What did the creature want? Had the dog gone mad?

Then, suddenly, he understood. Bimbo was telling him the way out—urging him there. The sea gate,[9] of course. The sea gate—and then the sea. Far from falling buildings, heaving ground. He turned, Bimbo guiding him across open pits and dangerous pools of bubbling mud, away from buildings that had caught fire and were dropping their burning beams. Tito could no longer tell whether the noises were made by the shrieking sky or the **agonized** people. He and Bimbo ran on—the only silent beings in a howling world.

New dangers threatened. All Pompeii seemed to be thronging toward the marine gate; and, squeezing among

9. **sea gate:** a gate in the city wall, leading to the sea.

Monitor Your Comprehension

HISTORICAL FICTION
Reread lines 263–284. Which details show you how the eruption has affected the forum and the town? Add them to your chart.

Event
a volcanic eruption

↓

Details

agonize (ăg′ə-nīz′) *v.* to suffer extreme physical or mental pain

Monitor Your Comprehension

PAUSE & REFLECT
Reread lines 301–314 and underline the phrase the stranger uttered in the forum days before. What warnings should the people of Pompeii have heeded?

THEME VERSUS TOPIC
Why does Bimbo bite Tito and snap at his heels?

the crowds, there was the chance of being trampled to death. But the chance had to be taken. It was growing harder and harder to breathe. What air there was choked him. It was all dust now—dust and pebbles, pebbles as large as beans. They fell on his head, his hands—pumice stones[10] from the black heart of Vesuvius. The mountain was turning itself inside out. Tito remembered a phrase that the stranger had said in the forum two days ago: "Those who will not listen to men must be taught by the gods." The people of Pompeii had refused to heed the warnings; they were being taught now—if it was not too late. **PAUSE & REFLECT**

Suddenly it seemed too late for Tito. The red hot ashes blistered his skin; the stinging vapors tore his throat. He could not go on. He staggered toward a small tree at the side of the road and fell. In a moment Bimbo was beside him. He coaxed. But there was no answer. He licked Tito's hands, his feet, his face. The boy did not stir. Then Bimbo did the last thing he could—the last thing he wanted to do. He bit his comrade, bit him deep in the arm. With a cry of pain, Tito jumped to his feet, Bimbo after him. Tito was in despair, but Bimbo was determined. He drove the boy on, snapping at his heels, worrying his way through the crowd; barking, baring his teeth, heedless of kicks or falling stones. Sick with hunger, half dead with fear and sulphur[11] fumes, Tito pounded on, pursued by Bimbo. How long he never knew. At last he staggered through the marine gate and felt soft sand under him. Then Tito fainted. . . .

Someone was dashing seawater over him. Someone was carrying him toward a boat.

"Bimbo," he called. And then louder, "Bimbo!" But Bimbo had disappeared.

---

10. **pumice** (pŭm′ĭs) **stones:** lightweight rocks formed from lava.
11. **sulphur** (sŭl′fər): a pale yellow substance that produces a choking fume when burned.

Voices jarred against each other. "Hurry—hurry!" "To the boats!" "Can't you see the child's frightened and starving!" "He keeps calling for someone!" "Poor boy, he's out of his mind." "Here, child—take this!"

They tucked him in among them. The oarlocks creaked; the oars splashed; the boat rode over toppling waves. Tito was safe. But he wept continually.

"Bimbo!" he wailed. "Bimbo! Bimbo!"

He could not be comforted. (K)

Eighteen hundred years passed. Scientists were restoring the ancient city; excavators were working their way through the stones and trash that had buried the entire town. Much had already been brought to light—statues, bronze instruments, bright mosaics,[12] household articles; even delicate paintings had been preserved by the fall of ashes that had taken over two thousand lives. Columns were dug up, and the forum was beginning to **emerge**.

It was at a place where the ruins lay deepest that the director paused.

"Come here," he called to his assistant. "I think we've discovered the remains of a building in good shape. Here are four huge millstones that were most likely turned by slaves or mules—and here is a whole wall standing with shelves inside it. Why! It must have been a bakery. And here's a curious thing. What do you think I found under this heap where the ashes were thickest? The skeleton of a dog!"

"Amazing!" gasped his assistant. "You'd think a dog would have had sense enough to run away at the time. And what is that flat thing he's holding between his teeth? It can't be a stone."

12. **mosaics** (mō-zā'ĭks): designs formed from inlaid pieces of stone or glass.

Monitor Your Comprehension

(K) THEME VERSUS TOPIC
Reread lines 331–343. What does Tito realize? What does the fact that Tito is safe, but unable to be comforted suggest about the story's theme? How would you state the theme?

____

____

____

____

____

____

____

emerge (ĭ-mûrj') *v.* to come into view

Ⓛ HISTORICAL FICTION
What abrupt change has occurred in the setting of the story, beginning at line 344? Underline the words in the text that signal this change. Explain how this final passage helps you draw conclusions about how the cultural and historical setting builds the story's theme and makes it more powerful.

"No. It must have come from this bakery. You know it looks to me like some sort of cake hardened with the years. And, bless me, if those little black pebbles aren't raisins. A raisin cake almost two thousand years old! I wonder what made him want it at such a moment." Ⓛ

"I wonder," murmured the assistant.

Literary Analysis: Theme Versus Topic

The **topic** of a story is one or two words that sum up what the story is about. The **theme** is the writer's message *about* the topic. Use the topic and the story elements shown in the chart to help you figure out the theme of "The Dog of Pompeii." Write your ideas in the chart.

READING 3 Draw conclusions about theme and genre in different historical contexts. **3A** Infer the implicit theme of a work of fiction, distinguishing theme from topic.

Topic:	
What I Learn from . . .	
the title:	
the plot:	
the characters:	
the setting/ images:	
Theme:	

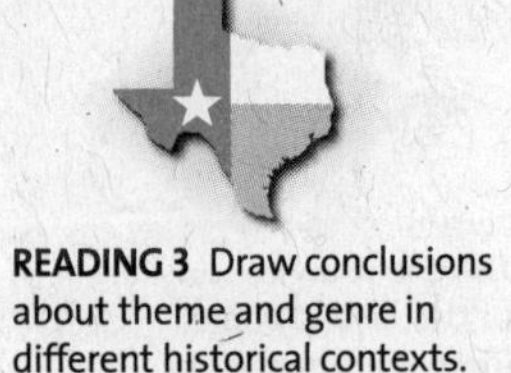

READING 3 Draw conclusions about theme and genre in different historical contexts.

Reading Strategy: Reading Historical Fiction

The historical setting and the eruption of Vesuvius are very important to the story. Review the details you recorded in your charts as you read. Choose one setting detail and one event detail and explain how they contribute to the story's theme.

SETTING DETAIL	
This detail is important because: ______________________	
EVENT DETAIL	
This detail is important because: ______________________	

What would you RISK for someone else?

What do you think about the risk Bimbo took for Tito? Would you do the same for someone you cared about? Explain.

____

____

Vocabulary Practice

Choose the letter of the situation you associate with each boldfaced word.

1. **agonize:** **(a)** sleeping in on a weekend, **(b)** suffering through a death in the family, **(c)** listening to an amusing speaker
2. **corrupt:** **(a)** a dad working overtime, **(b)** a politician taking bribes, **(c)** a child swimming
3. **dislodge:** **(a)** visiting a national park, **(b)** loosening a stone from a wall, **(c)** lending a friend cash
4. **emerge:** **(a)** birds building nests, **(b)** tulips growing in spring, **(c)** cars entering a tunnel
5. **ponder:** **(a)** making a hard decision, **(b)** canoeing in a lake, **(c)** missing a meeting

Academic Vocabulary in Speaking

READING 3 Draw conclusions about theme and genre in different historical contexts. **3A** Infer the implicit theme of a work of fiction, distinguishing theme from topic.

attitude	context	communicate	illustrate	implicit

TURN AND TALK Take notes on the lines below on how the author conveys the theme of "The Dog of Pompeii." With a partner, discuss the various ways the author helps you discover the **implicit** theme of this story. How do Bimbo's actions throughout the story **illustrate** the depth of his devotion to Tito? Use at least two Academic Vocabulary words in your discussion. Definitions of these words are on page 113.

____

____

____

Texas Assessment Practice

DIRECTIONS Use "The Dog of Pompeii" to answer questions 1–6.

1 Why does Bimbo leave Tito alone three times a day?

(A) He has to go home.
(B) He visits the forum.
(C) He fights off danger.
(D) He leaves to find food.

2 A plot event that is a clue to the theme is —

(F) the discussion about a recent earthquake
(G) Bimbo's daily search for food
(H) Tito and Bimbo attending a play
(J) the celebration of Caesar's birthday

3 Which of the following is an example of historical context given in the story?

(A) *Bimbo had never left his side.*
(B) *Tito was never an unhappy boy.*
(C) *The streets were always lively with shining chariots.*
(D) *The cries were even more animal-like than before.*

4 Where do the people of Pompeii go for safety?

(F) the sea
(G) the forum
(H) the bazaar
(J) the inner roads

5 Which of the following best shows Tito's feelings for Bimbo?

(A) They enjoyed the celebration of Caesar's birthday together.
(B) Tito could not be comforted after Bimbo was gone.
(C) Tito enjoyed the raisin cakes Bimbo brought.
(D) Bimbo brought Tito to the forum for safety.

6 What do Bimbo's last actions tell you about him?

(F) He was confused.
(G) He was afraid to swim.
(H) He was thinking of Tito at the end.
(J) He was trying to save other people.

READING 9 Analyze author's purpose in cultural, historical, and contemporary contexts. Compare and contrast the stated or implied purposes of different authors writing on the same topic. **12B** Interpret factual, quantitative, or technical information presented in illustrations, diagrams, and graphs.

Pompeii and Vesuvius

- Nonfiction Book Excerpt, page 133
- Online Article, page 138

Background

You've just read "The Dog of Pompeii," a story that takes place on the day that Mount Vesuvius erupts and buries Pompeii in ash. Now you will learn more about this historical event and what the future may hold for those currently living in the shadow of Mount Vesuvius.

Skill Focus: Author's Purpose and Main Idea

In nonfiction, the most important idea that a writer communicates is the **main idea.** The main idea can be stated directly in the form of a **topic sentence,** which is sometimes the first sentence in a paragraph. Usually, though, you have to determine the main idea by noting the smaller ideas developed in sections of the selection.

To really understand the message a nonfiction writer wants to communicate, you need to determine the **author's purpose,** or reason for writing. The author's purpose is often implied, or suggested by evidence in the text that you must find and analyze. Ask yourself questions to make inferences and draw conclusions about the author's purpose:

- *Why* is the writer telling me this?
- *What* does the writer want me to think about this topic?

Different writers will likely have different purposes and main ideas, even when they are writing about the same topic. As you read the following selections about Pompeii, notes in the side column will ask you to identify main ideas and the author's purpose for writing.

Source	Main Ideas	Author's Purpose
"In Search of Pompeii" Section 1: "Pompeii: The Evidence" Section 2: "Uncovering Pompeii" Section 3: "A Tragic Day"		
"Italians Trying to Prevent a Modern Pompeii"		

from IN SEARCH OF POMPEII

BY GIOVANNI CASELLI

Pompeii: The Evidence

Much of our knowledge of Roman life comes from the evidence uncovered at Pompeii. Splendid houses, beautiful paintings, sculptures of bronze and marble, fine glass, metal, and pottery bear witness not only to a city that perished in one day, but also to a long-vanished civilization.

A visit to Pompeii is like entering a time machine: you can see wide streets still with the ruts cut in the paving stones by the wheels of chariots, the entrance to a shop with graffiti on the wall beside it, the baths and grand houses with their wall paintings and colonnaded gardens. But, above all, there are the people of Pompeii, overwhelmed as they tried to escape the horror that overtook their city. Across nearly 2,000 years, their twisted bodies are vivid witnesses of what happened on August 24, A.D. 79. Ⓐ

SET A PURPOSE FOR READING

Read the selection from *In Search of Pompeii* to find out what Pompeii was like when the volcano erupted.

FOCUS ON FORM

An **informational text** is written material that provides factual information. News articles, encyclopedia entries, timelines, and nonfiction books are examples of informational texts. **Text features,** such as titles, subheadings, photos, captions, maps, and diagrams, often appear in informational texts.

Ⓐ MAIN IDEA

Circle the subheading and underline the topic sentence in the first paragraph. What is the main idea of this first section? Add it to your chart.

Source
Section 1: "Pompeii: The Evidence"

↓

Main Idea

B INFORMATIONAL TEXT
Main ideas in informational texts are often supported with visual information. This diagram shows the layout of Pompeii. What do you learn about Pompeii by studying this diagram? Why do you think the author presented this information in visual form?

Uncovering Pompeii

In December 1860, Victor Emmanuel II, king of the newly united Italy, appointed Giuseppe Fiorelli Director of the Excavations at Pompeii. The era of scientific excavation had begun.

FORUM BATHS
Much of Pompeii had running water, carried in by lead pipes under the streets. Public bath complexes used central furnaces to heat the water. B

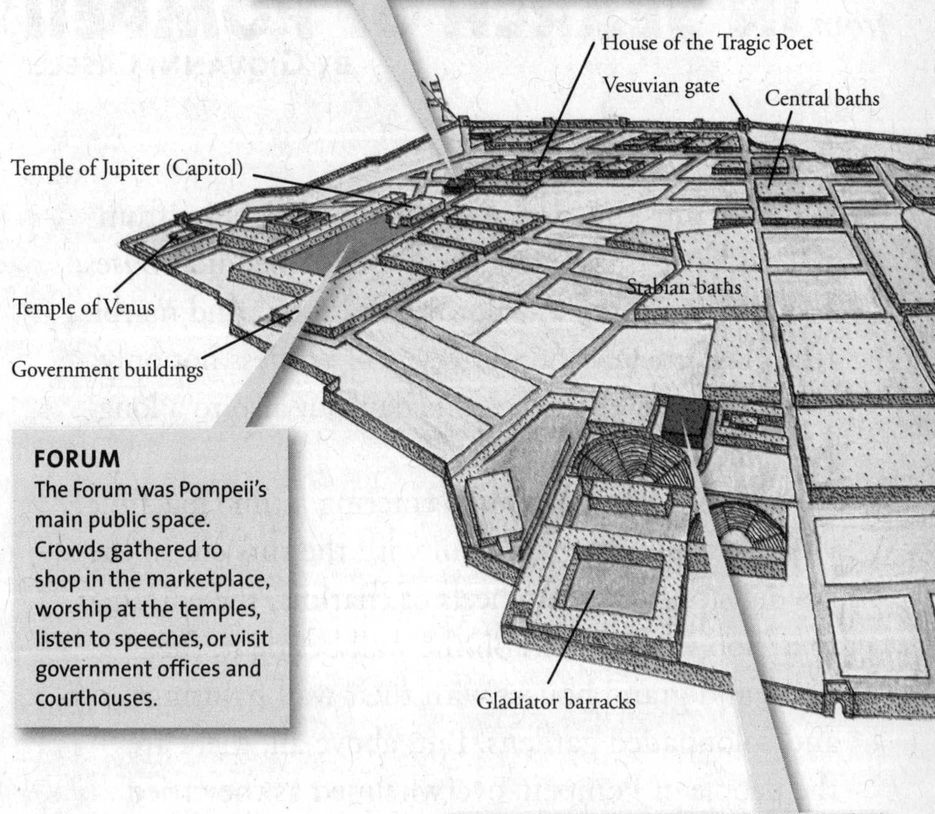

FORUM
The Forum was Pompeii's main public space. Crowds gathered to shop in the marketplace, worship at the temples, listen to speeches, or visit government offices and courthouses.

TEMPLE OF ISIS
Ancient Pompeiians participated in a variety of religions. This temple was dedicated to an Egyptian goddess.

Fiorelli divided the city into quarters, or regions, and gave every block and building a number—a system which is still used today. Archaeologists from all over the world came to see Fiorelli's work at Pompeii.

Slowly and carefully, soil and volcanic debris were removed. The position of every fragment of plaster and brickwork was recorded and then restored to its original place. Charred wood was replaced by fresh timber. C

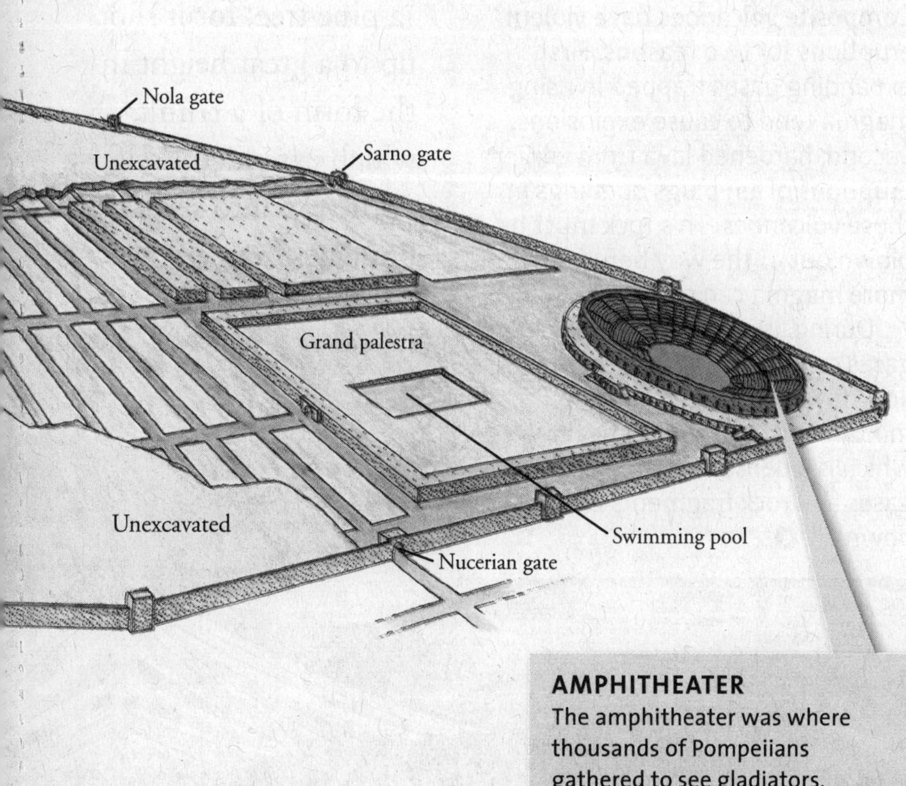

AMPHITHEATER
The amphitheater was where thousands of Pompeiians gathered to see gladiators, athletic competitions, and other forms of entertainment.

C MAIN IDEA
The topic of this second section is the excavation of Pompeii. Underline the topic sentence in the last paragraph and identify the main idea about the excavation. Record this information in your chart.

Source
Section 2: "Uncovering Pompeii"

↓

Main Idea

D MAIN IDEA
What is the main idea of this section, titled "A Tragic Day"? Underline the topic sentence in the first paragraph and use it to help you decide. Record the main idea in your chart.

Source
Section 3: "A Tragic Day"

↓

Main Idea

E AUTHOR'S PURPOSE
What is the author's purpose for presenting information in the form of a diagram and an illustration with a caption, instead of as part of the regular text?

A Tragic Day

When the volcano Vesuvius erupted on August 24, A.D. 79, it destroyed a rich and thickly populated part of southern Italy. We know this from the archaeological discoveries at Herculaneum and Pompeii. But, more remarkably, we know what the disaster was actually like for the people who lived in the region.

The young Roman nobleman Pliny the Younger witnessed the eruption and wrote a letter that is the earliest known account of such a tragedy. As people screamed and struggled to escape the horror, Pliny described the eruption as looking like "a pine tree, for it shot up to a great height in the form of a trunk, which extended itself at the top into several branches." D

Composite Volcano

A composite volcano is a cone-shaped volcano built up of layers of lava and layers of rock fragments. Composite volcanoes have violent eruptions for two reasons. First, expanding gases trapped in rising magma tend to cause explosions. Second, hardened lava from earlier eruptions often plugs openings in these volcanoes. This rock must be blown out of the way before any more magma can escape.

During an eruption, volcanic gases can mix with rock fragments and stay near the ground. The mixture forms a pyroclastic flow, which is a dense cloud of superhot gases and rock fragments that races downhill. E

A Survivor's Letter

"Ashes now fall upon us, though as yet not in great quantity. I looked behind me; gross darkness pressed upon our rear, and came rolling over the land after us like a torrent . . . darkness overspread us, not like that of a moonless or cloudy night, but of a room when it is shut up, and the lamp is put out. You could hear the shrieks of women, the crying of children, and the shouts of men; some were seeking their children, others their parents, others their wives or husbands . . . one lamenting his own fate, another that of his family . . . many lifting their hands to the gods; but the greater part imagining that there were no gods left and that the last and eternal night was come upon the world." F

This description from Pliny the Younger's letter to Tacitus is as vivid now as when he wrote it almost 2,000 years ago. **PAUSE & REFLECT**

F AUTHOR'S PURPOSE
Why does the author include this letter? Consider what you learn from the letter that you can't learn from other sources.

PAUSE & REFLECT
How is the description of events in Pliny's letter similar to that in "The Dog of Pompeii" (page 116)?

SET A PURPOSE FOR READING

Read "Italians Trying to Prevent a Modern Pompeii" to find out what authorities are doing to prevent another tragedy.

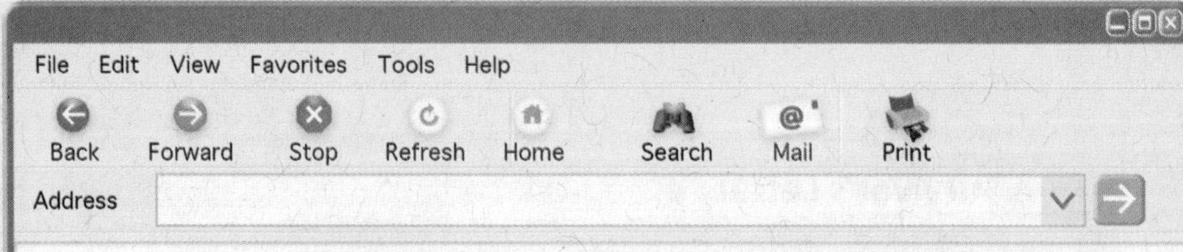

Italians Trying to Prevent a Modern Pompeii G

by Ellen Hale, USA TODAY

SAN SEBASTIANO AL VESUVIO, Italy — Concerned that too many people now crowd the sides of the active volcano, authorities here have launched a bold plan to prevent a repeat of the catastrophic explosion that wiped out Pompeii and smothered thousands of its residents nearly 2,000 years ago.

Authorities hope to thin the ranks of residents so they can be evacuated when Mount Vesuvius erupts

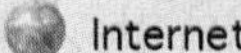

G AUTHOR'S PURPOSE
An author's purpose may be to inform, to persuade, to express feelings, or to entertain. Based on the title of this article, explain which of the four purposes best expresses the author's purpose.

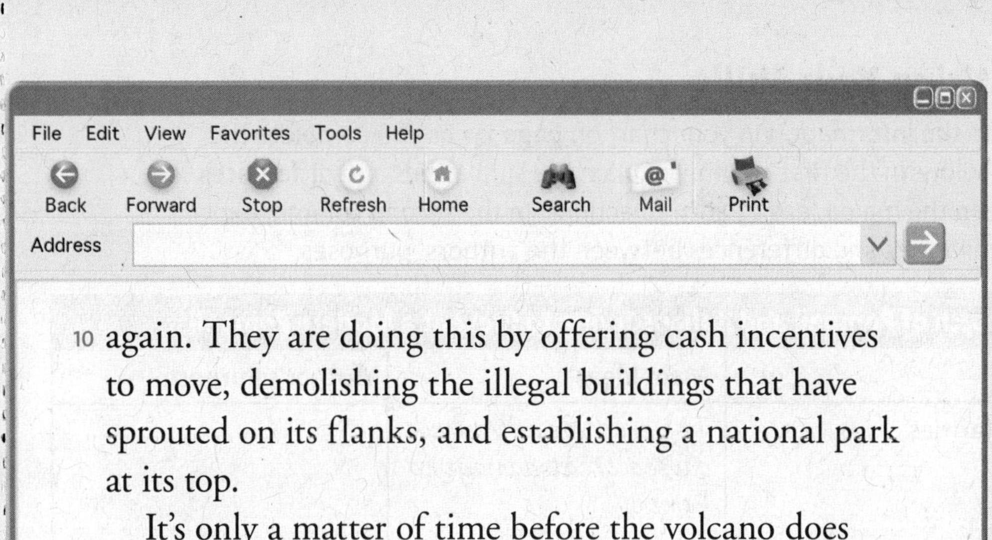

again. They are doing this by offering cash incentives to move, demolishing the illegal buildings that have sprouted on its flanks, and establishing a national park at its top.

It's only a matter of time before the volcano does erupt, scientists say.

"It won't be tomorrow, it won't be next month, and maybe it won't be next year. But it is overdue," says Giovanni Macedonio, director of Vesuvius Observatory, the institute responsible for monitoring the volcano. When it blows, Macedonio warns, it could be with the power of "tens of hundreds of atomic bombs."

Vesuvius last erupted in 1944. Lava destroyed some orchards and homes and 26 people were killed. . . . Residents put pots on their heads to protect against rocks shooting through the air, but the rumblings soon stilled. Vesuvius has been quiet since. . . .

During the volcano's 60-year slumber, however, sprawl from nearby Naples has spilled out; nearly 600,000 people now live in the 18 towns in the shadow of the volcano. H PAUSE & REFLECT

Internet

H AUTHOR'S PURPOSE
Is the author's purpose in writing this article stated or implied? Explain.

PAUSE & REFLECT
How does the writer strengthen her point by bringing up the historical context of a contemporary threat?

READING 9 Analyze author's purpose in cultural, historical, and contemporary contexts. Compare and contrast the stated or implied purposes of different authors writing on the same topic.

Practicing Your Skills

Refer to the information in your chart on page 132 as you complete the chart below. In the first column, explain the similarities and differences between the main ideas of both selections. In the second column, explain the similarities and differences between the authors' purposes.

In Search of Pompeii and Italians Trying to Prevent a Modern Pompeii		
	Main Ideas	Author's Purpose
Similarities	*The eruption of Vesuvius caused great damage to Pompeii.*	
Differences		*Many lives are in danger if Vesuvius erupts again.*

Author's Purpose and Main Idea

How are the main ideas of the two selections connected? How is each author's purpose for writing similar or different?

Academic Vocabulary in Writing

attitude	communicate	context	illustrate	implicit

READING 9 Analyze author's purpose in cultural, historical, and contemporary contexts. Compare and contrast the stated or implied purposes of different authors writing on the same topic. **12B** Interpret factual, quantitative, or technical information presented in illustrations, diagrams, and graphs.

These two selections provide **context** for the story "The Dog of Pompeii." What new information did you learn about Pompeii from these two selections that you did not find in the story? Use at least one Academic Vocabulary word in your response. Definitions of these words are on page 113.

____

____

____

____

Texas Assessment Practice

DIRECTIONS Use "In Search of Pompeii" and "Italians Trying to Prevent a Modern Pompeii" to answer questions 1–4.

1 The most important idea that a nonfiction writer communicates is the —

- (F) theme
- (G) main idea
- (H) topic sentence
- (J) author's purpose

2 "In Search of Pompeii" describes Fiorelli's excavation system. Why was it important?

- (A) His system ensured that artifacts could be returned to their original locations.
- (B) His system was the first to use modern excavation tools and procedures.
- (C) His system divided the city into regions.
- (D) His system gave every building a name.

3 What part of the volcano's eruption might Pliny have been describing in his letter?

- (A) magma
- (B) layers of lava
- (C) pyroclastic flow
- (D) expanding gases

4 A fact that the author includes to inform readers about the danger of another eruption of Mount Vesuvius is that —

- (F) authorities want to establish a national park
- (G) Vesuvius erupted in 1944
- (H) the Vesuvius Observatory monitors the volcano
- (J) nearly 600,000 people live near the volcano

READING 3 Analyze, make inferences, and draw conclusions about theme in different cultural and contemporary contexts. **3A** Infer the implicit theme of a work of fiction.

Scout's Honor

Short Story by **Avi**

When is a trip an ADVENTURE?

When we think of an adventure, we usually think of something big, like an African safari. But even a trip across town can be an adventure if you're going somewhere you've never been before. In "Scout's Honor," three boys get more adventure than they bargained for when they try to earn a merit badge from their Boy Scout troop.

DISCUSS How could a simple trip—a visit to a distant relative or friend, for example—become an adventure? Think about what might happen and who you might meet along the way. List some ideas about how you imagine your potential adventure. Then use your list to share your adventure with a partner.

My Adventure

What might happen:

Who I might meet:

Literary Analysis: Character and Theme

When you read a story, you often feel as though you are experiencing the events along with its characters. Characters can help reveal the **theme,** or implicit message about life, that a writer wishes to share with the reader.

CLUES TO THEME	
CHARACTERS AND ACTIONS	**Characters can reflect a theme through their actions, thoughts, and words. Ask yourself:** • What do the main characters do and say? • How do the characters deal with conflicts? • What lessons do the characters learn? • Do the characters change in any way? How?

As you read "Scout's Honor," study the characters to see how they help express the story's theme.

Reading Strategy: Predict

When you **predict**, you use details and clues from a story to make a reasonable guess about events in the story that haven't happened yet. As you read, record important details and clues in a graphic organizer like the one shown. Use the clues to make predictions about what will happen next in the story.

Clues		Predictions
The narrator has never left Brooklyn before.	→	He might get lost.

Vocabulary in Context

Note: Words are listed in the order in which they appear in the story.

khaki (kăk'ē) *n.* cloth made of light yellowish brown cotton or wool
*Boy Scouts wear **khaki** uniforms.*

compass (kŭm'pəs) *n.* a device used to determine geographical direction
*Max's **compass** is broken—it only points north.*

retort (rĭ-tôrt') *v.* to reply, especially in a quick or unkind way
*When anyone challenges Horse, he **retorts** in a threatening tone.*

discard (dĭ-skärd') *v.* to throw away
*The boys urge Horse to **discard** his wet mattress.*

retrieve (rĭ-trēv') *v.* to get back again
*Horse **retrieved** the hatchet Max dropped.*

congeal (kən-jēl') *v.* to make into a solid mass
*The spilled beans and mustard **congeal** into a lumpy mess.*

simultaneously (sī'məl-tā'nē-əs-lē) *adv.* at the same time
*The boys **simultaneously** knock over the tent and the frying pan.*

Vocabulary Practice

Review the vocabulary words and think about their meanings. Discuss with a partner what you think "Scout's Honor" will be about based on the words above. Share your prediction with the class.

Monitor Your Comprehension

SET A PURPOSE FOR READING

Read "Scout's Honor" to find out what happens when the narrator and his city friends go camping.

Ⓐ PREDICT

Reread lines 1–14. Underline details that tell you about the narrator's experience with the "country." Write one clue in the chart and make a prediction about how easy camping will be for the narrator.

Clues

Prediction

Scout's Honor

Short Story by

AVI

BACKGROUND The Boy Scouts of America is an organization that strives to develop young people's character, physical fitness, and sense of citizenship. Boy Scouts are asked to meet requirements by participating in outdoor activities and educational challenges. When Boy Scouts meet these requirements, they receive a new title and rank. In "Scout's Honor," a group of boys try to complete the requirements that will move them to Second Class.

Back in 1946, when I was nine, I worried that I wasn't tough enough. That's why I became a Boy Scout. Scouting, I thought, would make a man of me. It didn't take long to reach Tenderfoot rank. You got that for joining. To move up to Second Class, however, you had to meet three requirements. Scout Spirit and Scout Participation had been cinchy. The third requirement, Scout Craft, meant I had to go on an overnight hike in the *country.* In other words, I had to leave Brooklyn, on my own, for the first time in my life.

Since I grew up in Brooklyn in the 1940s, the only grass I knew was in Ebbets Field[1] where the Dodgers played. Otherwise, my world was made of slate pavements, streets of asphalt (or cobblestone), and skies full of tall buildings. The only thing "country" was a puny pin oak tree at our curb, which was noticed, mostly, by dogs. Ⓐ

1. **Ebbets Field:** The Los Angeles Dodgers were the Brooklyn Dodgers until the late 1950s. They played in the Ebbets Field stadium.

I asked Scoutmaster Brenkman where I could find some country. Now, whenever I saw Mr. Brenkman, who was a church pastor, he was dressed either in church black or Scout **khaki**. When he wore black, he'd warn us against hellfire. When he wore khaki, he'd teach us how to build fires.

"Country," Scoutmaster Brenkman said in answer to my question, "is anywhere that has lots of trees and is not in the city. Many boys camp in the Palisades."

"Where's that?"

"Just north of the city. It's a park in Jersey."

"Isn't that a zillion miles from here?"

"Take the subway to the George Washington Bridge, then hike across."

I thought for a moment, then asked, "How do I prove I went?"

Mr. Brenkman looked deeply shocked. "You wouldn't *lie*, would you? What about Scout's honor?"

"Yes, sir," I replied meekly. (B)

My two best friends were Philip Hossfender, whom we nicknamed Horse, and Richard Macht, called Max because we were not great spellers. They were also Scouts, Tenderfoots like me.

Horse was a skinny little kid about half my size whose way of arguing was to ball up his fist and say, "Are you saying . . . ?" in a threatening tone.

Max was on the pudgy side, but he could talk his way out of a locked room. More importantly, he always seemed to have pocket money, which gave his talk real power. (C)

I wasn't sure why, but being best friends meant we were rivals too. One of the reasons for my wanting to be tougher was a feeling that Horse was a lot tougher than I was, and that Max was a little tougher.

Monitor Your Comprehension

khaki (kăk'ē) *n.* cloth made of light yellowish brown cotton or wool

(B) PREDICT

What do you predict will happen? Record your thoughts in your graphic organizer.

Clues

↓

Prediction

(C) CHARACTER AND THEME

Reread lines 36–45. Underline words that describe Horse and Max and write a description of them on the lines below.

Horse: __________

Max: __________

D CHARACTER AND THEME
Reread lines 50–63. What do you learn about Horse and Max, based on what they say?

E PREDICT
Why do the boys think it is okay that they are telling a lie? What does this lead you to predict about how the adventure will turn out?

"I'm going camping in the Palisades next weekend," I casually informed them.

"How come?" Max challenged.

"Scout Craft," I replied.

"Oh, *that*," Horse said with a shrug.

"Look," I said, "I don't know about you, but I don't intend to be a Tenderfoot all my life. Anyway, doing stuff in the city is for sissies. Scouting is real camping. Besides, I like roughing it."

"You saying I don't?" Horse snapped.

"I'm not saying nothing," I said.

They considered my idea. Finally, Horse said, "Yeah, well, I was going to do that, but I didn't think you guys were ready for it." D

"I've been ready for *years*," Max protested.

"Then we're going, right?" I said.

They looked around at me. "If you can do it, I can do it," Max said.

"Yeah," Horse said thoughtfully.

The way they agreed made me nervous. Now I really was going to have to be tough.

We informed our folks that we were going camping overnight (which was true) and that the Scoutmaster was going with us—which was a lie. We did remember what Mr. Brenkman said about honesty, but we were baseball fans too, and since we were prepared to follow Scout law—being loyal, helpful, friendly, courteous, kind, obedient, cheerful, thrifty, brave, clean, *and* reverent—we figured a 900 batting average[2] was not bad. E

So Saturday morning we met at the High Street subway station. I got there first. Stuffed in my dad's army surplus

2. **900 batting average:** In baseball, a batting average is the number of times a batter gets a hit compared to the number of times he bats. A batting average of .900 is nearly perfect, since it means the batter gets a hit 90% of the time. The boys use this term to mean that since they have followed most of Scout law, they are above-average Scouts, even if they tell a lie.

knapsack was a blanket, a pillow, and a paper bag with three white-bread peanut-butter-and-jelly sandwiches—that is, lunch, supper, and Sunday breakfast. My pockets were full of stick matches. I had an old flashlight, and since I lived by the Scout motto—Be Prepared—I had brought along an umbrella. Finally, being a serious reader, I had the latest Marvel Family comics.

Horse arrived next, his arms barely managing to hold on to a mattress that seemed twice his size. As for food, he had four cans of beans jammed into his pockets.

Max came last. He was lugging a new knapsack that contained a cast-iron frying pan, a packet of hot dogs, and a box of saltine crackers—plus two bottles. One bottle was mustard, the other, celery soda. He also had a bag of Tootsie Rolls and a shiny hatchet. “To build a lean-to,”[3] he explained.

Max’s prize possession, however, was an official Scout **compass**. “It’s really swell,” he told us. “You can’t ever get lost with it. Got it at the Scout store.”

“I hate that place,” Horse informed us. “It’s all new. Nothing real.”

“This compass is real,” Max **retorted**. “Points north all the time. You can get cheaper ones, but they point all different directions.”

“What’s so great about the north?” Horse said.

“That’s always the way to go,” Max insisted. (F)

“Says who?” I demanded.

“Mr. Brenkman, dummy,” Horse cried. “Anyway, there’s always an arrow on maps pointing the way north.”

“Cowboys live out west,” I reminded them. They didn’t care.

On the subway platform, we realized we did not know which station we were heading for. To find out, we studied

3. **lean-to:** a shelter with a flat, sloping roof.

Monitor Your Comprehension

VISUAL VOCABULARY
compass *n.* a device used to determine geographic direction

From what Max says, do you think he understands how to use his **compass**? Explain.

retort (rĭ-tôrt′) *v.* to reply, especially in a quick or unkind way

(F) PREDICT
Reread lines 79–105. Circle the items the boys bring with them for the camping trip. How effective do you predict their camping gear will be?

the system map, which looked like a noodle factory hit by a bomb. The place we wanted to go (north) was at the top of the map, so I had to hoist Horse onto my shoulders for a closer look. Since he refused to let go of his mattress—or the tin cans in his pockets—it wasn't easy. I asked him—in a kindly fashion—to put the mattress down.

No sooner did he find the station—168th Street—than our train arrived. We rushed on, only to have Horse scream, "My mattress!" He had left it on the platform. Just before the doors shut, he and I leaped off. Max, however, remained on the train. Helplessly, we watched as his horror-stricken face slid away from us. "Wait at the next station!" I bellowed. "Don't move!"

The next train took forever to come. Then it took even longer to get to the next stop. There was Max. All around him—like fake snow in a glass ball—were crumbs. He'd been so nervous he had eaten all his crackers.

"Didn't that make you thirsty?"

"I drank my soda."

I noticed streaks down his cheeks. Horse noticed them too. "You been crying?" he asked.

"Naw," Max said. "There was this water dripping from the tunnel roof. But, you said don't move, right? Well, I was just being obedient." G

G CHARACTER AND THEME
Is Max telling the truth about crying? How do you know?

By the time we got on the next train—with all our possessions—we had been traveling for an hour. But we had managed to go only one stop.

During the ride, I got hungry. I pulled out one of my sandwiches. With the jelly soaked through the bread, it looked like a limp scab.

Horse, envious, complained *he* was getting hungry.

"Eat some of your canned beans," I suggested.

He got out one can without ripping his pocket too badly. Then his face took on a mournful look.

Monitor Your Comprehension

"What's the matter?" I asked.

"Forgot to bring a can opener."

Max said, "In the old days, people opened cans with their teeth."

"You saying my teeth aren't strong?"

"I'm just talking about history!"

"You saying I don't know history?"

Always kind, I plopped half my sandwich into Horse's hand. He squashed it into his mouth and was quiet for the next fifteen minutes. It proved something I'd always believed: The best way to stop arguments is to get people to eat peanut butter sandwiches. They can't talk.

Then we became so absorbed in our Marvel Family comics we missed our station. We got to it only by coming back the other way. When we reached street level, the sky was dark.

"I knew it," Max announced. "It's going to rain."

"Don't worry," Horse said. "New Jersey is a whole other state. It probably won't be raining there."

"I brought an umbrella," I said smugly, though I wanted it to sound helpful. **PAUSE & REFLECT**

PAUSE & REFLECT
Why does the narrator frequently describe himself with positive adjectives and adverbs, such as "always kind" (line 154) and "helpful" (line 166)?

As we marched down 168th Street, heading for the George Washington Bridge, we looked like European war refugees.[4] Every few paces, Horse cried, "Hold it!" and adjusted his arms around his mattress. Each time we paused, Max pulled out his compass, peered at it, then announced, "Heading north!"

I said, "The bridge goes from east to west."

"Maybe the bridge does," Max insisted with a show of his compass, "but guaranteed, we are going north."

About then, the heel of my left foot, encased in a heavy rubber boot over an earth-crushing Buster Brown shoe,

4. **European war refugees:** people who fled Europe to escape World War II (1939–1945) and its effects.

Monitor Your Comprehension

H PREDICT
Underline Max's statement in lines 183–184. What do you predict the boys will do at this point?

I CHARACTER AND THEME
Reread lines 180–200. In what ways do the boys try to hide their fear from one another?

started to get sore. Things weren't going as I had hoped. Cheerfully, I tried to ignore the pain.

The closer we drew to the bridge, the more immense it seemed. And the clouds had become so thick, you couldn't see the top or the far side.

Max eyed the bridge with deep suspicion. "I'm not so sure we should go," he said. **H**

"Why?"

"Maybe it doesn't have another side."

We looked at him.

"No, seriously," Max explained, "they could have taken the Jersey side away, you know, for repairs."

"Cars are going across," I pointed out.

"They could be dropping off," he suggested.

"You would hear them splash," Horse argued.

"I'm going," I said. Trying to look brave, I started off on my own. My bravery didn't last long. The walkway was narrow. When I looked down, I saw only fog. I could feel the bridge tremble and sway. It wasn't long before I was convinced the bridge was about to collapse. Then a ray of hope struck me: Maybe the other guys had chickened out. If they had, I could quit because of *them*. I glanced back. My heart sank. They were coming. **I**

After they caught up, Horse looked me in the eye and said, "If this bridge falls, I'm going to kill you."

A quarter of a mile farther across, I gazed around. We were completely fogged in.

"I think we're lost," I announced.

"What do we do?" Horse whispered. His voice was jagged with panic. That made me feel better.

"Don't worry," Max said. "I've got my compass." He pulled it out. "North is that way," he said, pointing in the direction we had been going.

Horse said, "You sure?"

"A Scout compass never lies," Max insisted.

"*We* lied," I reminded him.

"Yeah, but this is an *official* Scout compass," Max returned loyally.

"Come on," Max said and marched forward. Horse and I followed. In moments, we crossed a metal bar on the walkway. On one side, a sign proclaimed: NEW YORK; on the other, it said: NEW JERSEY.

"Holy smoke,"[5] Horse said with reverence as he straddled the bar. "Talk about being tough. We're in two states at the same time."

It began to rain. Max said, "Maybe it'll keep us clean."

"You saying I'm not clean?" Horse shot back.

Ever friendly, I put up my umbrella.

We went on—Max on one side, Horse on the other, me in the middle—trying to avoid the growing puddles. After a while, Max said, "Would you move the umbrella? Rain is coming down my neck."

"We're supposed to be roughing it," I said.

"Being in the middle isn't roughing it," Horse reminded me.

I folded the umbrella up so we all could get soaked equally. [J]

"Hey!" I cried. "Look!" Staring up ahead, I could make out tollbooths[6] and the dim outlines of buildings.

"Last one off the bridge is a rotten egg!" Horse shouted and began to run. The next second, he tripped and took off like an F-36 fighter plane. Unfortunately, he landed like a Hell-cat dive-bomber[7] as his mattress unspooled before him and then slammed into a big puddle.

5. **Holy smoke:** an old slang expression meaning "My goodness."

6. **tollbooths:** booths at which drivers must stop to pay a toll, or small fee.

7. **Hell-cat dive-bomber:** a World War II plane that took off from and returned to an aircraft carrier.

Monitor Your Comprehension

J CHARACTER AND THEME

Reread lines 230–234. What do the boys' definitions of "roughing it" tell you about them?

Max and I ran to help. Horse was damp. His mattress was soaked. When he tried to roll it up, water cascaded like Niagara Falls.

"Better leave it," Max said.

"It's what I sleep on at home," Horse said as he slung the soaking, dripping mass over his shoulder.

When we got off the bridge, we were in a small plaza. To the left was the roadway, full of roaring cars. In front of us, aside from the highway, there was nothing but buildings. Only to the right were there trees.

"North is that way," Max said, pointing toward the trees. We set off.

"How come you're limping?" Horse asked me. My foot *was* killing me. All I said, though, was, "How come you keep rubbing your arm?"

"I'm keeping the blood moving."

We approached the grove of trees. "Wow," Horse exclaimed. "Country." But as we drew closer, what we found were **discarded** cans, bottles, and newspapers—plus an old mattress spring.

"Hey," Max cried, sounding relieved, "this is just like Brooklyn." (K)

I said, "Let's find a decent place, make camp, and eat."

It was hard to find a campsite that didn't have junk. The growing dark didn't help. We had to settle for the place that had the least amount of garbage.

Max said, "If we build a lean-to, it'll keep us out of the rain." He and Horse went a short distance with the hatchet. Seeing a tree they wanted, Max whacked at it. The hatchet bounced right out of his hand. There was not even a dent in the tree. Horse **retrieved** the hatchet and checked the blade. "Dull," he said.

discard (dĭ-skärd′) *v.* to throw away

(K) CHARACTER AND THEME
Why is Max relieved to find the campsite full of garbage?

____

____

____

____

retrieve (rĭ-trēv′) *v.* to get back again

"Think I'm going to carry something sharp and cut myself?" Max protested. They contented themselves with picking up branches.

I went in search of firewood, but everything was wet. When I finally gathered some twigs and tried to light them, the only thing that burned was my fingers.

Meanwhile, Horse and Max used their branches to build a lean-to directly over me. After many collapses—which didn't help my work—they finally got the branches to stand in a shaky sort of way.

"Uh-oh," Horse said. "We forgot to bring something for a cover."

Max eyed me. "Didn't you say you brought a blanket?"

"No way!" I cried.

"All in favor of using the blanket!"

Horse and Max both cried, "Aye."

Only after I built up a mound of partially burned match sticks and lit *them*, did I get the fire going. It proved that where there's smoke there doesn't have to be much fire. The guys meanwhile draped my blanket over their branch construction. It collapsed twice. **PAUSE & REFLECT**

About an hour after our arrival, the three of us were gathered inside the tiny space. There was a small fire, but more light came from my flickering flashlight.

"No more rain," Horse said with pride.

"Just smoke," I said, rubbing my stinging eyes.

"We need a vent hole," Horse pointed out.

"I could cut it with the hatchet," Max said.

"It's my mother's favorite blanket."

"And you took it?" Max said.

I nodded.

"You *are* tough," Horse said.

Monitor Your Comprehension

PAUSE & REFLECT

How do the boys' experiences so far reflect the prediction you made on page 147?

Monitor Your Comprehension

L PREDICT
Reread lines 306–309 and circle the adjective the narrator uses to describe the other guys. Make a prediction about whether the narrator's statement will turn out to be true.

Besides having too much smoke in our eyes and being wet, tired, and in pain, we were starving. I almost said something about giving up, but as far as I could see, the other guys were still tough. L

Max put his frying pan atop my smoldering smoke. After dumping in the entire contents of his mustard bottle, he threw in the franks. Meanwhile, I bolted down my last sandwich.

"What am I going to eat?" Horse suddenly said.

"Your beans," I reminded him.

Max offered up his hatchet. "Here. Just chop off the top end of the can."

"Oh, right," Horse said. He selected a can, set it in front of him, levered himself onto his knees, then swung down—hard. There was an explosion. For a stunned moment, we just sat there, hands, face, and clothing dripping with beans.

Suddenly Max shouted, "Food fight! Food fight!" and began to paw the stuff off and fling it around.

Having a food fight in a cafeteria is one thing. Having one in the middle of a soaking wet lean-to with cold beans during a dark, wet New Jersey night is another. In seconds, the lean-to was down, the fire kicked over, and Max's frankfurters dumped on the ground.

"The food!" Max screamed, and began to snatch up the franks. Coated with mustard, dirt, grass, and leaves, they looked positively prehistoric. Still, we wiped the franks clean on our pants then ate them—the franks, that is. Afterward, we picked beans off each other's clothes—the way monkeys help friends get rid of lice.

For dessert, Max shared some Tootsie Rolls. After Horse swallowed his sixteenth piece, he announced, "I don't feel so good."

The thought of his getting sick was too much. "Let's go home," I said, ashamed to look at the others. To my surprise—and relief—nobody objected.

Wet and cold, our way lit by my fast-fading flashlight, we gathered our belongings—most of them, anyway. As we made our way back over the bridge, gusts of wind-blown rain pummeled us until I felt like a used-up punching bag. By the time we got to the subway station, my legs were melting fast. The other guys looked bad too. Other riders moved away from us. One of them murmured, "Juvenile delinquents." To cheer us up, I got out my comic books, but they had **congealed** into a lump of red, white, and blue pulp.

congeal (kən-jēl') *v.* to make into a solid mass

With the subways running slow, it took hours to get home. When we emerged from the High Street Station, it was close to midnight.

Before we split up to go to our own homes, we just stood there on a street corner, embarrassed, trying to figure out how to end the day gracefully. I was the one who said, "Okay, I admit it. I'm not as tough as you guys. I gave up first."

Max shook his head. "Naw. I wanted to quit, but I wasn't tough enough to do it." He looked to Horse.

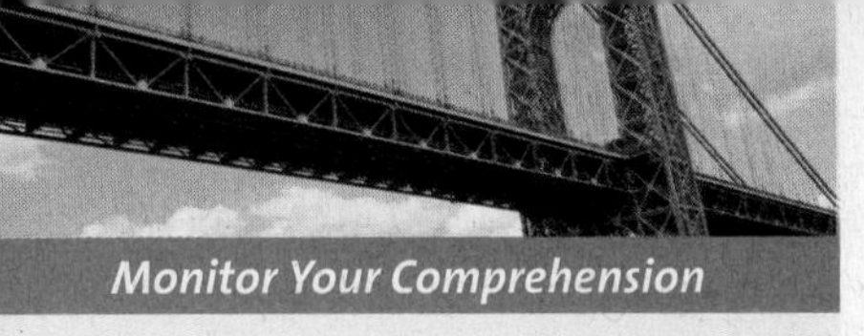

Horse made a fist. "You saying I'm the one who's tough?" he demanded. "I hate roughing it!"

"Me too," I said quickly.

"Same for me," Max said.

Horse said, "Only thing is, we just have to promise not to tell Mr. Brenkman."

Grinning with relief, we **simultaneously** clasped hands.

"No matter what," Max reminded us.

To which I added, "Scout's Honor." Ⓜ

simultaneously (sī'məl-tā'nē-əs-lē) *adv.* at the same time

Ⓜ CHARACTER AND THEME

Reread lines 353–368. Pay attention to how Horse and Max react to the narrator's confession. In what ways have their attitudes changed?

The boys agree to not tell Mr. Brenkman that they gave up. How have the boys stayed the same?

Literary Analysis: Character and Theme

READING 3 Analyze, make inferences, and draw conclusions about theme in different cultural and contemporary contexts. **3A** Infer the implicit theme of a work of fiction.

In the chart below, record each character's important statements and actions, what lessons he learns, and how he changes. Then, write a theme statement.

	Narrator	Horse	Max
Statements/ Actions	"I like roughing it."		
What He Learns			
How He Changes			

Theme Statement:

Reading Strategy: Predict

Look back at the predictions you made as you read. Write three of your predictions in the chart and then tell what really happened.

Prediction #1:
What Really Happened:
Prediction #2:
What Really Happened:
Prediction #3:
What Really Happened:

When is a trip an ADVENTURE?

Was the trip the boys took in this story a true adventure, or was it something else? Explain.

____

____

____

Vocabulary Practice

Synonyms are words that mean the same thing, while **antonyms** are words that mean the opposite. Next to each word pair below, write *S* if the words are synonyms and *A* if they are antonyms.

__________ **1.** retrieve/lose

__________ **2.** retort/reply

__________ **3.** discard/keep

__________ **4.** khaki/cloth

__________ **5.** congeal/separate

__________ **6.** simultaneously/together

Academic Vocabulary in Speaking

READING 3 Draw conclusions about theme and genre in different historical contexts. 3A Infer the implicit theme of a work of fiction, distinguishing theme from topic.

attitude	context	communicate	illustrate	implicit

TURN AND TALK With a partner, discuss how historical **context** influences the theme of Avi's story. (Remember that the story takes place in 1946.) How would the events be different if the story were set in modern times? Use at least two Academic Vocabulary words in your discussion. Definitions of these words are on page 113.

Texas Assessment Practice

DIRECTIONS Use "Scout's Honor" to answer questions 1–6.

1 Why do the boys need to take a camping trip?
- (A) to overcome their fears
- (B) to earn the Scout Craft badge
- (C) to advance to the Tenderfoot rank
- (D) to impress Scoutmaster Brenkman

2 What makes the narrator finally decide it is time to go home?
- (F) the rain
- (G) the lack of dinner
- (H) the possibility of Horse getting sick
- (J) the destruction of the shelter and his mother's blanket

3 How is the narrator different from his friends?
- (A) He is more of a leader.
- (B) He is not as tough.
- (C) He lies to people.
- (D) He is funnier.

4 What word best describes how the narrator feels when his friends agree to go home?
- (F) upset
- (G) excited
- (H) relieved
- (J) confused

5 How do the boys change by the end of the story?
- (A) They are no longer friends.
- (B) They now appreciate camping.
- (C) They are now Second Class scouts.
- (D) They are no longer competing to be the toughest.

6 Which of the following is not a clue to a story's theme?
- (F) what the characters say and do
- (G) what lessons the characters learn
- (H) whether the characters face conflict
- (J) whether the characters change in any way

READING 12 Understand how to use information in procedural texts. **12A** Follow multi-tasked instructions to complete a task, solve a problem, or perform procedures. **RC-6(E)** Synthesize texts in ways that maintain meaning and logical order within a text.

How to Build a Bat House

Instruction Manual

Background

In "Scout's Honor," you saw how three boys made a disastrous and comical attempt to earn a Boy Scout merit badge. To earn merit badges today, Boy Scouts can choose from many activities. All of these activities require the ability to follow instructions. A Scout might even try building a house for bats, using the how-to instructions in the following manual.

Skill Focus: Follow Instructions

Instructions are a type of **procedural text,** a text that tells you how to do something. Good instructions consist of multi-step directions that explain how to complete a task, solve a problem, or perform a procedure, such as repairing a bicycle, downloading music files, or building a bookcase. Well-written instructions communicate information in a logical order, using very few words. To follow instructions successfully, follow these strategies in order:

- Preview the task by reading all the directions carefully so you know the scope of the project. Make sure you have everything you'll need before you begin. If there are any safety precautions, work with adult supervision.
- Study any illustrations, diagrams, or charts that show the materials you'll need, recommended methods of working, or examples of the finished product.
- Follow the steps in order, and do exactly what the instructions say.

As you read "How to Build a Bat House," you will take notes in a chart like the one shown to keep track of what you'll need to consider for each step of the process.

How to Build a Bat House	
Step	**Things to Consider**
1	*I'll need to get enough plywood to cut into pieces the exact size of these measurements before I begin.* *I live in a cold climate, so read Step 7 now.*

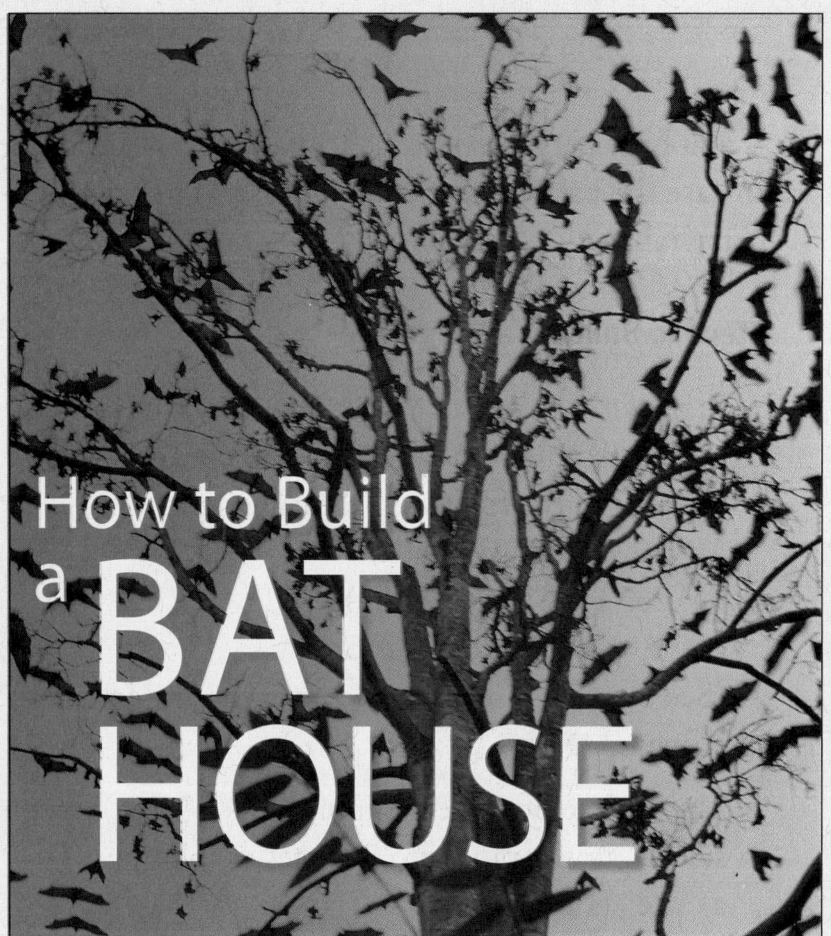

Bats have gotten a bad name from horror stories and movies. That's too bad, because bats can be great little guys to have around. Give a bat a nice place to live, and it will help you cut down on mosquitoes and other insect nuisances. These tiny creatures, the world's only flying mammals, don't ask for much in the way of shelter. They want a warm, enclosed space where they can "hang" out. Yes, bats do sleep upside-down, and they also climb the walls, which means they need a surface they can grip with their tiny claws. They also like a place that stays dark at night and is near water. **A**

This easy-to-build structure will welcome a small colony of bats. (Caution: Do not build a bat house

SET A PURPOSE FOR READING

Read "How to Build a Bat House" to find out what steps are involved in the process.

FOCUS ON FORM

Procedural texts, such as how-to guides and instruction manuals, communicate with more than words. They have certain **text features**—such as titles, subheadings, photos, captions, illustrations, and diagrams—that make it easy to find information at a glance. But unlike many other forms of informational text, procedural texts use the fewest possible words. They are usually not written in paragraphs. Instead they present information in clearly numbered steps. Each step focuses on one specific task that is an essential part of the whole procedure.

A PROCEDURAL TEXT

Reread lines 1–11. Why do you think the text begins by explaining why it's good to have bats to live nearby?

B PROCEDURAL TEXT
Reread Step 1 and circle the later step it references. Why do you think the writer didn't simply combine the two steps?

C INSTRUCTIONS
Take notes in your chart explaining what you'll need to consider for steps 2–4.

Step 2

Things to Consider:

Step 3

Things to Consider:

Step 4

Things to Consider:

if you have pets. Never touch a bat, alive or dead, in case the bat is sick. Report dead bats in case they carry rabies.)

Steps to Building a Bat House

1 Start with 1 sheet of ½″ exterior-grade untreated plywood, at least 2′ × 4′. Cut the plywood into 3 pieces of the following measurements:
a) 26 ½″ × 24″ (1 back)
b) 26″ × 24″ (1 front-top)
c) 5″ × 24″ (1 front-bottom)
(See Step 7 for measurements if you live in a cold climate.) B

2 Use 1 piece of untreated pine (1″ × 2″ × 8′) for the sides. Cut the pine into 3 pieces as follows:
a) 24″ (1 ceiling)
b) 20 ½″ (2 side walls)

3 Paint or stain the wood with a dark-colored, water-based stain or paint. The dark color will absorb the sunlight and keep the bat house warm.

4 To give the bats a way to grab onto a wall of their house, use a staple gun to secure window screen or mesh to one side of the back panel. C

5 Use exterior-grade 1″ screws (you'll need 20–30) to attach the side walls to the longer sides of the back panel. Line up the walls and sides correctly. There will be ½″ of extra back panel at the bottom for the

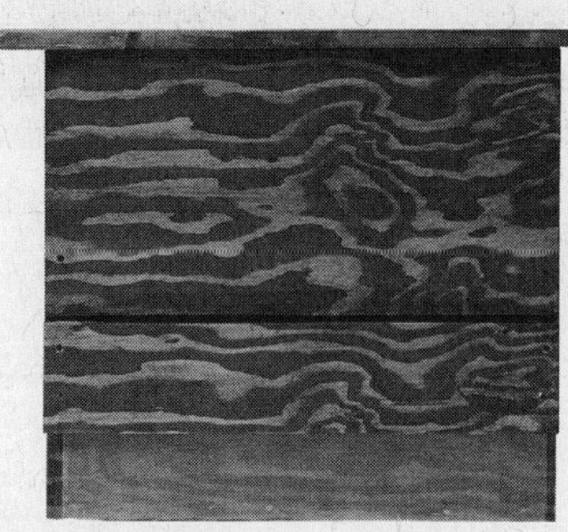

will be ½″ of extra back panel at the bottom for the bats to land on.

6 Place the ceiling at the top of the back panel, between the side walls. Screw into place.

7 Place the top front panel on the house. Line it up with the ceiling and screw into place. Place the bottom front panel on the house, leaving a ½″ vent space between the top and bottom front panels. If you live in a cold climate, you can eliminate this vent. Simply cut a single front piece that is 23″ long. C

8 Using 1″ nails (you'll need a small box), carefully nail the roof over the top.

9 For best results, use a caulk gun to apply caulk to the joints.

10 When your bat house is ready, look for a place to hang it that faces south or east and has a nearby water source. Using heavy-duty hanging hooks and wire, hang your bat house at least 12 feet off the ground (to help keep other critters out). Choose an area that's away from lighting, such as porch lights or street lights.

PAUSE & REFLECT

C INSTRUCTIONS
Reread step 7. If you lived in a warm climate, why would you be sure to include this vent?

PAUSE & REFLECT
What could be some consequences of not following these instructions precisely?

READING 12 Understand how to use information in procedural texts. **12A** Follow multi-tasked instructions to complete a task, solve a problem, or perform procedures. **RC-6(E)** Synthesize texts in ways that maintain meaning and logical order within a text.

Practicing Your Skills

Review "How to Build a Bat House" and complete the chart below. In column 1, write down the materials that are needed for each step. In column 2, restate the actions involved in each step.

Step	Materials, Tools, or Ingredients Needed	What Actions are Involved
1	*1 sheet of plywood*	
2		
3		
4		
5		
6		
7		
8		
9		*Apply caulk to joints*
10		

Academic Vocabulary in Writing

READING 12 Understand how to use information in procedural texts. **12A** Follow multi-tasked instructions to complete a task, solve a problem, or perform procedures. **RC-6(E)** Synthesize texts in ways that maintain meaning and logical order within a text.

attitude	communicate	context	illustrate	implicit

Were the instructions in the document **communicated** clearly? If you followed the steps, do you think you could construct a bat house? Tell why or why not, using at least one Academic Vocabulary word in your response. Definitions of these words are on page 113.

____

____

____

____

____

____

____

Texas Assessment Practice

DIRECTIONS Use "How to Build a Bat House" to answer questions 1–4.

1 Why are bats good to have around?

- (A) They eat mosquitoes.
- (B) They make good pets.
- (C) They are enjoyable to watch.
- (D) They appear in horror movies.

2 You should paint or stain the bat house's wood a dark color because —

- (F) bats can't see light colors
- (G) predators will be less likely to find the bat house
- (H) it will make the bat house blend in with its environment
- (J) the dark color will absorb the sunlight and keep the bat house warm

3 Which of the following is the best reason to preview a set of directions carefully?

- (A) to decide if you really need the directions to complete the task
- (B) to make sure you have everything you'll need
- (C) to look for errors and omissions
- (D) to find shortcuts and steps you can skip

4 Why can this document be classified a procedural text?

- (F) It includes text features.
- (G) It shows what a bat looks like.
- (H) It explains how to complete a task.
- (J) It is written in paragraphs and has a clear beginning and end.

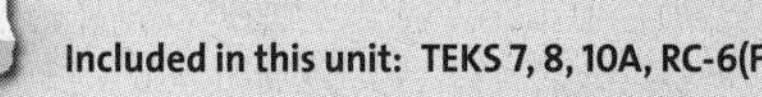

Included in this unit: TEKS 7, 8, 10A, RC-6(F)

UNIT 4 Writer's Craft

SENSORY LANGUAGE, IMAGERY, AND STYLE

Be sure to read the Reader's Workshop on pp. 436–441 in *Holt McDougal Literature*.

Academic Vocabulary for Unit 4

Academic Vocabulary is the language you use to discuss literary and informational texts. Preview the following Academic Vocabulary words. You will use these words as you write and talk about the selections in this unit.

aspect (as′pekt′) *n.* a quality, part, or element

*Which **aspect** of the story do you find most intriguing?*

distinctive (di-stink′tiv) *adj.* unique; clearly different

*The author's word choice helps create a **distinctive** style.*

interpret (in-tər′prət) *v.* to explain the meaning of something

*How do you **interpret** the metaphor the author used in the story?*

perceive (pər-sēv′) *v.* to grasp mentally; understand

*Does the story's ending change what you **perceive** its theme to be?*

sensory (sen′ser-ē) *adj.* of or relating to the senses

*Explain how the use of **sensory** language helps you picture the setting.*

Think of a book or story you've read. Write a brief paragraph explaining what made the book or story **distinctive**, using at least two Academic Vocabulary words in your response.

Before Reading

READING 8 Understand, make inferences, and draw conclusions about how an author's sensory language creates imagery in a literary text.

Tuesday of the Other June

Short Story by **Norma Fox Mazer**

How do you deal with a BULLY?

A bully can turn your life into a nightmare. All your thoughts become focused on the next awful encounter. Advice for dealing with a bully is often to "walk away." When actually dealing with a bully, however, many people dream of standing up for themselves. In "Tuesday of the Other June," you'll read about a girl who becomes the target of a bully.

LIST IT Imagine that your best friend is being bothered by a bully and has come to you for help. What advice would you give? Prepare a short list of suggestions.

Advice for Dealing with a Bully

1. Tell your parents about what is happening.
2. ______
3. ______
4. ______

Literary Analysis: Sensory Language and Imagery

Authors use many techniques to help readers imagine characters, conflicts, and other parts of a story. For example, an author describing a character or setting might use **sensory language,** words or phrases that appeal to the reader's senses of sight, hearing, touch, smell, and taste. These sensory details create **imagery** that helps the reader imagine how something looks, feels, or tastes.

Sensory Language	Imagery
Sensory language is language writers use to create images.	**Imagery** is language that appeals to the senses. Vivid imagery helps us see, smell, and feel a scene.
EXAMPLE: These descriptive words help you imagine the bully. "She had a deep growly voice."	EXAMPLE: The highlighted phrases help you picture the narrator's mother. "She had little emerald eyes that warmed me like the sun."

As you read, pay attention to specific details that help you picture what is happening and how a character feels.

Reading Strategy: Connect

When you read a story, you might find characters or events similar to those you know in real life. You may even find two texts that focus on similar themes. As you read this story, think about **connections** you can make to your own personal experiences, current events, and other texts.

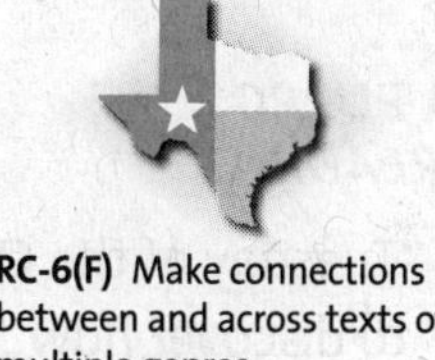

RC-6(F) Make connections between and across texts of multiple genres.

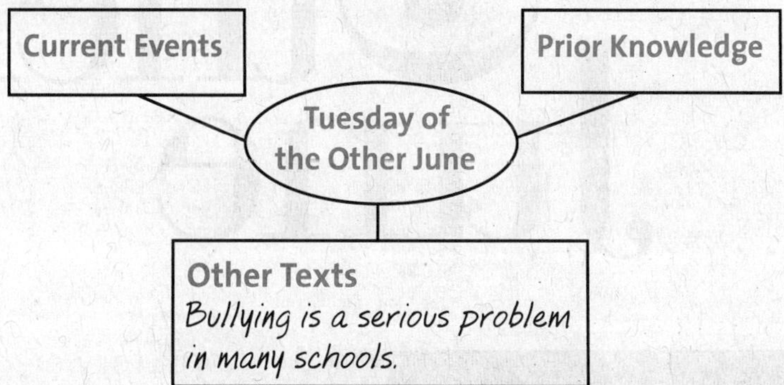

Vocabulary in Context

Note: Words are listed in the order in which they appear in the story.

emerald (ĕm′ər-əld) *adj.* of a rich green color
Fear was reflected in her ***emerald*** *eyes.*

rigid (rĭj′ĭd) *adj.* stiff; not moving
The young girl's body went ***rigid*** *with terror.*

torment (tôr′mĕnt′) *v.* to cause severe distress to the body or mind
Her enemy loved to ***torment*** *her.*

dazzling (dăz′lĭng) *adj.* beautiful; amazing **dazzle** *v.*
Finally, she put on a ***dazzling*** *display of courage.*

daze (dāz) *n.* a condition in which one cannot think clearly
The scary situation put her in a ***daze.***

devoted (dĭ-vō′tĭd) *adj.* very loyal; faithful **devote** *v.*
June had no ***devoted*** *friends to help her out.*

Vocabulary Practice

Review the vocabulary words and think about their meanings. Then use at least two of the words to describe how someone might respond to a bully.

____

____

____

SET A PURPOSE FOR READING

Read "Tuesday of the Other June" to discover how June deals with a bully.

Tuesday of the Other June

Short Story by

NORMA FOX MAZER

BACKGROUND Norma Fox Mazer is a well-known prize-winning writer of fiction for young adults. Her novels and stories usually address real problems teenagers face.

"Be good, be good, be good, be good, my Junie," my mother sang as she combed my hair; a song, a story, a croon, a plea. "It's just you and me, two women alone in the world, June darling of my heart, we have enough troubles getting by, we surely don't need a single one more, so you keep your sweet self out of fighting and all that bad stuff. People can be little-hearted, but turn the other cheek, smile at the world, and the world'll surely smile back."

We stood in front of the mirror as she combed my hair, combed and brushed and smoothed. Her head came just above mine, she said when I grew another inch she'd stand on a stool to brush my hair. "I'm not giving up this pleasure!" And she laughed her long honey laugh. Ⓐ

My mother was April, my grandmother had been May, I was June. "And someday," said my mother, "you'll have a daughter of your own. What will you name her?"

"January!" I'd yell when I was little. "February! No, November!" My mother laughed her honey laugh. She had little **emerald** eyes that warmed me like the sun.

Every day when I went to school, she went to work. "Sometimes I stop what I'm doing," she said, "lay down my tools, and stop everything, because all I can think about is you. Wondering what you're doing and if you need me. Now, Junie, if anyone ever bothers you—"

"—I walk away, run away, come on home as fast as my feet will take me," I recited.

"Yes. You come to me. You just bring me your trouble, because I'm here on this earth to love you and take care of you."

I was safe with her. Still, sometimes I woke up at night and heard footsteps slowly creeping up the stairs. It wasn't my mother, she was asleep in the bed across the room, so it was robbers, thieves, and murderers, creeping slowly . . . slowly . . . slowly toward my bed.

I stuffed my hand into my mouth. If I screamed and woke her, she'd be tired at work tomorrow. The robbers and thieves filled the warm darkness and slipped across the floor more quietly than cats. **Rigid** under the covers, I stared at the shifting dark and bit my knuckles and never knew when I fell asleep again. Ⓑ

In the morning we sang in the kitchen. "Bill Grogan's goat! Was feelin' fine! Ate three red shirts, right off the line!" I made sandwiches for our lunches, she made pancakes for breakfast, but all she ate was one pancake and a cup of coffee. "Gotta fly, can't be late."

Monitor Your Comprehension

Ⓐ IMAGERY
Reread lines 9–13. Underline details that help you form a mental picture of what is happening. To what senses do these details appeal?

____

____

____

____

____

____

____

____

emerald (ĕm'ər-əld) *adj.* of a rich green color

rigid (rĭj'ĭd) *adj.* stiff; not moving

Ⓑ SENSORY LANGUAGE
Reread lines 30–40. What details help you picture the nights when June gets scared? Underline them.

Monitor Your Comprehension

Ⓒ CONNECT
What does June want for her mother?

Explain whether you connect with her feelings in the diagram below.

Prior Knowledge

I wanted to be rich and take care of her. She worked too hard; her pretty hair had gray in it that she joked about. "Someday," I said, "I'll buy you a real house, and you'll never work in a pot factory again." Ⓒ

"Such delicious plans," she said. She checked the windows to see if they were locked. "Do you have your key?"

I lifted it from the chain around my neck.

"And you'll come right home from school and—"

"—I won't light fires or let strangers into the house, and I won't tell anyone on the phone that I'm here alone," I finished for her.

"I know, I'm just your old worrywart mother." She kissed me twice, once on each cheek. "But you are my June, my only June, the only June."

She was wrong; there was another June. I met her when we stood next to each other at the edge of the pool the first day of swimming class in the Community Center.

"What's your name?" She had a deep growly voice.

"June. What's yours?"

She stared at me. "June."

"We have the same name."

"No we don't. June is my name, and I don't give you permission to use it. Your name is Fish Eyes." She pinched me hard. "Got it, Fish Eyes?"

The next Tuesday, the Other June again stood next to me at the edge of the pool. "What's your name?"

"June."

"Wrong. Your—name—is—Fish—Eyes."

"June."

"Fish Eyes, you are really stupid." She shoved me into the pool.

The swimming teacher looked up, frowning, from her chart. "No one in the water yet."

Monitor Your Comprehension

Later, in the locker room, I dressed quickly and wrapped my wet suit in the towel. The Other June pulled on her jeans. "You guys see that bathing suit Fish Eyes was wearing? Her mother found it in a trash can."

"She did not!"

The Other June grabbed my fingers and twisted. "Where'd she find your bathing suit?"

"She bought it, let me go."

"Poor little stupid Fish Eyes is crying. Oh, boo hoo hoo, poor little Fish Eyes."

After that, everyone called me Fish Eyes. And every Tuesday, wherever I was, there was also the Other June—at the edge of the pool, in the pool, in the locker room. In the water, she swam alongside me, blowing and huffing, knocking into me. In the locker room, she stepped on my feet, pinched my arms, hid my blouse, and knotted my braids together. She had large square teeth; she was shorter than I was, but heavier, with bigger bones and square hands. If I met her outside on the street, carrying her bathing suit and towel, she'd walk toward me, smiling a square, friendly smile. "Oh well, if it isn't Fish Eyes." Then she'd punch me, blam! her whole solid weight hitting me. D

I didn't know what to do about her. She was training me like a dog. After a few weeks of this, she only had to look at me, only had to growl, "I'm going to get you, Fish Eyes," for my heart to slink like a whipped dog down into my stomach. My arms were covered with bruises. When my mother noticed, I made up a story about tripping on the sidewalk. E

My weeks were no longer Tuesday, Wednesday, Thursday, and so on. Tuesday was Awfulday. Wednesday was Badday. (The Tuesday bad feelings were still there.) Thursday was Betterday and Friday was Safeday. Saturday was Goodday, but Sunday was Toosoonday, and Monday—Monday was nothing but the day before Awfulday.

D IMAGERY

Reread lines 84–100. Underline the sensory language the author uses to help you imagine the bully's behavior toward June.

E CONNECT

Have you read any other stories in which a character is bullied? Is June's reaction to her bully similar or different from what has happened in other stories? Explain.

Monitor Your Comprehension

F IMAGERY
Reread lines 117–126. What images help you understand how June feels about her situation?

torment (tŏr'mĕnt) *v.* to cause sever distress to the body or mind

What does the Other June do to **torment** June?

I tried to slow down time. Especially on the weekends, I stayed close by my mother, doing everything with her, shopping, cooking, cleaning, going to the laundromat. "Aw, sweetie, go play with your friends."

"No, I'd rather be with you." I wouldn't look at the clock or listen to the radio (they were always telling you the date and the time). I did special magic things to keep the day from going away, rapping my knuckles six times on the bathroom door six times a day and never, ever touching the chipped place on my bureau. But always I woke up to the day before Tuesday, and always, no matter how many times I circled the worn spot in the living-room rug or counted twenty-five cracks in the ceiling, Monday disappeared and once again it was Tuesday. F

The Other June got bored with calling me Fish Eyes. Buffalo Brain came next, but as soon as everyone knew that, she renamed me Turkey Nose.

Now at night it wasn't robbers creeping up the stairs, but the Other June, coming to **torment** me. When I finally fell asleep, I dreamed of kicking her, punching, biting, pinching. In the morning I remembered my dreams and felt brave and strong. And then I remembered all the things my mother had taught me and told me.

Be good, be good, be good; it's just us two women alone in the world . . . Oh, but if it weren't, if my father wasn't long gone, if we'd had someone else to fall back on, if my mother's mother and daddy weren't dead all these years, if my father's daddy wanted to know us instead of being glad to forget us—oh, then I would have punched the Other June with a frisky heart, I would have grabbed her arm at poolside and bitten her like the dog she had made of me.

One night, when my mother came home from work, she said, "Junie, listen to this. We're moving!"

Alaska, I thought. Florida. Arizona. Someplace far away and wonderful, someplace without the Other June.

"Wait till you hear this deal. We are going to be caretakers, trouble-shooters for an eight-family apartment building. Fifty-six Blue Hill Street. Not janitors; we don't do any of the heavy work. April and June, Trouble-shooters, Incorporated. If a tenant has a complaint or a problem, she comes to us and we either take care of it or call the janitor for service. And for that little bit of work, we get to live rent free!" She swept me around in a dance. "Okay? You like it? I do!"

So. Not anywhere else, really. All the same, maybe too far to go to swimming class? "Can we move right away? Today?"

"Gimme a break, sweetie. We've got to pack, do a thousand things. I've got to line up someone with a truck to help us. Six weeks, Saturday the fifteenth." She circled it on the calendar. It was the Saturday after the last day of swimming class. PAUSE & REFLECT

Soon, we had boxes lying everywhere, filled with clothes and towels and glasses wrapped in newspaper. Bit by bit, we cleared the rooms, leaving only what we needed right now. The dining-room table staggered on a bunched-up rug, our bureaus inched toward the front door like patient cows. On the calendar in the kitchen, my mother marked off the days until we moved, but the only days I thought about were Tuesdays—Awfuldays. Nothing else was real except the too fast passing of time, moving toward each Tuesday . . . away from Tuesday . . . toward Tuesday. . . . G

And it seemed to me that this would go on forever, that Tuesdays would come forever and I would be forever trapped by the side of the pool, the Other June whispering Buffalo Brain Fish Eyes Turkey Nose into my ear, while she ground her elbow into my side and smiled her square smile at the swimming teacher.

Monitor Your Comprehension

PAUSE & REFLECT
Why is June at first so excited to move away? Why does the moving date of Saturday the fifteenth change her mood?

G IMAGERY
Reread lines 164–173. Underline words in the descriptions of the table and bureaus that help you picture the objects in your mind. What does the image of the bureaus help you to imagine?

Monitor Your Comprehension

Ⓗ CONNECT

Underline the phrase that June yells to the Other June as she runs out the door. Then think back to a time when you finished a task or activity that you hated. How did it feel to be done?

And then it ended. It was the last day of swimming class. The last Tuesday. We had all passed our tests, and, as if in celebration, the Other June only pinched me twice. "And now," our swimming teacher said, "all of you are ready for the Advanced Class, which starts in just one month. I have a sign-up slip here. Please put your name down before you leave." Everyone but me crowded around. I went to the locker room and pulled on my clothes as fast as possible. The Other June burst through the door just as I was leaving. "Goodbye," I yelled, "good riddance to bad trash!" Before she could pinch me again, I ran past her and then ran all the way home, singing, "Goodbye . . . goodbye . . . goodbye, good riddance to bad trash!" Ⓗ

Later, my mother carefully untied the blue ribbon around my swimming class diploma. "Look at this! Well, isn't this wonderful! You are on your way, you might turn into an Olympic swimmer, you never know what life will bring."

"I don't want to take more lessons."

"Oh, sweetie, it's great to be a good swimmer." But then, looking into my face, she said, "No, no, no, don't worry, you don't have to."

The next morning, I woke up hungry for the first time in weeks. No more swimming class. No more Baddays and Awfuldays. No more Tuesdays of the Other June. In the kitchen, I made hot cocoa to go with my mother's corn muffins. "It's Wednesday, Mom," I said, stirring the cocoa. "My favorite day."

"Since when?"

"Since this morning." I turned on the radio so I could hear the announcer tell the time, the temperature, and the day. Thursday for breakfast I made cinnamon toast, Friday my mother made pancakes, and on Saturday, before we moved, we ate the last slices of bread and cleaned out the peanut butter jar.

"Some breakfast," Tilly said. "Hello, you must be June." She shook my hand. She was a friend of my mother's from work; she wore big hoop earrings, sandals, and a skirt as **dazzling** as a rainbow. She came in a truck with John to help us move our things.

John shouted cheerfully at me, "So you're moving." An enormous man with a face covered with little brown bumps. Was he afraid his voice wouldn't travel the distance from his mouth to my ear? "You looking at my moles?" he shouted, and he heaved our big green flowered chair down the stairs. "Don't worry, they don't bite. Ha, ha, ha!" Behind him came my mother and Tilly balancing a bureau between them, and behind them I carried a lamp and the round, flowered Mexican tray that was my mother's favorite. She had found it at a garage sale and said it was as close to foreign travel as we would ever get.

The night before, we had loaded our car, stuffing in bags and boxes until there was barely room for the two of us. But it was only when we were in the car, when we drove past Abdo's Grocery, where they always gave us credit,[1] when I turned for a last look at our street—it was only then that I understood we were truly going to live somewhere else, in another apartment, in another place mysteriously called Blue Hill Street. ❶

Tilly's truck followed our car.

"Oh, I'm so excited," my mother said. She laughed. "You'd think we were going across the country."

Our old car wheezed up a long steep hill. Blue Hill Street. I looked from one side to the other, trying to see everything.

---

1. **credit:** an agreement to trust in someone's ability and intention to pay for something at a later date.

Monitor Your Comprehension

dazzling (dăz'lĭng) *adj.* beautiful; amazing **dazzle** *v.*

❶ CONNECT

Reread lines 231–238. Draw a box around the lines that tell what June realizes when she takes her last look at their street. Have you ever had to move? How did you feel about moving to a new place?

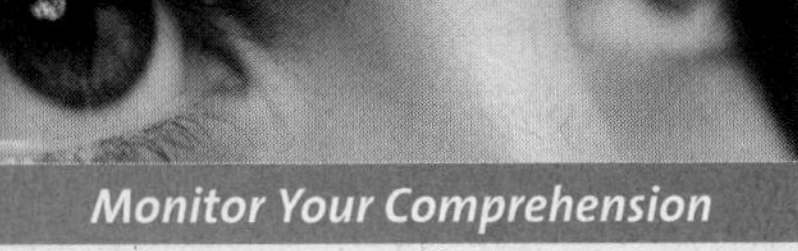

Monitor Your Comprehension

My mother drove over the crest of the hill. "And now—ta da!—our new home."

"Which house? Which one?" I looked out the window and what I saw was the Other June. She was sprawled on the stoop of a pink house, lounging back on her elbows, legs outspread, her jaws working on a wad of gum. I slid down into the seat, but it was too late. I was sure she had seen me.

My mother turned into a driveway next to a big white building with a tiny porch. She leaned on the steering wheel. "See that window there, that's our living-room window . . . and that one over there, that's your bedroom. . . ."

We went into the house, down a dim, cool hall. In our new apartment, the wooden floors clicked under our shoes, and my mother showed me everything. Her voice echoed in the empty rooms. I followed her around in a **daze**. Had I imagined seeing the Other June? Maybe I'd seen another girl who looked like her. A double. That could happen. J

daze (dāz) *n.* a condition in which one cannot think clearly

J SENSORY LANGUAGE
Reread lines 257–262. Underline details that help you picture what it looks like inside the house. Is June happy to be there? Why or why not?

"Ho yo, where do you want this chair?" John appeared in the door-way. We brought in boxes and bags and beds and stopped only to eat pizza and drink orange juice from the carton.

"June's so quiet, do you think she'll adjust all right?" I heard Tilly say to my mother.

"Oh, definitely. She'll make a wonderful adjustment. She's just getting used to things."

But I thought that if the Other June lived on the same street as I did, I would never get used to things.

That night I slept in my own bed, with my own pillow and blanket, but with floors that creaked in strange voices and walls with cracks I didn't recognize. I didn't feel either happy or unhappy. It was as if I were waiting for something.

Monday, when the principal of Blue Hill Street School left me in Mr. Morrisey's classroom, I knew what I'd been waiting for. In that room full of strange kids, there was one person I knew. She smiled her square smile, raised her hand, and said, "She can sit next to me, Mr. Morrisey."

"Very nice of you, June M. OK, June T, take your seat. I'll try not to get you two Junes mixed up."

I sat down next to her. She pinched my arm. "Good riddance to bad trash," she mocked.

I was back in the Tuesday swimming class, only now it was worse, because every day would be Awfulday. The pinching had already started. Soon, I knew, on the playground and in the halls, kids would pass me, grinning. "Hiya, Fish Eyes." **PAUSE & REFLECT**

The Other June followed me around during recess that day, droning in my ear, "You are my slave, you must do everything I say, I am your master, say it, say, 'Yes, master, you are my master.'"

I pressed my lips together, clapped my hands over my ears, but without hope. Wasn't it only a matter of time before I said the hateful words?

"How was school?" my mother said that night.

"OK."

She put a pile of towels in a bureau drawer. "Try not to be sad about missing your old friends, sweetie; there'll be new ones."

The next morning, the Other June was waiting for me when I left the house. "Did your mother get you that blouse in the garbage dump?" She butted me, shoving me against a tree. "Don't you speak anymore, Fish Eyes?"

Monitor Your Comprehension

PAUSE & REFLECT
What does June mean when she says that she is "back in the Tuesday swimming class" and that now every day will be Awfulday?

Monitor Your Comprehension

Ⓚ IMAGERY
Reread lines 313–315. To what does the author compare the sharpened pencil? Underline the answer in the text. What does this image suggest that June expects?

Ⓛ CONNECT
Knowing what you do about bullies, what do you think June is going to do if the Other June attacks her?

Grabbing my chin in her hands, she pried open my mouth. "Oh, ha ha, I thought you lost your tongue."

We went on to school. I sank down into my seat, my head on my arms. "June T, are you all right?" Mr. Morrisey asked. I nodded. My head was almost too heavy to lift.

The Other June went to the pencil sharpener. Round and round she whirled the handle. Walking back, looking at me, she held the three sharp pencils like three little knives. Ⓚ

Someone knocked on the door. Mr. Morrisey went out into the hall. Paper planes burst into the air, flying from desk to desk. Someone turned on a transistor radio. And the Other June, coming closer, smiled and licked her lips like a cat sleepily preparing to gulp down a mouse.

I remembered my dream of kicking her, punching, biting her like a dog.

Then my mother spoke quickly in my ear: Turn the other cheek, my Junie; smile at the world, and the world'll surely smile back.

But I had turned the other cheek and it was slapped. I had smiled and the world hadn't smiled back. I couldn't run home as fast as my feet would take me, I had to stay in school—and in school there was the Other June. Every morning, there would be the Other June, and every afternoon, and every day, all day, there would be the Other June. Ⓛ

She frisked down the aisle, stabbing the pencils in the air toward me. A boy stood up on his desk and bowed. "My fans," he said, "I greet you." My arm twitched and throbbed, as if the Other June's pencils had already poked through the skin. She came closer, smiling her Tuesday smile.

"No," I whispered, "no." The word took wings and flew me to my feet, in front of the Other June. "Noooooo." It flew out of my mouth into her surprised face.

The boy on the desk turned toward us. "You said something, my **devoted** fans?"

"No," I said to the Other June. "Oh, no! No. No. No. No more." I pushed away the hand that held the pencils.

The Other June's eyes opened, popped wide like the eyes of somebody in a cartoon. It made me laugh. The boy on the desk laughed, and then the other kids were laughing, too.

"No," I said again, because it felt so good to say it. "No, no, no, no." I leaned toward the Other June, put my finger against her chest. Her cheeks turned red, she squawked something—it sounded like "Eeeraaghyou!"—and she stepped back. She stepped away from me.

The door banged, the airplanes disappeared, and Mr. Morrisey walked to his desk. "OK. OK. Let's get back to work. Kevin Clark, how about it?" Kevin jumped off the desk and Mr. Morrisey picked up a piece of chalk. "All right, class—" He stopped and looked at me and the Other June. "You two Junes, what's going on there?"

I tried it again. My finger against her chest. Then the words. "No—more." And she stepped back another step. I sat down at my desk.

"June M," Mr. Morrisey said.

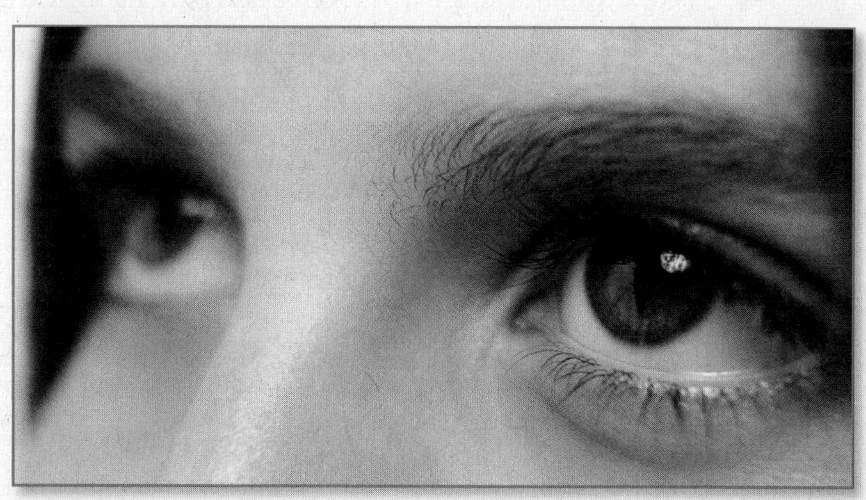

Monitor Your Comprehension

devoted (dĭ vō′tĭd) *adj.* very loyal; faithful **devote** *v.*

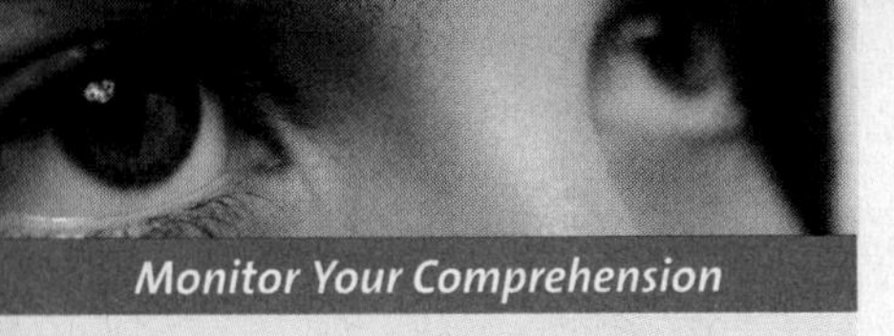

Monitor Your Comprehension

Ⓜ SENSORY LANGUAGE
Underline sensory language in lines 358–364. How do these details help you imagine the scene?

PAUSE & REFLECT
What does June mean by "the last Tuesday of the Other June"?

She turned around, staring at him with that big-eyed cartoon look. After a moment she sat down at the desk with a loud slapping sound. Ⓜ

Even Mr. Morrisey laughed.

And sitting at my desk, twirling my braids, I knew this was the last Tuesday of the Other June. **PAUSE & REFLECT**

After Reading

Literary Analysis: Sensory Language and Imagery

In the chart below, record three examples of imagery or sensory language from the story. Then, explain what senses each image appeals to (sight, hearing, touch, smell, and/or taste). Finally, tell how the imagery or sensory language helps you imagine part of the story.

READING 8 Understand, make inferences, and draw conclusions about how an author's sensory language creates imagery in a literary text. Explain how authors create meaning through figurative language emphasizing the use of personification.

Image/Details	Senses	What I Imagine

Reading Strategy: Connect

RC-6(F) Make connections between and across texts of multiple genres.

Review the chart that you filled out as you read "Tuesday of the Other June." Does the story remind you of any other events, personal or fictional? Explain.

____

____

____

____

____

____

How do you deal with a BULLY?

What do you think June will do the next time she is bothered by a bully? Support your answers with evidence from the text.

____

____

____

____

____

Vocabulary Practice

Circle the letter of the word or phrase you would associate with each boldfaced vocabulary word.

1. **Emerald** is a shade of **(a)** gray, **(b)** blue, **(c)** green.

2. A person in a **daze** is **(a)** excited, **(b)** confused, **(c)** good at sports.

3. **(a)** An enemy, **(b)** A vacation, **(c)** A prize might **torment** you.

4. The **rigid** flagpole **(a)** sways in the wind, **(b)** does not move, **(c)** falls over.

5. A **dazzling** light is **(a)** dim, **(b)** harsh, **(c)** bright.

6. Someone who is **devoted** to you is **(a)** very fond of you, **(b)** confused by your decisions, **(c)** unwilling to stick up for you.

Academic Vocabulary in Writing

aspect	distinctive	interpret	perceive	Sensory

READING 8 Understand, make inferences, and draw conclusions about how an author's sensory language creates imagery in a literary text.

Norma Fox Mazer uses **sensory** language to create a **distinctive** bully in the character of the "Other June." What is your interpretation of this character? Use at least two Academic Vocabulary words to describe June and explain her behavior. Definitions of these words are on page 167.

____

____

____

Texas Assessment Practice

DIRECTIONS Use "Tuesday of the Other June" to answer questions 1–6.

1 What is June's mother's approach to dealing with life's difficulties?

(A) She gets help from family members.
(B) She says to be good and run from trouble.
(C) She hides away from unpleasant situations.
(D) She expects people to stand up for themselves.

2 What unpleasant discovery does June make on moving day?

(F) The Other June has followed her.
(G) The Other June lives in her neighborhood.
(H) The Other June has vowed to get her back.
(J) She will have to go to the Other June's school.

3 What does June mean when she says that the Other June has made a dog of her?

(A) The Other June calls her dog-face.
(B) The Other June demands her loyalty.
(C) The Other June controls her reactions and feelings.
(D) The Other June makes her do tricks in front of the other swimmers.

4 How has June changed by the end of the story?

(F) She is stronger.
(G) She loves swimming class.
(H) She helps people who are bullied.
(J) She doesn't care what others think of her.

5 Which of the following is an example of sensory language?

(A) *I didn't know what to do about her.*
(B) *She was wrong; there was another June.*
(C) *The robbers and thieves filled the warm darkness and slipped across the floor more quietly than cats.*
(D) *Saturday was Goodday, but Sunday was Toosoonday, and Monday—Monday was nothing but the day before Awfulday.*

6 Which of the following images does not describe the "Other June"?

(F) *She had little emerald eyes.*
(G) *She had large square teeth.*
(H) *She had a deep growly voice.*
(J) *She swam alongside me, blowing and huffing.*

READING 10A Summarize the main ideas and supporting details in text, demonstrating an understanding that a summary does not include opinions. **RC-6(F)** Summarize texts in ways that maintain meaning and logical order within a text.

The Problem with Bullies

Feature Article

Background

Discussing the topic of bullying may make some of us uncomfortable, but growing numbers of people feel that it needs to be addressed. In the feature article you are about to read, Sean Price takes a closer look at the problem of bullying.

Skill Focus: Take Notes

When you **take notes,** you record the most important information from whatever you are reading. **Previewing** the article—looking at its title, subheadings, topic sentences, and graphic aids—can help you determine its **main idea,** the central or most important idea that the writer conveys. By previewing "The Problem with Bullies," you can see that it covers the following information:

- statistics about bullying
- forms of bullying
- the roots of bullying
- the effects of bullying
- programs for stopping bullying

Using a graphic organizer like the one below will help you record facts and supporting details that develop the main ideas. As you read Price's article, add information to the different parts of the organizer. You will use your completed organizer to help you write a summary.

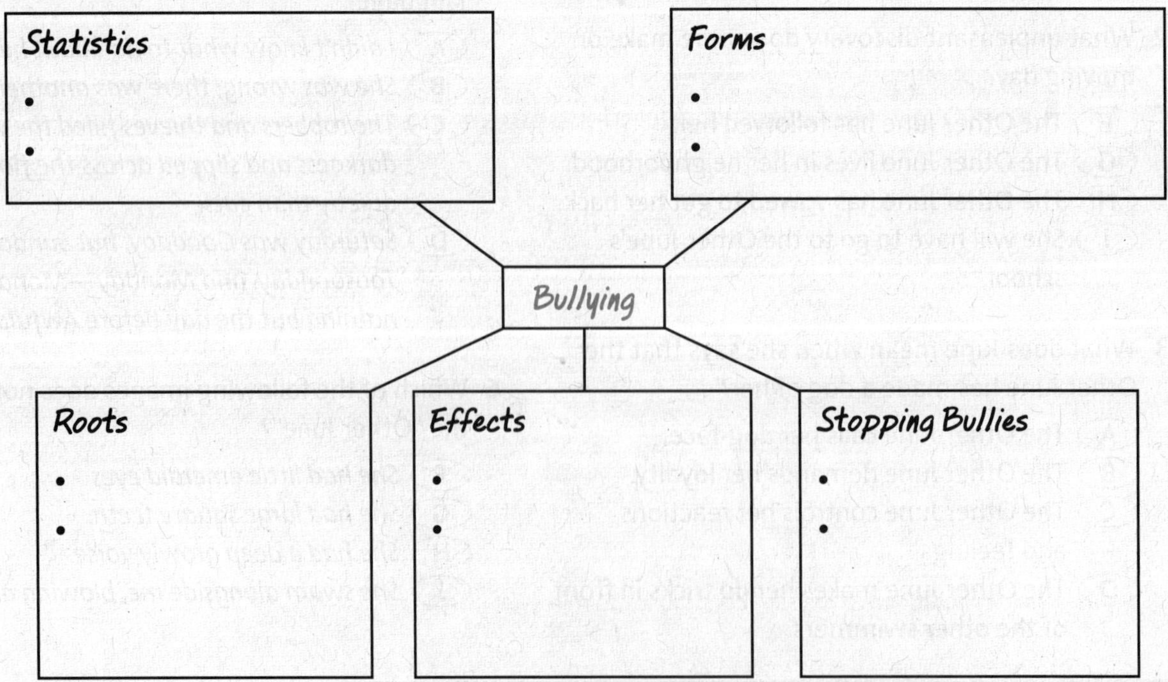

The PROBLEM with BULLIES

by Sean Price

By sixth grade, Karen had experienced her share of hardships. She had just been adopted by a family in Chattanooga, Tennessee, after spending six years in foster care. Naturally shy and quiet, Karen also struggled with a slight speech impediment.[1] She had only one good friend.

All this made Karen (not her real name) an easy target for a bully. Her tormentor,[2] a popular girl at school, loved to taunt Karen about the way she spoke and about her home life. Ⓐ

1. **speech impediment:** a physical condition that makes it difficult for a person to speak clearly.
2. **tormentor:** a person who is the source of harassment, annoyance, or pain.

SET A PURPOSE FOR READING

Read "The Problem with Bullies" to learn about how bullying happens, who it hurts, and ways to prevent it.

Ⓕ FOCUS ON FORM

"The Problem with Bullies" is a **feature article,** a nonfiction article found in a newspaper or magazine. This article gives readers information on a specific topic and offers some solutions.

Ⓐ TAKE NOTES

Reread lines 1–10. What do you learn about the roots of bullying in these lines?

B TAKE NOTES
Reread lines 18–27. In your organizer, take notes on the statistics the author provides on bullying that you find especially important.

Statistics
•
•
•

C TAKE NOTES
Reread the subhead. What kinds of information do you think this section will contain? In which parts of your organizer would you write notes from this section?

"She made fun of the fact that I was a foster kid and that my mother didn't take care of me," says Karen.

Sometimes the abuse was physical. The bully might shove Karen or throw one of her shoes in the toilet. Even after the other girl received several suspensions and detentions for her bullying, she refused to give Karen a break.

Millions of U.S. teens understand what Karen went through. A study by the National Institute of Children's Health and Human Development found that more than 16 percent of students in grades 6–12 say that they have been bullied. Nineteen percent said that they had been bullies themselves.

It's not just the victims who are hurt by bullying. Another study found that 60 percent of the bullies in grades 6–9 will be convicted of a criminal act by age 24! B

At one time, bullying was considered just a natural part of growing up. Today, authorities see it as a serious health crisis. It is estimated that bullying keeps 160,000 kids out of school each day.

What Is Bullying? C

Bullying takes many forms: gossip, snubbing, put-downs, threats, and violent attacks. Its roots lie in the difference of power between the bullies and their victims. Bullies tend to be confident, impulsive, and popular. Victims tend to be withdrawn and have few friends. Many bullies come from homes where they are neglected or abused. Bullying allows them to exercise power that's denied to them at home.

Boys and girls bully differently. Boys tend to use threats and physical violence. Girl bullies rely more on backbiting (cruel comments), social exclusion, and spreading false rumors. Cyberbullying, a newer form of harassment, allows bullies to humiliate[3] their peers with e-mail and blog postings.

For victims, being bullied damages self-esteem. Bullying expert Marlene Snyder says that fear of bullies also makes class time much more trying for the victims. "They're sitting there trying to survive, not being able to really learn," she says.

Karen's frequent complaints about the bullying finally brought her some relief. She and her tormentor were given separate class schedules for eighth grade.

Karen believes the other girl may have been threatened with expulsion. Whatever happened, the bully now ignores Karen. Life is easier to handle. And yet the bullying has left its mark.

"School's still stressful," Karen says. "I'm always on the watch to see who's coming toward me." D

PAUSE & REFLECT

Stopping Bullies

In recent years, many schools have implemented[4] effective antibullying programs. Denny Middle School in Seattle, Washington, launched such a program recently. Already there have been signs of progress. Craig Little, a student, saw a new student being taunted by a group of fellow seventh-graders. The lead bully wouldn't let the boy pass.

Instead of standing by, Craig acted. He said, "You guys leave him alone, and let him go." Craig then escorted the boy away from the group. The lead bully and the new student have since made up. "I talked to both of them [later], and they're all right with each other," Craig said. "They're kind of becoming friends."

3. **humiliate:** to lower the pride, dignity, or self-respect of another.
4. **implemented:** put into effect or carried out.

D TAKE NOTES
Reread lines 46–59. In your organizer, take notes on the effects of bullying.

Effects
•
•
•

PAUSE & REFLECT
What measures does the author suggest to stop bullying? How effective do you think they will be?

READING 10A Summarize the main ideas and supporting details in text, demonstrating an understanding that a summary does not include opinions. **RC-6(F)** Summarize texts in ways that maintain meaning and logical order within a text.

Practicing Your Skills

Use the text, your notes, and your graphic organizer to summarize ideas from "The Problem with Bullies." Follow these steps to summarize the article.

1. Review your notes and your organizer. If necessary, review the article to add details that you might have missed the first time.
2. Use your own words to restate ideas from text to summarize why bullying is a problem. Then use your own words to restate the solutions that the author presents. Keep in mind that a summary does not include your own ideas or opinions.

Summary

Evaluate how the author organized "The Problem with Bullies." Do you think he presents information in a way that makes sense, or would you present the information differently?

Academic Vocabulary in Writing

aspect	distinctive	interpret	perceive	sensory

How did this article affect your **perception** of bullies? Include at least one Academic Vocabulary word in your response. Definitions of these words are on page 167.

Texas Assessment Practice

DIRECTIONS Use "The Problem with Bullies" to answer questions 1–4.

1 One solution to bullying presented in the article is to —

- (A) tell someone in authority
- (B) convict bullies of criminal acts
- (C) withdraw and have few friends
- (D) distract others from learning

2 The author says that bullies tend to be —

- (F) shy and have few friends
- (G) boastful and opinionated
- (H) popular and self-assured
- (J) pleasant and helpful

3 In which category of a notes organizer would you record information about cyberbullying?

- (A) statistics
- (B) roots
- (C) effects
- (D) forms

4 What is one way that Denny Middle School's program provides an effective solution to bullying?

- (F) It punishes the bully in front of everyone.
- (G) It gives students tools to stop bullying when they see it happening.
- (H) It gets adults involved right away.
- (J) It sets up a circle of friends for the victim.

READING 7 Identify the literary language and devices used in personal narratives.

The Jacket

Personal Narrative by **Gary Soto**

What builds CONFIDENCE?

If you have confidence, that means you believe in yourself and in what you can accomplish. Confidence can help you speak in front of a group, meet new people, or make difficult choices. Real confidence comes from within. Still, as Gary Soto expresses in "The Jacket," outside pressures can sometimes bring you down.

LIST IT Brainstorm with classmates to list kinds of experiences that can build confidence. Then identify some ways that a person's confidence can be damaged.

Confidence Builders	Confidence Busters
doing well on a test	

Literary Analysis: Similes and Metaphors

Personal narratives allow writers to share their experiences with readers. As in fiction, nonfiction writers use descriptive language and literary devices such as similes and metaphors. The graphic below explains how similes and metaphors are alike and different.

Both similes and metaphors
- compare two things.
- can help readers see things in a new way.
- can reveal the writer's emotions and attitudes toward their subject.

A **simile** is a comparison that uses the words *like* or *as.*

Example:
I stared at the jacket, like an enemy, thinking bad things. . . .

A **metaphor** is a comparison that does not use the words *like* or *as.*

Example:
I glared at the jacket, my burden, feeling too weak to take it up again.

As you read "The Jacket" look for similes and metaphors and notice what they help you understand.

Reading Strategy: Summarize

One way to check your understanding of a work is to summarize it. A good **summary** provides a brief retelling of the main ideas. It uses your own words, but does not include your opinions, or personal views, about the subject. As you read "The Jacket," notes in the side column will ask you to record key events of the story in a log like the one below. Make sure you maintain the same meaning and a logical order in your notes.

READING 10A Summarize the main ideas and supporting details in text, demonstrating an understanding that a summary does not include opinions. **RC-6(F)** Summarize texts in ways that maintain meaning and logical order within a text.

Key Event
• *Soto asks his mother for a black leather jacket.*
• *Soto wanted a jacket that would make him look cool and tough, like a biker.*

Vocabulary in Context

Note: Words are listed in the order in which they appear in the personal narrative.

profile (prō′fīl′) *n.* a side view of an object, especially of the human head
I faced the mirror and then turned in ***profile*** *to see how I looked.*

propeller (prə-pĕl′ər) *n.* a spinning blade used to move a boat or airplane forward **propel** *v.*
The baby's hat has a tiny ***propeller*** *on top that spins in the wind.*

shrivel (shrĭ′vəl) *v.* to shrink or wrinkle
My wool gloves were ***shriveled*** *when they came out of the dryer.*

vicious (vĭsh′əs) *adj.* severe or fierce
Kent felt a ***vicious*** *envy when he eyed Tom's new skates.*

Vocabulary Practice

Review the vocabulary words and think about their meanings. Then, use at least one of the words to tell about an article of clothing you once loved—or hated.

SET A PURPOSE FOR READING

Read "The Jacket" to discover how an article of clothing shaped Gary Soto's perception of himself.

Personal Narrative by

GARY SOTO

BACKGROUND To create lively, poetic images in his writing, Gary Soto often draws upon childhood memories of growing up in a Mexican-American community in Fresno, California. "The Jacket" is a personal narrative about this time in Soto's life.

My clothes have failed me.

I remember the green coat that I wore in fifth and sixth grades when you either danced like a champ or pressed yourself against a greasy wall, bitter as a penny toward the happy couples.

When I needed a new jacket and my mother asked what kind I wanted, I described something like bikers wear: black leather and silver studs[1] with enough belts to hold down a small town. We were in the kitchen, steam on the windows from her cooking. She listened so long while stirring dinner that I thought she understood for sure the

1. **studs:** small ornamental metal buttons mounted on fabric.

kind I wanted. The next day when I got home from school, I discovered draped on my bedpost a jacket the color of day-old guacamole.[2] I threw my books on the bed and approached the jacket slowly, as if it were a stranger whose hand I had to shake. I touched the vinyl sleeve, the collar, and peeked at the mustard-colored lining. **A**

From the kitchen mother yelled that my jacket was in the closet. I closed the door to her voice and pulled at the rack of clothes in the closet, hoping the jacket on the bedpost wasn't for me but my mean brother. No luck. I gave up. From my bed, I stared at the jacket. I wanted to cry because it was so ugly and so big that I knew I'd have to wear it a long time. I was a small kid, thin as a young tree, and it would be years before I'd have a new one. I stared at the jacket, like an enemy, thinking bad things before I took off my old jacket whose sleeves climbed halfway to my elbow. **B**

I put the big jacket on. I zipped it up and down several times, and rolled the cuffs up so they didn't cover my hands. I put my hands in the pockets and flapped the jacket like a bird's wings. I stood in front of the mirror, full face, then **profile**, and then looked over my shoulder as if someone had called me. I sat on the bed, stood against the bed, and combed my hair to see what I would look like doing something natural. I looked ugly. I threw it on my brother's bed and looked at it for a long time before I slipped it on and went out to the backyard, smiling a "thank you" to my mom as I passed her in the kitchen. With my hands in my pockets I kicked a ball against the fence, and then climbed it to sit looking into the alley. I hurled orange peels at the mouth of an open garbage can and when the peels were gone I watched the white puffs of my breath thin to nothing.

2. **guacamole** (gwä'kə-mō'lē): a thick paste made from avocados, citrus juice, onions, and seasoning, often served as a dip.

Monitor Your Comprehension

A SUMMARIZE

When you summarize, you note the most important events and ideas. Reread lines 6–14. Complete the log entry about getting the jacket.

Key Events
•
•

B SIMILES AND METAPHORS

Underline two similes Soto uses in lines 24–26. What do these comparisons tell you about how he feels about the jacket?

profile (prō'fīl') *n.* a side view of an object, especially of the human head

Monitor Your Comprehension

I jumped down, hands in my pockets, and in the backyard on my knees I teased my dog, Brownie, by swooping my arms while making bird calls. He jumped at me and missed. He jumped again and again, until a tooth sunk deep, ripping an L-shaped tear on my left sleeve. I pushed Brownie away to study the tear as I would a cut on my arm. There was no blood, only a few loose pieces of fuzz. Dumb dog, I thought, and pushed him away hard when he tried to bite again. I got up from my knees and went to my bedroom to sit with my jacket on my lap, with the lights out.

That was the first afternoon with my new jacket. The next day I wore it to sixth grade and got a D on a math quiz. During the morning recess Frankie T., the playground terrorist, pushed me to the ground and told me to stay there until recess was over. My best friend, Steve Negrete, ate an apple while looking at me, and the girls turned away to whisper on the monkey bars.[3] The teachers were no help: they looked my way and talked about how foolish I looked in my new jacket. I saw their heads bob with laughter, their hands half-covering their mouths. (C)

Even though it was cold, I took off the jacket during lunch and played kickball in a thin shirt, my arms feeling like braille[4] from goose bumps. But when I returned to class I slipped the jacket on and shivered until I was warm. I sat on my hands, heating them up, while my teeth chattered like a cup of crooked dice. Finally warm, I slid out of the jacket but a few minutes later put it back on when the fire bell rang. We paraded out into the yard where we, the sixth graders, walked past all the other grades to stand against the back fence. Everybody saw me. Although they didn't say out loud, "Man, that's ugly,"

(C) SUMMARIZE
Reread lines 56–65. How do other people treat the narrator now that he is wearing the jacket? Record key events in the log.

Key Events
• ______
______
______
______
______
• ______
______
______
______
______

3. **monkey bars:** a structure of poles and bars for climbing, often found in playgrounds.
4. **braille** (brāl): a system of writing or printing for blind people, made up of arrangements of raised dots representing letters and numbers.

I heard the buzz-buzz of gossip and even laughter that I knew was meant for me.

And so I went, in my guacamole-colored jacket. So embarrassed, so hurt, I couldn't even do my homework. I received Cs on quizzes, and forgot the state capitals and the rivers of South America, our friendly neighbor. Even the girls who had been friendly blew away like loose flowers to follow the boys in neat jackets. **D**

I wore that thing for three years until the sleeves grew short and my forearms stuck out like the necks of turtles. All during that time no love came to me—no little dark girl in a Sunday dress she wore on Monday. At lunchtime I stayed with the ugly boys who leaned against the chainlink fence and looked around with **propellers** of grass spinning in our mouths. We saw girls walk by alone, saw couples, hand in hand, their heads like bookends pressing air together. We saw them and spun our propellers so fast our faces were blurs. **E**

I blame that jacket for those bad years. I blame my mother for her bad taste and her cheap ways. It was a sad time for the heart. With a friend I spent my sixth-grade year in a tree in the alley, waiting for something good to happen to me in that jacket, which had become the ugly brother who tagged along wherever I went. And it was about that time that I began to grow. My chest puffed up with muscle and, strangely, a few more ribs. Even my hands, those fleshy hammers, showed bravely through the cuffs, the fingers already hardening for the coming fights. But that L-shaped rip on the left sleeve got bigger, bits of stuffing coughed out from its wound after a hard day of play. I finally Scotch-taped it closed, but in rain or cold

Monitor Your Comprehension

D SIMILES AND METAPHORS
Underline the simile Soto uses in lines 79–84. How does this simile help you understand Soto's frustration?

____

____

____

____

____

____

propeller (prə-pĕl′ər) *n.* a spinning blade used to move a boat or airplane forward
propel *v.*

E SUMMARIZE
Reread lines 85–94. What does the narrator blame the jacket for? Use your log to summarize the key events that contributed to his feelings about the jacket.

Key Events
• ______________________
____
____
____
• ______________________
____
____
____

Monitor Your Comprehension

shrivel (shrĭ′vəl) *v.* to shrink or wrinkle

vicious (vĭsh′əs) *adj.* severe or fierce

F SUMMARIZE
Reread lines 119–124. Record a key event in the log to tell how long Soto wore the jacket. Then note an important idea about how Soto feels the jacket shaped his life during that time.

Key Events
• ______________________
____
____
____
• ______________________
____
____
____

PAUSE & REFLECT
Underline the metaphor Soto uses in lines 132–134. What final thought does the metaphor help Soto convey?

____

____

____

____

____

weather the tape peeled off like a scab and more stuffing fell out until that sleeve **shriveled** into a palsied arm.[5] That winter the elbows began to crack and whole chunks of green began to fall off. I showed the cracks to my mother, who always seemed to be at the stove with steamed-up glasses, and she said that there were children in Mexico who would love that jacket. I told her that this was America and yelled that Debbie, my sister, didn't have a jacket like mine. I ran outside, ready to cry, and climbed the tree by the alley to think bad thoughts and watch my breath puff white and disappear.

But whole pieces still casually flew off my jacket when I played hard, read quietly, or took **vicious** spelling tests at school. When it became so spotted that my brother began to call me "camouflage," I flung it over the fence into the alley. Later, however, I swiped the jacket off the ground and went inside to drape it across my lap and mope. **F**

I was called to dinner: steam silvered my mother's glasses as she said grace;[6] my brother and sister with their heads bowed made ugly faces at their glasses of powdered milk. I gagged too, but eagerly ate big rips of buttered tortilla that held scooped-up beans. Finished, I went outside with my jacket across my arm. It was a cold sky. The faces of clouds were piled up, hurting. I climbed the fence, jumping down with a grunt. I started up the alley and soon slipped into my jacket, that green ugly brother who breathed over my shoulder that day and ever since. **PAUSE & REFLECT**

5. **palsied** (pôl′zēd) **arm:** a paralyzed or weakened arm.
6. **grace:** a short prayer or blessing said before or after a meal.

Literary Analysis: Similes and Metaphors

Recall that metaphors and similes are literary devices that use comparisons to help readers see things in a new way. A simile uses the words *like* or *as*. Use the chart below to gather similes and metaphors that Soto uses in "The Jacket."

READING 7 Identify the literary language and devices used in personal narratives.

Simile/Metaphor	Basic Description	Positive or Negative
"I stared at the jacket, like an enemy."	He stared meanly or cautiously at it.	negative

Review the similes and metaphors that Soto uses in "The Jacket." What overall tone, or attitude toward the jacket, do these comparisons convey? What else do they contribute to the essay?

____

____

____

____

____

After Reading

READING 10A Summarize the main ideas and supporting details in text, demonstrating an understanding that a summary does not include opinions. **RC-6(F)** Summarize texts in ways that maintain meaning and logical order within a text.

Reading Strategy: Summarize

Use your notes about key events in "The Jacket" to write a summary of the selection. Remember that a summary is a brief retelling of a text's main ideas and that it should not include **opinions**, or personal views. Make sure you maintain the same order and meaning as the original text.

____

____

____

____

____

____

____

What builds CONFIDENCE?

Reread lines 56–65, and review your notes from page 192. Do you think that the jacket was entirely responsible for damaging Soto's self-confidence? Explain.

____

____

____

Vocabulary Practice

Complete each sentence with the vocabulary word that best completes it.

profile	propeller	shrivel	vicious

1. The airplane made an emergency landing when its __________ broke.
2. It was sad to see my favorite sweater __________ and shrink with each wash.
3. I know he was upset, but he didn't need to be so __________.
4. Many portraits show only the person's __________, not the whole face.

Academic Vocabulary in Writing

aspect	distinctive	interpret	perceive	sensory

READING 7 Identify the literary language and devices used in personal narratives. **10A** Summarize the main ideas and supporting details in text, demonstrating an understanding that a summary does not include opinions.

Review "The Jacket" to find **distinctive** phrases such as "day-old guacamole" and "green ugly brother," and vivid verbs such as "paraded" and "silvered." How does Soto's use of memorable words and phrases affect the way you **perceive** the jacket? Include at least one Academic Vocabulary word in your response. Definitions of these words are on page 167.

___

___

___

___

Texas Assessment Practice

DIRECTIONS Use "The Jacket" to answer questions 1–4.

1 Why is Soto disappointed by his sixth-grade year?

- (A) His mother doesn't understand him.
- (B) He doesn't do well in school.
- (C) He has to wear an ugly jacket.
- (D) Girls don't pay attention to him.

2 From his writing, you can tell that Soto feels that —

- (F) the jacket made him a failure
- (G) the jacket will look better when he gets older
- (H) no one understands him, no matter how hard he tries
- (J) other people's clothes are just as ugly as his

3 Which of the following is an example of a metaphor?

- (A) *my chest puffed up with muscle*
- (B) *flapped the jacket like a bird's wings*
- (C) *that sleeve shriveled into a palsied arm*
- (D) *I watched the white puffs of my breath thin to nothing*

4 What does Soto mean when he calls his jacket "that green ugly brother who breathed over my shoulder"?

- (F) He knows he will defeat it some day.
- (G) The jacket smells bad.
- (H) He thinks his siblings get better clothes.
- (J) He dislikes it intensely but he can't get away from it.

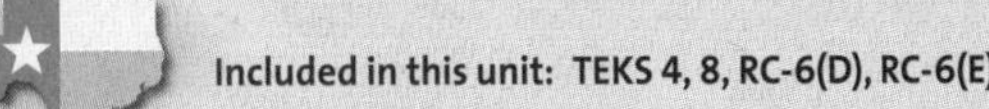

Included in this unit: TEKS 4, 8, RC-6(D), RC-6(E)

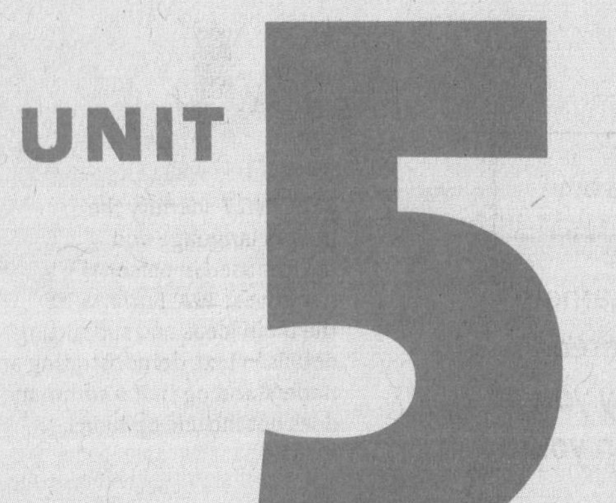

UNIT 5 Word Pictures

THE LANGUAGE OF POETRY

Be sure to read the Reader's Workshop on pp. 578–583 in *Holt McDougal Literature.*

Academic Vocabulary for Unit 5

Academic Vocabulary is the language you use to discuss literary and informational texts. Preview the following Academic Vocabulary words. You will use these words as you write and talk about the selections in this unit.

associations (ə-sō´sē-ā'shəns) *n.* connections or relations between thoughts, ideas, or images
*The poet made interesting **associations** between things that appeared to have little in common.*

•

device (dĭ-vīs') *n.* a way of achieving a particular purpose
*Repeating a word or phrase is a **device** writers use to highlight an important idea.*

•

insight (ĭn'sīt´) *n.* a clear understanding of the true nature of something
*Reading this poem gave me new **insight** into the subject of love.*

•

reaction (rē-ăk'shən) *n.* response
*Each student in the class may have a different **reaction** to the same poem.*

•

specific (spə-sĭf'ĭk) *adj.* detailed; exact
*Every word in the poem was carefully chosen to create a **specific** effect on readers.*

Think of a book, a movie, or a song to which you have a strong **reaction**. What **specific** parts do you especially like or dislike? Write your response on the lines below, using at least two Academic Vocabulary words.

____

____

____

READING 4 Understand, make inferences, and draw conclusions about the structure and elements of poetry.

Sea-Fever

Poem by John Masefield

The Village Blacksmith

Poem by Henry Wadsworth Longfellow

How can WORK affect our lives?

What do you think of when you hear the word *work?* If your experience with projects or chores hasn't been pleasant, then words like *boring* and *dull* might come to mind. When you love what you do, however, work can be more than just a job. For the people in the following two poems, the work they do each day becomes a part of who they are.

DISCUSS What jobs might be interesting enough to build your life around? With a small group, discuss the characteristics that would make a job more meaningful than just a paycheck. Record your ideas at left.

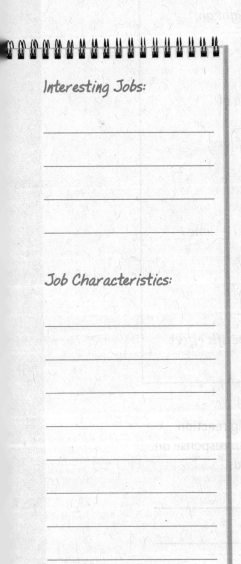

Interesting Jobs:

Job Characteristics:

Literary Analysis: Rhyme

Rhyme is the repetition of sounds at the end of words. A poet may use rhyme loosely, or develop a pattern of rhyme throughout a poem. In this example from "The Village Blacksmith," lines that rhyme are labeled with the same letter:

Under a spreading chestnut-tree *a*
The village smithy stands; *b*
The smith, a mighty man is he, *a*
With large and sinewy hands; *b*

As you read "Sea-Fever" and "The Village Blacksmith," look for the end words that rhyme.

Reading Skill: Recognize Meter

Poems and songs often have a regular rhythm, called meter. **Meter** creates a pattern of stressed (´) and unstressed (˘) syllables. Read aloud this first line of "Sea-Fever" to hear its beat:

˘ ´ ˘ ´ ˘ ˘ ´ ˘ ´ ˘ ˘ ´ ˘ ´ ˘ ˘ ´

I must go down to the seas again, to the lonely sea and the sky,

As you read the following poems, notice how the poets have arranged the words to create regular patterns of stressed and unstressed syllables.

READING 4 Understand, make inferences, and draw conclusions about the structure and elements of poetry.

Vocabulary in Context

Note: Words are listed in the order in which they appear in "The Village Blacksmith."

sinewy (sĭn′yo͞o-ē) *adj.* lean and tough

The crowd watched with anticipation as the ***sinewy*** *horses raced toward the finish line.*

brawny (brô′nē) *adj.* strong and muscular

He is a ***brawny*** *fellow who participated in difficult physical activities.*

repose (rĭ-pōz′) *n.* freedom from work or worry; rest

He looked forward to a brief ***repose*** *after a hard day of work.*

Vocabulary Practice

Review the vocabulary words and their meanings. Then write a brief description of a physically demanding job using at least two of the vocabulary words.

SET A PURPOSE FOR READING

Read to find out how the speaker feels about being at sea.

Sea-Fever

Poem by

JOHN MASEFIELD

BACKGROUND In "Sea-Fever," John Masefield uses terms related to sailing that may be unfamiliar to you. Although supertankers and cruise ships are much taller than sailing ships, the term *tall ship* is used in line 2 to describe a sailing boat with high masts. In line 3, the "wheel's kick" is a reference to what can happen when a sudden shift in the wind or tide causes a ship to spin out of control. In line 6, the word *trick* is a sailing term for a round-trip voyage. Years ago, a "long trick" might have involved a voyage from England to China and back, a trip that could last for more than a year.

I must go down to the seas again, to the lonely sea and
 the sky,
And all I ask is a tall ship and a star to steer her by,
And the wheel's kick and the wind's song and the white
 sail's shaking,
And a grey mist on the sea's face and a grey dawn breaking. Ⓐ

Ⓐ METER

Read aloud lines 1–4, labeling each syllable with a stressed or unstressed mark. Is the pattern the same in each line? Explain.

I must go down to the seas again, for the call of the running tide
Is a wild call and a clear call that may not be denied;
And all I ask is a windy day with the white clouds flying,
And the flung spray and the blown spume,[1] and the sea-gulls crying.

I must go down to the seas again to the vagrant[2] gypsy life,
To the gull's way and the whale's way where the wind's like a whetted[3] knife;
And all I ask is a merry yarn[4] from a laughing fellow-rover,
And a quiet sleep and a sweet dream when the long trick's[5] over. B PAUSE & REFLECT

1. **spume** (spyo͞om): foam or froth on a liquid.
2. **vagrant** (vā'grənt): wandering from place to place; unrestrained.
3. **whetted** (hwĕt-ĭd): sharpened.
4. **yarn:** long, entertaining tale.
5. **trick:** term of work or duty.

Monitor Your Comprehension

B RHYME
Reread lines 1–12. Underline the rhyming pairs in each stanza and record the words below.

Rhyming Words

What is the pattern of rhyme?

PAUSE & REFLECT
How would you describe the speaker's personality, based on the details mentioned in the poem?

SET A PURPOSE FOR READING

Read to find out about the life of a village blacksmith.

The Village Blacksmith

Poem by

HENRY WADSWORTH LONGFELLOW

BACKGROUND A blacksmith makes and repairs iron objects by hammering them against an anvil, which is a heavy iron block. Using the roaring fire in his forge, the blacksmith would shape iron into horseshoes, weapons, and tools. Because of improvements in the production of such objects, blacksmiths are rare today.

Under a spreading chestnut-tree
    The village smithy stands;
The smith, a mighty man is he,
    With large and sinewy hands;
And the muscles of his brawny arms
    Are strong as iron bands.

His hair is crisp, and black, and long,
    His face is like the tan;
His brow is wet with honest sweat,
    He earns whate'er he can,
And looks the whole world in the face,
    For he owes not any man. C

sinewy (sĭn'yo͞o-ē) *adj.* lean and tough

brawny (brô'nē) *adj.* strong and muscular

C RHYME

Reread lines 1–12, underlining the rhyming words. Which lines in the first two stanzas rhyme?

Monitor Your Comprehension

Week in, week out, from morn till night,
You can hear his bellows[1] blow;
You can hear him swing his heavy sledge,
With measured beat and slow,
Like a sexton[2] ringing the village bell,
When the evening sun is low.

And children coming home from school
Look in at the open door;
They love to see the flaming forge,
And hear the bellows roar,
And catch the burning sparks that fly
Like chaff from a threshing-floor.[3]

PAUSE & REFLECT

He goes on Sunday to the church,
And sits among his boys;
He hears the parson pray and preach,
He hears his daughter's voice,
Singing in the village choir,
And it makes his heart rejoice. D

It sounds to him like her mother's voice,
Singing in Paradise!
He needs must think of her once more,
How in the grave she lies;
And with his hard, rough hand he wipes
A tear out of his eyes.

1. **bellows**: a device for providing air to feed a fire.
2. **sexton**: an employee of a church, responsible for maintaining the building and ringing the church bells.
3. **chaff from a threshing-floor**: Chaff is the dry coating on grains of wheat. It is discarded during threshing, when the wheat and straw are separated.

PAUSE & REFLECT
Reread lines 13–24. What is the speaker's attitude toward the blacksmith?

D METER
Read aloud lines 25–30, marking the pattern of stressed and unstressed syllables. What do you notice about the pattern of the rhythm?

Monitor Your Comprehension

repose (rĭ-pōz′) *n.* freedom from work or worry; rest

PAUSE & REFLECT
Reread lines 43–48. Why does the speaker express gratitude toward the blacksmith?

Toiling, —rejoicing, —sorrowing,
Onward through life he goes;
Each morning sees some task begin,
Each evening sees it close;
Something attempted, something done,
Has earned a night's **repose**.

Thanks, thanks to thee, my worthy friend,
For the lesson thou hast taught!
Thus at the flaming forge of life
Our fortunes must be wrought;
Thus on its sounding anvil[4] shaped
Each burning deed and thought.

PAUSE & REFLECT

4. **sounding anvil:** An anvil is a heavy block of iron on which metals are hammered into shape. *Sounding* refers to the ringing noise the hammering makes.

Literary Analysis: Rhyme

In addition to creating a pattern of sound, rhyme can help emphasize and connect important ideas or words in a poem. Look back at the rhyming words you listed as you read. In the chart below, describe the effects of rhyme on each poem's meaning.

READING 4 Understand, make inferences, and draw conclusions about the structure and elements of poetry.

"Sea-Fever"	
Rhyming words:	Effects of rhyme:

"The Village Blacksmith"	
Rhyming words:	Effects of rhyme:

Do you think rhyme has a greater effect on "Sea-Fever" or on "The Village Blacksmith"? Explain.

READING 4 Understand, make inferences, and draw conclusions about the structure and elements of poetry.

Reading Skill: Recognize Meter

The meter in "Sea-Fever" and in "The Village Blacksmith" seems to mimic the movements involved in the work each speaker does. Use the charts below to identify this relationship.

"Sea-Fever"

Subject:	Meter:
How they relate:	

"The Village Blacksmith"

Subject:	Meter:
How they relate:	

How can WORK affect our lives?

What jobs would mean more to you than just a paycheck? What does the way we feel about work reveal about our values?

Vocabulary Practice

Circle the part of each sentence that answers the question.

1. If you wanted a day's **repose,** would you go to a cabin in the woods or a busy train station?
2. Who would be more likely to be described as **sinewy,** a pie-eating champion or a track star?
3. Does a **brawny** person have a slender build or large muscles?

Academic Vocabulary in Writing

associations	device	insight	reaction	specific

What **associations** do you make with the life of a sailor and the life of a blacksmith? What **insights** into these occupations do you get from the poems? Use at least two Academic Vocabulary words in your response. Definitions of these words are on page 203.

READING 4 Understand, make inferences, and draw conclusions about the structure and elements of poetry.

Texas Assessment Practice

DIRECTIONS **Use "Sea-Fever" and "The Village Blacksmith" to answer questions 1–4.**

1 The "call" that the speaker refers to in lines 5–6 of "Sea-Fever" means —

- (A) the desire to sail on the sea
- (B) the noise of a foghorn
- (C) the orders of the captain
- (D) the need to earn a living

2 In line 12 of "Sea-Fever," the "long trick" refers to —

- (F) the sail mast
- (G) the trip at sea
- (H) a caught fish
- (J) a crew member

3 What brings the village blacksmith to tears in lines 35–36?

- (A) His mother's singing sounds like an angel.
- (B) The difficulties of his job make him want to quit.
- (C) The children who visit make him long for his youth.
- (D) His daughter's voice reminds him of his deceased wife.

4 The speakers of "Sea-Fever" and "The Village Blacksmith" both —

- (F) express how work can bring satisfaction
- (G) lament over the harshness of everyday life
- (H) take pleasure in not knowing what each day will bring
- (J) feel nervous about the dangerous aspects of work

READING 4 Explain how figurative language contributes to the meaning of a poem.
8 Understand how an author's sensory language creates imagery in a literary text.

Message from a Caterpillar

Poem by **Lilian Moore**

Fog

Poem by **Carl Sandburg**

Two Haiku

Poems by **Bashō**

How much can one WORD say?

Sometimes a single word can be very powerful. Words like *peace, freedom, friendship,* and *love* might express strong feelings and ideas or remind you of significant memories. In each of the following short poems, the poet has created a great amount of meaning in just a few of words.

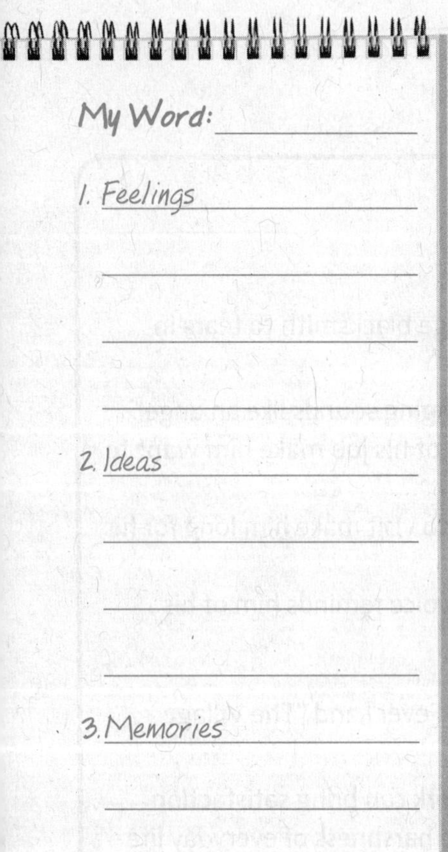

LIST IT Choose a small word that is meaningful to you. Write the word at the top of the notebook at left. Then, list the feelings, ideas, and memories that you connect to the word.

Literary Analysis: Imagery and Metaphor

Imagery is the use of sensory language—language that appeals to our senses of sight, hearing, smell, taste, and touch. Imagery is a central element of poetry that helps readers see the world in a fresh light.

Figurative language is the use of imaginative comparisons to help readers understand something in a new way. Figurative language is not literally true. One common figure of speech is a metaphor. A **metaphor** compares one thing to another different thing. As you read the poems, note examples of sensory language and metaphors

Explanation	Example
A **metaphor** is a comparison between two unlike things that does not include the word *like* or *as*.	"The road was a ribbon of moonlight," a line from a poem by Alfred Noyes, presents a vivid visual image. It also contains a metaphor: the road at night, flooded with moonlight, is compared to a ribbon.

Reading Strategy: Paraphrase

RC-6(E) Paraphrase texts in ways that maintain meaning and logical order within a text and across texts.

Paraphrasing means restating someone else's ideas in your own words. A paraphrase often helps clarify ideas that are expressed in complicated terms. Putting someone else's words into your own words can help you understand a poem.

As you read each of the poems, paraphrase the ideas in your own familiar vocabulary and write your notes in the chart below. List the ideas in the order they appear in the poem so that you keep the meaning and order of each poem.

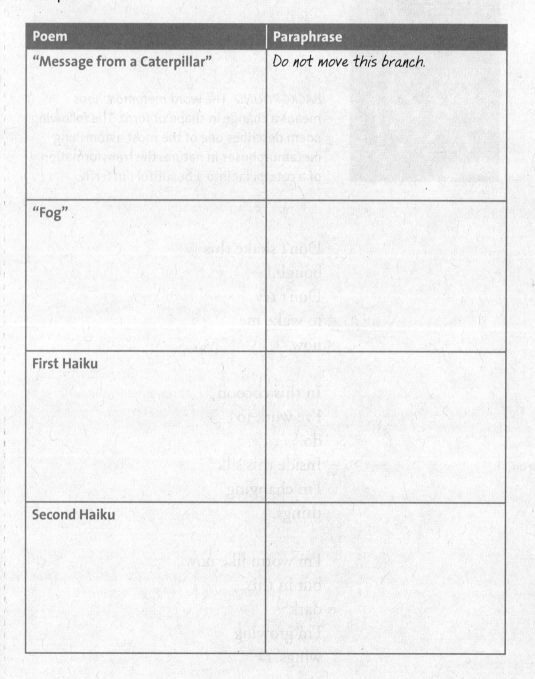

Poem	Paraphrase
"Message from a Caterpillar"	*Do not move this branch.*
"Fog"	
First Haiku	
Second Haiku	

Monitor Your Comprehension

SET A PURPOSE FOR READING

Read to interpret the caterpillar's message.

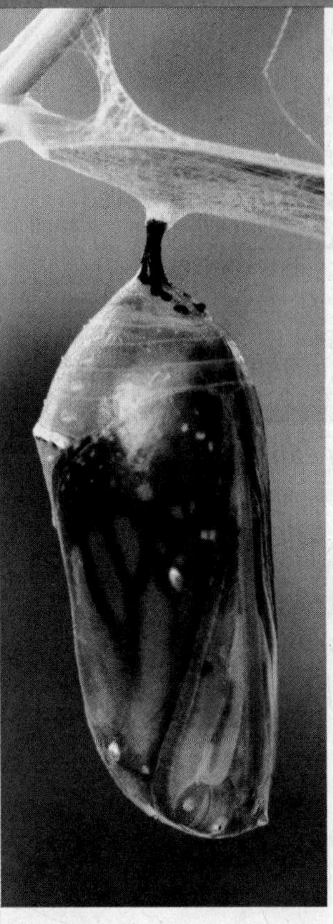

Message from a Caterpillar

Poem by

LILIAN MOORE

BACKGROUND The word *metamorphosis* means a change in shape or form. The following poem describes one of the most astonishing metamorphoses in nature: the transformation of a caterpillar into a beautiful butterfly.

Don't shake this
bough.
Don't try
to wake me
now.

In this cocoon
I've work to
do.
Inside this silk
I'm changing
things.

I'm worm like now
but in this
dark
I'm growing
wings. Ⓐ

Ⓐ **PARAPHRASE**
Reread lines 12–16. Restate in your own words what is going on inside the cocoon.

FOG

Poem by

CARL SANDBURG

BACKGROUND Much of Carl Sandburg's poetry centers on the city of Chicago, Illinois, where he worked as a reporter. In addition to poems, he wrote a two-volume biography of Abraham Lincoln and assembled *The American Songbag,* a collection of folk songs.

The fog comes
on little cat feet. (B)

It sits looking
over harbor and city
on silent haunches[1]
and then moves on. (C)

1. **haunches:** the hind legs of a four-legged animal.

Monitor Your Comprehension

SET A PURPOSE FOR READING

Consider what fog reminds you of as you read this poem.

(B) METAPHOR

What is the fog compared to?

(C) IMAGERY

What does this poem help you see and even hear?

Monitor Your Comprehension

SET A PURPOSE FOR READING

Read to determine the seasonal imagery in each haiku.

Two Haiku

Poems by

BASHŌ

BACKGROUND Matsuo Bashō set the rules for haiku, poems that describe a single moment of enlightenment or discovery, using only 17 syllables.

Winter solitude—
in a world of one color
the sound of the wind. PAUSE & REFLECT

A field of cotton—
as if the moon
had flowered. D

PAUSE & REFLECT

In the first haiku, what does "a world of one color" refer to?

____

____

D PARAPHRASE

In the chart, explain in your own words the images in these haiku that appeal to your senses of sight and sound.

Paraphrase
First Haiku:
Second Haiku:

After Reading

Literary Analysis: Imagery and Metaphor

READING 4 Explain how figurative language contributes to the meaning of a poem. **8** Understand how an author's sensory language creates imagery in a literary text.

Sensory language and metaphors are important elements of many poems. Reread each poem and pay close attention to the images or word pictures each poem creates. In the Sensory Language column of the chart below, write down words and phrases from each poem that appeal to the sense of sight, hearing, smell, taste, or touch. Write any metaphors from the poems in the Metaphor column.

	Sensory Language	Metaphor
"Message from a Caterpillar"		
"Fog"		
First Haiku		
Second Haiku		

Each poet uses language to create images or ideas through their poetry. Choose an image from one of the poems and explain why you thought it was effective. Consider the sense that the image appeals to. Remember that metaphors can work as sensory language to create imagery, too.

RC-6(E) Paraphrase texts in ways that maintain meaning and logical order within a text and across texts.

Reading Strategy: Paraphrase

Review the chart you completed on page 215, and write a paraphrase of each poem below. In a paraphrase, you express every idea in each poem in your own words. Follow the order of the ideas used in each poem.

"Message from a Caterpillar"	First Haiku

"Fog"	Second Haiku

How much can one WORD say?

Review the list you created on page 214. Using the list for ideas, write a haiku. Try to express as much as you can in three short lines.

Academic Vocabulary in Speaking

READING 4 Explain how figurative language contributes to the meaning of a poem. **8** Understand how an author's sensory language creates imagery in a literary text. **RC-6(E)** Paraphrase texts in ways that maintain meaning and logical order within a text and across texts.

associations	device	insight	reaction	specific

TURN AND TALK Which poem contained the most effective imagery? What **insights** did you have into the ideas that the poets were trying to convey? Discuss your **specific** thoughts with a partner. Use at least two Academic Vocabulary words in your discussion. Definitions of these words are on page 203.

Texas Assessment Practice

DIRECTIONS Use "Message from a Caterpillar," "Fog," and the two haiku to answer questions 1–6.

1 Which of the following is a good summary of the caterpillar's message in "Message from a Caterpillar"?

- (A) I need to wake up as soon as possible to fly away.
- (B) I think my cocoon is a hard place to grow up.
- (C) I already have wings and am ready to fly.
- (D) I am busy transforming, and cannot be disturbed.

2 Both "Fog" and the first haiku by Bashō have —

- (F) from three to seven syllables in a line
- (G) imagery that compares two things
- (H) two stanzas and titles
- (J) no titles and three lines

3 Which senses does the word *haunches* in the poem "Fog" appeal to as it supports the cat metaphor?

- (A) smell and taste
- (B) hear and smell
- (C) sight and touch
- (D) taste and sight

4 Which of these phrases best describes the tone in lines 1–5 and 6–11 in "Message from a Caterpillar"?

- (F) forceful and commanding
- (G) timid and shy
- (H) happy and upbeat
- (J) sad and depressed

5 In Bashō's two haiku, which word does the poet use to create an image of melancholy, or gentle thought?

- (A) flowered
- (B) solitude
- (C) moon
- (D) sound

6 Which of the following is the most accurate paraphrase of "Fog"?

- (F) The fog rushes quickly into the harbor and city before moving on.
- (G) The fog overwhelms the harbor and city and stays for a long time.
- (H) The fog enters the harbor and city noisily making its presence known.
- (J) The fog stops for a quiet rest over the harbor and city before it moves on.

READING 4 Explain how figurative language contributes to the meaning of a poem. **8** Explain how authors create meaning through figurative language emphasizing the use of personification and hyperbole.

I'm Nobody! Who are You?

Poem by Emily Dickinson

Is the Moon Tired?

Poem by Christina Rossetti

Mooses

Poem by Ted Hughes

Possible Surprising Ideas About . . .

Being a nobody:

The moon:

A moose:

How can POETRY surprise you?

Have you ever felt completely surprised by the way a story ended? Poetry is often full of surprises, too. For example, a poet might compare two things that seem totally unrelated. Such comparisons can give you a fresh outlook on a familiar subject.

DISCUSS In this lesson you will read three poems. One is about being a nobody, one is about the moon, and one is about a moose. What surprising things might each poet say about his or her topic? Write your ideas in the notebook at left, and then discuss them with a small group.

Literary Analysis: Figurative Language

Writers use figurative language to describe an aspect of life in a surprising or original way. As you read the poems, look for the specific types of figurative language defined in the chart below.

Figurative Language

Figure of Speech	What It Does	Example
Simile	Compares two things using the word *like* or *as*	Her eyes were like green emeralds.
Metaphor	Compares two things without the word *like* or *as*	Her eyes were green emeralds.
Personification	Gives human qualities to something that is not human	The sun smiled down on us.
Hyperbole	Uses exaggeration to create an effect	The sun burned us to a crisp.

Reading Skill: Make Inferences

When you read poetry, you need to make **inferences,** or educated guesses, about the poem's meaning. To make an inference, you note details in the text and add what you know from your own experience. As you read the poems, record each inference you make in a graphic organizer like this one.

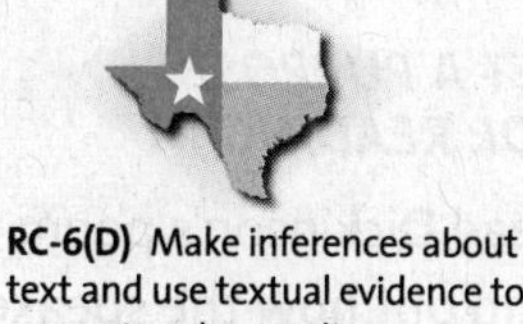

RC-6(D) Make inferences about text and use textual evidence to support understanding.

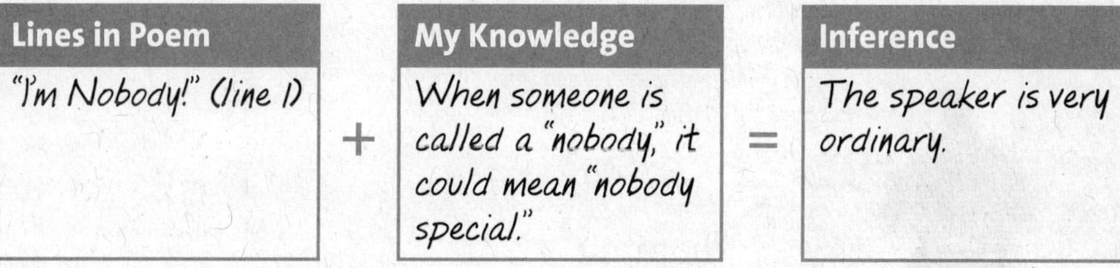

Lines in Poem		My Knowledge		Inference
"I'm Nobody!" (line 1)	+	When someone is called a "nobody," it could mean "nobody special."	=	The speaker is very ordinary.

Vocabulary in Context

Note: Words are listed in the order in which they appear in the poems.

dreary (drîr'ē) *adj.* dismal, bleak, or boring
*We spent a **dreary** afternoon staring out the window and waiting for the rain to stop.*

blunder (blŭn'dər) *v.* to move clumsily
*The animal **blundered** along because he was lost.*

lectern (lĕk'tərn) *n.* a stand that holds papers for someone standing up to deliver a speech or lecture
*The poet placed her poem on the **lectern** at the front of the auditorium.*

cackle (kăk'əl) *v.* to make a sound of shrill laughter or chatter
*It's rude to **cackle** when someone has made an honest mistake.*

Vocabulary Practice

Review the vocabulary words and their meanings. Then work with a partner to brainstorm ways in which each word could relate to one of the poem topics—being a nobody, the moon, or a moose. Write your two best ideas on the lines below.

SET A PURPOSE FOR READING

Read Dickinson's poem to find out how the speaker feels about being a "nobody."

I'M NOBODY! WHO ARE YOU?

Poem by

EMILY DICKINSON

BACKGROUND Today Emily Dickinson is regarded as one of America's greatest poets. During her lifetime, however, she was not famous at all. Only seven of her poems were published while she was alive. She even refused to have her name put on any of them. Dickinson's attitude toward fame comes through in "I'm Nobody! Who are You?"

dreary (drîr'ē) *adj.* dismal, bleak, or boring

I'm Nobody! Who are you?
Are you—Nobody—Too?
Then there's a pair of us!
Don't tell! they'd advertise—you know!

How **dreary**—to be—Somebody!
How public—like a Frog—
To tell one's name—the livelong June—
To an admiring Bog![1] Ⓐ

Ⓐ **FIGURATIVE LANGUAGE**
Reread lines 5–8. Underline the **simile** that tells what being a "Somebody" is like. Circle the thing Dickinson compares, using a **metaphor,** to the people who admire the Somebody. Are these comparisons meant to be flattering, or positive? Explain.

1. **bog:** an area of soft, waterlogged ground.

Is the Moon Tired?

Poem by
CHRISTINA ROSSETTI

BACKGROUND Christina Rossetti came from a talented family of poets, writers, and artists. However, she avoided fame just as Emily Dickinson did. Poor health was one reason for Rossetti's solitary life.

Is the moon tired? she looks so pale
Within her misty veil: B
She scales the sky from east to west,
And takes no rest.

Before the coming of the night
The moon shows papery white;
Before the dawning of the day
She fades away. C

Monitor Your Comprehension

SET A PURPOSE FOR READING

Read Rossetti's poem to discover what makes the speaker wonder if the moon is tired.

B MAKE INFERENCES
What is the "misty veil" mentioned in line 2? Complete the chart to make an **inference** about the meaning of this phrase.

Lines in Poem
↓
My Knowledge
↓
Inference
The "misty veil" is

C FIGURATIVE LANGUAGE
Circle the words Rossetti uses to **personify** the moon. (Ask yourself: What can a person do or feel that the real moon cannot?)

SET A PURPOSE FOR READING
Read this poem to find examples of humor in Hughes's description of the moose.

MOOSES

Poem by
TED HUGHES

BACKGROUND Ted Hughes grew up hunting in the woods of rural England. Later, he avoided hunting, preferring to write poetry about the "aliveness of animals in their natural states." You may be surprised by Hughes's view of the animals in "Mooses."

The goofy Moose, the walking-house frame, (D)
Is lost
In the forest. He bumps, he **blunders**, he stands.

With massy bony thoughts sticking out near his ears—
Reaching out palm upwards, to catch whatever might be
falling from heaven—
He tries to think,
Leaning their huge weight
On the **lectern** of his front legs.

(D) FIGURATIVE LANGUAGE
Reread line 1 and underline the metaphor used to describe the moose. How does this metaphor help you imagine what the moose looks like?

____

____

____

blunder (blŭn′dər) *v.* to move clumsily

lectern (lĕk′tərn) *n.* a stand that holds papers for someone standing up to deliver a speech or lecture

He can't find the world!
Where did it go? What does a world look like?
The Moose
Crashes on, and crashes into a lake, and stares at the
mountain and cries
"Where do I belong? This is no place!"

He turns and drags half the lake out after him
And charges the **cackling** underbrush— E

He meets another Moose.
He stares, he thinks "It's only a mirror!"
"Where is the world?" he groans, "O my lost world!
And why am I so ugly?
And why am I so far away from my feet?"

He weeps.
Hopeless drops drip from his droopy lips.

The other Moose just stands there doing the same.

Two dopes of the deep woods. PAUSE & REFLECT

Monitor Your Comprehension

cackle (kăk'əl) *v.* to make a sound of shrill laughter or chatter

E FIGURATIVE LANGUAGE
Circle the **hyperbole,** or exaggeration, in line 14. Which of the moose's traits does the hyperbole emphasize?

PAUSE & REFLECT
Consider whether this poem is simply about moose. If the "deep woods" represent life, who are the "dopes" who cannot understand anything about it? Support your answer with details from the poem.

After Reading

READING 4 Explain how figurative language contributes to the meaning of a poem. **8** Explain how authors create meaning through figurative language emphasizing the use of personification and hyperbole. **RC-6(D)** Make inferences about text and use textual evidence to support understanding.

Literary Analysis: Figurative Language

In each of the poems you have just read, the poet uses figurative language to make an interesting point about his or her subject. Review your notes and select one example of each kind of figurative language. Record your examples in the chart below. Then explain the meaning of each one.

Figurative Language

Figure of Speech	Example from Poem	Meaning of Example
Simile		
Metaphor		
Personification		
Hyperbole		

Reading Skill: Make Inferences

Think about the attitude of the speaker in "I'm Nobody! Who are You?" and what you know about Emily Dickinson's life. What can you infer about Dickinson's attitude toward fame?

How can POETRY surprise you?

What was the most surprising idea or comparison you encountered in the three poems? Explain why it was surprising.

Vocabulary Practice

Circle the word that is most closely related to each boldfaced vocabulary word.

1. **blunder:** **(a)** dance, **(b)** cook, **(c)** stumble, **(d)** mumble
2. **lectern:** **(a)** voter, **(b)** guide, **(c)** desk, **(d)** chair
3. **cackle:** **(a)** laugh, **(b)** gather, **(c)** cry, **(d)** punish
4. **dreary:** **(a)** heavy, **(b)** gloomy, **(c)** ready, **(d)** old

READING 4 Explain how figurative language contributes to the meaning of a poem. **8** Explain how authors create meaning through figurative language emphasizing the use of personification and hyperbole. **RC-6(D)** Make inferences about text and use textual evidence to support understanding.

Academic Vocabulary In Speaking

associations	device	insight	reaction	specific

TURN AND TALK Is the poem "Mooses" mostly sad or mostly humorous? With a partner, discuss the poet's **insights** about people who spend a lot of time thinking about difficult questions. Cite **specific** details from the poem, and use at least one Academic Vocabulary word in your discussion. Definitions of these words are on page 203.

Texas Assessment Practice

DIRECTIONS Use the three poems to answer questions 1–4.

1 The speaker in "I'm Nobody! Who are You?" thinks that the life of a famous person is —

- (A) similar to living in a swamp
- (B) exciting and glamorous
- (C) better than being ignored
- (D) boring and unappealing

2 "Is the Moon Tired?" uses personification to describe —

- (F) the moon's appearance and actions
- (G) a night when the moon is full
- (H) a woman with a moon-shaped face
- (J) the moment before dawn breaks

3 Which of the following is an example of hyperbole from "Mooses"?

- (A) *He bumps, he blunders, he stands*
- (B) *Where did it go? What does a world look like?*
- (C) *He turns and drags half the lake out after him*
- (D) *Hopeless drops drip from his droopy lips*

4 In "Mooses," the moose is sad because —

- (F) his antlers are very heavy
- (G) he doesn't know the answers to his questions
- (H) the underbrush cackles at him
- (J) the other moose doesn't want to be his friend

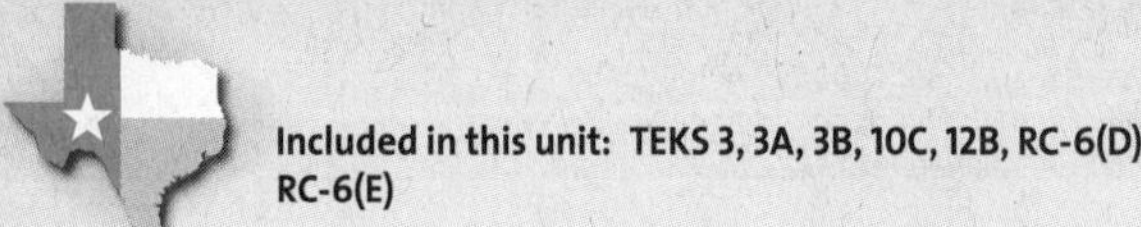

Included in this unit: TEKS 3, 3A, 3B, 10C, 12B, RC-6(D), RC-6(E)

UNIT 6 Timeless Tales

MYTHS, LEGENDS, AND TALES

Be sure to read the Reader's Workshop on pp. 676–681 in *Holt McDougal Literature.*

Academic Vocabulary for Unit 6

Academic Vocabulary is the language you use to discuss literary and informational texts. Preview the following Academic Vocabulary words. You will use these words as you write and talk about the selections in this unit.

circumstance (sər'kəm-stans) *n.* an event or condition that affects a person

*The character was in a difficult **circumstance** when the monster reached for her.*

•

contribute (kən-trib'yo͞ot) *v.* to give or add something, such as resources or ideas

*What does this story event **contribute** to the development of the plot?*

•

element (el'ə-mənt) *n.* a separate, identifiable part of something

*Each **element** of the myth was important to conveying the theme.*

•

significant (sig-nif'ə-kənt) *adj.* important; meaningful

*It is **significant** that the character who treats others with kindness is rewarded.*

•

tradition (trə-dish'ən) *n.* a set of beliefs or customs that have been handed down for generations

*The **traditions** of a culture are often reflected in its myths and legends.*

What are some **traditions** that are important in your school? How are these traditions **significant?** Write about these traditions, using at least three Academic Vocabulary words in your response.

____

____

____

READING 3 Analyze, make inferences, and draw conclusions about theme and genre in different cultural, historical, and contemporary contexts.

Apollo's Tree: The Story of Daphne and Apollo

Classical Myth Retold by **Mary Pope Osborne**

Arachne

Classical Myth Retold by **Olivia E. Coolidge**

Event

Consequence

Event

Consequence

Can PRIDE ever hurt you?

It's good to have pride in yourself as well as in your accomplishments. But when pride turns to boasting, it can get you into trouble. Some classical myths, such as the two you are about to read, serve as warnings about the dangers of being overly sure of yourself.

DISCUSS With a group of classmates, discuss some times when you or someone you know witnessed the dangers of pride. What events took place? What were the consequences, or effects? Take turns discussing the effects it had on those involved. Complete the chart at left with information from your discussion.

Literary Analysis: Cultural Values in Myths

Cultural values are the standards of behavior that a society expects from its people. Myths and their themes reflect the cultural values of the societies in which they were first told. As the events in a myth or a folk tale take place, the main character often learns an important lesson. This lesson reflects ideas and beliefs that are important to the culture in which the story developed. The chart below shows some values often taught in Greek and Roman myths.

Important Values in Greek and Roman Myths
• respecting your elders
• respecting and obeying the gods, who are often involved in humans' everyday lives
• knowing your place

As you read "Apollo's Tree" and "Arachne," notice what happens to the characters who do not maintain these values. Then determine what lessons are being taught by the myths.

Reading Strategy: Predict

When you **predict,** you make reasonable guesses about what will happen next based on clues in a story and your own experiences. As you read the myths that follow, you will use a chart like the one shown to record your predictions.

Myth	My Prediction	Clues in Story
"Apollo's Tree"	*Cupid will shoot Apollo with an arrow.*	

Vocabulary in Context

Note: Words are listed in the order in which they appear in the myths.

ominous (ŏm′ə-nəs) *adj.* threatening; frightening
As they gathered in the sky, the ***ominous*** *storm clouds promised a thunderstorm.*

exquisite (ĕk′skwĭ-zĭt) *adj.* of extraordinary beauty or charm
The ***exquisite*** *quilt was stunningly beautiful.*

sacred (sā′krĭd) *adj.* worthy of great respect; holy
The museum had a large collection of ***sacred*** *objects from ancient history.*

obscure (ŏb-skyo͝or′) *adj.* far from cities or other areas of human population
Even though the family lived in an ***obscure*** *village, they knew many famous stories.*

immensely (ĭ-mĕns′lē) *adv.* extremely; very
Athena was ***immensely*** *angry when she saw the way Arachne behaved.*

indignantly (ĭn-dĭg′nənt-lē) *adv.* angrily; in annoyance
He replied ***indignantly*** *after Zeus questioned his wisdom.*

obstinacy (ŏb′stə-nə-sē) *n.* the act of being stubborn or disobedient
Many figures in myths act with ***obstinacy*** *when the Gods confront them.*

distorted (dĭ-stôrt′əd) *adj.* twisted out of shape; misshapen
The old mirror made people's faces seem ***distorted.***

Vocabulary Practice

Review the vocabulary words and their meanings. Work with a partner to predict what the myths will be about based on the list above. Write your prediction below.

Monitor Your Comprehension

SET A PURPOSE FOR READING

Read to discover the positive and negative aspects of pride in this myth.

APOLLO'S TREE

The Story of Daphne and Apollo

Classical Myth Retold by

MARY POPE OSBORNE

BACKGROUND The myths told by the ancient Greeks and Romans are known as classical mythology. The earliest Greek myths appeared almost 3,000 years ago. When Rome conquered Greece around 178 B.C., the Romans adopted the Greek myths but changed the names of the gods to Roman names.

One day when Apollo, the god of light and truth, was a young man, he came upon Cupid, the god of love, playing with one of his bows. "What are you doing with my bow?" Apollo asked angrily. "Don't try to steal my glory, Cupid! I've slain a great serpent with that weapon. Play with your own little bow and arrows!"

"Your arrows may slay serpents, Apollo," said the god of love, "but *my* arrows can do worse harm! Even you can be wounded by them!" **A**

A PREDICT

Reread lines 1–9. What do you think Cupid is going to do? Use clues from the text to help you make reasonable guesses about what will happen next. For example, Apollo speaks angrily to Cupid (lines 3–6), and Cupid threatens Apollo (lines 7–9).

My Prediction

↓

Clues in the Story

With that **ominous** threat, Cupid flew into the sky and landed on top of a high mountain. Then he pulled two arrows from his quiver:[1] One had a blunt tip filled with lead. Whomever was hit by this arrow would run from anyone professing love. The second arrow was sharp and made of gold. Whomever was hit with this arrow would instantly fall in love.

Cupid aimed his first arrow at Daphne, a beautiful nymph[2] hunting deep in the woods. Daphne was a follower of Diana, Apollo's twin sister and the goddess of wild things. Like Diana, Daphne loved her freedom, as she roamed the woods and fields with her hair in wild disarray and her limbs bare to the sun and rain.

Cupid pulled the bowstring back and shot the blunt-tipped arrow at Daphne. When the arrow flew through the air, it became invisible. And when it pierced Daphne's heart, she felt a sharp pain, but knew not why.

Holding her hands over her wound, Daphne rushed to her father, the river god. "Father!" she shouted. "You must make me a promise!"

"What is it?" called the god who stood in the river, surrounded by water nymphs.

"Promise I will never have to get married!" Daphne cried.

The river god, confused by his daughter's frantic request, called back, "But I wish to have grandchildren!"

"No, Father! No! I *never* want to get married! Please, let me always be as free as Diana!"

"But I want you to marry!" cried the god.

"No!" screamed Daphne. And she beat the water with her fists, then rocked back and forth and sobbed.

"All right!" shouted the river god. "Do not grieve so, Daphne! I promise I'll never make you marry!" B

---

1. **quiver** (kwĭv′ər): a portable case for holding arrows.
2. **nymph** (nĭmf): any of a number of minor gods represented as beautiful maidens in Greek and Roman mythology.

Monitor Your Comprehension

ominous (ŏm′ə-nəs) *adj.* threatening; frightening

B CULTURAL VALUES
Reread lines 32–42. In what way does Daphne's behavior show disrespect toward elders?

Monitor Your Comprehension

PAUSE & REFLECT
Is Cupid's pride causing positive or negative consequences? Explain.

"And promise you'll help me escape my suitors!" cried the huntress.

"I promise, I will!" called the river god.

After Daphne secured this promise from her father, Cupid aimed his second arrow—the sharp, gold-tipped one—at Apollo, who was wandering in the woods. Just as the young god came upon Daphne, Cupid pulled back the tight string of his bow and shot the golden arrow into Apollo's heart. PAUSE & REFLECT

The god instantly fell in love with Daphne. Even though the huntress's hair was wild and she wore only rough animal skins, Apollo thought she was the most beautiful woman he'd ever seen.

"Hello!" he cried. But Daphne gave him a startled look, then bolted into the woods like a deer.

Apollo ran after her, shouting, "Stay! Stay!" But Daphne fled as fast as the wind.

"Don't run, please!" cried Apollo. "You flee like a dove flees an eagle. But I'm not your enemy! Don't run from me!"

Daphne continued to run.

"Stop!" Apollo cried.

Daphne did not slow down.

"Do you know who I am?" said the god. "I am not a farm boy or a shepherd. I am Lord of Delphi! Son of Jupiter! I've slain a great serpent with my arrow! But alas, I fear Cupid's weapons have wounded me worse!"

Daphne continued to run, her bare limbs lit by the sun and her soft hair wild in the wind.

Apollo grew tired of begging her to stop, so he began to pick up speed. On the wings of love, running more swiftly than he'd ever run before, the god of light and truth gave the girl no rest, until soon he was close upon her.

Her strength gone, Daphne could feel Apollo's breath on her hair. "Help me, Father!" she cried to the river god. "Help me!" (C)

No sooner had she spoken these words, than her arms and legs grew heavy and turned to wood. Then her hair became leaves, and her feet became roots growing deep into the ground. She had become a laurel tree;[3] and nothing was left of her, but her exquisite loveliness.

Apollo embraced the tree's branches as if they were Daphne's arms. He kissed her wooden flesh. Then he pressed his hands against the tree's trunk and wept.

"I feel your heart beating beneath this bark," Apollo said, tears running down his face. "Since you can't be my wife, you'll be my sacred tree. I'll use your wood for my harp and for my arrows. I'll weave your branches into a wreath for my head. Heroes and scholars will be crowned with your leaves.[4] You'll always be young and green—my first love, Daphne." (D)

3. **laurel tree:** a Mediterranean evergreen tree with fragrant leaves and small, blackish berries.

4. **Heroes and scholars . . . your leaves:** In ancient times, a wreath of laurel leaves was often given to poets, heroes, and victors in athletic contests as a mark of honor.

Monitor Your Comprehension

(C) PREDICT

Review lines 52–77. Predict what will happen next. Underline clues in the selection that support your prediction.

exquisite (ĕk'skwĭ-zĭt) *adj.* of extraordinary beauty or charm

sacred (sā'krĭd) *adj.* worthy of great respect; holy

(D) CULTURAL VALUES

Think about how the events of the myth start with Apollo's disrespect of another god—his boastful pride about his accomplishments and his insults toward Cupid. What lessons does the myth teach?

SET A PURPOSE FOR READING

Read to find out how pride affects Arachne's life.

ARACHNE

Classical Myth Retold by

OLIVIA E. COOLIDGE

BACKGROUND Most myths teach morals, or lessons on how to behave. You can figure out the moral of a myth by examining the choices characters make and the consequences they face. In "Arachne," the title character crosses Athena, the goddess of wisdom and crafts, and learns a difficult lesson.

Arachne was a maiden who became famous throughout Greece, though she was neither wellborn nor beautiful and came from no great city. She lived in an **obscure** little village, and her father was a humble dyer of wool. In this he was very skillful, producing many varied shades, while above all he was famous for the clear, bright scarlet which is made from shellfish and which was the most glorious of all the colors used in ancient Greece. Even more skillful than her father was Arachne. It was her task to spin the fleecy wool into a fine, soft thread and to weave it into cloth on the high-standing loom within the cottage. Arachne was small and pale from much working. Her eyes were light

obscure (ŏb-skyŏŏr') *adj.* far from cities or other areas of human population

and her hair was a dusty brown, yet she was quick and graceful, and her fingers, roughened as they were, went so fast that it was hard to follow their flickering movements. So soft and even was her thread, so fine her cloth, so gorgeous her embroidery,[1] that soon her products were known all over Greece. No one had ever seen the like of them before. E

At last Arachne's fame became so great that people used to come from far and wide to watch her working. Even the graceful nymphs would steal in from stream or forest and peep shyly through the dark doorway, watching in wonder the white arms of Arachne as she stood at the **loom** and threw the shuttle[2] from hand to hand between the hanging threads or drew out the long wool, fine as a hair, from the distaff[3] as she sat spinning. "Surely Athena herself must have taught her," people would murmur to one another. "Who else could know the secret of such marvelous skill?"

Arachne was used to being wondered at, and she was **immensely** proud of the skill that had brought so many to look on her. Praise was all she lived for, and it displeased her greatly that people should think anyone, even a goddess, could teach her anything. Therefore, when she heard them murmur, she would stop her work and turn round **indignantly** to say, "With my own ten fingers I gained this skill, and by hard practice from early morning till night. I never had time to stand looking as you people do while another maiden worked. Nor if I had, would I give Athena credit because the girl was more skillful than I. As for Athena's weaving, how could there be finer cloth or more beautiful embroidery than mine? If Athena herself

1. **embroidery:** the decoration of fabric with needlework.
2. **shuttle:** a device used in loom weaving to carry thread back and forth between other threads held lengthwise.
3. **distaff:** an attachment for a spinning wheel that holds unspun wool, cotton, or flax.

Monitor Your Comprehension

E PREDICT
Review lines 1–19. Use clues in the text to make a prediction about how pride might cause problems for Arachne or her father.

VISUAL VOCABULARY
loom *n.* a device for making cloth by weaving strands of yarn or thread together.

How does the detail of Arachne at the loom contrast with the description of her as small and pale with dusty brown hair?

immensely (ĭ-mĕns'lē) *adv.* extremely; very

indignantly (ĭn-dĭg'nənt-lē) *adv.* angrily; in annoyance

Monitor Your Comprehension

F PREDICT
Reread lines 20–45. Underline Arachne's boasts in the text. Then, make a prediction about what will happen next.

G CULTURAL VALUES
Reread lines 55–62. What value does Arachne fail to show respect for? Explain.

obstinacy (ŏb'stə-nə-sē) *n.* the act of being stubborn or disobedient

were to come down and compete with me, she could do no better than I." **F**

One day when Arachne turned round with such words, an old woman answered her, a grey old woman, bent and very poor, who stood leaning on a staff and peering at Arachne amid the crowd of onlookers.

"Reckless girl," she said, "how dare you claim to be equal to the immortal gods themselves? I am an old woman and have seen much. Take my advice and ask pardon of Athena for your words. Rest content with your fame of being the best spinner and weaver that mortal eyes have ever beheld."

"Stupid old woman," said Arachne indignantly, "who gave you a right to speak in this way to me? It is easy to see that you were never good for anything in your day, or you would not come here in poverty and rags to gaze at my skill. If Athena resents my words, let her answer them herself. I have challenged her to a contest, but she, of course, will not come. It is easy for the gods to avoid matching their skill with that of men." **G**

At these words the old woman threw down her staff and stood erect. The wondering onlookers saw her grow tall and fair and stand clad in long robes of dazzling white. They were terribly afraid as they realized that they stood in the presence of Athena. Arachne herself flushed red for a moment, for she had never really believed that the goddess would hear her. Before the group that was gathered there she would not give in; so pressing her pale lips together in **obstinacy** and pride, she led the goddess to one of the great looms and set herself before the other. Without a word both began to thread the long woolen strands that hung from the rollers and between which the shuttle would move back and forth. Many skeins[4] lay heaped beside them to use, bleached white, and gold, and scarlet, and other

4. **skeins** (skānz): lengths of thread or yarn wound in long, loose coils.

shades, varied as the rainbow. Arachne had never thought of giving credit for her success to her father's skill in dyeing, though in actual truth the colors were as remarkable as the cloth itself. **H**

Soon there was no sound in the room but the breathing of the onlookers, the whirring of the shuttles, and the creaking of the wooden frames as each pressed the thread up into place or tightened the pegs by which the whole was held straight. The excited crowd in the doorway began to see that the skill of both in truth was very nearly equal but that, however the cloth might turn out, the goddess was the quicker of the two. A pattern of many pictures was growing on her loom. There was a border of twined branches of the olive, Athena's favorite tree, while in the middle, figures began to appear. As they looked at the glowing colors, the spectators realized that Athena was weaving into her pattern a last warning to Arachne. The central figure was the goddess herself, competing with Poseidon[5] for possession of the city of Athens; but in the four corners were mortals who had tried to strive with gods and pictures of the awful fate that had overtaken them. The goddess ended a little before Arachne and stood back from her marvelous work to see what the maiden was doing.

Never before had Arachne been matched against anyone whose skill was equal, or even nearly equal, to her own. As she stole glances from time to time at Athena and saw the goddess working swiftly, calmly, and always a little faster than herself, she became angry instead of frightened, and an evil thought came into her head. Thus, as Athena stepped back a pace to watch Arachne finishing her work, she saw that the maiden had taken for her design a pattern of scenes which showed evil or unworthy actions of the

5. **Poseidon** (pō-sīd'n): in Greek mythology, the god of waters, earthquakes, and horses.

Monitor Your Comprehension

H PREDICT
Who do you think will win the weaving contest? Record this prediction in the chart below.

My Prediction

↓

Clues in Story

Monitor Your Comprehension

CULTURAL VALUES
In what ways does Arachne's behavior show disrespect for the gods?

gods, how they had deceived fair maidens, resorted to trickery, and appeared on earth from time to time in the form of poor and humble people. When the goddess saw this insult glowing in bright colors on Arachne's loom, she did not wait while the cloth was judged but stepped forward, her grey eyes blazing with anger, and tore Arachne's work across. Then she struck Arachne across the face. Arachne stood there a moment, struggling with anger, fear, and pride. "I will not live under this insult," she cried, and seizing a rope from the wall, she made a noose and would have hanged herself.

The goddess touched the rope and touched the maiden. "Live on, wicked girl," she said. "Live on and spin, both you and your descendants.[6] When men look at you, they may remember that it is not wise to strive with Athena." At that the body of Arachne shriveled up; and her legs grew tiny, spindly, and **distorted**. There before the eyes of the spectators hung a little dusty brown spider on a slender thread.

distorted (dĭ-stôrt'əd) *adj.* twisted out of shape; misshapen

All spiders descend from Arachne, and as the Greeks watched them spinning their thread wonderfully fine, they remembered the contest with Athena and thought that it was not right for even the best of men to claim equality with the gods. PAUSE & REFLECT

PAUSE & REFLECT
What factors contributed to the downfall of Apollo and Arachne? How might they have avoided their fates?

6. **descendants** (dĭ-sĕn'dənts): persons whose ancestry can be traced to a particular individual.

Literary Analysis: Cultural Values in Myths

Characters in Greek myths did not always behave in ways that reflect the values of Ancient Greek culture. Under each of the three values in the chart, list details that show how characters in each myth demonstrate or disregard the value.

READING 3 Analyze, make inferences, and draw conclusions about theme and genre in different cultural, historical, and contemporary contexts.

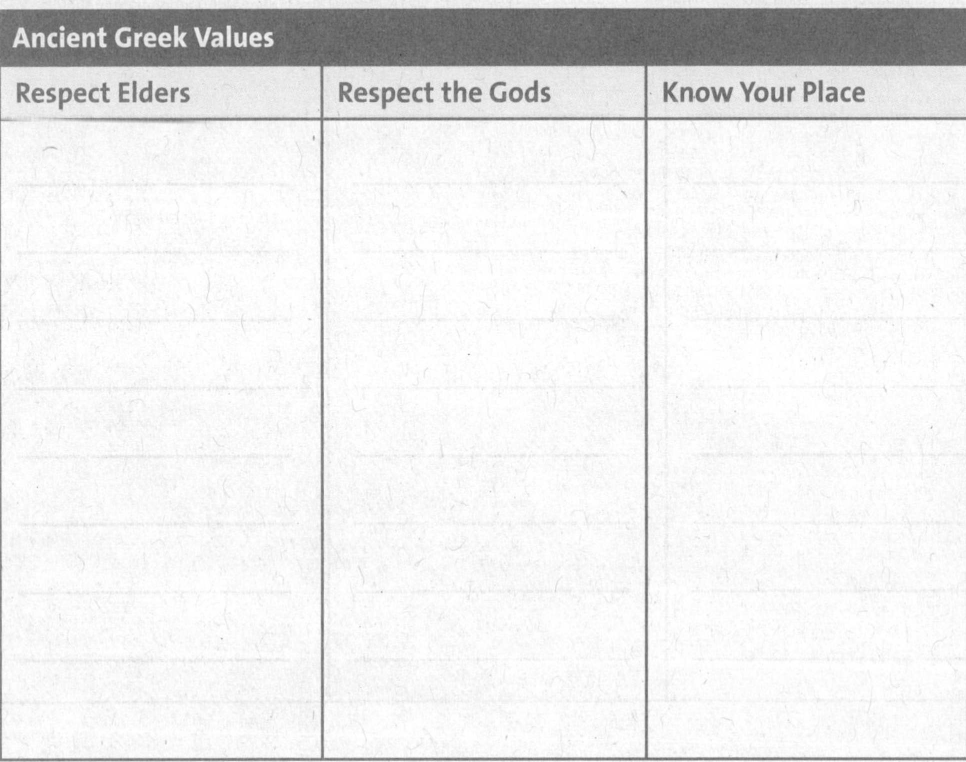

Ancient Greek Values		
Respect Elders	Respect the Gods	Know Your Place

Review your notes for "Apollo's Tree" and "Arachne," as well as the chart above. What do you now know about how the ancient Greeks viewed pride? Write your conclusions below.

READING 3 Analyze, make inferences, and draw conclusions about theme and genre in different cultural, historical, and contemporary contexts.

Reading Strategy: Predict

Review the predicting notes you took as you read the myths. Write two of your predictions and what actually happened on the chart. Then explain why your prediction was accurate or inaccurate.

My Prediction	What Actually Happened	Explanation of My Prediction
1. ____________	1. ____________	1. ____________
2. ____________	2. ____________	2. ____________

Can PRIDE ever hurt you?

Recall your discussion with classmates about the dangers of pride. How did your examples of the negative effects of too much pride compare with the events of the myth of Arachne? Explain whether you think the myth is a powerful warning against the dangers of pride.

____

____

Vocabulary Practice

Circle the vocabulary word that best completes each sentence.

1. The funhouse mirror made her body look strangely **distorted/exquisite**.
2. The site of the grave was considered **sacred/ominous** by the mourners.
3. When asked if she was lying, Lola denied it **immensely/indignantly**.
4. Kyle's **obstinacy/obscurity** often got him in trouble at school.

Academic Vocabulary in Writing

circumstance	contribute	element	significant	tradition

READING 3 Analyze, make inferences, and draw conclusions about theme and genre in different cultural, historical, and contemporary contexts.

What **contributes** to how people learn cultural values today? For instance, do people learn from television, newspapers, or in some other way? In a few sentences, discuss how people learn cultural values. Use at least two Academic Vocabulary words in your response. Definitions of these words are on page 203.

Texas Assessment Practice

DIRECTIONS Use "Apollo's Tree" and "Arachne" to answer questions 1–4.

1 In addition to her skill as a weaver, what makes Arachne's work beautiful?

- (A) a loom and shuttle that she made of special wood
- (B) the friendly way that she allows visitors to help
- (C) the skeins of wool her father dyes in beautiful colors
- (D) a chair that makes it easy for her to weave quickly

2 What does Apollo mean when he says that the wounds from Cupid's weapons are worse than those from his own arrows?

- (F) Apollo's arrows cause people to run away, while Cupid's arrows kill people.
- (G) Apollo's arrows are deadly, but Cupid's arrows cause love that can't be attained.
- (H) Cupid's arrows hurt serpents, but Apollo's can harm everyone.
- (J) Cupid's arrows work only on gods, while Apollo's work only on mortals.

3 Athena tries to give Arachne a final warning by —

- (A) trying to explain again why Arachne should respect the gods
- (B) asking the people to convince her that she is wrong
- (C) praising Arachne for her wonderful weaving and going away
- (D) weaving a design showing the suffering of people who challenge the gods

4 What message do both "Apollo's Tree" and "Arachne" have in common?

- (F) Being too proud can have negative consequences.
- (G) Challenges happen often when dealing with gods.
- (H) Mortals should be proud of their accomplishments.
- (J) Gods and mortals should live only for praise.

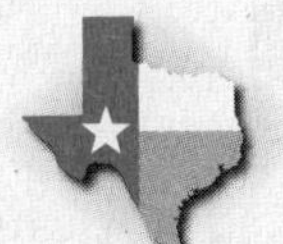

READING 10C Explain how different organizational patterns develop the main idea and the author's viewpoint. **12B** Understand how to glean and use information in documents.

Spider Webs

Online Science Article

Background

This **science article** explains how to identify different kinds of spiders by their webs. Examples include the common orb spider, whose web is shaped like spirals on lines, and the less well-known sheetweb spider, whose web is made of sheets of silk.

Skill Focus: Organizational Patterns—Classification

Expository text is informational text written to explain, define, persuade, or inform. Newspaper, magazine, and Web site articles are examples of expository texts. Expository text is built on text features and organizational patterns. **Text features** are the design elements: headings, layout, graphics, and captions. **Organizational patterns** are patterns writers use to organize the information they write. Comparison-and-contrast, cause-and-effect, and proposition-and-support are examples of organizational patterns. Writers choose the best organizational pattern for developing their main ideas and presenting their viewpoint—how the writer feels about the subject matter. Knowing the organizational pattern of an expository text can help you understand the information more easily.

Classification is an organizational pattern you'll often find in scientific writing. In classification, the writer organizes the text by sorting related information into categories. As you read "Spider Webs," make an outline of the article's structure so that you can understand the organizational pattern of classification. Start by writing what the article is about (its main idea), and then list the parts into which the article is divided.

Main Idea of Article
1. Subheading
A. Detail
B. Detail
2. Subheading
A. Detail
B. Detail
3. Subheading
A. Detail
B. Detail

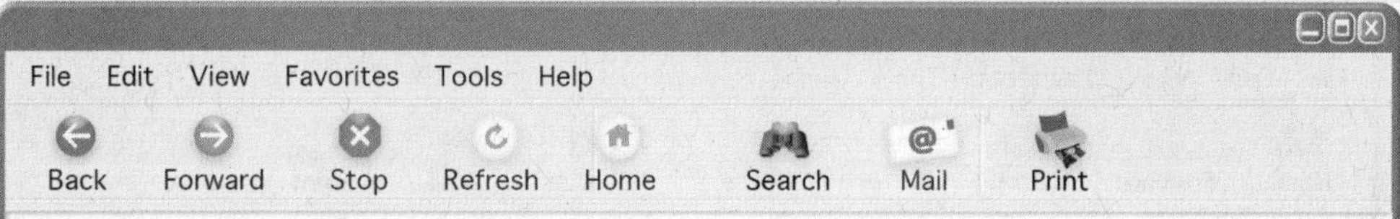

Online Science Article

You know there are many kinds of spiders, but did you know there are also many kinds of spider webs? In fact, a spider web can be a big clue to the kind of spider that made it. When you know the different kinds of webs that spiders commonly make, you can make a pretty accurate guess about the kind of spider that created it. Ⓐ

Internet

SET A PURPOSE FOR READING

Read to find out about spiders and spider webs.

FOCUS ON FORM

A **science article** is a short piece of expository writing on a scientific subject. The author's purpose for writing a science article is usually to inform or to explain.

Ⓐ CLASSIFICATION

Reread lines 1–7. How does the organizational pattern of classification support the writer's purpose?

PAUSE & REFLECT
Why do you think the writer begins with the kind of spider web readers are most likely to be familiar with?

B CLASSIFICATION
Why does it help to have the names of the spiders, such as "Triangle Spiders," boldfaced?

File Edit View Favorites Tools Help

Back Forward Stop Refresh Home Search Mail Print

▶ The kind of web that you are probably most familiar with is made by **ORB SPIDERS** (*Araneidae* family). Their webs are shaped like spirals on lines and are often very beautiful. To maintain that beauty, orb spiders have to repair their webs at least once every day. As the web loses its stickiness, the spider will eat it as it spins new threads. **PAUSE & REFLECT**

▶ **TRIANGLE SPIDERS** (*Uloboridae* family) make triangular webs. These webs resemble a slice of the webs made by orb spiders. B

▶ **FUNNEL SPIDERS** (*Agelenidae* family) make webs that might look like a bird's nest made of silk. The spiders make sheets of silk and shape them into funnels. The funnels have one

Internet

big opening to catch prey. They also have one small opening in the back in case the spider needs to escape. These webs are not actually sticky. The spiders that make them are just better at moving around in the smooth funnel shape than their prey.

Sometimes, funnel spider webs aren't cupped. Instead, spiders may make flat sheets with a small funnel-shaped retreat off to one side. Ⓒ

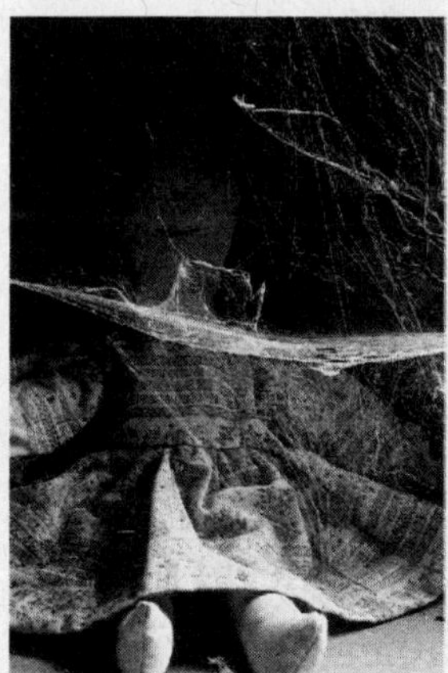

▶ **COBWEB SPIDERS** (*Theriidae* family) make small, random messes of silk string that are attached to their surroundings by long strings. Cobweb spiders are also called comb-footed spiders.

Internet

Ⓒ **CLASSIFICATION**

Complete the outline below with details about triangle spiders and funnel spiders.

II. Triangle Spiders

A. ______________________

B. ______________________

III. Funnel Spiders

A. ______________________

B. ______________________

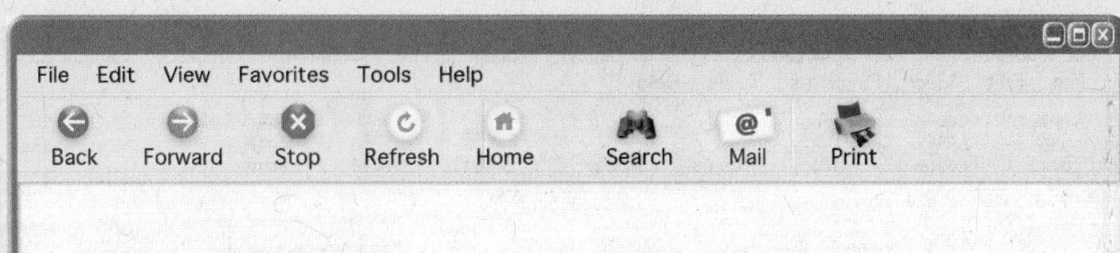

D CLASSIFICATION
Reread lines 43–58. Explain the comparison the writer makes between the meshweb spiders and the cobweb spiders. Why might such comparisons be helpful in a text that uses the classification organizational pattern?

E SCIENCE ARTICLE
How do the photographs on this page help you understand what the author describes? In addition to photographs, what other kinds of visuals could the writer have included? How might they have helped you?

▶ **MESHWEB SPIDERS** (*Dictynidae* family) make webs that are similar to those of cobweb spiders but have a little more structure. The spiders are usually found in small, messy webs at the tips of vegetation, especially in grassy fields. They can also be found under stones and dead leaves. D

E

▶ **SHEETWEB SPIDERS** (*Linyphiidae* family) make many kinds of webs that are formed out of sheets of silk. The sheets are a maze of threads, and don't have many large gaps.

There are several kinds of sheetweb spiders. *Platform spiders* make thickly interwoven sheets of silk. *Filmy dome spiders* make dome-shaped sheets that are secured by a network of silk strings. *Bowl and doily*[1] *spiders*

1. **doily** (doi'lē): a small mat, often round and made of lace, that is used as a protective or decorative cover on furniture.

File Edit View Favorites Tools Help

Back Forward Stop Refresh Home Search Mail Print

make unusual webs. The tops look like bowls that are secured by strings to something above them. The bowl appears to be sitting on a doily that is the second part of the web and is attached horizontally. These kinds of webs make very effective booby-traps for unsuspecting insects. F

► Spider webs are a sign that spiders have been nearby, but they aren't the only sign. Spiders also spin webs to protect their eggs and developing young. These **EGG CASES** look like eggs but actually contain hundreds of tiny spider eggs.

Some spiders don't make webs at all. However, these spiders do use silk to make a little hiding place for themselves, especially females with eggs. G

Internet

F CLASSIFICATION
Underline the different kinds of sheetweb spiders the author describes (lines 65–80). What are the similarities and differences between them? Why do you think the author presents the spiders in this particular order?

G CLASSIFICATION
How do you think the author feels about the topic? How does the classification pattern of organization support the author's viewpoint about the topic?

READING 10A Summarize the main ideas and supporting details in a text, demonstrating an understanding that a summary does not include opinions. **10C** Explain how different organizational patterns develop the main idea and the author's viewpoint. **RC-6(E)** Summarize texts in ways that maintain meaning and logical order within a text.

Practicing Your Skills

Now that you have read the science article, think about how the author organized the text by classifying the information. Fill in the chart below with a main idea statement for "Spider Webs." Then list one detail from each section of the article that supports the main idea.

Main Idea: ______________________________
Detail about Orb Spiders: ______________________________
Detail about Triangle Spiders: ______________________________
Detail about Funnel Spiders: ______________________________
Detail about Cobweb Spiders: ______________________________
Detail about Meshweb Spiders: ______________________________
Detail about Sheetweb Spiders: ______________________________
Detail about Egg Cases: ______________________________

Use the outline you created and the chart above to write a short summary of the article. Remember that a summary is a short restatement of the main idea and the most important details in a text.

____

____

____

____

Academic Vocabulary in Speaking

READING 10C Explain how different organizational patterns develop the main idea and the author's viewpoint.

circumstance	contribute	element	significant	tradition

TURN AND TALK With a partner, discuss how the various **elements** of a scientific article **contribute** to understanding the information. Before your discussion, take notes on how the text features such as the photographs and subheadings helped clarify the information in the text. Use at least two Academic Vocabulary words. Definitions of these words are on page 231.

Texas Assessment Practice

DIRECTIONS Use "Spider Webs" to answer questions 1–4.

1 What are the three kinds of sheetweb spiders mentioned in the article?

- (A) filmy dome, triangle, orb
- (B) sheetweb, bowl and doily, platform
- (C) orb, funnel, filmy dome
- (D) platform, filmy dome, bowl and doily

2 From the text details, you can assume the writer—

- (F) includes many opinions about spiders
- (G) cares only about certain types of spiders
- (H) knows very little about spiders
- (J) is very interested in spiders

3 The boldfaced words in the article —

- (A) show the reader where information about a topic ends.
- (B) tell the reader that a new topic is starting.
- (C) give the reader unnecessary information.
- (D) answer questions stated in the text.

4 One inference you can make from the information in this article is that spiders are named for the —

- (F) areas where they live
- (G) kinds of webs they make
- (H) markings on their bodies
- (J) colors of their webs

READING 3 Analyze, make inferences, and draw conclusions about theme and genre in different cultural and historical contexts. **3B** Analyze the function of stylistic elements in traditional literature from various cultures.

The Chenoo

Native American Legend Retold by **Joseph and James Bruchac**

Is FEAR ever fun?

What do scary movies, amusement-park haunted houses, and roller coasters have in common? Though they cause chills, screams, and fear, we turn to them again and again because they are fun. In "The Chenoo," you'll meet a monster—so prepare yourself for some fearful fun.

CHART IT The chart at left lists two fearful activities you may have experienced. Rate their fear and fun levels on a scale of 1 to 5 (with 5 being the highest). Then add three more activities and rate them. Compare your answers with those of your classmates.

Fear and Fun Levels for Various Activities

Activity	Fear Level	Fun Level
roller coaster		
reading a scary story		

Literary Analysis: Characteristics of Legends

A **legend** is a traditional tale about a hero or heroine's struggle against a powerful force. Look for the following characteristics of legends as you read "The Chenoo."

- Legends are often based on real people and events from history.
- The hero or heroine of a legend shows uncommon courage and cleverness in the face of danger.
- Many events in a legend could not actually happen in the real world.
- Everyday objects or events in a legend can take on special meaning, becoming **symbols** of something else.

Reading Skill: Make Inferences

When you **make inferences** as you read, you make educated guesses about the events or characters in a story. For example, if a character helps someone in need, you might infer that the character is kind and considerate. As you read "The Chenoo," use a chart like this one to record inferences you make about Nolka based on her words and actions.

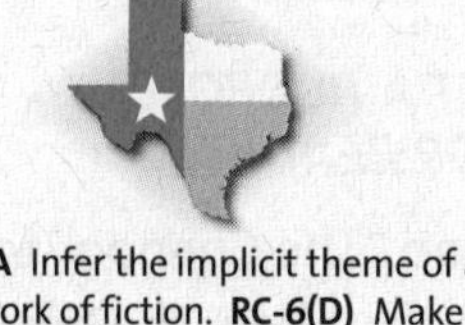

3A Infer the implicit theme of a work of fiction. **RC-6(D)** Make inferences about text.

Nolka's Words and Actions	Inferences About Nolka
cleans an elk hide and heats rocks for a sweat lodge	*She is hard-working and takes good care of her brothers.*

Making inferences can help you identify a story's **theme**—its message about life or human nature. As you learn what happens to the characters in this legend, ask yourself what message is suggested by the ways they act and change.

Vocabulary in Context

Note: Words are listed in the order in which they appear in the story.

inspect (ĭn-spĕkt') *v.* to examine carefully
*Awasos bent down to **inspect** the tracks on the ground.*

clearing (klîr'ĭng) *n.* an open area of land, as in the middle of a forest
*They walked through the forest into a **clearing.***

proceed (prō-sēd') *v.* to go forward or onward; continue
*She wanted to **proceed,** but she was frozen by fear.*

sibling (sĭb'lĭng) *n.* a brother or sister
*The brothers were worried about their **sibling,** Nolka.*

Vocabulary Practice

Review the vocabulary words and think about their meanings. Then, use at least two words in original sentences. Try to create sentences that could be part of a legend about a brave hero or heroine.

Monitor Your Comprehension

SET A PURPOSE FOR READING

Read "The Chenoo" to find out how the heroine, Nolka, will handle the danger she faces.

The Chenoo

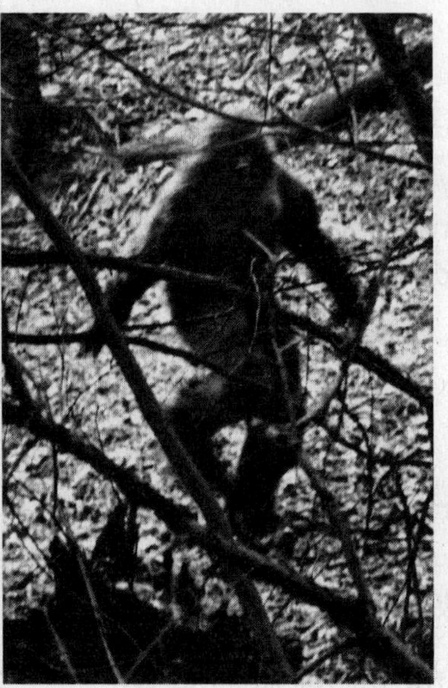

Native American Legend Retold by

JOSEPH AND JAMES BRUCHAC

BACKGROUND Monster stories are a popular type of legend passed down in Native American culture. In many monster stories, a hero or heroine defeats a foe by using his or her wits and courage. Often, the lesson of these stories is that bravery and intelligence can triumph over evil.

Long ago, during the Moon of Falling Leaves,[1] a woman and her two brothers traveled to the north to set up a hunting camp. Hoping to bring back enough furs and meat for the winter, they went far away from their village, much farther than anyone had gone in a long time.

During the first two days after making camp the hunting was very good. Each day the two brothers would go hunting. The sister, whose name was Nolka, would stay behind to tend their camp and prepare any game

1. **Moon of Falling Leaves:** In many Native American cultures, the Moon of Falling Leaves is the name given to the tenth of the thirteen cycles of the moon each year. The Moon of Falling Leaves usually begins in October.

caught the day before. On the third day, however, while out hunting, the brothers came across a very large set of footprints. Those footprints were over two feet long and ten feet apart. Kneeling down, Awasos, the older of the two brothers, carefully **inspected** each track. **A**

"Great grandfather told me of a creature that makes tracks like this. It is called a Chenoo."[2] Awasos lifted his head to scan the forest around them.

"Yes, I remember," answered Kasko, Awasos's younger brother. "He said they were giant cannibals[3] with sharp teeth and hearts made of ice. Consuming the spirit of a human being makes them stronger."

Looking closer at the tracks, the two men realized the huge footprints were headed in the direction of their camp.

"We must return and check on our sister," said Awasos. Both men began to run back toward camp.

Meanwhile, back at camp, unaware of any danger, Nolka was busy cleaning an elk hide. Several yards away, in a large fire pit, a pile of rocks was being heated up for her brothers' evening sweat lodge.

Having finished the hide, Nolka slowly stood up to add more wood to the fire. As she did so, she heard a sudden sound of breaking branches. She turned and looked up. There stood a huge Chenoo. Its large gray body was covered with pine pitch[4] and leaves, and it wore a necklace of human skulls. Its legs and arms were as thick as tree stumps. Its open mouth revealed a sharp set of teeth, and its eyes were darker than a starless night. The Chenoo raised its arms, preparing to grasp Nolka in its long, bony fingers. **B**

Knowing there was nowhere to hide, Nolka thought quickly.

---

2. **Chenoo** (chā'no͞o).
3. **cannibals:** people or animals that feed on others of their own kind.
4. **pine pitch:** the thick, sticky sap of a pine tree.

Monitor Your Comprehension

inspect (ĭn-spĕkt') *v.* to examine carefully

A MAKE INFERENCES
Reread lines 10–14 and underline details that describe the footprints. What inference can you make about the creature that made the footprints?

B LEGENDS
Reread the descriptions of the Chenoo in lines 18–39. Circle details that show it is a legendary creature that does not exist in the real world. Underline details that show how powerful the Chenoo is.

Monitor Your Comprehension

C MAKE INFERENCES
Reread lines 40–58. In the chart below, note what Nolka says and does. Use this information to make one or more inferences about her.

Nolka's Words and Actions

↓

Inferences About Nolka

clearing (klîr′ĭng) *n.* an open area of land, as in the middle of a forest

"Grandfather!" she said with a smile. "Where have you been?"

"GRANDFATHER?" the Chenoo growled. It stopped in its tracks and looked confused. No human being had ever dared to speak to it this way before.

"Yes, Grandfather. I have been waiting here all day for you. Don't you even remember me?" Nolka said. There was a long pause. Nolka did her best to appear calm.

"GRANDDAUGHTER?!" roared the Chenoo. "I have a granddaughter?!"

"Yes, of course you do. I have been preparing this sweat lodge for you all day," Nolka said, motioning toward the large pile of rocks glowing in the fire. She hoped to delay the Chenoo from trying to eat her until her brothers returned from hunting. So far the plan was working.

"Grandfather, please come into the lodge," she said, lifting up the door flap. C

"THANK YOU, GRANDDAUGHTER," the Chenoo rumbled as it walked over to the sweat lodge and bent down. Crawling in on its hands and knees, the giant squeezed through the door. Sitting down, his legs around the fire pit, the Chenoo filled the entire lodge.

Walking over to the fire, Nolka picked up a large forked stick and carried one hot rock after another and began placing them in the center of the lodge. She was just pulling another rock out of the fire when she heard someone coming.

"Sister, what are you doing?" called Awasos as he and Kasko, both completely out of breath, came running into the **clearing**.

"We saw huge tracks headed toward our camp," Kasko said. "We were afraid that you—"

Nolka held up a hand to her mouth, and her brothers stopped talking. She looked over toward the lodge.

"Our grandfather has finally arrived!" Nolka said. "Come and greet him." Then she picked up another glowing rock. As she walked over to the lodge, her brothers, totally confused, followed her. **PAUSE & REFLECT**

"Grandfather, your grandsons have returned to greet you," said Nolka to the Chenoo, through the door of the lodge.

"GRANDSONS? I HAVE GRANDSONS?" roared the Chenoo. Looking into the lodge, Awasos and Kasko could not believe it. There sat the very same monster whose tracks they had seen headed toward camp.

"HELLO, MY GRANDSONS!" the Chenoo rumbled.

"Oh, ah, yes. Hello, grandfather . . . it is good to see you," Kasko said, after being nudged in the ribs by Nolka.

"THIS LODGE FEELS GOOD. BRING ME MORE ROCKS!"

"Yes, Grandfather," Kasko said.

The two men and their sister piled one glowing rock after another in the center of the lodge. Then, after placing a large birch-bark bucket full of water just inside the door of the lodge, they closed the flap. Moments later, a loud hissing sound came from inside the lodge as the Chenoo began to pour water on the rocks.

"Now is our chance to make a run for it," Nolka whispered to her brothers. The three of them began to quietly sneak out of camp. But they had not moved quickly enough.

"MORE ROCKS! BRING ME MORE ROCKS! OPEN THE DOOR!" roared the Chenoo.

Monitor Your Comprehension

PAUSE & REFLECT

Do you believe that Nolka is behaving courageously? Support your answer with details from the text.

Monitor Your Comprehension

proceed (prō-sēd') *v.* to go forward or onward; continue

What might have happened if Nolka and her brothers had **proceeded** to run away from the Chenoo instead of bringing him more rocks?

sibling (sĭb'lĭng) *n.* a brother or sister

D MAKE INFERENCES
Why might the Chenoo's voice seem softer now?

Nolka ran over and swung open the flap of the lodge. Awasos and Kasko **proceeded** to bring in four more loads of rocks. Then, after the fourth load, the flap to the lodge was again closed. As soon as the door was closed, the sound of hissing steam came again from within the lodge. And just as before, just when they began to sneak away, the Chenoo shouted for them again.

"OPEN THE DOOR. MORE ROCKS, MORE WATER!"

"Yes, Grandfather. We are coming!"

Quickly Awasos and Kasko brought more rocks as Nolka ran to a nearby stream to refill the birch-bark bucket. When they opened the door to the lodge, huge gusts of steam flowed out so thickly that the only thing in the lodge they could see was the Chenoo's huge arm as it reached out to grab the freshly filled bucket of water.

Closing the flap again, all three **siblings** agreed it was no use trying to run. The Chenoo would only call for them again. And sure enough, it did.

"OPEN THE DOOR. MORE ROCKS. MORE WATER."

This time, they brought in every rock from the fire, even the rocks from the fire circle. They hoped the heat would be so great that the Chenoo would pass out. Standing by the lodge, they listened closely. But, to their surprise, as the hissing sound of the water hitting the rocks got louder and louder, the Chenoo began to sing.

"WAY-YAA, WAY-YAA, WAY-YAA, HOOO!!
WAY-YAA, WAY-YAA, WAY-YAA, HOOO!!"

Then it paused to pour more water on the rocks before it sang again.

"WAY-YAA, WAY-YAA, WAY-YAA, HOOO!!
WAY-YAA, WAY-YAA, WAY-YAA, HOOO!!"

This time, as the Chenoo sang, they noticed that its voice did not seem as loud. Again they heard the sounds of steam rising as water was poured on the stones. D

"Way-yaa, way-yaa, way-yaa, hooo!!
Way-yaa, way-yaa, way-yaa, hooo!!"

That voice was much softer now, so soft that it sounded like the voice of an old man.

"Way-yaa, way-yaa, way-yaa, hooo!!
Way-yaa, way-yaa, way-yaa, hooo!!"

Then it was silent.

"Grandchildren, open the door," a little voice called from inside the sweat lodge.

Awasos lifted up the door flap. A huge gust of steam blew out from the lodge, knocking him backward. As the steam rose into the air, a little old man crawled out from the lodge. As he stood up, the little old man began to cough. He coughed and coughed until he coughed up a huge piece of ice in the shape of a human heart. Falling to the ground, the heart-shaped piece of ice that was the bad spirit of the Chenoo shat tered on a rock. E

"Thank you, my grandchildren. You have saved me. I am no longer a monster. Now I am truly your grandfather," said the old man with a smile.

E LEGENDS
A symbol is an object that stands for something other than itself. Circle the symbol in lines 150–154. What does it stand for?

Monitor Your Comprehension

PAUSE & REFLECT
In what way is the ending of this legend similar to that of other traditional tales you have read?

So Nolka and her two brothers took the old man who had been a Chenoo as their grandfather. They brought him back to their village, where he quietly and peacefully lived out the rest of his days. **PAUSE & REFLECT**

After Reading

Literary Analysis: Characteristics of Legends

READING 3 Analyze, make inferences, and draw conclusions about theme and genre in different cultural and historical contexts. **3B** Analyze the function of stylistic elements in traditional literature from various cultures.

How does "The Chenoo" display the characteristics of a legend? For each characteristic in the chart below, provide an example from the story.

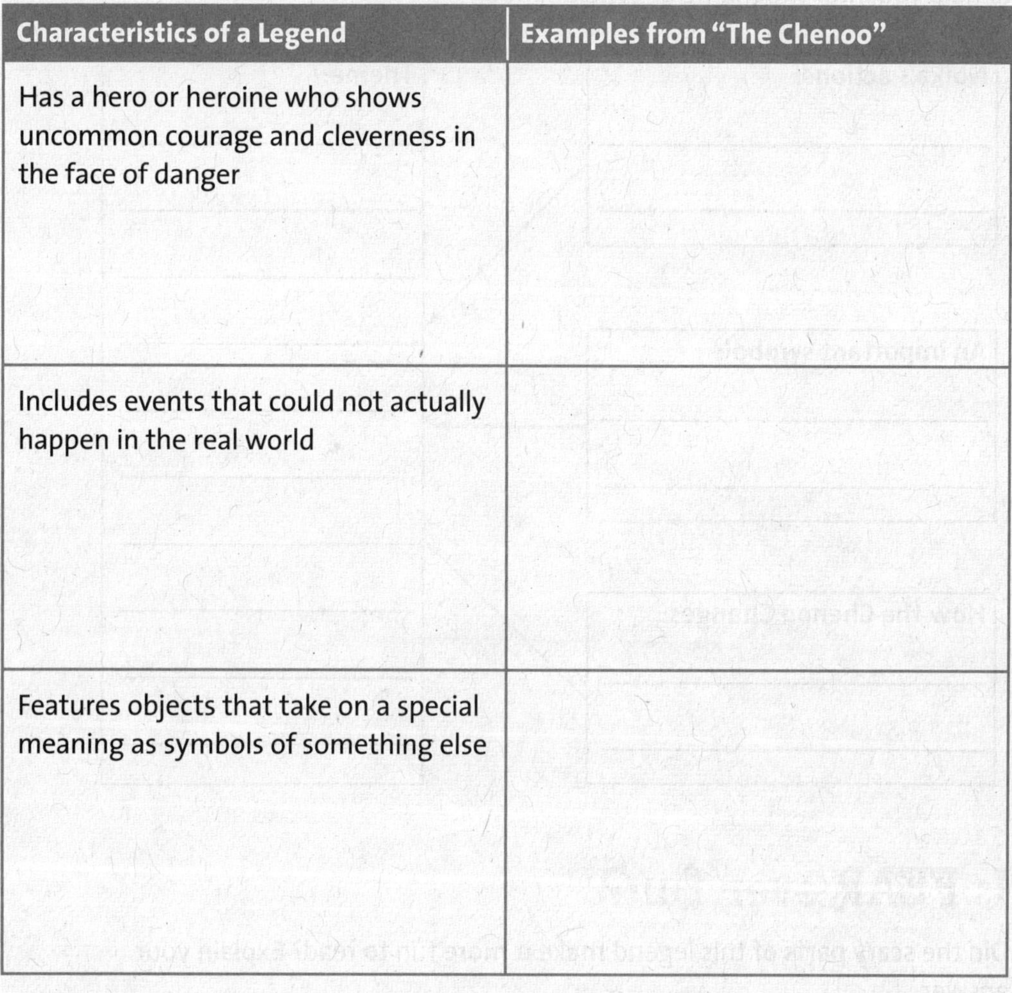

Characteristics of a Legend	Examples from "The Chenoo"
Has a hero or heroine who shows uncommon courage and cleverness in the face of danger	
Includes events that could not actually happen in the real world	
Features objects that take on a special meaning as symbols of something else	

Review your notes for "The Chenoo" and the chart you have just completed. Which part of the legend did you find the most interesting or memorable? Explain why it captured your attention.

____

____

____

____

____

____

____

READING 3A Infer the implicit theme of a work of fiction. **RC-6(D)** Make inferences about text.

Reading Skill: Make Inferences

Thinking about the characters, events, and symbols in a legend can help you infer its **theme,** or message about life or human nature. Complete this chart to help you infer the theme of "The Chenoo."

Nolka's actions:

____

____

An important symbol:

____

____

How the Chenoo Changes:

____

____

Theme:

____

____

____

____

____

____

____

____

____

Is FEAR ever fun?

Did the scary parts of this legend make it more fun to read? Explain your answer.

____

____

____

Vocabulary Practice

Circle the word or phrase that is most closely related to each boldfaced vocabulary word.

1. **proceed:** **(a)** continue, **(b)** halt, **(c)** pause
2. **sibling:** **(a)** friend, **(b)** father, **(c)** brother
3. **inspect:** **(a)** ignore, **(b)** refuse, **(c)** examine
4. **clearing:** **(a)** grove of trees, **(b)** open land, **(c)** thick jungle

Academic Vocabulary in Writing

READING 3 Analyze, make inferences, and draw conclusions about theme and genre in different cultural and historical contexts. 3A Infer the implicit theme of a work of fiction. 3B Analyze the function of stylistic elements in traditional literature from various cultures. RC-6(D) Make inferences about text.

circumstance	contribute	element	significant	tradition

Think about the character Nolka. What is her most **significant** trait, and what does it **contribute** to the legend as a whole? Use at least two Academic Vocabulary words in your response. Definitions of these words are on page 231.

____

____

____

____

Texas Assessment Practice

DIRECTIONS Use "The Chenoo" to answer questions 1–6.

1 The brothers infer from the Chenoo's footprints that he is —

(A) an old man in disguise
(B) a huge monster that eats people
(C) an animal they would like to hunt
(D) a member of their family

2 Why do the brothers run back to camp after inspecting the footprints?

(F) They are running away from the Chenoo.
(G) They are eager to meet their grandfather.
(H) They want to get their weapons.
(J) They want to protect their sister.

3 Nolka's plan to escape the Chenoo shows that she is —

(A) generous
(B) clever
(C) fearful
(D) powerful

4 The siblings cannot run away from the Chenoo because —

(F) he has trapped them in the sweat lodge
(G) they have forgotten how to get home
(H) he keeps demanding more rocks and water
(J) they are too frightened to move

5 The icy heart that the Chenoo coughs up is a symbol of —

(A) the evil part of the monster's character
(B) the siblings' grandfather who has died
(C) the love that Nolka feels for the Chenoo
(D) the Chenoo's desire to eat the siblings

6 Which of the following helps reveal the legend's theme?

(F) the brothers' fear of the Chenoo
(G) the way the Chenoo changes
(H) Nolka's cleaning of the elk hide
(J) the Chenoo's loud, rumbling voice

READING 12B Interpret factual, quantitative, or technical information presented in maps and timelines.

The Passamaquoddy

Article

Background

"The Chenoo" is a legend from the Passamaquoddy, a northeast American Indian people. The following article presents information about the Passamaquoddy. As you read, note the information conveyed by the map and timeline.

Skill Focus: Interpret Maps and Timelines

Information can be communicated not only with words but also with **graphic aids**—visual tools that are printed, handwritten, or drawn. Graphic aids make complex information easier to understand because you can immediately see how facts are related to each other. Maps and timelines are two examples of graphic aids. A **map** represents a geographic region, such as a state or a country.

- Physical maps illustrate the natural landscape of an area. They often use shading to indicate **relief** (mountains, hills, and valleys).
- Maps often include a **legend,** or key, that explains symbols, lines, and shadings used on the map.
- A map's **compass rose,** or directional indicator, shows north, south, east, and west.

A **timeline** shows events in chronological order, or the order in which they happened. Events are listed along a horizontal or vertical line, and each event is usually labeled with the year in which it occurred.

As you read, use a chart like the one below to record key facts you learn about the Passamaquoddy from the map and from the timeline.

Information About The Passamaquoddy	
From the Map	From the Timeline

The PASSAMAQUODDY

The legend of "The Chenoo" has been passed down from generation to generation by the Passamaquoddy people of northeastern North America. The early Passamaquoddy moved from place to place throughout the year to follow the herds of animals they hunted.

Despite their frequent movement, the Passamaquoddy remained within one general region. Their eastern location allowed them to be among the first to see the rising sun each day. Because of this, they became known as "People of the Dawn."

A

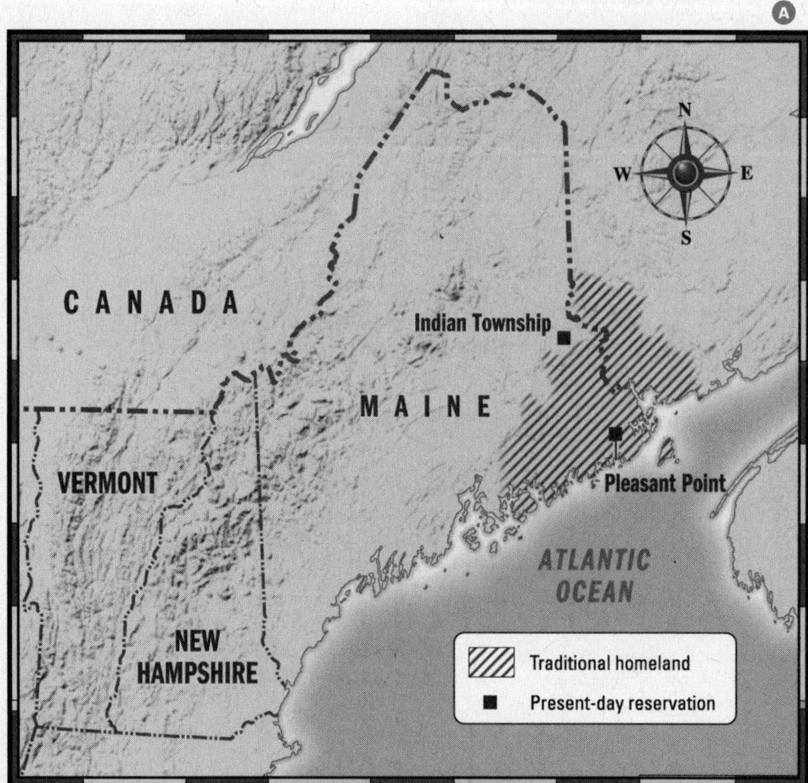

SET A PURPOSE FOR READING

Read the article and timeline to learn what caused the Passamaquoddy lands to shrink over time.

FOCUS ON FORM

The purpose of a nonfiction **article** is to present facts about a specific topic. This article is combined with a map and a timeline to give readers information about the Passamaquoddy people.

A INTERPRET MAPS

On the **map,** label the following features: **relief, legend, compass rose.** Then underline the facts in the article (lines 1–16) that are illustrated by the map. What else do you learn about the lands of the Passamaquoddy from the map? Record two facts in the chart below.

From the Map

Today, Passamaquoddy reservations are located in eastern Maine in two locations: Pleasant Point and Indian Township. These reservations are within the same region where previous generations of Passamaquoddy people lived and traveled.

PAUSE & REFLECT

PAUSE & REFLECT
What facts about the Passamaquoddy surprised you? Explain.

Timeline of Passamaquoddy History B

1400 Passamaquoddy are part of 20,000 Native Americans living in the area now known as Maine.

1604 French explorer Samuel de Champlain makes contact with Passamaquoddy, opening up period of trade with Europe. Passamaquoddy population is about 2,000.

1616 European diseases spread among Passamaquoddy and other Maine tribes, causing a pandemic called the "Great Dying." Passamaquoddy population goes down to about 150.

1701 Passamaquoddy join with other Maine tribes to form Wabanaki Confederacy, a protection against enemies.

1776 Many Passamaquoddy fight alongside American Colonists against the British in the Revolutionary War.

1820 Maine becomes a state; Passamaquoddy reservations are created at Indian Township and Pleasant Point.

1954 Passamaquoddy are granted right to vote in national elections.

1972 Passamaquoddy, together with Penobscot Nation, file a lawsuit against the Federal government, claiming that over 12 million acres of their land were taken in treaties that violated the law.

1980 President Jimmy Carter signs Maine Indian Land Claims Settlement Act. Penobscots and Passamaquoddys are given a 27 million dollar trust fund and 300,000 acres of land.

Present Passamaquoddy number about 3,500 and own more than 200,000 acres of land in Maine. A strong cultural revival seeks to keep alive the language, stories, and customs of the people.

B INTERPRET TIMELINES
As you read the timeline, circle two entries that match what you have already learned about the Passamaquoddy from the article and the map. Then place a star next to two entries that give you new information about the Passamaquoddy.

READING 12B Interpret factual, quantitative, or technical information presented in maps and timelines.

Practicing Your Skills

You've now gathered information about the Passamaquoddy from the article. Think about what each text element added to your understanding of Passamaquoddy history and culture. In the chart below, briefly describe the information presented in each source. Then tell why the source was especially useful.

Source	Information It Provides	Why Source Is Useful
Text		
Map		
Timeline		

Academic Vocabulary In Speaking

circumstance	contribute	element	significant	tradition

READING 12B Interpret factual, quantitative, or technical information presented in maps and timelines.

TURN AND TALK Which text **element**—the article, the map, or the timeline—**contributed** the most to your understanding of Passamaquoddy history and culture? Explain your answer to a partner. Use at least two Academic Vocabulary words in your discussion. Definitions of these words are on page 231.

Texas Assessment Practice

DIRECTIONS Use the article about the Passamaquoddy to answer questions 1–6.

1 The Passamaquoddy became known as "People of the Dawn" because they —

- (A) liked to begin their hunting at dawn
- (B) were the first to see the morning light
- (C) arrived in North America at the dawning of a new age
- (D) held religious ceremonies in the early morning

2 The map shows that the two Passamaquoddy reservations are —

- (F) placed in the center of their traditional homeland
- (G) slightly larger than their traditional homeland
- (H) located in the same region as their traditional homeland
- (J) far away from their traditional homeland

3 According to the map, the traditional Passamaquoddy homeland covered areas known today as —

- (A) Maine and New Hampshire
- (B) Vermont and New Hampshire
- (C) Vermont and Canada
- (D) Maine and Canada

4 According to the timeline, which event happened first?

- (F) The Passamaquoddy could vote in national elections.
- (G) The Passamaquoddy joined the Wabanaki Confederacy.
- (H) A pandemic reduced the Passamaquoddy population to 150.
- (J) Indian Township and Pleasant Point reservations were created.

5 Both the map and the timeline indicate that —

- (A) the Passamaquoddy lived in the region now called Maine
- (B) Pleasant Point is farther east than Indian Township
- (C) the early Passamaquoddy moved from place to place
- (D) Maine became a state in 1820

6 About how many Passamaquoddy live in the United States today?

- (F) 20,000
- (G) 3,500
- (H) 2,000
- (J) 150

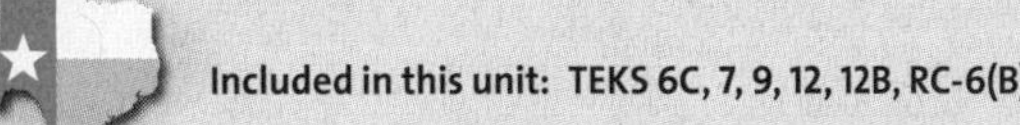
Included in this unit: TEKS 6C, 7, 9, 12, 12B, RC-6(B)

Life Stories

BIOGRAPHY AND AUTOBIOGRAPHY

Be sure to read the Reader's Workshop on pp. 802–807 in *Holt McDougal Literature*.

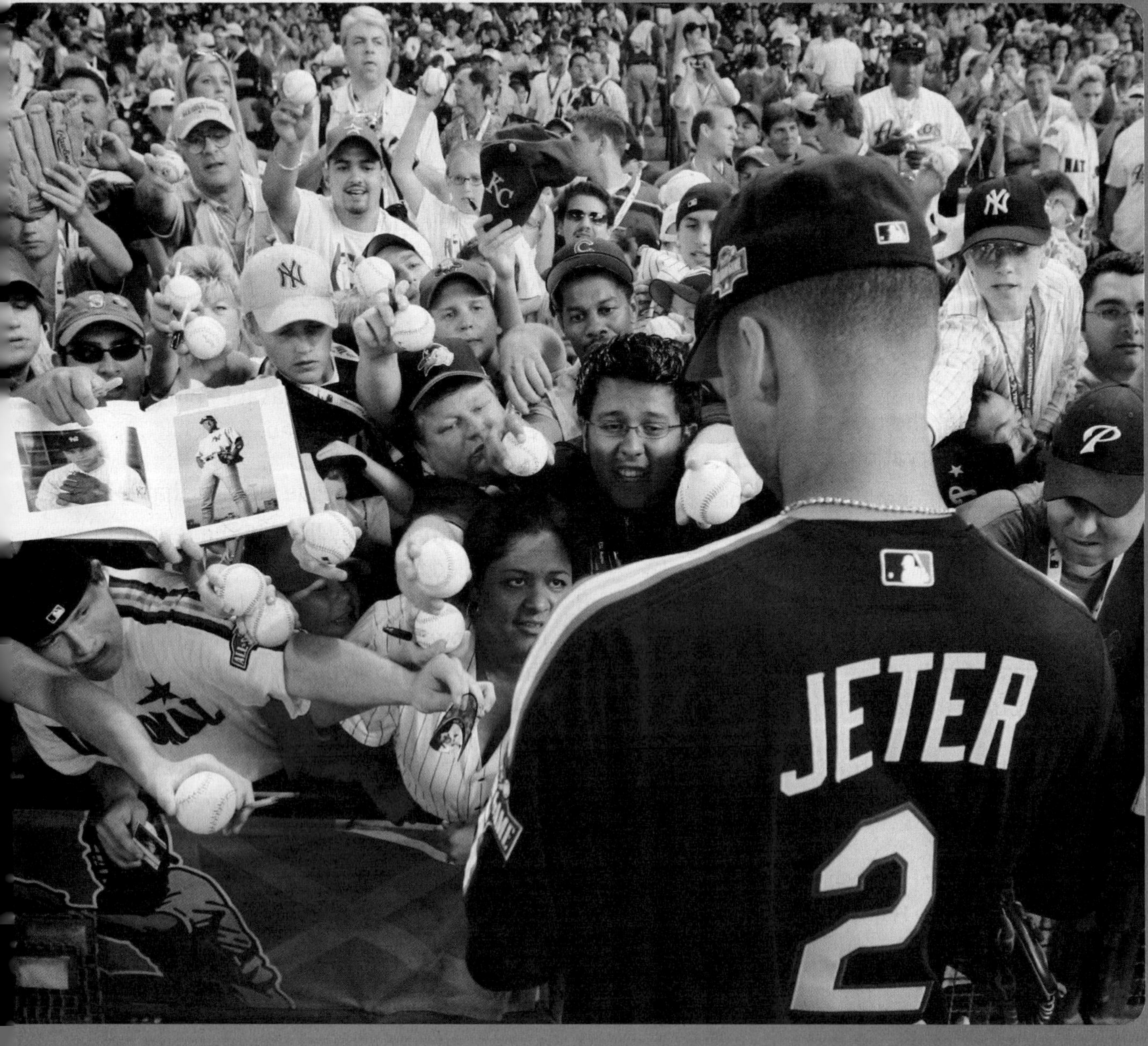

Academic Vocabulary for Unit 7

Academic Vocabulary is the language you use to discuss literary and informational texts. Preview the following Academic Vocabulary words. You will use these words as you write and talk about the selections in this unit.

achieve (ə-chēv′) *v.* to bring about an intended result; accomplish

*Did the writer **achieve** his goal of showing readers what this person was like?*

appreciate (ə-prē′shē-āt) *v.* to think highly of; to recognize favorably the quality or value of

*Many people **appreciate** this author's style.*

characteristics (kăr′ək-tər-ĭs′tĭks) *n.* features or qualities that help identify, describe, or recognize something

*Compare the **characteristics** of each type of nonfiction.*

conclude (kən-klo͞od′) *v.* to form an opinion about something based on evidence, experience, or reasoning

*Based on the dialogue, what can you **conclude** about the conflict between the characters?*

obvious (ŏb′vē-əs) *adj.* easy to see or understand

*Although the answer may seem **obvious,** reread the question to make sure you have understood it correctly.*

Think about a book or movie you recently enjoyed. What did you **appreciate** about it? Describe why you liked it on the lines below. Use at least one Academic Vocabulary word in your response.

____

____

____

Before Reading

READING 7 Understand, make inferences, and draw conclusions about the varied structural patterns and features of literary nonfiction.

Matthew Henson at the Top of the World

Biography by **Jim Haskins**

Why attempt the IMPOSSIBLE?

Sailing across the ocean. Taking a walk on the moon. Once, these things were thought to be impossible. Then someone had the courage to try what had never been done. In the following selection, you will see how a young explorer's determination helped him achieve something nobody had done before.

LIST IT What do you want to accomplish in your lifetime? Write down one of your biggest ambitions in the notebook at the left. Then brainstorm different things you could do to make that possible.

My Ambition

____

Steps I Could Take

1. read books about space
2. __________
3. __________
4. __________
5. __________

Literary Analysis: Biography

A **biography** is a true account of a person's life, written by another person. Since no two writers are the same, every biography is unique—even two different biographies about the same person. Still, all biographies share some characteristics.

Characteristics of a Biography
• written from the third-person point of view
• based on information from many sources, including books about the subject, the subject's journals and letters, and interviews
• sometimes includes details provided by the subject

As you read the biography of Matthew Henson, look for these elements.

Reading Skill: Compare and Contrast

When you **compare and contrast,** you identify the ways in which two or more subjects are alike and different. As you read the following biography, you will be asked to compare and contrast the explorers Matthew Henson and Robert Peary, as shown in the example below. Some points you may want to consider are family background, education, and personal motivation.

Henson	Both	Peary
grew up in Washington,	love the Sea	grew up in Maine

Vocabulary in Context

Note: Words are listed in the order in which they appear in the selection.

expedition (ĕk'spĭ-dĭsh'ən) *n.* a journey taken by a group with a definite goal
*Their **expedition** to the North Pole began in 1908.*

manifestation (măn'ə-fĕ-stā'shən) *n.* evidence that something is present
*His lack of money was a **manifestation** of prejudice.*

resourcefulness (rĭ-sôrs'fəl-nĕs) *n.* the ability to act effectively, even in difficult situations
*His difficult early years taught him **resourcefulness.***

ardent (är'dnt) *adj.* having strong enthusiasm or devotion
*This biography will show you that Matthew Henson was an **ardent** adventurer.*

feasibility (fē'zə-bĭl-ə-tē') *n.* the possibility of something's being accomplished
*First, Henson studied the **feasibility** of the expedition.*

prestige (prĕ-stēzh') *n.* recognition; fame
*If they succeeded, they would win **prestige** and fame.*

Vocabulary Practice

Review the vocabulary words and their meanings, and use at least two of the words to describe an expedition taken by two adventurers.

SET A PURPOSE FOR READING

Read this biography to find out about Matthew Henson's achievements.

Matthew Henson

AT THE TOP OF THE WORLD

Biography by

JIM HASKINS

BACKGROUND The Arctic is the area north of the Arctic Circle, 66° north latitude. The Dutch and the English began exploring the Arctic in the early 1500s. They hoped to find a trade route to Asia. In early Arctic exploration, ships often became trapped in the ice, and many sailors lost their lives. By the late 1800s, nearly all of the Arctic had been explored. Groups began to set records, pushing farther north each time. The race to reach the North Pole became an international competition.

While the explorers of the American West faced many dangers in their travels, at least game and water were usually plentiful; and if winter with its cold and snow overtook them, they could, in time, expect warmth and spring. For Matthew Henson, in his explorations with Robert Peary at the North Pole, this was hardly the case. In many ways, to forge ahead into the icy Arctic took far greater stamina[1] and courage than did the earlier explorers' travels, and Henson possessed such hardiness. As Donald

1. **stamina** (stăm′ə-nə): physical strength or endurance.

MacMillan, a member of the **expedition**, was later to write: “Peary knew Matt Henson’s real worth. . . . Highly respected by the Eskimos, he was easily the most popular man on board ship. . . . Henson . . . was of more real value to our Commander than [expedition members] Bartlett, Marvin, Borup, Goodsell and myself all put together. Matthew Henson went to the Pole with Peary because he was a better man than any one of us.” A

Matthew Henson was born on August 8, 1866, in Charles County, Maryland, some forty-four miles south of Washington, D.C. His parents were poor, free tenant farmers[2] who barely eked a living from the sandy soil. The Civil War had ended the year before Matthew was born, bringing with it a great deal of bitterness on the part of former slave-owners. One **manifestation** of this hostility was the terrorist activity on the part of the Ku Klux Klan in Maryland. Many free and newly freed blacks had suffered at the hands of this band of night riders. Matthew’s father, Lemuel Henson, felt it was only a matter of time before the Klan turned its vengeful eyes on his family. That, and the fact that by farming he was barely able to support them, caused him to decide to move north to Washington, D.C.

At first, things went well for the Henson family, but then Matthew’s mother died and his father found himself unable to care for Matthew. The seven-year-old boy was sent to live with his uncle, a kindly man who welcomed him and enrolled him in the N Street School. Six years later, however, another blow fell; his uncle himself fell upon hard times and could no longer support Matthew. The boy couldn’t return to his father, because Lemuel had recently died. Alone, homeless, and penniless, Matthew was forced to fend for himself. B

2. **tenant farmers:** farmers who rent the land they work and live on and pay rent in cash or crops.

Monitor Your Comprehension

expedition (ĕk′spĭ-dĭsh′ən) *n.* a journey taken by a group with a definite goal

A COMPARE AND CONTRAST

Reread lines 11–17. Underline details that tell how Henson compared to other expedition members. What does this quotation tell you about Henson's contributions to the expedition?

manifestation (măn′ə-fĕ-stā′shən) *n.* evidence that something is present

B BIOGRAPHY

Reread lines 18–42. What events shaped Henson's early life?

resourcefulness (rĭ-sôrs'fəl-nĕs) *n.* the ability to act effectively, even in difficult situations

C BIOGRAPHY
Circle words and phrases that describe Henson's thoughts and feelings in lines 50–62. What inspired Henson to become an explorer?

Matthew Henson was a bright boy and a hard worker, although he had only a sixth-grade education. Calling upon his own **resourcefulness**, he found a job as a dishwasher in a small restaurant owned by a woman named Janey Moore. When Janey discovered that Matthew had no place to stay, she fixed a cot for him in the kitchen; Matthew had found a home again.

Matthew Henson didn't want to spend his life waiting on people and washing dishes, however, no matter how kind Janey was. He had seen enough of the world through his schoolbooks to want more, to want adventure. This desire was reinforced by the men who frequented the restaurant—sailors from many ports, who spun tales of life on the ocean and of strange and wonderful places. As Henson listened, wide-eyed, to their stories, he decided, as had so many boys before him, that the life of a sailor with its adventures and dangers was for him. Having made up his mind, the fourteen-year-old packed up what little he owned, bade good-bye to Janey, and was off to Baltimore to find a ship. **C**

Although Matthew Henson's early life seems harsh, in many ways he was very lucky. When he arrived in Baltimore, he signed on as a cabin boy on the *Katie Hines*, the master of which was a Captain Childs. For many sailors at that time, life at sea was brutal and filled with hard work, deprivation, and a "taste of the cat": whipping. The captains of many vessels were petty despots,[3] ruling with an iron hand and having little regard for a seaman's health or safety. Matthew was fortunate to find just the opposite in Childs.

Captain Childs took the boy under his wing. Although Matthew of course had to do the work he was assigned, Captain Childs took a fatherly interest in him. Having an excellent private library on the ship, the captain saw to Matthew's education, insisting that he read widely in

3. **petty despots** (dĕs'pəts): leaders who insist on absolute power and mistreat people.

Monitor Your Comprehension

geography, history, mathematics, and literature while they were at sea.

The years on the *Katie Hines* were good ones for Matthew Henson. During that time he saw China, Japan, the Philippines, France, Africa, and southern Russia; he sailed through the Arctic to Murmansk. But in 1885 it all ended; Captain Childs fell ill and died at sea. Unable to face staying on the *Katie Hines* under a new skipper, Matthew left the ship at Baltimore and found a place on a fishing schooner bound for Newfoundland. D

Now, for the first time, Henson encountered the kind of unthinking cruelty and tyranny so often found on ships at that time. The ship was filthy, the crew surly and resentful of their black shipmate, and the captain a dictator. As soon as he was able, Matthew left the ship in Canada and made his way back to the United States, finally arriving in Washington, D.C., only to find that things there had changed during the years he had been at sea.

Opportunities for blacks had been limited when Henson had left Washington in 1871, but by the time he returned they were almost nonexistent. Post—Civil War reconstruction had failed, bringing with its failure a great deal of bitter resentment toward blacks. Jobs were scarce, and the few available were menial ones. Matthew finally found a job as a stock clerk in a clothing and hat store, B. H. Steinmetz and Sons, bitterly wondering if this was how he was to spend the rest of his life. But his luck was still holding. E

Steinmetz recognized that Matthew Henson was bright and hardworking. One day Lieutenant Robert E. Peary, a young navy officer, walked into the store, looking for tropical hats. After being shown a number of hats, Peary unexpectedly offered Henson a job as his personal servant. Steinmetz had recommended him, Peary said, but the job

D BIOGRAPHY
Reread lines 72–86. Underline details about Henson's first job on a ship. Which details seem most significant?

E BIOGRAPHY
The biographer emphasizes Henson's luck in lines 64 and 103. Do you think Henson's character may have contributed to his luck? Explain.

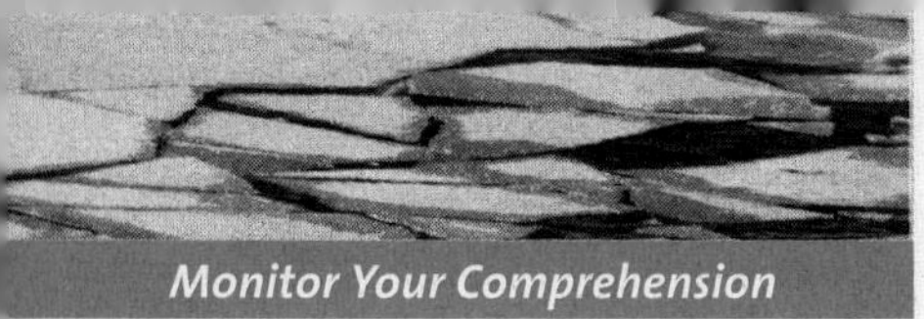

wouldn't be easy. He was bound for Nicaragua to head an engineering survey team. Would Matthew be willing to put up with the discomforts and hazards of such a trip? Thinking of the adventure and opportunities offered, Henson eagerly said yes, little realizing that a partnership had just been formed that would span years and be filled with exploration, danger, and fame.

Robert E. Peary was born in Cresson, Pennsylvania, in 1856, but was raised in Maine, where his mother had returned after his father's death in 1859. After graduating from Bowdoin College, Peary worked as a surveyor[4] for four years and in 1881 joined the navy's corps of civil engineers. One result of his travels for the navy and of his reading was an **ardent** desire for adventure. "I shall not be satisfied," Peary wrote to his mother, "until my name is known from one end of the earth to the other." This was a goal Matthew Henson could understand. As he later said, "I recognized in [Peary] the qualities that made me willing to engage myself in his service." In November 1887, Henson and Peary set sail for Nicaragua, along with forty-five other engineers and a hundred black Jamaicans.

Peary's job was to study the **feasibility** of digging a canal across Nicaragua (that canal that would later be dug across the Isthmus of Panama). The survey took until June of 1888, when the surveying party headed back to the United States. Henson knew he had done a good job for Peary, but, even as they started north, Peary said nothing to him about continuing on as his servant. It was a great surprise, then, when one day Peary approached Henson with a proposition. He wanted to try to raise money for an expedition to the Arctic, and he wanted Henson to accompany him. Henson quickly accepted, saying he would go whether Peary could pay him or not.

ardent (är′dnt) *adj.* having strong enthusiasm or devotion

According to Peary's letter to his mother (lines 123–125), what else besides adventure did he have an **ardent** desire for?

feasibility (fē′zə-bĭl-ə-tē′) *n.* the possibility of something's being accomplished

4. **surveyor:** one who measures the boundaries of lands, areas, or surface features.

“It was in June, 1891, that I started on my first trip to the Arctic regions, as a member of what was known as the ‘North Greenland Expedition,’” Matthew Henson later wrote. So began the first of five expeditions on which Henson would accompany Peary. (F)

During this first trip to Greenland, on a ship named *Kite*, Peary discovered how valuable Henson was to any expedition. He reported that Henson was able to establish “a friendly relationship with the Eskimoes, who believed him to be somehow related to them because of his brown skin. . . .” Peary’s expedition was also greatly aided by Henson’s expert handling of the Eskimoes, dogs, and equipment. Henson also hunted with the Eskimoes for meat for the expedition and cooked under the supervision of Josephine Peary, Robert’s wife. On the expedition’s return to New York, September 24, 1892, Peary wrote, “Henson, my faithful colored boy, a hard worker and apt at anything, . . . showed himself . . . the equal of others in the party.” (G)

This first expedition to the Arctic led to several others, but it was with the 1905 expedition that Peary first tried to find that mystical[5] point, the North Pole, the sole goal of the 1908 expedition.

On July 6, 1908, the *Roosevelt* sailed from New York City. Aboard it were the supplies and men for an expedition to reach the North Pole. Accompanying Peary were Captain Robert Bartlett and Ross Marvin, who had been with Peary on earlier expeditions; George Borup, a young graduate from Yale and the youngest member of the group; Donald MacMillan, a teacher; and a doctor, J. W. Goodsell. And, of course, Matthew Henson. In Greenland the group was joined by forty-one Eskimos and 246 dogs, plus the supplies. “The ship,” Henson wrote, “is now in a most

5. **mystical:** associated with a sense of wonder or mystery.

Monitor Your Comprehension

(F) COMPARE AND CONTRAST

Reread lines 117–147. Use the graphic below to explain similarities and differences between Peary and Henson. Compare and contrast Henson's childhood, education, and motivations for becoming an explorer.

Similarities

↓

Differences

(G) BIOGRAPHY

Reread lines 148–161. Circle the qualities that Peary says make Henson a valuable member of the expedition team.

Monitor Your Comprehension

PAUSE & REFLECT

Reread lines 182–202. How did Henson and Peary react to difficulties on the expedition?

perfect state of dirtiness." On September 5, the Roosevelt arrived at Cape Sheridan and the group began preparing for their journey, moving supplies north to Cape Columbia by dog sled to establish a base camp. Peary named the camp Crane City in honor of Zenas Crane, who had contributed $10,000 to the expedition.

The plan was to have two men, Bartlett and Borup, go ahead of the rest of the group to cut a trail stretching from the base camp to the North Pole. On February 28, the two men set out, and on March 1, the remainder of the expedition started north, following the trail Bartlett and Borup had cut the day before. At first, trouble seemed to plague them. On the first day, three of the sledges broke, Henson's among them. Fortunately, Henson was able to repair them, despite the fact that it was nearly 50 degrees below zero.

As the days passed, further trouble came the way of the expedition. Several times they encountered leads—open channels of water—and were forced to wait until the ice closed over before proceeding. On March 14, Peary decided to send Donald MacMillan and Dr. Goodsell back to the base camp. MacMillan could hardly walk, because he had frozen a heel when his foot had slipped into one of the leads. Dr. Goodsell was exhausted. As the expedition went on, more men were sent back due to exhaustion and frostbite. George Borup was sent back on March 20, and, on the 26th, so was Ross Marvin. PAUSE & REFLECT

Although the expedition had encountered problems with subzero temperatures, with open water, and in handling the dogs, they had had no real injuries. On Ross Marvin's return trip to the base camp, however, he met with tragedy. On his journey, Marvin was accompanied by two Eskimos.

Monitor Your Comprehension

He told them that he would go ahead to scout the trail. About an hour later, the Eskimos came upon a hole in the ice; floating in it was Marvin's coat. Marvin had gone through thin ice and, unable to save himself, had drowned or frozen. The Peary expedition had suffered its first—and fortunately its last—fatality.

By April 1, Peary had sent back all of the original expedition except for four Eskimos and Matthew Henson. When Bartlett, the last man to be sent back, asked Peary why he didn't also send Henson, Peary replied, "I can't get along without him." The remnant of the original group pushed on. Ⓗ

We had been travelling eighteen to twenty hours out of every twenty-four. Man, that was killing work! Forced marches all the time. From all our other expeditions we had found out that we couldn't carry food for more than fifty days, fifty-five at a pinch. . . .

We used to travel by night and sleep in the warmest part of the day. I was ahead most of the time with two of the Eskimos.

So Matthew Henson described the grueling[6] journey. Finally, on the morning of April 6, Peary called a halt. Henson wrote: "I was driving ahead and was swinging around to the right. . . . The Commander, who was about 50 feet behind me, called to me and said we would go into camp. . . ." In fact, both Henson and Peary felt they might have reached the Pole already. That day, Peary took readings with a **sextant** and determined that they were within three miles of the Pole. Later he sledged ten miles north and found he was traveling south; to return to camp, Peary would have to return north and then head south in another direction—something that could only happen at the North Pole. To be absolutely sure, the next day Peary

Ⓗ BIOGRAPHY
Reread lines 214–219, underlining the words in quotation marks. Why do you think the author uses Peary's exact words?

VISUAL VOCABULARY
sextant (sĕk′stənt) *n.* a tool that measures one's location based on the position of the sun, the moon, or a star

6. **grueling** (gro͞o′ə-lĭng): physically or mentally demanding; exhausting.

again took readings from solar observations. It was the North Pole, he was sure.

On that day Robert Peary had Matthew Henson plant the American flag at the North Pole. Peary then cut a piece from the flag and placed it and two letters in a glass jar that he left at the Pole. The letters read:

90 N. Lat., North Pole
April 6, 1909
Arrived here today, 27 marches from C. Columbia.

I have with me 5 men, Matthew Henson, colored, Ootah, Egingwah, Seegloo, and Ooqueah, Eskimos; 5 sledges and 38 dogs. My ship, the S.S. Roosevelt, is in winter quarters at Cape Sheridan, 90 miles east of Columbia.

*The expedition under my command which has succeeded in reaching the Pole is under the auspices[7] of the Peary Arctic Club of New York City, and has been fitted out and sent north by members and friends of the Club for the purpose of securing this geographical prize, if possible, for the honor and **prestige** of the United States of America.*

The officers of the Club are Thomas H. Hubbard of New York, President; Zenas Crane, of Mass., Vice-president; Herbert L. Bridgman, of New York, Secretary and Treasurer.

I start back for Cape Columbia tomorrow.

Robert E. Peary
United States Navy ❶

prestige (prĕ-stēzh′) *n.* recognition; fame

❶ **BIOGRAPHY**
Recall that biographers often include quotations by people who know the subject. Why do you think the author includes this letter in Henson's biography?

90 N. Lat., North Pole
April 6, 1909

I have today hoisted the national ensign[8] of the United States of America at this place, which my observations indicate to be the North Polar axis of the earth, and have formally

7. **auspices** (ô′spĭ-sĭz): protection or support.
8. **hoisted the national ensign:** raised the flag.

taken possession of the entire region, and adjacent,[9] *for and in the name of the President of the United States of America.*

I leave this record and United States flag in possession.

Robert E. Peary
United States Navy

Having accomplished their goal, the small group set out on the return journey. It was, Matthew Henson wrote, "17 days of haste, toil, and misery. . . . We crossed lead after lead, sometimes like a bareback rider in the circus, balancing on cake after cake of ice." Finally they reached the *Roosevelt*, where they could rest and eat well at last. The Pole had been conquered!

During the return trip to New York City, Henson became increasingly puzzled by Peary's behavior. "Not once in [three weeks]," Henson wrote, "did he speak a word to me. Then he . . . ordered me to get to work. Not a word about the North Pole or anything connected with it." Even when the *Roosevelt* docked in New York in September of 1909, Peary remained withdrawn and silent, saying little to the press and quickly withdrawing to his home in Maine. The ostensible reason for his silence was that when the group returned to New York, they learned that Dr. Frederick A. Cook was claiming that he had gone to the North Pole—and done so before Peary reached it. Peary told his friends that he wished to wait for his own proofs to be validated by the scientific societies before he spoke. He felt sure that Cook would not be able to present the kinds of evidence that he could present, and so it proved. **PAUSE & REFLECT**

On December 15, Peary was declared the first to reach the North Pole; Cook could not present adequate evidence that he had made the discovery. Peary and Bartlett

9. **adjacent** (ə-jā'sənt): close to or next to.

Monitor Your Comprehension

PAUSE & REFLECT
Reread lines 282–297, underlining the words in quotations. What does the quote suggest about how Peary's behavior may have made Henson feel?

Monitor Your Comprehension

J COMPARE AND CONTRAST

Reread lines 298–314. Circle details that identify how Peary and Henson were recognized for their achievement. What is the difference between the way the men on the expedition view Henson's contributions and the way the public viewed them?

were awarded gold medals by the National Geographic Society; Henson was not. Because Henson was black, his contributions to the expedition were not recognized for many years.

After 1909, Henson worked in a variety of jobs. For a while, he was a parking-garage attendant in Brooklyn, and at the age of forty-six, he became a clerk in the U.S. Customs House in Lower Manhattan. In the meantime, friends tried again and again to have his contributions to the expedition recognized. At last, in 1937, nearly thirty years after the expedition, he was invited to join the Explorers Club in New York, and in 1944, Congress authorized a medal for all of the men on the expedition, including Matthew Henson. J

After his death in New York City on March 9, 1955, another lasting tribute was made to Henson's endeavors. In 1961, his home state of Maryland placed a bronze tablet in memory of him in the State House. It reads, in part:

MATTHEW ALEXANDER HENSON
Co-Discoverer of the North Pole
with
Admiral Robert Edwin Peary
April 6, 1909

Son of Maryland, exemplification of courage, fortitude[10] *and patriotism, whose valiant deeds of noble devotion under the command of Admiral Robert Edwin Peary, in pioneer arctic exploration and discovery, established everlasting prestige and glory for his State and Country. . . .*

10. **fortitude:** strength of mind; courage.

Literary Analysis: Biography

READING 7 Understand, make inferences, and draw conclusions about the varied structural patterns and features of literary nonfiction.

Biographies draw their information from a variety of sources. These sources may include diaries, letters, reference books, or even photographs. In the chart below, list some of the sources Jim Haskins uses in "Matthew Henson at the Top of the World." Then tell how each source adds to your understanding of Henson's life.

Source	How It Adds to My Understanding
Quotation from Donald Macmillan	*Explained that he was liked and respected by Peary and all members of the crew.*

Based on the reading and your notes above, explain which source you think revealed the most about Henson's character.

___

___

___

___

___

Reading Skill: Compare and Contrast

Look back at the notes you took as you read. Which similarities and differences between Henson and Peary helped make them a good team? Give examples and explain your reasoning in the graphic below.

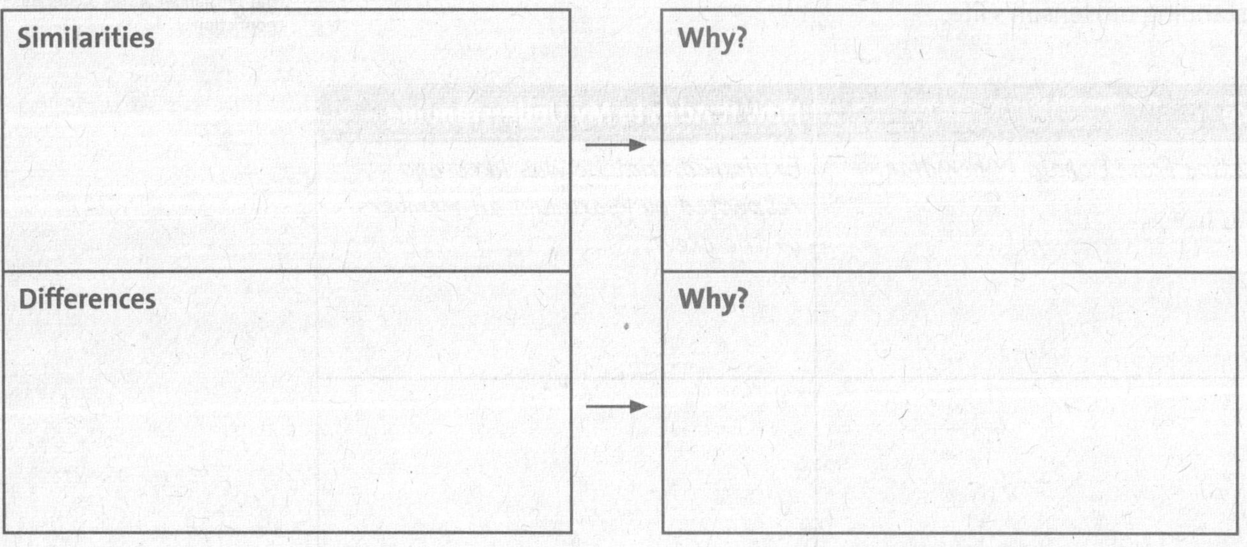

Why attempt the IMPOSSIBLE?

How do you think Matthew Hanson would answer this question?

___

___

___

Vocabulary Practice

Write the word from the box that best completes each sentence.

WORD LIST

ardent
expedition
feasibility
manifestation
prestige
resourcefulness

1. After getting lost three times, we abandoned our ________ to the lake.
2. Bill is a(n) ________ fan of that writer and has read all of her books.
3. Lucy's ________ helped her find her way back to the camp.
4. Fame and ________ are not the only reasons to be ambitious.
5. The project's ________ depends upon how much time is available.
6. The time she gives to her students is one ________ of her love of teaching.

Academic Vocabulary in Writing

READING 7 Understand, make inferences, and draw conclusions about the varied structural patterns and features of literary nonfiction.

achieve	appreciate	characteristics	conclude	obvious

What did Robert Peary hope to **achieve** in the 1908 expedition to the Arctic? Use at least two Academic Vocabulary words in your response. Definitions of these words are on page 273.

____

____

____

____

Texas Assessment Practice

DIRECTIONS Use "Matthew Henson at the Top of the World" to answer questions 1–5.

1 The author uses the first paragraph of the biography to —

- (A) explain how Captain Childs influenced Henson to return home
- (B) introduce Henson as a courageous explorer
- (C) describe the hardships of exploring the American West
- (D) provide differing viewpoints of Henson's achievements

2 Henson was inspired to become a sailor when he —

- (F) went sailing with his father as a child
- (G) heard stories about life at sea where he worked
- (H) worked as a cabin boy under Captain Childs
- (J) met a young navy officer named Robert Peary

3 The quotation in lines 151–153 is by —

- (A) Henson
- (B) Peary
- (C) Bartlett
- (D) Marvin

4 The author includes details about Henson's experience on the Katie Hines to —

- (F) explain how Captain Childs influenced Henson
- (G) describe the harshness and cruelty of life at sea
- (H) contrast the way Captain Childs and Steinmetz treated Henson
- (J) compare how black shipmates and other crew members were treated

5 Based on details in the text, Henson and Peary were both strongly influenced by —

- (A) a desire for fame
- (B) a love for adventure
- (C) living in poverty
- (D) working as cabin boys

READING 9 Analyze, make inferences, and draw conclusions about the author's purpose in cultural, historical, and contemporary contexts.

from Over the Top of the World

Journal Entries, page 291

Up and Over the Top

Personal Narrative, page 296

Background

You just learned about the hardships and challenges that faced Arctic explorers in the early 1900s. In the journal entries you are about to read you will learn how **contemporary,** or present-day, explorers led by Will Steger tackle the same journey. Then you will read a personal narrative by Bill Cosby about a challenge he set for himself when he was in middle school. As you study these selections, try to determine each author's purpose in writing about the topic of facing challenges.

Skill Focus: Analyzing an Author's Purpose

Authors write for a number of reasons. An **author's purpose** may be to

- inform
- describe
- entertain
- persuade
- reveal a truth about life
- share an experience

Authors often write nonfiction narratives—such as biographies, journals, and personal narratives—for more than one purpose. However, one purpose is usually more important than the others.

Authors rarely state their reasons for writing. To figure out an author's purpose, notice the details and descriptions the author includes and consider what these details tell you about the author's reasons for writing. As you read the following selections, notes in the side column will prompt you to record information from the text to help you determine the author's purpose. A sample is shown below.

Text	Author's Purpose
"Here are the conditions we face most days"	*to inform the audience about the conditions in the Arctic*

from Over the Top of the World by Will Steger

APRIL 10

Here are the conditions we face most days: The ice is more than three years old and thick, so leads are usually less than three feet wide. Each time we come to one we have to decide whether to try to cross over it or find a way around. There's roughly two feet of snow covering the ice, and we're traveling through an area filled with 10-to-15-foot-tall pressure ridges. . . .

APRIL 16

The temperatures continue to drop, and today was a very cold, difficult day. . . . By day's end, we and the dogs were all very tired. Ⓐ

Our goal now is to reach land in Canada sometime in July. That will mean another 100 days living in tents, eating the same frozen food, rarely bathing

SET A PURPOSE FOR READING

Read to find out about the obstacles that a modern-day Arctic explorer faces.

FOCUS ON FORM

A **journal** is a personal record of thoughts, activities, and feelings. While a journal reveals a lot about the person writing, it can also give information about the time and place in which it was written.

Ⓐ AUTHOR'S PURPOSE

Circle details that describe the conditions on the expedition. Why does the author include these details?

or changing clothes. I see why some people can't understand why we do these expeditions!

APRIL 17

We passed 89 degrees north latitude, which means we are less than 60 miles from the pole! Unlike explorers who traveled to the North Pole at the turn of the century, we are able to find out exactly where we are at any moment using a handheld computer called a Global Positioning System, or GPS. By communicating with a satellite orbiting Earth, in just minutes it can tell us our exact latitude and longitude. We use it every night to see how far we've traveled—and every morning to see how far we've drifted. . . . B

APRIL 22

We have reached the North Pole exactly as planned, on Earth Day. It's been nine years since I first dogsledded here, and I've seen and learned a lot since then. I've now traveled to both poles, North and South, and find something calm and peaceful about being at the top, or the bottom, of the world. . . .

We were greeted by a small group of friends who had flown up for the occasion with our resupply. We spent the morning having our pictures taken while our fingers and toes nearly froze. . . .

Our friends have brought supplies with them, including letters and small gifts from our families, whom we haven't seen for two months. In addition, they carried with them 15 more days of food and fuel, a half-dozen waterproof bags, and some boards and plastic necessary for repairing our sleds, which have been quite punished by the rough ice. . . . But I got the

B AUTHOR'S PURPOSE
What do you learn in the April 17 entry? Why does Steger provide this information?

best present—an apple pie baked by my mother back in Minneapolis.

APRIL 24

So far, the most surprising aspect of the whole trip is all the snow. Most years the Arctic is like a desert, with very little precipitation. This year is different. It snows almost every day! Even when the skies are clear, there is a light sprinkling. Some storms dump five or six inches overnight. On top of that, the winds have been incredible. Temperatures have gone as low as –40°F, but the average is –20°F. Since we left Siberia, the warmest temperature was 0°F. . . . C

MAY 3

Outside this morning it's clear, –20°F, with a north wind, which is good because it is at our back. I'm looking forward to the days now, as are the dogs, who are strong and excited. It's a very simple existence we lead when we're traveling like this. . . .

One of the reasons we're here is to draw attention to the environmental problems that affect the Arctic. We are collecting snow samples along the way for scientists back home to test. On most days it's hard to believe there's pollution out here in the middle of the Arctic Ocean. But there is. In the air, the water, and the ice and, unfortunately, in the wildlife.

The pollution problems that scientists study in the Arctic are created in big industrial cities and on farms in North America, Asia, and Europe. Pollution travels through the air and water, carried by wind, river, and ocean currents. Once in the Arctic, pollutants "live" longer because of the cold conditions. Studies have

C AUTHOR'S PURPOSE

List three significant details the author includes in lines 29–58 below. Then tell which author's purpose these details support.

Details/Description
1.
2.
3.

Author's Purpose(s)

Ⓓ AUTHOR'S PURPOSE
Underline details that support the main idea of lines 60–81. How are these details different from those presented in earlier journal entries? Check which author's purpose(s) these details support below.

- [ ] to inform
- [ ] to describe
- [ ] to entertain
- [ ] to persuade
- [ ] to reveal a truth about life
- [ ] to share an experience

shown that man-made pollutants are starting to show up in Arctic animals, like seals and polar bears. So we're not affecting just the air and the water, but the animals, too. . . . Ⓓ

MAY 13

Early this morning, at 4 o'clock, we were awakened by the sound of dogs howling. All 22 of them in unison. They don't howl for no reason, so I was sure there was a polar bear nearby.

They soon quieted down, though, and I fell back asleep—only to be awakened again a half-hour later when a gigantic snap in the ice sent a shockwave rolling through camp. A tremor lifted our tents, like an earthquake rolling right beneath our sleeping bags. The air was filled with a thundering, grinding, rumbling roar, a very frightening sound, one we had not heard before. I shot out of my bag and quickly unzipped the tent door, ready to jump out in my long underwear to pull the tent to safety.

What I saw amazed me. A wall of ice, 20 feet tall and as long as a football field, was moving our way as if being pushed by the blade of a giant bulldozer. Blocks of ice as big as cars were falling off the top of the moving wall and being crushed beneath it. It moved toward us, threatening to crush us, too.

The dogs were in shock, standing perfectly still and quiet. All five of us were out of our tents, and we, too, were in shock. All we could do was watch, helplessly. Just as suddenly as it began, the wall of ice stopped, only 100 feet from our tents.

Julie has compared traveling on the Arctic Ocean to traveling on a big, floating jigsaw puzzle. This morning we watched as some of the bigger pieces shifted around. It was very powerful, and very beautiful, too. And, I admit, quite frightening. . . . **PAUSE & REFLECT**

JUNE 24

Another miserable day of hauling. It snowed throughout the day, dumping more than a foot, resulting in deep drifts coming up over our knees. All day long we slaved in a complete whiteout, pulling the sleds forward just inches at a time. In six hours, we made only three miles. No one is saying it out loud, but we're all wondering if we'll ever make it to land. . . .

JULY 3

Our last morning was spent pulling the canoe-sleds up a 200-foot ridge and then riding them down the other side like toboggans. I was on the front, pushing with one leg as if I were riding a scooter, and Victor was sitting in the back, pushing with his ski poles and yelling like a little boy. It was a perfect way to end the trip—slipping and sliding and laughing.

As we pulled the last couple of miles, I could feel all the tension of the past months lift off my shoulders. I picked up the first stones I saw and rolled them in my hand, feeling their smooth hardness. When we finally saw dirt and small flowers, we kneeled and pulled them to our faces. It was perhaps the best smell I have ever had! We made it! We were all safe, finally on solid ground.

PAUSE & REFLECT

Describe Steger's thoughts and feelings about the event discussed in the May 13 entry.

SET A PURPOSE FOR READING

Read to find out about a challenge Bill Cosby faced as a boy.

FOCUS ON FORM

A **personal narrative** is an autobiographical essay written from the first-person point of view. It reflects the writer's experiences, feelings, and personality. It usually deals with a single subject and offers a snapshot of a moment in the writer's life. Personal narratives often appear in magazines and newspapers.

E PERSONAL NARRATIVE

Reread lines 1–10. What do you think the subject of Cosby's personal narrative will be?

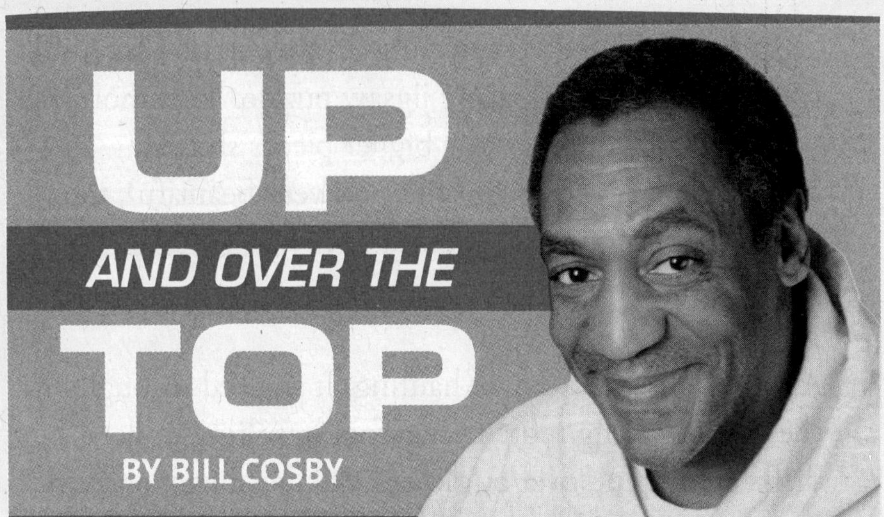

UP
AND OVER THE
TOP
BY BILL COSBY

When I was in junior high school in Philadelphia, I wasn't really interested in any other activity than watching this fellow named Sporty. That was his nickname.

One day after school I saw Sporty high-jumping. He had both high-jump stands up, three old mats to break his fall, and a bamboo pole. Sporty was jumping at 4'6". Well, at the time I was only about 5'3" and very wiry. I watched him jump, and it looked simple enough. I wanted to do it. E

Now, the way Sporty jumped and the way I jumped were two different styles. Let's say my style was a sort of running-away-from-the-scene-of-the-crime jump. Sporty's was the classic Eastern Roll.

Sporty approached his target with a certain number of steps, planted his right foot (because he was left-footed) and threw the left leg up. Then as he began to clear the bar, he flattened his body out and kicked his back leg up to keep from knocking the bar off. He also landed smoothly on his back.

So now I tried my style. Coming from the side of the bar, I ran up, stopped, planted both legs and jumped straight up. Then, bringing my knees to my chin, I came down with my behind crashing the bamboo pole. One broken pole!

This, of course, made Sporty very upset. So, I apologized and asked him if he would show me how to do it right. **PAUSE & REFLECT**

At that particular point, Mr. Richard Lister came over and offered to teach us. Mr. Lister was our gym teacher, a very kind gentleman, who had high-jumped for Temple University. I think his record was 6'9". Of course, to Sporty and me that was out of this world.

I notified my mother I would be home late because Sporty and I were high-jumping. My mother wanted to know if there was a high-jumping team. I said, "No, but Sporty and I have a great time just jumping over this bamboo pole." Then she asked me whether I had finished my homework.

I showed up after school, quickly changed my clothes, came out and saw Sporty in a gray sweat suit. First thing: Warm up! Mr. Lister gave us this set of exercises, showing us how we must bend over and do the same things we had done in gym class earlier that day. I notified Mr. Lister that I had done these exercises. Mr. Lister said, "You're going to have to do them again. You have to warm up properly. Get the blood flowing. Loosen up." This, he said, was warning

PAUSE & REFLECT
How did Cosby react to his initial failure? What do you think of this reaction?

the body that it was about to get involved in something special.

Mr. Lister decided to work on my style, because the school couldn't afford any more broken poles. I had a lot of energy and drive. This was something I really wanted to do, and I enjoyed doing it.

I knew I had the coordination, because I was one of the top gym-class athletes. Mr. Lister said, "Son, the thing you are going to have to learn is that in order to do anything well, you must start from lesson one. Then we go to lessons two, three, four, and five. After you have learned these, it may come to you that this is not necessarily the right way for you. You may then, perhaps, make some adjustments. But in the meantime, you are fighting yourself." F

So Mr. Lister and I worked on a very smooth approach to the bar at the very embarrassing height of two feet. I made my five-step approach, stopped, lifted my leg, threw my arms up, cleared the bar, and fell on my back.

Mr. Lister said, "Good." And I protested, "Yes, but look! A two-foot bar!" He said, "It is better for you to miss at two feet than to break another bar at four feet two. Look how many bars we've saved. You jump twenty times, you save twenty bars."

As the months passed, Sporty and I were both jumping at 4'6". Then Sporty moved the bar to 4'9". This was indeed a challenge. At 5'3", you may be looking eye-to-eye with a 4'9" bar. I made the approach, and as I approached I became frightened.

F AUTHOR'S PURPOSE
Underline what Mr. Lister says to Cosby in lines 56–63. What is Cosby's purpose in telling readers what his teacher said?

Not that I would hurt myself, not that I would break the bar—I became frightened because this looked like something I couldn't do.

The closer I got to the bar, the more I realized I couldn't do it. The more I accepted the fact I couldn't, the more I didn't prepare myself physically. In other words, as my mind said no, it allowed certain things to happen so my body would not give its all.

And I did exactly what I thought. I knocked the bar off. G

As a matter of fact, the first time I tried it, I remember running up, planting my foot, starting to do it, and then snatching the bar off with my left hand. I never left the ground.

I put the bar back up. Sporty ran at it, jumped, and his trail leg nicked the bar. But it stayed up. He made 4'9". Of course, Sporty and I were now competing against each other, and I figured, if Sporty can do it, I *better* do it.

I stood on my mark, started with the right foot, and took three steps. Then came that thought again: "Awfully high. You can't make it." Again as I finished the last two steps, I grabbed the bar with my left hand and put it back up. Sporty approached again, made his jump, but knocked the bar over. I felt better.

After talking to myself, I decided I could do it now. Suddenly, I realized that in being afraid to fail I was making a halfhearted attempt. H

So I tried to block all negative thoughts and remembered everything positive about myself.

G AUTHOR'S PURPOSE
Circle details that identify Cosby's thoughts and feelings and their effect on him in lines 74–88. Why does he include these details?

H AUTHOR'S PURPOSE
Reread lines 104–106. Why does Cosby tell readers how his fear continued to affect him?

I approached the bar, and for some reason none of the negative thoughts came into play. I found myself looking down on the bar, six inches over it. I had cleared that bar, and I was happy.

(What I am doing now is freezing this moment so you can get the actual feeling of what happened: I approached the bar, I planted that foot, jumped with all my might, went up and went over. I am six inches over, and I say to myself, "I'm up. I'm over. I've actually done it." Hear the great burst of applause, the cheers from all those little people in my brain. "Yea! We've done it!")

However, I had forgotten to complete the jump, so as I sailed across the bar my trail leg hit and knocked the bar off. Still, I had made the height, and I had cleared it by a good six inches!

I put the bar up quickly, came back around, and Sporty said, "You know, you really made that." We were both excited, both talking fast, and Sporty, for some reason, felt very good about what I had done.

Again I made my approach with no negative thoughts. Up. Over. Six inches over. This time I remembered to kick and clear that leg. So 4'9" was no longer a problem. I felt secure. Now I began to think about the next height. If I could do 4'9", looking down on it, how high could I go? 5'2"? Impossible! I'm 5'3". How could I jump my height? Wouldn't it be wonderful if I could?

That was a great day for me because I learned something about myself. I learned to talk to myself, reason with myself, believe in myself.

AUTHOR'S PURPOSE
Reread lines 113–120. What is Cosby's purpose in including these lines? Check off all that apply.

- ☐ to inform
- ☐ to describe
- ☐ to entertain
- ☐ to persuade
- ☐ to reveal a truth about life
- ☐ to share an experience

Self-confidence has a lot to do with one's performance—how well you perform, how much success you have and, even if you do not succeed, how much progress you are making.

You can become successful at whatever you choose to do, but first you must have some sort of feeling for it. How do you get a feeling for it? Sometimes the answer is simply "try." If you don't, you'll never know. J

J AUTHOR'S PURPOSE
Reread lines 144–147. Why does Cosby give this advice at the end of his narrative?

READING 9 Analyze, make inferences, and draw conclusions about the author's purpose in cultural, historical, and contemporary contexts.

Practicing Your Skills

Review your notes from "Over the Top of the World" and "Up and Over the Top." Use your notes to identify the main purpose of each selection. Then add details that support the purpose you've chosen.

	"Over the Top of the World"	"Up and Over the Top"
Main Purpose		
Details		

Author's Purpose

What similarities and differences do you find among the reasons each author had for writing. Support your answer with details from your chart.

Academic Vocabulary in Speaking

READING 9 Analyze, make inferences, and draw conclusions about the author's purpose in cultural, historical, and contemporary contexts.

achieve	appreciate	characteristics	conclude	obvious

TURN AND TALK How does a journal differ from a personal narrative? Discuss the **characteristics** of "Over the Top of the World" and "Up and Over the Top" with a partner. Use at least one Academic Vocabulary word in your discussion. Definitions of these words are on page 273.

Texas Assessment Practice

DIRECTIONS Use "Over the Top of the World" and "Up and Over the Top" to answer questions 1–6.

1 According to Steger's May 3 journal entry, Arctic pollution comes from —

- (A) developing countries in the tropics
- (B) expeditions by scientists and explorers
- (C) oil refineries in the eastern hemisphere
- (D) cities and farms in the northern hemisphere

2 In "Over the Top of the World," Will Steger's main purpose is to —

- (F) describe
- (G) entertain
- (H) persuade
- (J) inform

3 In the July 3 entry, Steger describes his feelings of —

- (A) fear
- (B) relief
- (C) worry
- (D) suffering

4 Cosby describes Sporty in lines 1–10 of "Up and Over the Top" to —

- (F) explain the importance of exercise
- (G) introduce the subject of his challenge
- (H) contrast how people confront their fears
- (J) share a story about a humorous incident

5 After Cosby breaks the pole in line 25, Mr. Lister —

- (A) offers to fix it
- (B) tells him to leave
- (C) offers to teach him
- (D) calls the gym teacher

6 Cosby's main purpose in "Up and Over the Top" is to —

- (F) provide information
- (G) tell an entertaining story
- (H) share an experience
- (J) reveal a truth about life

READING 6C Describe different forms of point of view, including first- and third-person. **7** Identify the literary language and devices used in an autobiography.

from The Story of My Life

Autobiography by **Helen Keller**

Do we have to accept our LIMITS?

Sometimes the things we most want to do are the hardest to accomplish. It can be discouraging to discover our limits and frustrating to face unexpected challenges. Fortunately, many serious obstacles can be overcome with creativity and determination.

QUICKWRITE Helen Keller found a way to succeed despite being both blind and deaf. Think of someone else—from your life, a book, or a movie—who also had to deal with some type of limitation. Read the sentences in the notebook to the left and fill in your answers describing this person and his or her efforts to conquer a major difficulty.

Conquering Difficulties

I admire __________

because __________

____

____

This person has conquered a major difficulty by __________

____

____

____

____

____

____

____

____

____

Literary Analysis: Autobiography

The most personal kind of nonfiction writing is **autobiography**—a writer's account of his or her own life. In biographies, the subject is a person other than the writer. In autobiographies, the writer is the subject.

Characteristics of an Autobiography
• told from the first-person point of view, using first-person pronouns (*I, me, we, us, our, my, mine*)
• includes literary language and devices (such as imagery, metaphors, and similes) to provide descriptions of people and events that have influenced the writer
• shares the writer's personal thoughts and feelings about his or her experiences
• based primarily on details that come from the subject's own memories, but may include details provided by others

As you read *The Story of My Life,* think about the information the author decides to include about herself.

Reading Strategy: Monitor

Monitoring is the process of checking your understanding as you read. One way to do this is to **ask questions** about what you have just read. As you read Helen Keller's autobiography, you will be prompted to note any passages that you find confusing. Ask yourself questions about each passage to help you explore its meaning. Sample notes are shown below.

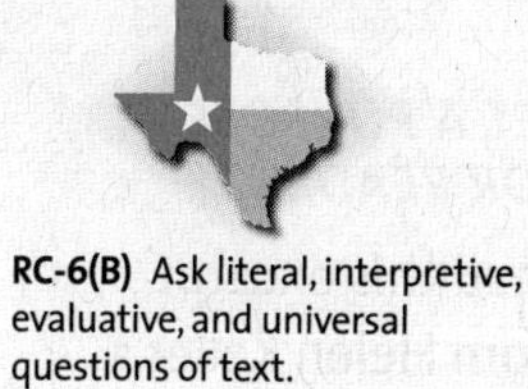

RC-6(B) Ask literal, interpretive, evaluative, and universal questions of text.

Keller's Words	My Questions
"Anger and bitterness had preyed upon me" (line 17).	Why is Helen Keller so bitter and angry?

Vocabulary in Context

Note: Words are listed in the order in which they appear in the selection.

tangible (tăn'jə-bəl) *adj.* possible to touch; real
*There was **tangible** evidence that the child was blind and deaf.*

uncomprehending (ŭn'kŏm-prĭ-hĕn'dĭng) *adj.* not understanding
*The student gave the teacher an **uncomprehending** stare after hearing the lecture.*

sensation (sĕn-sā'shən) *n.* a feeling
*The **sensation** of sitting in the rain can be very uncomfortable.*

consciousness (kŏn'shəs-nĭs) *n.* awareness of one's own thoughts
*A person can lose **consciousness** from a lack of oxygen, food, or water.*

repentance (rĭ-pĕn'təns) *n.* sorrow or regret
*Keller expresses **repentance** after she acts badly.*

Vocabulary Practice

Review the vocabulary words and think about their meanings. With a partner, discuss how the senses of sight and hearing affect our **consciousness.** What kinds of **sensations** do we experience through these senses? Write your ideas below.

___

___

___

___

___

Monitor Your Comprehension

SET A PURPOSE FOR READING

Read this excerpt from Helen Keller's autobiography to explore how you might overcome your own limits.

The Story *of* My Life

Autobiography by

HELEN KELLER

BACKGROUND **Before Helen Keller was two years old, she developed a fever that left her blind and deaf. The young girl was highly intelligent, but her parents did not know how to communicate with her properly. Anne Sullivan, a teacher from the Perkins Institution for the Blind, became Keller's tutor.**

Ⓐ MONITOR
Reread lines 1–6. What question comes to mind when you read lines 3–5? Explain.

The most important day I remember in all my life is the one on which my teacher, Anne Mansfield Sullivan, came to me. I am filled with wonder when I consider the immeasurable contrasts between the two lives which it connects. It was the third of March, 1887, three months before I was seven years old. Ⓐ

On the afternoon of that eventful day, I stood on the porch, dumb,[1] expectant. I guessed vaguely from my mother's signs and from the hurrying to and fro in the house that something unusual was about to happen, so I went to the door and waited on the steps. The afternoon

1. **dumb:** unable to speak; mute.

sun penetrated the mass of honeysuckle that covered the porch, and fell on my upturned face. My fingers lingered almost unconsciously on the familiar leaves and blossoms which had just come forth to greet the sweet southern spring. I did not know what the future held of marvel or surprise for me. Anger and bitterness had preyed upon me continually for weeks and a deep languor had succeeded[2] this passionate struggle. B

Have you ever been at sea in a dense fog, when it seemed as if a **tangible** white darkness shut you in, and the great ship, tense and anxious, groped her way toward the shore with plummet and sounding-line,[3] and you waited with beating heart for something to happen? I was like that ship before my education began, only I was without compass or sounding-line, and had no way of knowing how near the harbor was. "Light! Give me light!" was the wordless cry of my soul, and the light of love shone on me in that very hour. C

I felt approaching footsteps. I stretched out my hand as I supposed to my mother. Someone took it, and I was caught up and held close in the arms of her who had come to reveal all things to me, and, more than all things else, to love me.

The morning after my teacher came she led me into her room and gave me a doll. The little blind children at the Perkins Institution had sent it and Laura Bridgman[4] had dressed it; but I did not know this until afterward. When I had played with it a little while, Miss Sullivan slowly spelled into my hand the word "d-o-l-l." I was at once interested in this finger play and tried to imitate it. When I finally

2. **deep languor had succeeded:** a complete lack of energy had followed.
3. **plummet and sounding-line:** a weighted rope used to measure the depth of water.
4. **Perkins Institution . . . Laura Bridgman:** The Perkins Institution was a school for the blind, located in Massachusetts. Laura Bridgman (1829–1889), a student at the Perkins Institution, was the first deaf and blind child to be successfully educated. Like Keller, Bridgman became quite famous for her accomplishments.

Monitor Your Comprehension

B AUTOBIOGRAPHY
Reread lines 7–19. In what way does the first-person point of view help show Keller's thoughts and feelings?

tangible (tăn′jə-bəl) *adj.* possible to touch; real

Why does Keller describe fog as **tangible**?

C AUTOBIOGRAPHY
In lines 20–28, Keller describes her experience of being blind. What literary devices does Keller use in her description?

Monitor Your Comprehension

uncomprehending (ŭn'kŏm-prĭ-hĕn'dĭng) *adj.* not understanding

D MONITOR

Reread lines 34–50. Underline a quote from the text about what Keller thought about spelling. Then ask and try to answer a question about the passage in the box below.

My Question:

____

____

____

____

____

____

____

____

sensation (sĕn-sā'shən) *n.* a feeling

succeeded in making the letters correctly I was flushed with childish pleasure and pride. Running downstairs to my mother I held up my hand and made the letters for *doll*. I did not know that I was spelling a word or even that words existed; I was simply making my fingers go in monkey-like imitation. In the days that followed I learned to spell in this **uncomprehending** way a great many words, among them *pin, hat, cup* and a few verbs like *sit, stand* and *walk*. But my teacher had been with me several weeks before I understood that everything has a name. D

One day, while I was playing with my new doll, Miss Sullivan put my big rag doll into my lap also, spelled "d-o-l-l" and tried to make me understand that "d-o-l-l" applied to both. Earlier in the day we had had a tussle over the words "m-u-g" and "w-a-t-e-r." Miss Sullivan had tried to impress it upon me that "m-u-g" is *mug* and that "w-a-t-e-r" is *water*, but I persisted in confounding the two. In despair she had dropped the subject for the time, only to renew it at the first opportunity. I became impatient at her repeated attempts and, seizing the new doll, I dashed[5] it upon the floor. I was keenly delighted when I felt the fragments of the broken doll at my feet. Neither sorrow nor regret followed my passionate outburst. I had not loved the doll. In the still, dark world in which I lived there was no strong sentiment or tenderness. I felt my teacher sweep the fragments to one side of the hearth, and I had a sense of satisfaction that the cause of my discomfort was removed. She brought me my hat, and I knew I was going out into the warm sunshine. This thought, if a wordless **sensation** may be called a thought, made me hop and skip with pleasure.

5. **dashed:** threw or knocked with sudden violence.

We walked down the path to the well-house, attracted by the fragrance of the honeysuckle with which it was covered. Someone was drawing water and my teacher placed my hand under the spout. As the cool stream gushed over one hand she spelled into the other the word *water*, first slowly, then rapidly. I stood still, my whole attention fixed upon the motions of her fingers. Suddenly I felt a misty **consciousness** as of something forgotten—a thrill of returning thought; and somehow the mystery of language was revealed to me. I knew then that "w-a-t-e-r" meant the wonderful cool something that was flowing over my hand. That living word awakened my soul, gave it light, hope, joy, set it free! There were barriers still, it is true, but barriers that could in time be swept away. E

consciousness (kŏn'shəs-nĭs) *n.* awareness of one's own thoughts

E AUTOBIOGRAPHY
Reread lines 72–85. Underscore the literary language in this passage that might not have been included in a biography.

I left the well-house eager to learn. Everything had a name, and each name gave birth to a new thought. As we returned to the house every object which I touched seemed to quiver with life. That was because I saw everything with the strange, new sight that had come to me. On entering the door I remembered the doll I had broken. I felt my way to the hearth and picked up the pieces. I tried vainly[6]

6. **vainly:** without success.

Monitor Your Comprehension

repentance (rĭ-pĕn′təns) *n.* sorrow or regret

F MONITOR
Reread lines 86–95. Why does Keller suddenly feel sorry for breaking the doll?

PAUSE & REFLECT
How did reading about Keller affect your view of people with physical limits?

to put them together. Then my eyes filled with tears; for I realized what I had done, and for the first time I felt **repentance** and sorrow. F

I learned a great many new words that day. I do not remember what they all were; but I do know that *mother, father, sister, teacher* were among them—words that were to make the world blossom for me, "like Aaron's rod, with flowers."[7] It would have been difficult to find a happier child than I was as I lay in my crib at the close of that eventful day and lived over the joys it had brought me, and for the first time longed for a new day to come.

PAUSE & REFLECT

7. **like Aaron's rod, with flowers:** a reference to a story in the Bible in which a wooden staff suddenly sprouts flowers.

After Reading

Literary Analysis: Autobiography

In her autobiography, Helen Keller uses images that appeal to your senses of touch and smell to help you understand her experiences. In the chart below, record words and phrases that help you understand what she describes, despite her lack of sight and hearing. Then answer the question below.

READING 6C Describe different forms of point of view, including first- and third-person. **7** Identify the literary language and devices used in an autobiography.

Touch	Smell
"the wonderful cool something" (line 82)	

Review your notes for *The Story of My Life* and your graphic organizer. Are the descriptions that Keller uses in her autobiography an effective way for her to describe her feelings about her experiences? Explain.

___

___

___

___

After Reading

RC-6(B) Ask literal, interpretive, evaluative, and universal questions of text.

Reading Strategy: Monitor

Review the notes you took as you read. Write your questions in the chart below, as well as any other questions that you have. Then work with a partner to answer each question and record the answers in the chart. Make sure you both go back to the text to get details to support your answers.

My Questions	Answers

Do we have to accept our LIMITS?

How was Helen Keller able to overcome her disabilities?

___

___

___

Vocabulary Practice

Complete each sentence using the appropriate vocabulary word.

WORD LIST

consciousness
repentance
sensation
tangible
uncomprehending

1. After the ride ended, he still had the ______________ of being upside-down.
2. Her happiness was ______________, like a warm blanket wrapped around her.
3. The teacher looked at him in a(n) ______________ way, so he repeated himself.
4. A feeling of ______________ is natural after you do something hurtful or wrong.
5. When I hit my head, I lost ______________ and my mind went blank.

Academic Vocabulary in Writing

achieve	appreciate	characteristics	conclude	obvious

With a partner, list the **characteristics** of people who **achieve** their goals while facing challenges. Use at least one Academic Vocabulary word in your response. Definitions of these words are on page 273.

____

____

____

____

READING 6C Describe different forms of point of view, including first- and third-person. **7** Identify the literary language and devices used in an autobiography. **RC-6(B)** Ask literal, interpretive, evaluative, and universal questions of text.

Texas Assessment Practice

DIRECTIONS Use *The Story of My Life* to answer questions 1–4.

1 Helen Keller knows that something unusual is happening on the day Anne Sullivan arrives because she—

- (A) expects a surprise because it is close to her seventh birthday
- (B) hears people hurrying around the house and sees her mother preparing for guests
- (C) realizes that people are hurrying around the house and that her mother has tried to tell her about it
- (D) is angry and bored and wants something different to happen

2 The quote "When I finally succeeded in making the letters correctly I was flushed with childish pleasure and pride" (lines 40–43) is characteristic of an autobiography because it —

- (F) is written from the third-person point of view
- (G) tells a story about events that did not happen
- (H) describes Keller's thoughts from the first-person point of view
- (J) provides information from sources such as letters and other books

3 How would the story of Keller's life be different if Anne Sullivan had written it?

- (A) The events would be different, and readers would know more about Keller's thoughts and feelings.
- (B) The events would be the same, but readers would know less about Sullivan's thoughts and feelings.
- (C) The events would be different, and the readers would know less about Keller's thoughts and feelings.
- (D) The events would be the same, but readers would know about Sullivan's thoughts and feelings rather than Keller's.

4 In this excerpt, how does Keller feel about her limits?

- (F) She is angry, bitter, and tired of living with her limitations.
- (G) She feels resigned and calm about her life without sight or hearing.
- (H) She doesn't feel that she had any limits on what she could do.
- (J) She knows that she will never overcome the challenges to communication.

READING 12 Understand how to glean and use information in procedural texts and documents. **12B** Interpret factual, quantitative, or technical information presented in charts, illustrations, and diagrams.

American Sign Language

Procedural Text

Background

"American Sign Language" describes a common visual language, also known as ASL, used by people who are deaf. ASL has specific rules of grammar that are not identical with those of standard English usage. It is estimated that ASL is the fourth most common language in the United States.

Skill Focus: Interpret Information in Procedural Texts

Information on how to complete a task, or procedure, can be presented in a variety of ways. **Procedural information** may include

- a statement of the task to be performed
- a list of materials or tools needed
- a series of numbered or sequenced instructions
- a diagram or an illustration

By following the steps in a procedural document, you should be able to complete the task it describes. A procedural text should be written in simple, imperative sentences, such as "do this, do that." The steps must be given in chronological order, from the first to the last step. Sometimes, a procedural text may be a simple chart with illustrations or diagrams that show you what to do along with some descriptive text. Sometimes, all the information you need is in the visuals, and the illustrations or diagrams may have no additional text. If this is the case, you need to **glean**, or gather, information from the visuals to complete the task.

When reading procedural texts, first scan the text to identify the type of information. Then focus on the content of that information. As you read, take notes on what you learn from each type of information found in the text. An example is shown below.

Types of Information	Notes on Content
Title	*Tells me the topic of the procedural document*
Introductory or Explanatory Text	
Diagrams or Illustrations	
Numbered or sequenced items	

American Sign Language

American Sign Language (ASL) is a visual language that incorporates gestures, facial expressions, head movements, body language, and even the space around the speaker. Hand signs are the foundation of the language. Many signs are **iconic**, meaning the sign uses a visual image that resembles the concept it represents. For instance, to express the concept of "deer" in ASL, you would hold your hands up to either side of your head, fingers spread, to represent antlers.

SET A PURPOSE FOR READING

Read to learn about the structure of American Sign Language.

FOCUS ON FORM

A **procedural text** is written to describe how something is done. Recipes, repair manuals, and how-to instructions are all examples of procedural texts. To aid comprehension, many procedural texts include visuals, such as illustrations or diagrams. Procedural texts may also include titles, numbered or sequenced steps, and lists of materials.

Ⓐ INTERPRET INFORMATION

Reread lines 7–15 and review the diagrams on page 315. Then use the information in the text and the diagrams to sign the words *eat* and *deer.* Which of these two signs do you think would be more useful? Explain.

Ⓑ INTERPRET INFORMATION

With a partner, sign the letters in your names using the chart on this page. Say a letter, then sign a letter. Ask your partner to circle the letter you have signed in the chart. Repeat this process until both of you have signed your names.

Ⓒ INTERPRET INFORMATION

What do you think the arrows that accompany the "J" and the "Z" illustration represent?

Actions are often expressed through hand signals that mimic the action being communicated—if you wished to sign the concept "eat," you would bring your fingers and thumb of your dominant hand together as if holding food and then move your hand toward your mouth. Ⓐ

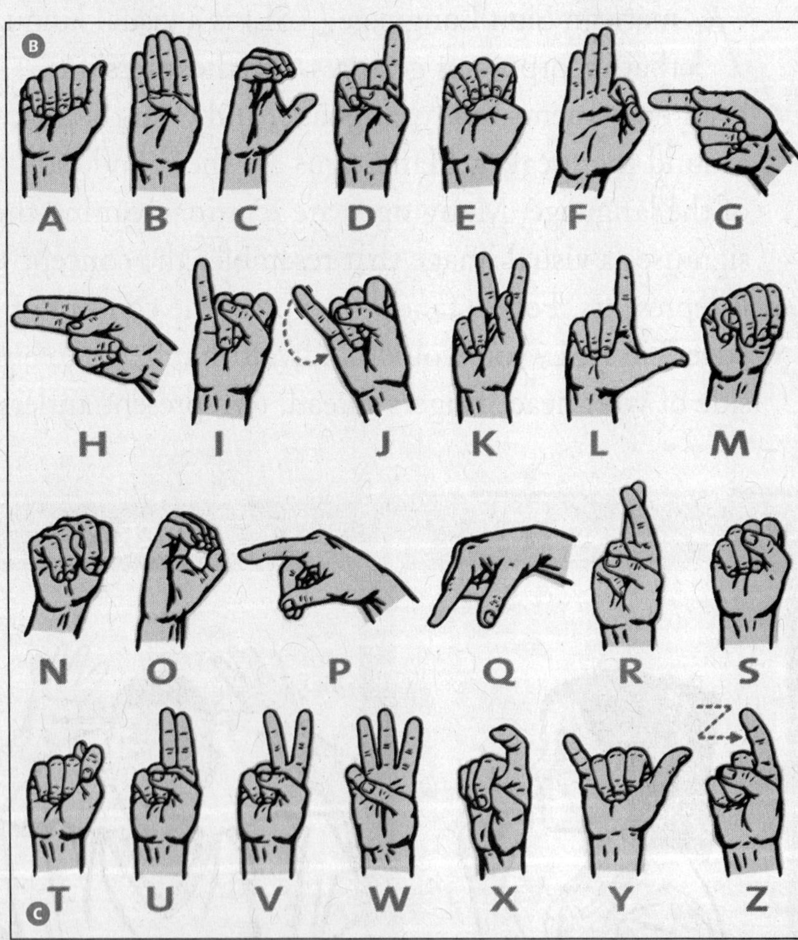

American Sign Language Alphabet.

The alphabet is an important series of signs. Some hand signs for letters resemble the written form of the respective letter. When you use the hand signs for letters to spell out a word, you are **finger spelling.** Finger spelling is useful to convey names or to ask someone the sign for a particular concept. ASL uses one-handed signals for each letter of the alphabet (some other sign languages use both hands for some letters). Many people find finger spelling the most challenging hurdle when learning to sign, as accomplished speakers are very fast finger spellers. D

PAUSE & REFLECT

D PROCEDURAL TEXT
What is the purpose of this procedural document? Complete the chart below with your notes on numbered or sequenced items and then answer the question on the lines.

Diagrams and Illustrations

↓

Notes on Content

PAUSE & REFLECT
Why was the development of American Sign Language important to the community of people who are deaf?

READING 12 Understand how to glean and use information in procedural texts and documents. **12B** Interpret factual, quantitative, or technical information presented in charts, illustrations, and diagrams.

Practicing Your Skills

An effective procedural text gives clear, detailed instructions on how to do something. However, sometimes information in this kind of text can be difficult to understand. What would you add or change to make the instruction about American Sign Language more clear? Complete the chart below with your ideas and your reasons for thinking the information could be useful.

Existing Information	Ideas for Improved Information	Reasons Information Could Be Useful
Title		
Introductory or Explanatory Text		
Diagrams or Illustrations		
Numbered or Sequenced Items		

How do the visuals add to your understanding of the text? Use your chart to help you explain your answer.

Academic Vocabulary in Writing

achieve	appreciate	characteristics	conclude	obvious

READING 12 Understand how to glean and use information in procedural texts and documents. **12B** Interpret factual, quantitative, or technical information presented in charts, illustrations, and diagrams.

What kind of effort would it take to **achieve** fluency in American Sign Language? Practice finger spelling "My name is ______." Then write your **conclusion** about how long it would take to become very good at signing. Use at least one Academic Vocabulary word in your answer. Definitions of these words are on page 273.

____

____

____

Texas Assessment Practice

DIRECTIONS Use "American Sign Language" to answer questions 1–5.

1 A procedural text —

- (A) is a form of fictional writing
- (B) often uses visuals to help readers understand the text
- (C) gives a general explanation about how to do something
- (D) rarely includes visuals to help the readers understand the text

2 American Sign Language is different from some other sign languages because it uses —

- (F) two-handed signs for each letter of the alphabet
- (G) one- and two-handed signs for each letter of the alphabet
- (H) only iconic signs for each letter of the alphabet
- (J) one-handed signs for each letter of the alphabet

3 Which of the following is not a procedural text?

- (A) recipe
- (B) repair manual
- (C) graphic novel
- (D) how-to instructions

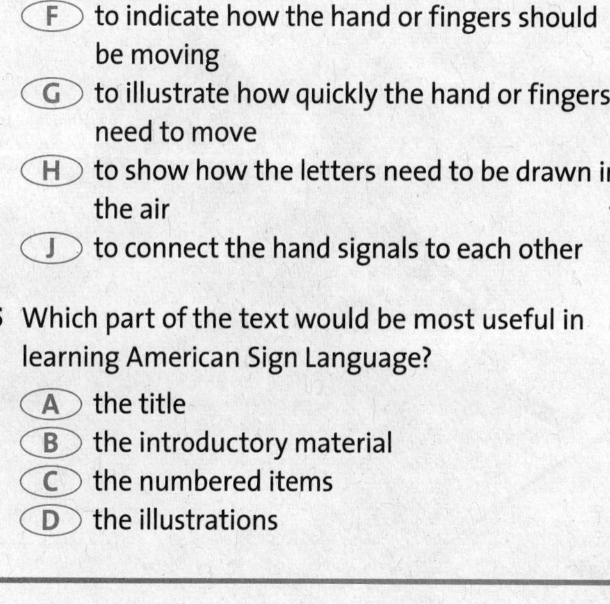

4 Why are arrows used in the illustrations in this procedural text?

- (F) to indicate how the hand or fingers should be moving
- (G) to illustrate how quickly the hand or fingers need to move
- (H) to show how the letters need to be drawn in the air
- (J) to connect the hand signals to each other

5 Which part of the text would be most useful in learning American Sign Language?

- (A) the title
- (B) the introductory material
- (C) the numbered items
- (D) the illustrations

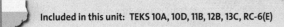

Included in this unit: TEKS 10A, 10D, 11B, 12B, 13C, RC-6(E)

UNIT 8

Know the Facts

INFORMATION, ARGUMENT, AND PERSUASION

Be sure to read the Reader's Workshops on pp. 894–897 and 936–941 in *Holt McDougal Literature.*

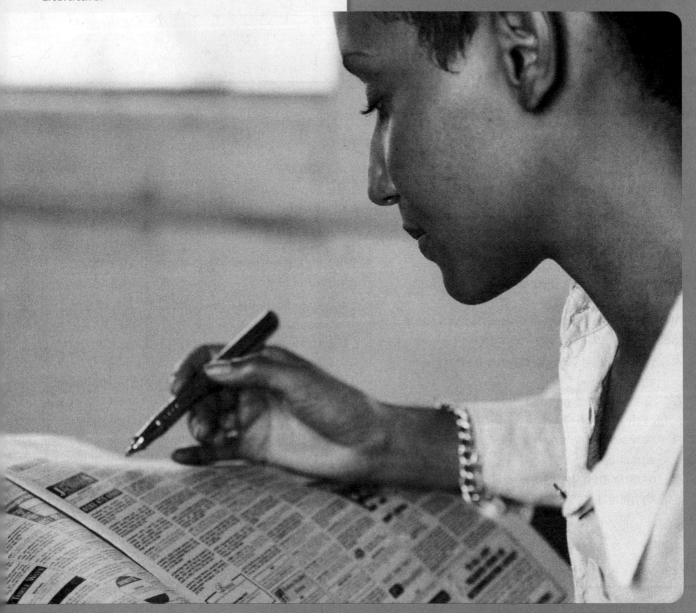

Academic Vocabulary for Unit 8

Academic Vocabulary is the language you use to discuss literary and informational texts. Preview the following Academic Vocabulary words. You will use these words as you write and talk about the selections in this unit.

adequacy (ad'i-kwə-sē) *n.* quality of being enough to meet a need or requirement

*I question the **adequacy** of the writer's evidence for his argument.*

•

authority (ə-thôr'ə-tē) *n.* someone who is respected because of his or her knowledge about a subject

*You can trust the information on this Web site because it was written by an **authority** on the topic.*

•

concept (kän'sept') *n.* an idea of how something is or could be

*The article explains a new **concept** for living an eco-friendly lifestyle.*

•

purpose (pər'pəs) *n.* the goal or desired outcome of something

*The author's **purpose** is to convince readers to accept her ideas about space travel.*

•

structural (struk'chər-al) *adj.* of or related to the manner of organization

*This essay has **structural** problems and needs to be reorganized to help readers understand it.*

Think of a book, an article, or a documentary film that gave you some new information about a topic. What did the writer or filmmaker do to achieve the **purpose** of making the work both informative and interesting? Write your response on the lines below, using at least two Academic Vocabulary words.

____

____

READING 12B Interpret factual, quantitative, or technical information presented in maps, illustrations, and timelines.

SuperCroc

Magazine Article by **Peter Winkler**

Are MONSTERS real?

Monsters have always existed in the world of imagination. Yet fierce, deadly creatures exist in reality, too. In the following article, you will read about a prehistoric "monster" scientists discovered that is so terrifying, even dinosaurs may have feared it.

LIST IT In the notebook, list some of your favorite monsters in two groups: imaginary creatures from stories and movies, and dangerous creatures from the real world that you've learned about from books, television programs, and nature magazines. Then share your lists with a small group of classmates. Discuss which list is more frightening, and why.

Imaginary Monsters

1. Godzilla

2. ______

3. ______

4. ______

Real Monsters

1. Komodo dragon

2. ______

3. ______

4. ______

Which list is scariest? Why?

______

______

______

______

Elements of Nonfiction: Text Features

The magazine article "SuperCroc" is an **expository text**—a text that explains something. Writers of expository texts often use **text features,** or design elements that present information visually, to convey their ideas. Text features highlight key points and provide more information about topics discussed in the main text. Read about several common text features in the chart below.

Text Feature	Definition
Subheading	A section title that hints at the main idea or topic of the section that follows
Graphic aid	A visual representation such as a map, a photograph, or a timeline
Caption	Brief text that provides information about a specific graphic aid

As you read the article, identify each text feature and notice the information it presents.

Reading Strategy: Summarize

When you **summarize** a text, you use your own words to restate the main ideas and important supporting details. A summary is usually no more than one-third the length of the original text. It includes only facts—not your personal opinions.

As you read "SuperCroc," you'll be prompted to record the most important information from each section of the article. You will use this information later to write a summary of the article. A sample is provided below.

READING 10A Summarize the main ideas and supporting details in text, demonstrating an understanding that a summary does not include opinions. **RC-6(E)** Summarize texts in ways that maintain meaning and logical order within a text.

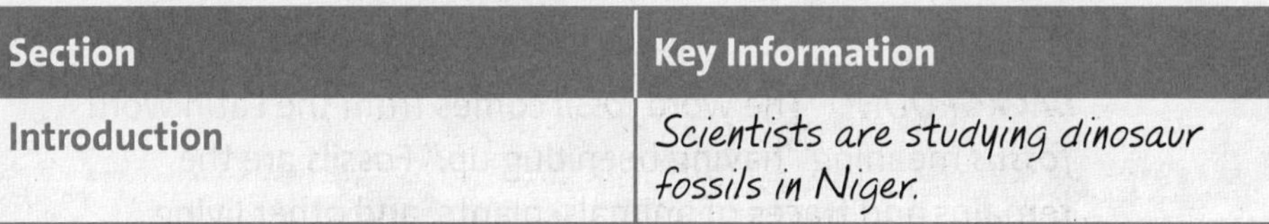

Section	Key Information
Introduction	*Scientists are studying dinosaur fossils in Niger.*

Vocabulary in Context

Note: Words are listed in the order in which they appear in the article.

fossil (fŏs'əl) *n.* the remains of a living thing, preserved in soil or rock
*The scientists found a dinosaur **fossil** buried in the earth.*

expert (ĕk'spûrt') *n.* one who is skilled in or knowledgeable about a particular thing
*Scientist Paul Sereno is a dinosaur **expert.***

extinct (ĭk-stĭngkt') *adj.* no longer existing
*Dinosaurs have been **extinct** for millions of years.*

predator (prĕd'ə-tər) *n.* an animal that feeds on other animals
*The large **predator** could have eaten anything it wanted.*

species (spē'shēz) *n.* a variety or type of something
*The team discovered a **species** of crocodile that was previously unknown.*

Vocabulary Practice

Review the vocabulary words and think about their meanings. Then write a few sentences that could begin an article about an exciting new scientific discovery. Use at least three vocabulary words.

SET A PURPOSE FOR READING

Read this article to find out what kind of creature the SuperCroc was.

SUPERCROC

PETER WINKLER

BACKGROUND The word *fossil* comes from the Latin word *fossus* meaning "having been dug up." Fossils are the remains and traces of animals, plants, and other living organisms. Scientists examine fossils to learn about the remote past. In this article, you will learn about a creature from the past that is so fearsome that one scientist calls him "the monster of them all."

Out of Africa comes a giant reptile that lived with dinosaurs—and ate them.

"We're stuck again!" Scientist Paul Sereno and his team said those words many times as they drove into a rugged part of Africa. Desert sand kept stopping their vehicles. It took 10 hours to go just 87 miles.

That long crawl ended at Gadoufaoua,[1] a dry region in the country of Niger.[2] To most eyes, the place looked empty. There was sand. There was wind. There was nothing else. Or so it seemed.

But Sereno saw much more. He saw a chance to find dinosaurs. Sereno, a paleontologist, knew that the region

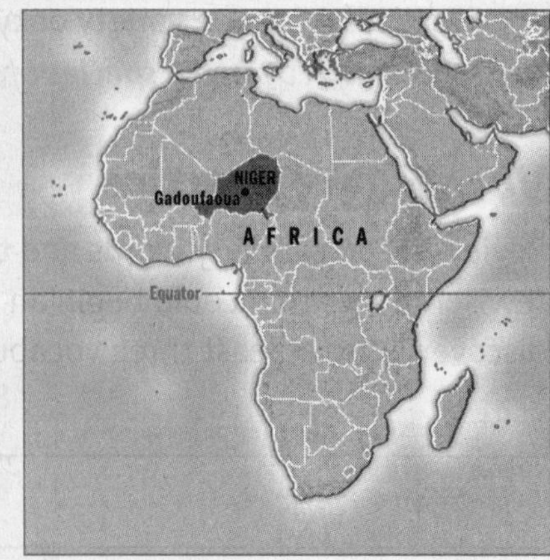

The country of Niger is in West Africa.

1. **Gadoufaoua** (gə-do͞o′fä′wŏh).
2. **Niger** (nī′jər).

contains countless **fossils** from ancient dinosaurs. Gadoufaoua is one of Africa's richest sources of dino fossils. A

Sereno found some fossils there in 1997. He came back in 2000 to seek more. The team spent four months in the desert. Crew members woke at 6:00 each morning, then explored the sand dunes for about 12 hours. They worked even when the temperature hit 125°F.

And they found fossils. By the end of the expedition, Sereno and his team had collected 20 tons of bones. Most of the fossils came from dinosaurs, including types never seen before. Others came from turtles, fish, and crocodiles.

One of those crocodiles was *Sarcosuchus imperator*,[3] a name that means "flesh crocodile emperor." Sereno's team nicknamed it "SuperCroc."

What Makes This Croc So Super? B

In a word, size. The skull alone was six feet long. Sereno says it's "about the biggest I've ever seen."

Naturally, Sereno wondered how big SuperCroc was overall. The team found only part of its skeleton, so Sereno had to make an estimate. To do that, he looked at crocodiles that live today. He and other **experts** compared the animals' skull and body sizes.

Based on his research, Sereno concluded that an adult SuperCroc could grow to be 40 feet long and probably weighed as much as 10 tons. That's heavier than an African elephant.

3. ***Sarcosuchus imperator*** (sär'kō-so͞o'kĭs ĭm-pîr'ā-tôr).

fossil (fŏs'əl) *n.* the remains of a living thing, preserved in soil or rock

A TEXT FEATURES
Reread lines 1–21 and underline text that tells about Gadoufaoua. Then study the map. What information about Gadoufaoua and Niger does the map present that the text does not? List three details below.

1. ______

2. ______

3. ______

B TEXT FEATURES
Preview the article's **subheadings.** What do you think the article will tell you about SuperCroc?

______

expert (ĕk'spûrt') *n.* one who is skilled in or knowledgeable about a particular thing

C SUMMARIZE
Reread lines 35–49. Circle the main idea of this section. Underline the most important details. Then state this information in your own words in the box below.

What Makes This Croc So Super?

Main Idea: ______________________

____

____

____

Supporting Details: ______________________

____

____

____

Those measurements make SuperCroc one of the largest crocodiles ever to walk Earth. Today's biggest crocs grow to about 20 feet. C

A Different-Looking Beast

SuperCroc's long head is wider in front than in the middle. That shape is unique. No other croc—living or **extinct**—has a snout quite like it.

At the front of SuperCroc's head is a big hole. That's where the nose would be. That empty space may have given the ancient **predator** a keen sense of smell. Or perhaps it helped SuperCroc make noise to communicate with other members of its **species**.

SuperCroc wore serious armor. Huge plates of bone, called scutes, covered the animal's back. Hundreds of them lay just below the skin. A single scute from the back could be a foot long!

extinct (ĭk-stĭngkt') *adj.* no longer existing

predator (prĕd'ə-tər) *n.* an animal that feeds on other animals

species (spē'shēz) *n.* a variety or type of something

When Did SuperCroc Live?

Estimating a fossil's age is a challenge. Sereno and his team looked carefully at the group of fossils they had found. They compared the fossils to others whose ages the scientists did know. Based on those comparisons, Sereno believes SuperCroc lived about 110 million years ago.

Gadoufaoua looked a bit different in those days. What is now a desert was a land of winding rivers. Plenty of trees grew along the banks. Huge fish swam the rivers, while various dinosaurs lived in the forests.

Five or more crocodile species lurked in the rivers. SuperCroc, Sereno says, was "the monster of them all." **D**

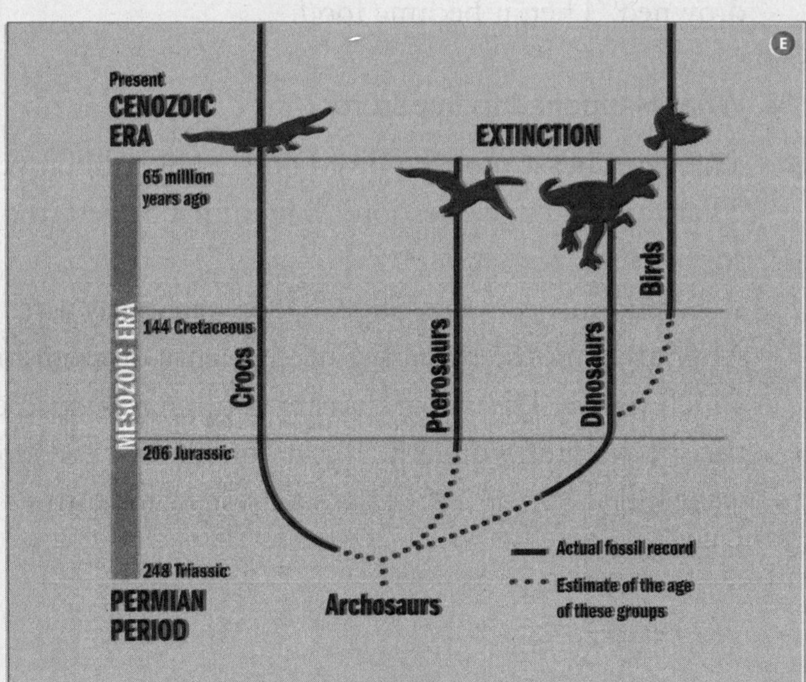

This timeline covers many millions of years, from the Permian Period (at the bottom of the graphic aid) to the present day. It shows some of the animals that descended from the ancient archosaurs. Not all of the archosaurs' descendants have survived. The line near the top of the graphic aid shows when some became extinct.

D SUMMARIZE
Reread lines 50–75. Circle the main idea of each section. Underline the most important details. You will use this information to help you **summarize** the article.

E TEXT FEATURES
A **timeline** shows events in chronological order (the order in which they happened). This timeline reads from bottom to top—the earliest events are on the bottom. There you see the name archosaurs, a very ancient kind of animal from which many others descended. On the timeline, circle the names of two animals that became extinct about 65 million years ago. Which two kinds of animal survived into the Cenozoic Era (the present era)?

F SUMMARIZE
Reread lines 76–99. Circle the main idea of each section. Underline important details. Then summarize each section in one sentence below.

What Did SuperCroc Eat?

What Happened to SuperCroc?

What Did SuperCroc Eat?

"Anything it wanted," Sereno says. SuperCroc's narrow jaws held about 130 teeth. The teeth were short but incredibly strong. SuperCroc's mouth was "designed for grabbing prey[4]—fish, turtles, and dinosaurs that strayed too close."

SuperCroc likely spent most of its life in the river. Water hid the creature's huge body. Only its eyes and nostrils poked above the surface.

After spotting a meal, the giant hunter moved quietly toward the animal. Then—wham! That huge mouth locked onto its prey. SuperCroc dragged the stunned creature into the water. There the animal drowned. Then it became food.

What Happened to SuperCroc?

The giant beast probably lived only a few million years. That raises a huge question: Why didn't SuperCroc survive?

Sereno suspects that SuperCrocs were fairly rare. After all, a monster that big needs plenty of room in which to live. Disease or disaster could have wiped out the species pretty quickly. But no one knows for sure what killed SuperCroc. That's a mystery for future scientists. F

4. **prey:** animals that become the food of another animal.

Elements of Nonfiction: Text Features

READING 12B Interpret factual, quantitative, or technical information presented in maps, illustrations, and timelines.

Review the notes you took about the text features in "SuperCroc." How did each type of text feature help you understand the article and learn about SuperCrocs? Write your answers in the chart.

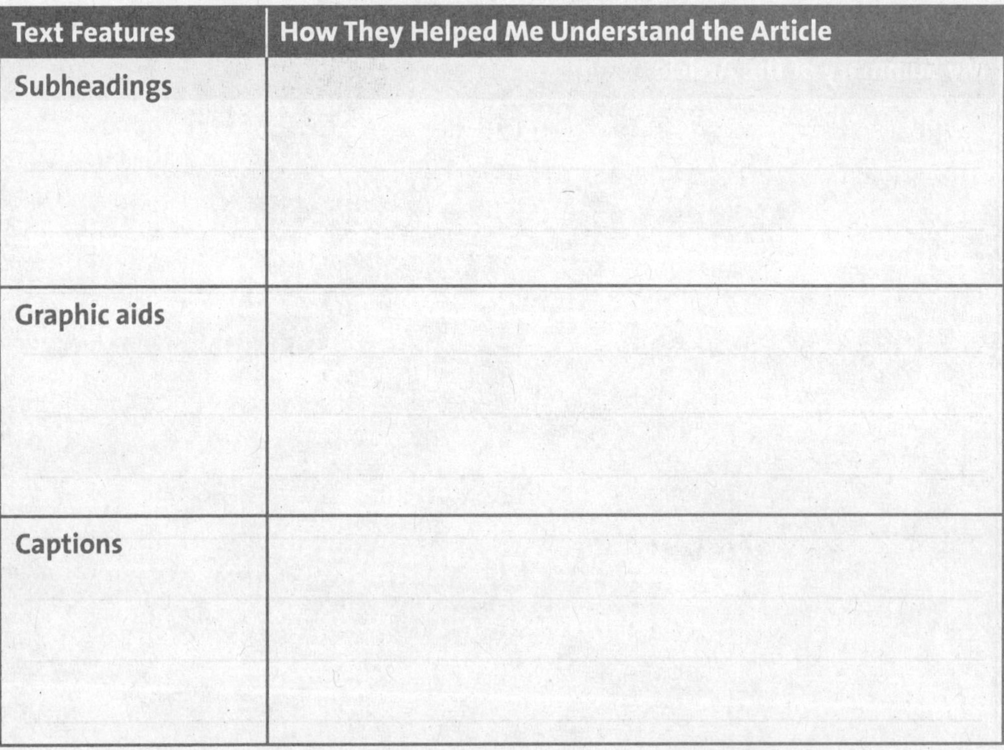

Text Features	How They Helped Me Understand the Article
Subheadings	
Graphic aids	
Captions	

What kinds of information do maps and timelines convey more clearly than regular text? Refer to the map and timeline from "SuperCroc" in your answer.

READING 10A Summarize the main ideas and supporting details in text, demonstrating an understanding that a summary does not include opinions.
RC-6(E) Summarize texts in ways that maintain meaning and logical order within a text.

Reading Strategy: Summarize

Review the main ideas and important details you noted in each section of "SuperCroc." Use this information to write a summary of the entire article. Your summary might include one sentence for each section. Remember that a summary does not include your opinions—only facts from the article.

My Summary of the Article

Are MONSTERS real?

Review the list of monsters you created on page 322. Which monster from your list is most similar to SuperCroc? Explain your answer.

Vocabulary Practice

Circle the word that is not related in meaning to the other words.

1. (a) skeleton, **(b)** fossil, **(c)** bone, **(d)** alive

2. **(a)** expert, **(b)** inexperienced, **(c)** authority, **(d)** knowledgeable

3. **(a)** kind, **(b)** species, **(c)** type, **(d)** desert

4. **(a)** extinct, **(b)** living, **(c)** active, **(d)** breathing

5. **(a)** slayer, **(b)** admirer, **(c)** predator, (d) killer

Academic Vocabulary in Writing

achieve	appreciate	characteristics	conclude	obvious

READING 10A Summarize the main ideas and supporting details in text, demonstrating an understanding that a summary does not include opinions. **12B** Interpret factual, quantitative, or technical information presented in maps, illustrations, and timelines. **RC-6(E)** Summarize texts in ways that maintain meaning and logical order within a text.

What was Paul Sereno's **purpose** in spending so much time in the desert of Gadoufaoua? Use at least two Academic Vocabulary words in your response. Definitions of these words are on page 321.

___

___

___

Texas Assessment Practice

DIRECTIONS Use "SuperCroc" to answer questions 1–5.

1 The Gadoufaoua region of Niger interests Paul Sereno because —

- (A) an ancient river once flowed through it
- (B) it is filled with dinosaur fossils
- (C) many crocodiles live there today
- (D) he is an expert on desert environments

2 The *Sarcosuchus imperator* is nicknamed "SuperCroc" because —

- (F) it had extremely long teeth
- (G) its head had an unusual shape
- (H) adults reached a length of 40 feet
- (J) it existed in greater numbers than other prehistoric animals

3 The map on page 324 shows —

- (A) the locations of Niger and Gadoufaoua
- (B) the rivers where many SuperCrocs lived
- (C) how far Sereno's team traveled to reach Africa
- (D) the way Africa looked in the Mesozoic Era

4 Which of the following is the best summary of the section "A Different-Looking Beast"?

- (F) SuperCroc's snout grew wider at the end and had a large hole in it, and the animal was covered in tough plates called scutes.
- (G) SuperCroc was one of the ugliest prehistoric animals, but its armor was impressive.
- (H) SuperCroc, a large predator with an unusually shaped head, lived about 110 million years ago and ate many different animals.
- (J) SuperCroc had a hole in its snout that may have given it a keen sense of smell or helped it communicate with other crocs.

5 The timeline on page 327 shows that —

- (A) archosaurs descended from ancient SuperCrocs
- (B) SuperCroc survived into the Cenozoic Era
- (C) birds are not related to crocodiles
- (D) pterosaurs become extinct about 65 million years ago

READING 10D Synthesize and make logical connections between ideas within a text and across two texts representing similar or different genres. **12B** Interpret factual, quantitative, or technical information presented in maps, illustrations, and graphs.

The First Emperor

Book Excerpt from *The Tomb Robbers* by Daniel Cohen

Digging Up the Past: Discovery and Excavation of Shi Huangdi's Tomb

Magazine Article by Helen Wieman Bledsoe

How can we uncover the PAST?

To learn about the recent past, we might ask older friends and relatives to recall events they lived through, or to talk about the way life used to be. To explore the very distant past, we have to dig deeper—literally! The two selections you are about to read describe an amazing discovery that has uncovered an important part of China's ancient history.

QUICKWRITE Think about a time period you would like to know more about. It might be when your parents were children, when your grandparents were children, or even thousands of years ago. In the notebook, write the span of years you would like to know about and then list facts that you already know.

Time Period

Things I Know

Elements of Nonfiction: Synthesizing Information

There can be many, many resources available on the same topic. However, not every source presents the same information on a topic. When you read multiple sources on the same topic, you **synthesize information;** that is, you combine information from different sources into a full understanding of a topic.

The texts you'll be reading are about the same topic. To create a synthesis, or combination, of the information that the texts convey you will make logical, or reasonable, connections across the texts. As you read these texts, think about how you can combine what you are learning to draw a conclusion about the texts.

Information from "The First Emperor"	Information from "Digging Up the Past"	Logical Connections
Ch'in Shih Huang Ti had the Great Wall of China built.	*He forced 700,000 laborers to build his elaborate tomb.*	*The emperor left China incredible artifacts.*

Reading Strategy: Set a Purpose for Reading

Your purpose for reading these two selections is to synthesize information. As you read, notes throughout the texts will help you synthesize information on different topics.

READING 10D Synthesize and make logical connections between ideas within a text and across two texts representing similar or different genres.

Vocabulary in Context

Note: Words are listed in the order in which they appear in the texts.

archaeological (är'kē-ə-lŏj'ĭ-kəl) *adj.* relating to the study of past human life and culture

The people on the ***archaeological*** *dig were hoping to find artifacts.*

barbarian (bär-bâr'ē-ən) *n.* a person considered by those of another group to have a primitive culture

The emperor struggled to defend his empire against ***barbarians.***

surpass (sər-păs') *v.* to become greater than; to go beyond

The precise stonework in ancient buildings can ***surpass*** *the construction of modern buildings.*

immortality (ĭm'ôr-tăl'ĭ-tē) *n.* endless life

Many people have looked for the secret of ***immortality*** *so that they can avoid death.*

ancestor (ăn'sĕs'tər) *n.* a person from whom another person or group is descended

Some people research their family to find out more about their ***ancestors.***

dedicate (dĕd'ĭ-kāt') *v.* to set apart for a particular use

Tools, such as a shovel or drill, are often ***dedicated*** *to a specific task.*

excavation (ĕk'skə-vā'shən) *n.* the act or process of exposing by digging away a covering

Workers protected the seaside ***excavation*** *from the tide and salt spray.*

preservation (prĕz'ər-vā'shən) *n.* the state of being mostly unchanged or kept from harm

The ***preservation*** *of the ceramic bowls was effective because no cracks showed where the bowls had been repaired.*

disintegrate (dĭs-ĭn'tĭ-grāt') *v.* to break down into smaller parts

In wet climates, wooden buildings ***disintegrate*** *quickly because they begin to rot.*

reconstruction (rē'kən-strŭk'shən) *n.* the act of building or assembling again

A large team of scientists worked on the ***reconstruction*** *of the ancient city.*

SET A PURPOSE FOR READING

Read to find out how each text presents information about the same topic.

(A) SYNTHESIZE INFORMATION

Preview the selection's title and and scan the text and graphic aids. What do you think the selection will be about?

THE FIRST EMPEROR (A)

Daniel Cohen

BACKGROUND An excavation is the recovery and recording of buried material. Archaeologists perform excavations to learn about the distant past. In the selection you are about to read, you will learn about the excavation of the emperor Ch'in Shih Huang Ti's tomb. He is the man who is regarded as the founder of China.

There is what may turn out to be the greatest **archaeological** find of modern times, one that may ultimately outshine even the discovery of the tomb of Tutankhamun.[1] It is the tomb of the emperor Ch'in Shih Huang Ti.[2] Now admittedly the name Ch'in Shih Huang Ti is not exactly a household word in the West. But then neither was Tutankhamun until 1922. The major difference is that while Tutankhamun himself was historically insignificant, Ch'in Shih Huang Ti was enormously important in Chinese history. In many respects he was really the founder of China.

The future emperor started out as the king of the small state Ch'in. At the time, the land was divided up among a number of small states, all constantly warring with one another. Ch'in was one of the smallest and weakest. Yet the king of Ch'in managed to overcome all his rivals, and in the year 221 B.C. he proclaimed himself emperor

1. **Tutankhamun** (to͞ot′äng-kä′mən): Egyptian pharaoh whose tomb was found intact in 1922.
2. **Ch'in Shih Huang Ti** (chĭn shĭh hwäng′ dē): The use of the word *Ch'in* (or *Qin*) at the beginning of the emperor's name is a formal title that refers to the place from which the emperor came.

archaeological (är′kē-ə-lŏj′ĭ-kəl) *adj.* relating to the study of past human life and culture

of the land that we now know as China. From that date until the revolution of 1912, China was always ruled by an emperor. The name China itself comes from the name Ch'in. B

Shih Huang Ti ruled his empire with ferocious efficiency. He had the Great Wall of China built to keep out the northern **barbarians**. The Great Wall, which stretches some fifteen hundred miles, is a building project that rivals and perhaps **surpasses** the Great Pyramid.[3] The Great Wall took thirty years to build and cost the lives of countless thousands of laborers. Today the Great Wall remains China's number one tourist attraction.

As he grew older, Shih Huang Ti became obsessed with the prospect of his own death. He had survived several assassination attempts and was terrified of another. He traveled constantly between his 270 different palaces, so that no one could ever be sure

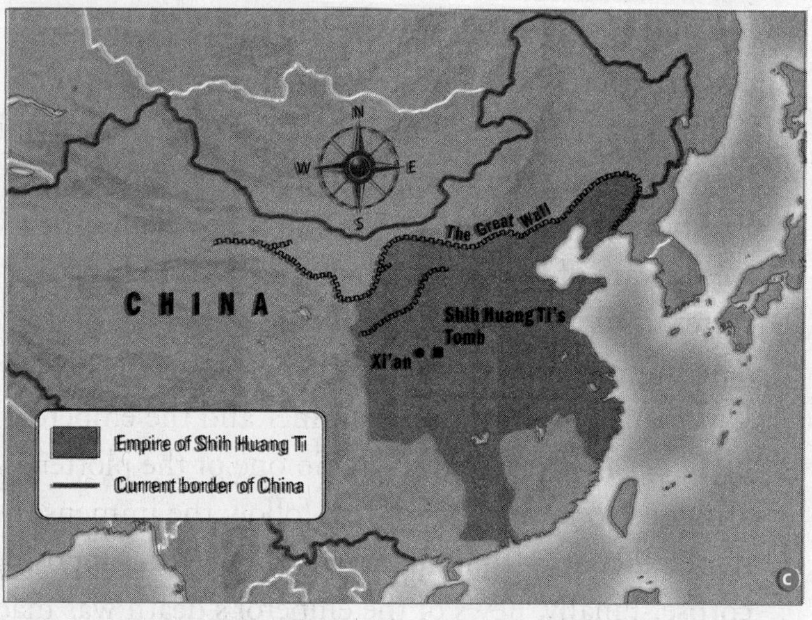

3. **Great Pyramid:** massive four-sided monument built around a tomb by people in ancient Egypt.

B SYNTHESIZE INFORMATION

What is the focus of the information presented in lines 12–21?

barbarian (bär-bâr'ē-ən) *n.* a person considered by those of another group to have a primitive culture

surpass (sər-păs') *v.* to become greater than; to go beyond

What is another word or phrase that could be used to express the same idea as surpasses in lines 24–27?

C SYNTHESIZE INFORMATION

Writers sometimes include information in graphic aids such as a map. What information does this map convey about the size of Shih Huang Ti's empire and the size of China? Circle the part of the map that tells you.

where he was going to be. He never slept in the same room for two nights in a row. Anyone who revealed the emperor's whereabouts was put to death along with his entire family.

Shih Huang Ti searched constantly for the secret of **immortality**. He became prey to a host of phony magicians and other fakers who promised much but could deliver nothing.

The emperor heard that there were immortals living on some far-off island, so he sent a huge fleet to find them. The commander of the fleet knew that if he failed in his mission, the emperor would put him to death. So the fleet simply never returned. It is said that the fleet found the island of Japan and stayed there to become the **ancestors** of the modern Japanese. D

In his desire to stay alive, Shih Huang Ti did not neglect the probability that he would die someday. He began construction of an immense tomb in the Black Horse hills near one of his favorite summer palaces. The tomb's construction took as long as the construction of the Great Wall—thirty years.

The emperor, of course, did die. Death came while he was visiting the eastern provinces.[4] But his life had become so secretive that only a few high officials were aware of his death. They contrived to keep it a secret until they could consolidate their own power. The imperial procession[5] headed back for the capital. Unfortunately, it was midsummer and the emperor's body began to rot and stink. So one of the plotters arranged to have a cart of fish follow the immense imperial chariot to hide the odor of the decomposing corpse. Finally, news of the emperor's death was made

4. **provinces:** districts, or parts, of a country.
5. **imperial procession:** a group of people traveling with an emperor.

immortality (ĭm′ôr-tăl′ĭ-tē) *n.* endless life

ancestor (ăn′sĕs′tər) *n.* a person from whom another person or group is descended

D SET A PURPOSE FOR READING
What do you learn about Shih Huang Ti in lines 44–50? Record this information in the chart below.

The First Emperor
What I learn about the emperor:

public. The body, or what was left of it, was buried in the tomb that he had been building for so long. . . .

PAUSE & REFLECT

There are two contradictory stories about the tomb of Ch'in Shih Huang Ti. The first says that it was covered up with earth to make it resemble an ordinary hill and that its location has remained unknown for centuries.

But a more accurate legend holds that there never was any attempt to disguise the existence of the tomb. Ch'in Shih Huang Ti had been building it for years, and everybody knew where it was. After his death the tomb was surrounded by walls enclosing an area of about five hundred acres. This was to be the emperor's "spirit city." Inside the spirit city were temples and all sorts of other sacred buildings and objects **dedicated** to the dead emperor.

Over the centuries the walls, the temples, indeed everything above ground was carried away by vandals. The top of the tomb was covered with earth and eventually came to resemble a large hill. Locally the hill is called Mount Li. But still the farmers who lived in the area had heard stories that Mount Li contained the tomb of Ch'in Shih Huang Ti or of some other important person. . . . Ⓔ

In the spring of 1974 a peasant plowing a field near Mount Li uncovered a life-sized clay statue of a warrior. Further digging indicated that there was an entire army of statues beneath the ground. Though **excavations** are not yet complete, Chinese authorities believe that there are some six thousand life-sized clay

PAUSE & REFLECT
Based on what you've read so far, how were the emperors in the ancient past different from leaders in the United States today?

dedicate (dĕd'ĭ-kāt') *v.* to set apart for a particular use

Ⓔ SET A PURPOSE FOR READING
Reread lines 51–90. What have you learned so far about the tomb? Underline details in the text. Then summarize the information in a sentence or two.

excavation (ĕk'skə-vā'shən) *n.* the act or process of exposing by digging away a covering

preservation (prĕz'ər-vā'shən) *n.* the state of being mostly unchanged or kept from harm

F SET A PURPOSE FOR READING

Reread lines 91–119. What have you learned from this selection about the excavation of the tomb? Take notes below.

statues of warriors, plus scores of life-sized statues of horses. Most of the statues are broken, but some are in an absolutely remarkable state of **preservation**. Each statue is finely made, and each shows a distinct individual, different from all the others.

This incredible collection is Shih Huang Ti's "spirit army." At one time Chinese kings practiced human sacrifice so that the victims could serve the dead king in the next world. Shih Huang Ti was willing to make do with models. Men and horses were arranged in a military fashion in a three-acre underground chamber. The chamber may have been entered at some point. The roof certainly collapsed. But still the delicate figures have survived surprisingly well. Most of the damage was done when the roof caved in. That is why the Chinese archaeologists are so hopeful that when the tomb itself is excavated, it too will be found to have survived surprisingly well.

The Chinese are not rushing the excavations. They have only a limited number of trained people to do the job. After all, the tomb has been there for over two thousand years. A few more years won't make much difference. F

Though once denounced as a tyrant, Ch'in Shih Huang Ti is now regarded as a national hero. His name is a household word in China. The Chinese government knows that it may have an unparalleled ancient treasure on its hands, and it wants to do the job well. Over the next few years we should be hearing much more about this truly remarkable find.

DIGGING UP THE PAST:

DISCOVERY AND EXCAVATION OF SHI HUANGDI'S TOMB G

Helen Wieman Bledsoe

BACKGROUND The information contained in a nonfiction work often depends on the time and place in which the piece was written. "The First Emperor" was written when the excavation of the emperor's tomb was just beginning. This article was written some years later, when more information was available. **PAUSE & REFLECT**

In March 1974, Chinese peasants digging a well near Xi'an in the central province of Shaanxi[1] found some unusual pottery fragments. Then, deeper down at 11 feet, they unearthed a head made of terra-cotta. They notified the authorities, and excavation of the site began immediately. To date, workers have dug up about 8,000 sculpted clay soldiers, and the site has proved to be one of the greatest archaeological discoveries of all time.

For over 2,000 years, these clay warriors have been guarding the tomb of Shi Huangdi,[2] the First Emperor of China. Tradition says that the First Emperor began building his tomb when he ascended to the throne at age 13, and that it was unfinished at his death,

1. **Xi'an** (shē′än′) **. . . Shaanxi** (shän′shē′): Xi'an is a city of central China. The former capital of the Qin (also called Ch'in) dynasty, it is now the capital of China's Shaanxi province.
2. **Shi Huangdi** (also **Shih Huang Ti**): The spelling of Chinese names and places can vary.

SET A PURPOSE FOR READING

While reading this article, compare how the two selections tell about the personal qualities of the emperor and the people under his rule.

G SYNTHESIZE INFORMATION

Remember that previewing a text means looking for clues about its subject matter before reading it. Preview the article's title and graphic aids. What do you think the article will focus on?

PAUSE & REFLECT

Reread the background note. Based on this note, make a prediction about the new information contained in this selection.

H SET A PURPOSE FOR READING
This graph presents information about four excavated pits. What kind of information does it convey? Circle the features of the graph that help you.

disintegrate (dĭs-ĭn'tĭ-grāt') *v.* to break down into smaller parts

What factors may have caused the wooden chariots to **disintegrate**?

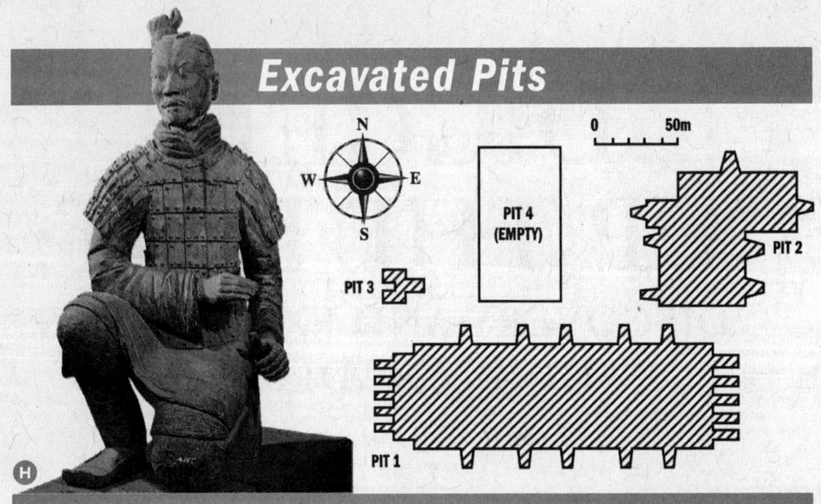

36 years later. The Chinese historian Sima Qian wrote in the *Shiji*, "Historical Records," that the emperor forced 700,000 laborers to work on his elaborate tomb.

The warriors stand guard in three pits (a fourth was found to be empty) that cover five-and-a-half acres and are 16 to 24 feet deep. The largest one contains 6,000 terra-cotta soldiers marching in military formation in 11 trenches, each as long as a football field. At the western end of the formation is a vanguard[3] of archers and bowmen. At the head of six of the trenches stand the remnants of chariots, each with four life-sized horses and 18 soldiers. The wooden chariots have largely **disintegrated**, unlike the well-preserved terra-cotta horses and men. Last come row upon row of soldiers.

Despite the enormous number of men, no two faces are alike. Their expressions display dignity, steadfastness, and intelligence. Each is tall, standing five-and-a-half to six feet high. Some people think the terra-cotta soldiers portray real-life men from the vast army of the First Emperor.

3. **vanguard** (văn'gärd): the troops that move at the head of an army.

The warriors' legs are solid columns of clay, with square-toed sandals on their feet. The hollow bodies are of coiled clay. The head and hands of each soldier were carefully molded and attached to the body in assembly-line fashion. Traces of pink, yellow, purple, blue, orange, green, brown, and black pigment show that the figures were once brightly painted. The horses were roan (reddish-brown), brown, or black with pink mouths.

The warriors' hair styles and topknots, and the tassels trimming their garments, denote their military rank. Many do not wear helmets or carry shields, a mark of bravery in battle. Their armor was probably of lacquered[4] leather; some pieces look like baseball catchers' pads. The soldiers' hands are positioned to hold weapons, but most of the weapons have disappeared. Very likely they were stolen when the pits were looted after the fall of the Qin Dynasty (the Dynasty founded by Shi Huangdi). Even so, bronze spears, halberds (a combination spear and battle-ax), swords, daggers, and about 1,400 arrowheads remain. Some of the blades are still very sharp. ❶

A second pit, only partially excavated, contains about 1,400 more soldiers. While the first pit holds mostly infantry,[5] the second has a more mobile attack force of horses and chariots. A third pit is thought to hold the high command of the army. The chariot

4. **lacquered** (lăk'ərd): covered with a glossy, protective coating.

5. **infantry:** foot soldiers.

❶ SET A PURPOSE FOR READING

Reread lines 36–58. In the chart below, note what you have learned from this passage about the excavation of the tomb.

Digging Up the Past
What I learned about the excavation of the tomb:

J SYNTHESIZE INFORMATION

Pages 339–342 contain additional information about the tomb. How does this information connect with what you learned in "The First Emperor"?

The First Emperor

↓

Digging Up the Past

↓

Logical Connections

of the Commander-in-Chief survives, with men surrounding it in protective formation. J

Covered by a wooden roof and ten feet of earth, these figures were not intended to be seen. When the pits were looted and burned, the roof fell in and damaged most of the sculptures. **Reconstruction** is a slow, delicate task. Today, a visitor to the site can walk on long wooden platforms 16 feet above the pits and gaze down with astonishment at the thousands of sculptured soldiers below.

Approximately a mile away from the pits is a gently sloping, rounded mountain covered with trees—the burial mound of the First Emperor. The four-sided, rammed—earth mound covers three quarters of a square mile and is 156 feet high. It once stood at 400 feet. Of the two great walls that enclosed the funerary park[6] only rubble remains. The perimeter[7] of the outer wall is almost four miles. Set into the strong thick walls were

6. **funerary park:** the place of a burial.
7. **perimeter:** the boundary or border of something.

reconstruction (rē'kən-strŭk'shən) *n.* the act of building or assembling again

four gates and four corner towers. Inside the walls were gardens, pavilions,[8] and a sacrificial palace, in addition to the burial mound. The burial chamber itself is still untouched, its contents as yet unknown.

Tradition based on the *Shiji* says that the emperor's body was buried in a suit of small jade pieces sewed together with gold thread and covered with a pearl and jade shroud. Also in the burial mound were bronze models of Shi Huangdi's palaces and government offices. These replicas featured such details as pearls to represent the sun and moon, and pools of mercury[9] to recreate rivers and seas.

According to the ancient Chinese, the soul of the dead continued living and therefore required all of life's necessities within the tomb. Kings especially needed many luxuries and that is why their tombs are treasure houses of jewels, gold, silver, and bronze. Ⓚ

The *Shiji* states that in order to prevent people from robbing the tomb, "Craftsmen built internal devices that would set off arrows should anyone pass through the tunnels." Because Sima Qian wrote his history a century after the death of the First Emperor, the accuracy of his statements is questionable. In fact, grave robbers did enter and loot Shi Huangdi's tomb for 30 years after the fall of the Qin Dynasty (four years after the Emperor's death). During this time, many precious relics most likely were stolen. **PAUSE & REFLECT**

8. **pavilions** (pə-vĭl′yənz): open-sided buildings used for shelter or recreation.
9. **mercury:** quicksilver; a chemical element that is a silvery liquid at room temperature.

Ⓚ SET A PURPOSE FOR READING

Reread lines 86–98. Underline the details that tell you about the emperor and his tomb, based on the *Shiji* and the other items that have been excavated so far.

PAUSE & REFLECT

Pause at line 108. How might excavations like this one encourage people to learn about the past?

L SYNTHESIZE INFORMATION
Now that you have read both selections, do you think the authors use details effectively to describe the tomb and its contents?

In 1980, additional smaller pits were discovered. One contains pottery coffins with bones of exotic birds and animals, probably from the royal zoo. Another has vessels inscribed with the words, "Belonging to the Officials in Charge of Food at Mount Li," and must be where food and sacrifices were offered to the dead emperor. Uncovered in the nearby Hall of Slumber were clothes and everyday objects for use by the soul of the Emperor. As the excavations continue, each find serves to remind us of the tremendous energy and genius of Shi Huangdi and his people. L

Elements of Nonfiction: Synthesizing Information

The first step in synthesizing information is taking notes on specific topics covered in each article. Add notes to the chart below.

READING 10D Synthesize and make logical connections between ideas within a text and across two texts representing similar or different genres. **RC-6(E)** Synthesize texts in ways that maintain meaning and logical order within a text and across texts.

What I learned about . . .	"The First Emperor"	"Digging Up the Past"
the emperor		
the tomb's history		
the tomb's excavation		

READING 10D Synthesize and make logical connections between ideas within a text and across two texts representing similar or different genres. **RC-6(E)** Synthesize texts in ways that maintain meaning and logical order within a text and across texts.

Reading Strategy: Set a Purpose for Reading

Review the chart you completed on page 345. Then, synthesize the information in it by completing the chart below.

	"The First Emperor"	"Digging Up the Past"
Main ideas		
What main ideas do the two selections share?		

How can we uncover the PAST?

Look back at the timeline you made on page 332. Now that you have read these selections about the emperor's tomb, do you have any more ideas about time periods you'd like to "uncover"? Explain.

____

____

____

Vocabulary Practice

Circle the word or phrase that is closest in meaning to each boldfaced word.

1. **preservation:** **(a)** demolition, **(b)** protection, **(c)** destruction
2. **disintegrate:** **(a)** fall apart, **(b)** combine with, **(c)** match up
3. **reconstruction:** **(a)** elimination, **(b)** cancellation, **(c)** restoration
4. **ancestor:** **(a)** older sister, **(b)** great-grandmother, **(c)** youngest daughter
5. **surpass:** **(a)** go beyond, **(b)** turn around, **(c)** fall back
6. **dedicate:** **(a)** dislike, **(b)** devote, **(c)** daydream
7. **barbarian:** **(a)** associate, **(b)** brute, **(c)** partner
8. **immortality:** **(a)** everlasting life, **(b)** short life, **(c)** temporary life
9. **archaeological:** **(a)** historical, **(b)** comical, **(c)** mystical
10. **excavation:** **(a)** an injury, **(b)** a vehicle, **(c)** a dig

Academic Vocabulary in Speaking

adequacy	authority	concept	purpose	structural

TURN AND TALK With a partner, discuss the **purpose** of an excavation and why the **authorities** often need to be involved in a major archaeological dig. Use at least one Academic Vocabulary word in your conversation. Definitions of these words are on page 321.

READING 10D Synthesize and make logical connections between ideas within a text and across two texts representing similar or different genres. **12B** Interpret factual, quantitative, or technical information presented in maps, illustrations, and graphs. **RC-6(E)** Synthesize texts in ways that maintain meaning and logical order within a text and across texts.

Texas Assessment Practice

DIRECTIONS Use "The First Emperor" and "Digging Up the Past" to answer questions 1–6.

1 According to the author of "The First Emperor," how was the emperor's tomb discovered?

- (A) Archaeologists were digging around some hills and found pottery fragments.
- (B) Peasants digging a well found pottery fragments and informed the authorities.
- (C) People building a house basement opened up the tomb.
- (D) Children playing a game found the tomb when their ball fell into a hole.

2 What was the emperor afraid of?

- (F) immortality
- (G) traveling
- (H) dying
- (J) poverty

3 What main idea do "The First Emperor" and "Digging Up the Past" share?

- (A) The emperor's tomb contained thousands of identical terra-cotta soldiers.
- (B) The emperor had the Great Wall of China built to keep out enemies.
- (C) The emperor's burial mound started out at 400 feet high, but it shrank to only 156 feet.
- (D) The emperor's tomb is a very important archaeological find.

4 Lines 15–17 in "Digging Up the Past" reinforce the idea from "The First Emperor" that the emperor was —

- (F) a tyrant
- (G) kind
- (H) afraid
- (J) poor

5 Both "The First Emperor" and "Digging Up the Past" —

- (A) give extensive details about the early history of the emperor
- (B) discuss the number of terra-cotta warriors found at the site
- (C) reveal the height of the burial mound of the emperor
- (D) refer to the *Shiji* to support the information provided

6 What is one important reason for synthesizing information found in different sources?

- (F) to avoid combining information about the same topic
- (G) to decide on one source for all information on a topic
- (H) to obtain information about many interesting topics
- (J) to gain a broad understanding of a particular topic

READING 13C Critique persuasive techniques used in media messages.

Start the Day Right!

Public Service Announcement Script

Background

"Start the Day Right!" is a script for a 30-second television advertisement about the value of eating a nutritious breakfast. It is informative and educational, but it is also **persuasive**—it aims to bring about a change in people's attitudes or behaviors.

Skill Focus: Persuasive Techniques

Though you may not realize it, you are exposed to dozens of persuasive messages every day. A magazine ad for jeans, a TV commercial for dishwashing liquid, a billboard promoting bicycle helmet safety—all of these messages try to influence you to accept a particular idea or to take a specific action. Writers use **persuasive techniques** such as logical and emotional appeals to convince their audience.

- **Logical appeals** present facts and evidence to support a **claim**, or message.
- **Emotional appeals** stir the feelings of an audience. They often use **loaded language**—words with either positive or negative connotations, or suggested meanings.

Notice persuasive techniques as you read "Start the Day Right!" Notes in the side column will prompt you to take notes about the logical and emotional appeals the script uses to support its claim.

"Start the Day Right!"	
Claim	
Logical Appeals and Evidence	
Emotional Appeals and Loaded Language	*"At most, they've eaten empty calories provided by junk foods."*

CAMPAIGN: *Start the Day Right!*

FOR: *Health for Kids and Other Important People*

TV: *30-second spot*

VIDEO	AUDIO
Camera opens on sunlit classroom with middle school students at desks. Most of them seem engaged, listening to a teacher at the front of the room, out of frame. The camera starts to focus on one boy, who looks like he is about to fall asleep.	Announcer: Every morning, in every classroom in America, students come to school without having eaten a nutritious breakfast. At most, they've eaten empty calories provided by junk foods. Maybe they haven't eaten anything at all. The result? They're tired, irritable, unable to concentrate in class. Ⓐ

SET A PURPOSE FOR READING

Read to learn what the announcement recommends for starting your day and why.

FOCUS ON FORM

"Start the Day Right!" is a **public service announcement,** a non-commercial media or print advertisement that seeks to inform the public about a social issue, such as safety, health, or education.

Ⓐ PERSUASIVE TECHNIQUES

What **claim,** or message, can you infer from this section of the script? Record your answer in the chart on page 348.

B PERSUASIVE TECHNIQUES
Public service ads often show situations that most people can identify with. Reread the Video description on this page. Do you think this sequence will be effective with television viewers? Explain.

VIDEO	AUDIO
Boy puts his head on his desk. His classmate looks over and pokes him in the arm. He looks up, a bit dazed, and realizes he is in class and should be taking notes. He shakes his head as if to wake himself, blinks his eyes a few times, and fights to stay awake. B	Announcer: Scientific studies show that the eating habits kids learn when they're young will affect them all their lives. Poor nutrition during the school years can lead to a variety of health problems in adulthood—everything from low energy and obesity to diabetes and heart disease. C

C PERSUASIVE TECHNIQUES
Reread the Audio script on this page. Circle the statement that makes a **logical appeal** about nutrition, and underline facts and evidence used to support the logical appeal. Add this information to the chart on page 348.

VIDEO	AUDIO
Camera shows same boy at kitchen table the next morning with his parents and infant brother. The boy and his parents are eating cereal; a banana is on the table.	Announcer: You wouldn't let them go out the door without their homework—don't let them go out the door without a good breakfast. No matter how rushed you are, there's always a way to fit in a nutritious breakfast—for every member of the family. For some handy tips on how to create healthy on-the-go breakfasts, visit our Web site, Health for Kids and Other Important People, at www.hkoip.org. D PAUSE & REFLECT

D PERSUASIVE TECHNIQUES
Underline the emotional appeals to persuade viewers used in the Video and Audio sections of the script.

PAUSE & REFLECT
What specific group of people does the ad seek to persuade, and how do you know?

READING 13C Critique persuasive techniques used in media messages.

Practicing Your Skills

Use the chart below to evaluate the effectiveness of the persuasive techniques in "Start the Day Right!" First, restate its claim. Then, record the strongest logical and emotional appeal included in the announcement. Finally, write a paragraph in which you discuss whether or not the public service announcement is effective.

"Start the Day Right!"

Claim:

Strongest Logical Appeal:

Strongest Emotional Appeal:

Whether the Ad Is Effective:

Academic Vocabulary in Speaking

adequacy	authority	concept	purpose	structural

READING 13C Critique persuasive techniques used in media messages.

TURN AND TALK Which **structural** features of the advertisement were more convincing: the video portion or the spoken portion? Discuss this question with a partner. Use at least two Academic Vocabulary words in your discussion. Definitions of these words are on page 321.

Texas Assessment Practice

DIRECTIONS Use "Start the Day Right!" to answer questions 1–6.

1 "Start the Day Right!" is a public service announcement because —

- (A) its purpose is to inform the public about an important issue
- (B) it tries to persuade viewers to buy a nutritious brand of cereal
- (C) its message is aimed at the parents of school-age children
- (D) it is a brief television spot with audio and video elements

2 Which of the following is the announcement's central claim?

- (F) Parents can use the Internet to find nutritious recipes.
- (G) Students who don't eat bananas will fall asleep in class.
- (H) Eating a good breakfast is more important than doing homework.
- (J) Children should eat a nutritious breakfast every day.

3 Which words from the ad are examples of loaded language?

- (A) classroom, students, breakfast
- (B) empty, junk, irritable
- (C) young, nutrition, adulthood
- (D) homework, every, family

4 The image of a student falling asleep in class is effective because —

- (F) viewers will be shocked that it could actually happen
- (G) many people can relate to the experience
- (H) the ad is aimed at teachers who struggle to engage students
- (J) it is a positive image that will appeal to many viewers

5 Which of the following is a logical appeal?

- (A) *At most, they've eaten empty calories provided by junk foods.*
- (B) *He looks up, a bit dazed, and realizes he is in class . . .*
- (C) *Poor nutrition during the school years can lead to a variety of health problems . . .*
- (D) *No matter how rushed you are, there's always a way to fit in a nutritious breakfast . . .*

6 What action do the creators of the ad want its audience to take?

- (F) try harder to stay awake in class
- (G) eat a nutritious breakfast every day
- (H) avoid being rushed in the morning
- (J) contribute recipes to a Web site

READING 11B Identify simply faulty reasoning used in persuasive texts.

Shine-n-Grow: Hair Repair That Really Works!

Advertisement

Background

"Shine-n-Grow: Hair Repair That Really Works!" is an advertisement designed to convince people to buy a particular brand of shampoo. When you read an advertisement, do not assume that all the information it presents is trustworthy. Sometimes, evidence that seems to be factual is not in reality.

Skill Focus: Faulty Reasoning

When reading any persuasive text, be sure not to confuse logic with faulty reasoning. **Logic** is correct reasoning backed by solid reasons and evidence. **Faulty reasoning** is flawed thinking. It often includes **logical fallacies,** or incorrect ways of reasoning. (When you see the word *fallacy,* think of the word *false.*) Here are four common logical fallacies that you will often see in advertising—especially dishonest advertising:

- **Hasty generalization**—a conclusion drawn from too little evidence
- **Overgeneralization**—a broad conclusion using all-or-nothing words like *every, always,* and *never*
- **Circular reasoning**—reasons that say the same thing over and over again using different words
- **False cause**—the assumption that one event caused another because it occurred earlier in time

As you read "Shine-n-Grow: Hair Repair That Really Works!" note any logical fallacies it uses to persuade you to buy its brand of shampoo. The chart below shows an example of the kind of notes you will be prompted to take.

Logical Fallacies in "Shine-n-Grow: Hair Repair That Really Works!"	
Hasty generalization	
Overgeneralization	*"Customers who use SHINE-N-GROW just once never go back to their old brands." (lines 32–34)*
Circular reasoning	
False cause	

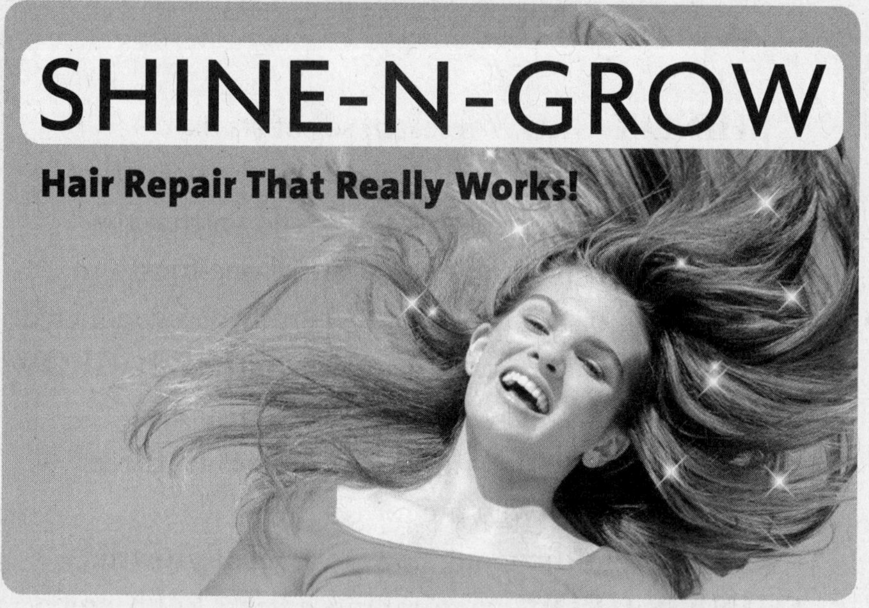
SHINE-N-GROW
Hair Repair That Really Works!

Have you ever suffered at the hands of a barber or careless hair stylist who cut your hair much shorter than you wanted? Have you ever envied your friends who have long hair? Now you no longer have to wait for weeks, months, or even years for your hair to grow back the way you want it to. With **SHINE-N-GROW** shampoo, your hair can grow faster than you ever dreamed possible. We guarantee that in no time at all, you can achieve the look everyone wants: a full head of hair that's long, healthy, and shiny. Ⓐ

SHINE-N-GROW shampoo contains a unique combination of vitamins, minerals, and hair-growth ingredients that

- directly provide nutrients to each strand of hair to help it grow
- wash away dullness and replace it with shine
- bring life back to dry or damaged hair

SET A PURPOSE FOR READING

Read the advertisement to find out why Shine-n-Grow is called "hair repair that really works"—and to decide whether you believe it.

FOCUS ON FORM

A **commercial advertisement** is intended to generate sales for a particular service or product. Commercial ads can appear almost anywhere, including on television and radio, in magazines, on billboards, on the Internet, and in movie theaters.

Ⓐ FAULTY REASONING

Reread lines 1–10 and underline the sentence that contains a **logical fallacy.** Write which type of logical fallacy it is and explain your answer. Then add the example to the chart on page 354.

SHINE-N-GROW research scientists have discovered a combination of natural ingredients that helps hair grow faster. Studies have shown that the average person's hair grows at a rate of one-fourth to one-half inch or less per month. A study was conducted to determine the effects of using the **SHINE-N-GROW** formula. The results were amazing! Test subjects reported hair growth of up to **five inches in three months!** (See our Web site for results.)

Bacteria and dirty oils slow down hair growth. **SHINE-N-GROW**'s natural ingredients kill bacteria, making it easier for hair to grow through the scalp. Thanks to our secret combination of ingredients, the cleansing value of the shampoo is far superior to that of any other products on the market. Customers who use **SHINE-N-GROW** just once never go back to their old brands. You'll love **SHINE-N-GROW,** too.

"My hair has never been so long before in my life. I've tried everything, but nothing has worked as well as **SHINE-N-GROW** ***to make my hair long and clean."***
—Susan Steinberg, actress, Brooklyn, New York

People who use **SHINE-N-GROW** shampoo have reported that their hair has grown faster and has been cleaner, shinier, and easier to manage. Happy customers agree that their hair feels better after it's been washed. "I just feel more confident," one customer said, "and I've been getting more dates ever since I started using your shampoo." B

B FAULTY REASONING
False cause is the belief that one event caused another when the events are actually unrelated. Reread lines 40–46 to find an example of false cause. Explain it in the chart below.

False Cause

SHINE-N-GROW is the only shampoo that actually speeds up hair growth while it makes your hair smooth, shiny, and spectacular! Using **SHINE-N-GROW** guarantees what no other shampoo can: that you'll always have long, shiny hair. (C)

Learn more about **SHINE-N-GROW** on our Web site at www.shine-n-grow.com, and download a coupon for 15% off your first purchase! **SHINE-N-GROW** is available now at better drugstores and supermarkets.

"My boyfriend mentioned the shine in my hair the first time I used* SHINE-N-GROW*. He really noticed how it helped my dry and damaged hair."

—Christine Martinez, nurse, Tucson, Arizona

"My last haircut was way too short, so I tried* SHINE-N-GROW*, and now my hair is long again—and clean! Finally my hair looks the way I like it."

—Roger Canter, accountant, Los Angeles, California

PAUSE & REFLECT

(C) FAULTY REASONING

Reread lines 47–51. What kind of logical fallacy is this statement? Underline words that provide clues, and write the name of the logical fallacy below. Add the example to the chart on page 354.

PAUSE & REFLECT

Explain how these testimonials influence your response to the product. How convincing are they?

After Reading

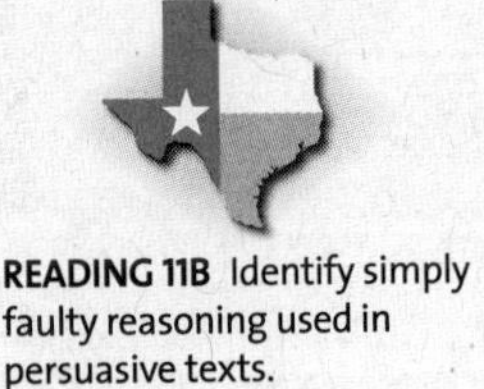

READING 11B Identify simply faulty reasoning used in persuasive texts.

Practicing Your Skills

Review your chart on page 354 and your notes for "Shine-n-Grow." Identify the ad's main claim for why people should buy the shampoo, and record it in the chart. Then complete the chart with examples of logical appeals, emotional appeals, and faulty reasoning that you found in the ad.

"Shine-n-Grow: Hair Repair That Really Works!"	
Claim	
Logical Appeals and Evidence	
Emotional Appeals and Loaded Language	
Faulty Reasoning • Hasty generalization • Overgeneralization • Circular reasoning • False cause	

Faulty Reasoning

Would you buy Shine-n-Grow shampoo? Explain your answer.

___

___

___

Academic Vocabulary in Writing

READING 11B Identify simply faulty reasoning used in persuasive texts.

adequacy	authority	concept	purpose	structural

Review the three boxed statements from happy customers on pages 356 and 357. Then write a similar statement on the lines below. Remember that your **purpose** is to convince others that Shine-n-Grow is a great product. Use at least one Academic Vocabulary word in your response. Definitions of these words are on page 321.

___

___

___

Texas Assessment Practice

DIRECTIONS Use "Shine-n-Grow: Hair Repair That Really Works!" to answer questions 1–5.

1 "Shine-n-Grow: Hair Repair That Really Works!" is a commercial advertisement because it —

- (A) is meant to be broadcast on television
- (B) seeks to sell a product to consumers
- (C) contains examples of faulty reasoning
- (D) informs the public about scientific studies

2 The advertisement's central claim is that Shine-n-Grow shampoo —

- (F) was developed by top scientists
- (G) helps the people who use it get more dates
- (H) is endorsed by both actresses and accountants
- (J) makes people's hair look shiny and grow faster

3 What action do the creators of the ad want its audience to take?

- (A) learn more about the science of clean hair
- (B) change their hair to a longer style
- (C) buy Shine-n-Grow shampoo
- (D) boycott barbers who cut hair too short

4 "A study was conducted. . . . Test subjects reported hair growth of up to five inches" is an example of —

- (F) a logical appeal with evidence
- (G) loaded language
- (H) a logical fallacy
- (J) an unsupported claim

5 According to the ad, hair grows faster with Shine-n-Grow because —

- (A) people with increased self-confidence have faster-growing hair
- (B) shiny hair grows faster than dry, damaged hair
- (C) the average person's hair grows less than half an inch each month
- (D) the shampoo washes away oils and kills bacteria to help hair grow through the scalp

READING 13C Critique persuasive techniques used in media messages.

Brain Breeze

Advertisement

Background

At a glance, the magazine advertisement that follows might seem to make a very strong case. But does it use techniques that actually prevent you from thinking for yourself? As you read "Brain Breeze," consider the effectiveness of the advertiser's techniques.

Skill Focus: Propaganda Techniques

When a persuasive text is extremely one-sided and appeals to people's emotions at the expense of reason, it can become propaganda. **Propaganda** is the attempt to convince an audience to accept ideas without considering other viewpoints. Advertisements can seldom be called propaganda. However, they sometimes use **propaganda techniques** such as the following:

- **Bandwagon appeal** takes advantage of people's desire to be part of a group or to be popular. Example: "Everyone else is doing it. Why aren't you?"
- A **stereotype** presents a narrow, fixed idea about all the members of a certain group. Example: "No politician can be trusted."
- **Name-calling** is the use of loaded words to create negative feelings about a person, group, or thing. Example: "Only a tree-hugger would try to protect that park from developers."
- **Snob appeal** sends the message that something is valuable because only "special" people appreciate it. Example: "Our jeans are designed for people who insist on quality."
- An **endorsement** is a recommendation made by someone who is well known but not necessarily an authority. For example, some celebrities use their fame to persuade you to believe in a cause, a candidate, or a product.

As you read "Brain Breeze," you'll be prompted to note examples of propaganda techniques used in the ad.

Propaganda Techniques in "Brain Breeze"	
Bandwagon Appeal	
Stereotype	
Name-calling	
Snob Appeal	*"High-achieving, high-income people appreciate the BRAIN BREEZE advantage."*
Endorsement	

The FIRST and ONLY Mental Power Booster that fits in the palm of your hand!

Uses music and air movement to sharpen your concentration and clear your clouded mind!

- **Study with No Effort!**
- **Finish Big Projects While You Relax!**
- **Feel Smarter and Less Stressed!**

Do you have a big test coming up? a big project to complete? Are you so wound up with stress that you can't think straight? Time to open the windows of your mind and let ***BRAIN BREEZE*** in!

Businesspeople, students, the guy who lives next door—everyone is looking for that competitive mental edge. Now, getting that edge is easier than you ever thought possible with ***BRAIN BREEZE***—the Mental Power Booster that uses scientifically researched music and the physics of airflow to make you more productive, less stressed—and smarter! Ⓐ

SET A PURPOSE FOR READING

Read this advertisement to find out what "Brain Breeze" is and why people might be tempted to buy it.

FOCUS ON FORM

"Brain Breeze" is a **commercial advertisement.** Its purpose is to persuade consumers to buy a particular product and to make money for the company that sells the product.

Ⓐ PROPAGANDA TECHNIQUES

Underline the sentence in this paragraph that uses a bandwagon appeal to engage readers. Add this example to the chart on page 360.

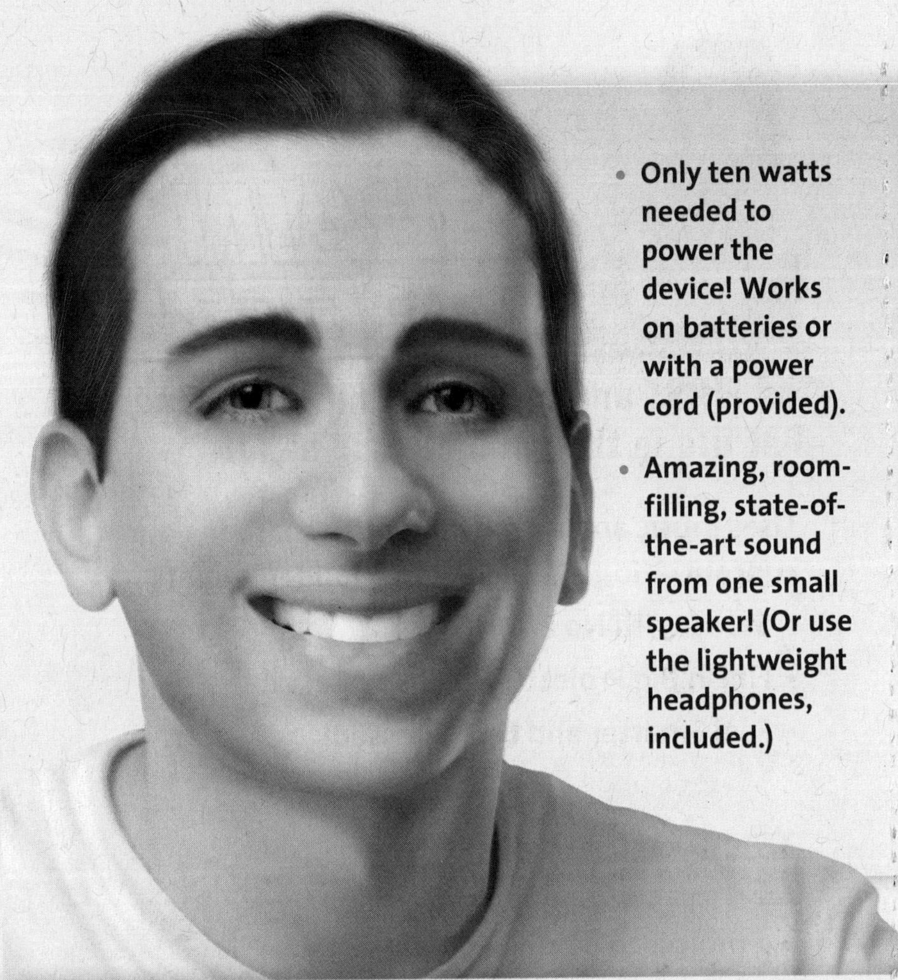

• Only ten watts needed to power the device! Works on batteries or with a power cord (provided).
• Amazing, room-filling, state-of-the-art sound from one small speaker! (Or use the lightweight headphones, included.)

B PERSUASIVE TECHNIQUES
Underline the words that the advertiser uses in this paragraph to make Brain Breeze seem like a desirable product for consumers.

BRAIN BREEZE is an amazing new technological breakthrough! It increases your concentration and keeps you at the top of your mental game while it soothes and relaxes you with a patented combination of moving air and music—all delivered from a device no larger than the palm of your hand! It's so easy to use that even the laziest couch potato can benefit. B

BRAIN BREEZE the Mental Power Booster, was developed by Professor Gary Fract of the University of Hadleyburg and was tested for effectiveness at Right Idea Labs, a scientific center for the advancement of learning. Researchers found that in a study of one hundred people aged sixteen to sixty-nine, scores

- Weighs 14.7 ounces—less than a digital camera! Completely portable! Use at home, in the library—on the road!
- Additional music tracks available through digital download. (See our Web site for details.)
- Available in five fashionable colors to reflect your lifestyle and personality: *Lively Lime, Tranquil Turquoise, Shimmering Silver, Awesome Orange, and Perky Pink.*
- Satisfaction guaranteed! You have fourteen days to try *BRAIN BREEZE*, risk free. Return it for a complete refund if you don't feel smarter and less stressed!
- 90-DAY WARRANTY. PAUSE & REFLECT

increased an average of five points overall on tests of memory and problem-solving ability among those who used ***BRAIN BREEZE***. PAUSE & REFLECT

High-achieving, high-income people appreciate the ***BRAIN BREEZE*** advantage. After using ***BRAIN BREEZE*** at his desk for two weeks, financial planner Tony Fine realized he was successfully dealing with two to three more clients per day than he had been before. "There's just something about the combination of the music and the airflow. It makes me feel more focused and organized," he says, "and I was already the most organized person I know." C

PAUSE & REFLECT
Which specific features of the Brain Breeze would appeal to you most if you were thinking about buying it? Underline three or four of the best features in this list.

PAUSE & REFLECT
Do you think including facts and evidence as well as propaganda techniques makes the ad more effective? Explain.

C PROPAGANDA TECHNIQUES
The paragraph begins with an example of **snob appeal.** What other propaganda technique can you find? Underline it in the text and then write the name of the technique below. Add this example to the chart on page 360.

THE DEVELOPMENT TEAM

Professor Gary Fract, specialist in cognitive advancement, is author of *The Effect of Music on Developing Thought*, a major study of the cognitive changes that individuals undergo when listening to certain types of music. Right Idea Labs pioneered important studies on the effects of indoor airflow on mental focus by testing thousands of participants in the Idea Room, a model controlled environment.

Find out more about *BRAIN BREEZE* at www.gobrainbreeze.com. **PAUSE & REFLECT**

PAUSE & REFLECT
Why is the information on Gary Fract included? Explain whether you find it convincing.

Emery Goodson, a medical student, had been using ***BRAIN BREEZE*** for just a week when she realized that studying no longer felt like a chore. "***BRAIN BREEZE*** is like this little treat I give myself," she says. "Now studying is something I look forward to. It's like a mental vacation, except I'm working!"

Even elderly people can enjoy the benefits of ***BRAIN BREEZE***. Studies have shown that using ***BRAIN BREEZE*** at least once a week can vastly improve people's memories. Imagine—no more forgetting relatives' birthdays!

BRAIN BREEZE comes fully programmed with thirty-nine different music tracks, each carefully

selected from a research database of music scientifically proven to enhance concentration and problem-solving abilities. Choose from five different airflow settings, from low to high, based on the complexity of the work you are doing.

For information about scientific research on ***BRAIN BREEZE,*** go to www.gobrainbreeze.com. Find out how you can try ***BRAIN BREEZE*** on a free trial basis—and order one today for overnight delivery. Don't be the last person in your office or school to act on this offer. Get the ***BRAIN BREEZE*** advantage now! D

D PROPAGANDA TECHNIQUES
What propaganda technique does the advertiser use in this paragraph? How will the audience respond to this technique? Explain.

READING 13C Critique persuasive techniques used in media messages.

Practicing Your Skills

Review your notes for "Brain Breeze." Which propaganda techniques did you find most and least effective? List examples of each of the propaganda techniques in the appropriate row of the chart below.

Propaganda Techniques in "Brain Breeze"	
Most Effective	
Least Effective	

Propaganda Techniques

Based on the advertisement, would you be interested in buying the Brain Breeze? Explain why or why not.

Academic Vocabulary in Speaking

adequacy	authority	concept	purpose	structural

READING 13C Critique persuasive techniques used in media messages.

TURN AND TALK With a partner, role-play an interview with Professor Gary Fract. One of you should ask questions about the **concept** and **purpose** of the Brain Breeze, while the other (in the role of Professor Fract) answers the questions. Use at least two Academic Vocabulary words in your interview. Definitions of these words are on page 321.

Texas Assessment Practice

DIRECTIONS Use "Brain Breeze" to answer questions 1–6.

1 The purpose of the selection "Brain Breeze" is to —

- (A) explain the relationship between music and thinking
- (B) entertain readers with the story of how the Brain Breeze was created
- (C) inform readers about the work of Right Idea Labs
- (D) persuade readers to buy the Brain Breeze device

2 What is the intended audience for the advertisement?

- (F) elderly people who forget birthdays
- (G) medical students who need to study more
- (H) anyone who wants to improve his or her memory
- (J) high-income people who can afford an expensive device

3 Which of the following is an example of name-calling?

- (A) *financial planner Tony Fine*
- (B) *even the laziest couch potato*
- (C) *BRAIN BREEZE the Mental Power Booster*
- (D) *no more forgetting relatives' birthdays!*

4 If someone buys the Brain Breeze and is not happy with it, what does the ad say the person should do?

- (F) get more information at the Web site
- (G) return it within 14 days for a full refund
- (H) exchange it for a more fashionable color
- (J) send an e-mail to Professor Gary Fract

5 Which of the following is an example of bandwagon appeal?

- (A) *Do you have a big test coming up? a big project to complete?*
- (B) *Emery Goodson, a medical student, . . . realized that studying no longer felt like a chore.*
- (C) *Airflow is silent. There's no fan and no motor, so there's nothing to make noise.*
- (D) *Don't be the last person in your office or school to act on this offer.*

6 According to the ad, how does the Brain Breeze work to help people concentrate?

- (F) It combines a controlled airflow with carefully selected music.
- (G) It simulates the environment of the Idea Room at Right Idea Labs.
- (H) It gives them memory tests and shows them how to improve their scores.
- (J) It includes lightweight headphones that can be used anywhere.

Glossary of Academic Vocabulary in English & Spanish

The Glossary of Academic Vocabulary in this section is an alphabetical list of the Academic Vocabulary words found in this textbook. Use this glossary just as you would use a dictionary—to find out the meanings of words used in your literature class, to talk about and write about literary and informational texts, and to talk about and write about concepts and topics in your other academic classes.

For each word, the glossary includes the pronunciation, syllabication, part of speech, and meaning. A Spanish version of each word and definition follows the English version. For more information about the words in this glossary, please consult a dictionary.

achieve (ə-chēv′) *v.* to bring about an intended result; accomplish
lograr *v.* obtener el resultado esperado; alcanzar un objetivo

adequacy (ad′i-kwə-sē) *n.* quality of being enough to meet a need or requirement
adecuación *s.* que cumple una necesidad o requisito

affect (a-fekt′) *v.* to produce a response or reaction
afectar *v.* producir una respuesta o una reacción

analyze (an′ə-līz′) *v.* to separate, or break into parts and examine
analizar *v.* separar o dividir en partes y examinar

appreciate (ə-prē′shē-āt) *v.* to think highly of; to recognize favorably the quality or value of
apreciar *v.* tener una buena opinión de algo o alguien; reconocer de manera favorable la calidad o el valor de algo o alguien

aspect (as′pekt′) *n.* a quality, part, or element
aspecto *s.* cualidad, parte o elemento

associations (ə-sō′sē-ā′shəns) *n.* connections or relations between thoughts, ideas, or images
asociaciones *s.* conexiones o relaciones entre pensamientos, ideas o imágenes

attitude (at′ə-to͞od′) *n.* a state of mind or feeling
actitud *s.* estado de ánimo o sentimiento

authority (ə-thôr′ə-tē) *n.* someone who is respected because of his or her knowledge about a subject
autoridad *s.* alguien que es respetado por su conocimiento acerca de un tema

characteristics (kar′ək-tər-is′tiks) *n.* features or qualities that help identify, describe, or recognize something
características *s.* rasgos o cualidades que ayudan a identificar, describir o reconocer algo

circumstance (sər′kəm-stans′) *n.* an event or condition that affects a person
circunstancia *s.* evento o condición que afecta a una persona

communicate (kə-myo͞o′ni-kāt′) *v.* to express thoughts or feelings clearly so that other people can understand them
comunicar *v.* expresar pensamientos o sentimientos de manera clara para que otras personas puedan comprenderlos

concept (kän′sept′) *n.* an idea of how something is or could be
concepto *s.* idea de cómo es o podría ser algo

conclude (kən-klo͞od′) *v.* to form an opinion about something based on evidence, experience, or reasoning
concluir *v.* formar una opinión sobre algo a partir de pruebas, experiencias o razonamientos

context (kän'tekst') *n.* words or phrases that become before and after a word in a passage that help explain its meaning
contexto *s.* palabras o frases que están antes y después de una palabra en un pasaje y que ayudan a explicar su significado

contribute (kən-trib'yo͞ot) *v.* to give or add something, such as resources or ideas
contribuir *v.* dar o añadir algo, como recursos o ideas

convey (kən-vā') *v.* to make known, express
transmitir *v.* dar a conocer, expresar

create (krē-āt') *v.* to produce something; to use imagination to invent things
crear *v.* producir algo; usar la imaginación para inventar cosas

device (di-vīs') *n.* a way of achieving a particular purpose
recurso *s.* manera de alcanzar un propósito particular

distinctive (di-stink'tiv) *adj.* unique; clearly different
distintivo *adj.* único; claramente diferente

element (el'ə-mənt) *n.* a separate, identifiable part of something
elemento *s.* parte individual e identificable de una cosa

evidence (ev'ə-dəns) *n.* specific information that supports a claim
prueba *s.* información específica que respalda una afirmación

formulate (fôr'myo͞o-lāt') *v.* to develop a plan, system, or method
formular *v.* desarrollar un plan, sistema o método

illustrate (il'ə-strāt') *v.* explain or make something clear
ilustrar *v.* explicar o aclarar algo

impact (im-pakt') *v.* to have a direct effect on
impactar *v.* tener un efecto directo en algo

implicit (im-plis'it) *adj.* not stated directly, but understood in what is expressed
implícito *adj.* no enunciado directamente, pero comprendido según lo expresado

influence (in-flo͞o'əns) *n.* ability or power to affect thought, behavior, or development
influencia *s.* capacidad o poder para afectar el pensamiento, la conducta o el desarrollo

insight (in'sīt') *n.* a clear understanding of the true nature of something
comprensión *s.* claro entendimiento de la verdadera naturaleza de algo

interact (in'tər-akt') *v.* to talk to and deal with others
interactuar *v.* hablar y tratar con otras personas

interpret (in-tər'prət) *v.* to explain the meaning of something
interpretar *v.* explicar el significado de algo

obvious (äb'vē-əs) *adj.* easy to see or understand
obvio *adj.* fácil de ver o comprender

perceive (pər-sēv') *v.* to grasp mentally; understand
percibir *v.* captar con la mente; comprender

provide (prə-vīd') *v.* to supply; make something available
proveer *v.* suministrar; hacer que algo esté disponible

purpose (pər'pəs) *n.* the goal or desired outcome of something
propósito *s.* objetivo o resultado deseado de algo

qualities (kwôl'ə-tēz) *n.* traits; distinguishing characteristics
cualidades *s.* rasgos; características distintivas

reaction (rē-ak'shən) *n.* response
reacción *s.* respuesta

refine (ri-fīn') *v.* to improve something to make it more effective
refinar *v.* mejorar algo para que sea más eficaz

relevant (rel'ə-vənt) *adj.* having a logical connection with something else
relevante *adj.* que tiene una conexión lógica con otra cosa

reliable (ri-lī'ə-bəl) *adj.* able to be trusted or accurate
confiable *adj.* que inspira confianza o es preciso

sensory (sen'ser-ē) *adj.* of or relating to the senses
sensorial *adj.* perteneciente o relativo a los sentidos

significant (sig-nif'ə-kənt) *adj.* important; meaningful
significativo *adj.* importante; coherente

specific (spə-sif'ik) *adj.* detailed, exact
específico *adj.* detallado, exacto

structural (struk'chər-al) *adj.* of or related to the manner of organization
estructural *s.* perteneciente o relativo a la disposición de partes

systematically (sis'tə-mat'ik-lē) *adv.* carried on by step-by-step procedures; orderly
sistemáticamente *adv.* paso a paso; en forma ordenada

tradition (trə-dish'ən) *n.* a set of beliefs or customs that have been handed down for generations
tradición *s.* conjunto de creencias o costumbres que se transmiten de generación en generación

Symbol	Examples	Symbol	Examples	Symbol	Examples
ă	**a**t, g**a**s	m	**m**an, see**m**	v	**v**an, sa**v**e
ā	**a**pe, d**ay**	n	**n**ight, mitte**n**	w	**w**eb, t**w**ice
ä	f**a**ther, b**a**rn	ng	si**ng**, ha**ng**er	y	**y**ard, law**y**er
âr	**fair**, **dare**	ŏ	**o**dd, n**o**t	z	**z**oo, rea**s**on
b	**b**ell, ta**b**le	ō	**o**pen, r**oa**d, gr**ow**	zh	trea**s**ure, gara**ge**
ch	**ch**in, lun**ch**	ô	**aw**ful, b**ough**t, h**o**rse	ə	**a**wake, ev**e**n, penc**i**l,
d	**d**ig, bore**d**	oi	c**oi**n, b**oy**		pil**o**t, foc**u**s
ĕ	**e**gg, t**e**n	o͝o	l**oo**k, f**u**ll	ər	p**er**form, lett**er**
ē	**e**vil, s**ee**, m**ea**l	o͞o	r**oo**t, gl**ue**, thr**ough**		
f	**f**all, lau**gh**, **ph**rase	ou	**ou**t, c**ow**	**Sounds in Foreign Words**	
g	**g**old, bi**g**	p	**p**ig, ca**p**	KH	*German* i**ch**, au**ch**;
h	**h**it, in**h**ale	r	**r**ose, sta**r**		*Scottish* lo**ch**
hw	**wh**ite, every**wh**ere	s	**s**it, fa**c**e	N	*French* e**n**tre, bo**n**, fi**n**
ĭ	**i**nch, f**i**t	sh	**sh**e, ma**sh**	œ	*French* f**eu**, c**œu**r;
ī	**i**dle, m**y**, tr**ie**d	t	**t**ap, hoppe**d**		*German* sch**ö**n
îr	**dear**, **here**	th	**th**ing, wi**th**	ü	*French* **u**tile, r**ue**;
j	**j**ar, **g**em, ba**dge**	*th*	**th**en, o**th**er		*German* gr**ü**n
k	**k**eep, **c**at, lu**ck**	ŭ	**u**p, n**u**t		
l	**l**oad, rattle	ûr	f**ur**, **ear**n, b**ir**d, w**or**m		

Stress Marks

ʹ This mark indicates that the preceding syllable receives the primary stress. For example, in the word *language*, the first syllable is stressed: lăngʹgwĭj.

ʹ This mark is used only in words in which more than one syllable is stressed. It indicates that the preceding syllable is stressed, but somewhat more weakly than the syllable receiving the primary stress. In the word *literature*, for example, the first syllable receives the primary stress, and the last syllable receives a weaker stress: lĭtʹər-ə-cho͝orʹ.

High-Frequency Word List

Would you like to build your word knowledge? If so, the word lists on the next six pages can help you. These lists contain the 600 most common words in the English language. The most common words are on the First Hundred Words list; the next most common are on the Second Hundred Words list; and so on.

Study tip: Read through these lists starting with the First Hundred Words list. For each word you don't know, make a flash card. Work through the flash cards until you can read each word quickly.

FIRST HUNDRED WORDS			
the	he	go	who
a	I	see	an
is	they	then	their
you	one	us	she
to	good	no	new
and	me	him	said
we	about	by	did
that	had	was	boy
in	if	come	three
not	some	get	down
for	up	or	work
at	her	two	put
with	do	man	were
it	when	little	before
on	so	has	just
can	my	them	long
will	very	how	here
are	all	like	other
of	would	our	old
this	any	what	take
your	been	know	cat
as	out	make	again
but	there	which	give
be	from	much	after
have	day	his	many

SECOND HUNDRED WORDS			
saw	big	may	fan
home	where	let	five
soon	am	use	read
stand	ball	these	over
box	morning	right	such
upon	live	present	way
first	four	tell	too
came	last	next	shall
girl	color	please	own
house	away	leave	most
find	red	hand	sure
because	friend	more	thing
made	pretty	why	only
could	eat	better	near
book	want	under	than
look	year	while	open
mother	white	should	kind
run	got	never	must
school	play	each	high
people	found	best	far
night	left	another	both
into	men	seem	end
say	bring	tree	also
think	wish	name	until
back	black	dear	call

THIRD HUNDRED WORDS			
ask	hat	off	fire
small	car	sister	ten
yellow	write	happy	order
show	try	once	part
goes	myself	didn't	early
clean	longer	set	fat
buy	those	round	third
thank	hold	dress	same
sleep	full	tell	love
letter	carry	wash	hear
jump	eight	start	eyes
help	sing	always	door
fly	warm	anything	clothes
don't	sit	around	through
fast	dog	close	o'clock
cold	ride	walk	second
today	hot	money	water
does	grow	turn	town
face	cut	might	took
green	seven	hard	pair
every	woman	along	now
brown	funny	bed	keep
coat	yes	fine	head
six	ate	sat	food
gave	stop	hope	yesterday

FOURTH HUNDRED WORDS			
told	yet	word	airplane
Miss	true	almost	without
father	above	thought	wear
children	still	send	Mr.
land	meet	receive	side
interest	since	pay	poor
feet	number	nothing	lost
garden	state	need	wind
done	matter	mean	Mrs.
country	line	late	learn
different	large	half	held
bad	few	fight	front
across	hit	enough	built
yard	cover	feet	family
winter	window	during	began
table	even	gone	air
story	city	hundred	young
I’m	together	week	ago
tried	sun	between	world
horse	life	change	kill
brought	street	being	ready
shoes	party	care	stay
government	suit	answer	won’t
sometimes	remember	course	paper
time	something	against	outside

FIFTH HUNDRED WORDS			
hour	grade	egg	spell
glad	brother	ground	beautiful
follow	remain	afternoon	sick
company	milk	feed	became
believe	several	boat	cry
begin	war	plan	finish
mind	able	question	catch
pass	charge	fish	floor
reach	either	return	stick
month	less	sir	great
point	train	fell	guess
rest	cost	fill	bridge
sent	evening	wood	church
talk	note	add	lady
went	past	ice	tomorrow
bank	room	chair	snow
ship	flew	watch	whom
business	office	alone	women
whole	cow	low	among
short	visit	arm	road
certain	wait	dinner	farm
fair	teacher	hair	cousin
reason	spring	service	bread
summer	picture	class	wrong
fill	bird	quite	age

SIXTH HUNDRED WORDS			
become	themselves	thousand	wife
body	herself	demand	condition
chance	idea	however	aunt
act	drop	figure	system
die	river	case	line
real	smile	increase	cause
speak	son	enjoy	marry
already	bat	rather	possible
doctor	fact	sound	supply
step	sort	eleven	pen
itself	king	music	perhaps
nine	dark	human	produce
baby	whose	court	twelve
minute	study	force	rode
ring	fear	plant	uncle
wrote	move	suppose	labor
happen	stood	law	public
appear	himself	husband	consider
heart	strong	moment	thus
swim	knew	person	least
felt	often	result	power
fourth	toward	continue	mark
I'll	wonder	price	voice
kept	twenty	serve	whether
well	important	national	president

UNIT 1

Random House, Inc.: "The School Play" by Gary Soto, from *Funny You Should Ask,* edited by David Gale. Copyright © 1992 by Gary Soto. Used by permission of Dell Publishing, a division of Random House, Inc.

Don Congdon Associates: "All Summer in a Day" by Ray Bradbury, published in *Magazine of Fantasy and Science Fiction,* March 1954. Copyright © 1954, renewed 1982 by Ray Bradbury. Reprinted by permission of Don Congdon Associates, Inc.

Carus Publishing Company: "Weather That's Out of this World!" adapted from "Getting Caught Up in Earth's Atmosphere" by Alan Dyer, from *Odyssey,* April 1993. Copyright © 1993 by Cobblestone Publishing, 30 Grove Street, Suite C, Peterborough, NH 03458. Used by permission of Carus Publishing Company.

NASA: "What Is an Orbital Space Colony?" by Al Globus. Copyright © NASA. Reprinted by courtesy of NASA.

PLAYS/Sterling Partners Inc.: "The Prince and the Pauper" by Mark Twain, adapted by Joellen Bland, from *Stage Plays from the Classics* and *PLAYS, the Drama Magazine for Young People.* Copyright © 1987, reprinted 1994 and 2005 and © 2000. Reprinted with the permission of the publisher PLAYS/Sterling Partners, Inc., P.O. Box 60016, Newton, MA 02460.

UNIT 2

Susan Bergholz Literary Services: "Eleven," from *Woman Hollering Creek* by Sandra Cisneros. Copyright © 1991 by Sandra Cisneros. Published by Vintage Books, a division of Random House, Inc., and originally in hardcover by Random House, Inc. Reprinted by permission of Susan Bergholz Literary Services, New York. All rights reserved.

Dell Publishing: "Jeremiah's Song" by Walter Dean Myers, from *Visions,* edited by Donald R. Gallo. Copyright © 1987 by Donald R. Gallo. Used by permission of Dell Publishing, a division of Random House, Inc.

Sheldon Fogelman Agency, Inc.: "Role-Playing and Discovery" by Jerry Pinkney, from *Guys Write for Guys Read* by Viking Books for Young Readers. Copyright © 2005 by Jerry Pinkney. All rights reserved. Used with permission of Sheldon Fogelman Agency, Inc.

UNIT 3

Professional Publishing Services Company: Excerpt from *The Donkey of God* by Louis Untermeyer. Copyright © 1932 by Harcourt, Brace and Company, Inc. Reprinted by arrangement with the Estate of Louis Untermeyer, Norma Anchin Untermeyer c/o Professional Publishing Services. The reprint is granted with the expressed permission by Laurence S. Untermeyer.

Hachette Children's Books: Excerpt from *In Search of Pompeii* by Giovanni Caselli. Copyright © 1999 by Giovanni Caselli. Reprinted by permission of Hachette Children's Books.

USA Today: "Italians trying to prevent a modern Pompeii" by Ellen Hale, from *USA Today,* October 21, 2003. Copyright © 2003 by USA Today. Reprinted with permission.

Brandt & Hochman Literary Agents, Inc.: "Scout's Honor," from *When I Was Your Age: Original Stories About Growing Up* by Avi. Copyright © 1996 by Avi. Reprinted by permission of Brandt & Hochman Literary Agents, Inc.

UNIT 4

Elaine Markson Agency: "Tuesday of the Other June" by Norma Fox Mazer, from *Short Takes,* selected by Elizabeth Segel. Copyright © 1986 by Norma Fox Mazer. Reprinted by permission of the Elaine Markson Agency. All rights reserved.

Scholastic Inc.: "The Problem with Bullies" by Sean Price, from *Junior Scholastic,* February 9, 2004. Copyright © 2004 by Scholastic Inc. Used by permission.

Persea Books: "The Jacket," from *The Effects of Knut Hamsun on a Fresno Boy: Recollections and Short Essays* by Gary Soto. Copyright © 1983, 2001 by Gary Soto. Reprinted by permission of Persea Books, Inc. (New York).

UNIT 5

Marian Reiner: "Message from a Caterpillar," from *Little Raccoon and Poems from the Woods* by Lilian Moore. Copyright © 1975 by Lilian Moore. All rights renewed and reserved. Used by permission of Marian Reiner.

HarperCollins: "Winter solitude" and "A field of cotton, " from *The Essential Haiku: Versions of Basho. Buson & Issa* by Robert Haas. Copyright © 1994 by Robert Haas. Reprinted by permission of HarperCollins Publishers.

Harvard University Press: "I'm Nobody! Who are You?" from *The Poems of Emily Dickinson,* Thomas H. Johnson, editor, Cambridge, Mass. Copyright © 1951, 1955, 1979, 1983 by the President and Fellows of Harvard College. Reprinted with the permission of Harvard University Press and the Trustees of Amherst College.

Farrar, Straus and Giroux: "Mooses," from *Under the North Star* by Ted Hughes. Copyright © 1981 by Ted Hughes. Used by permission of Farrar, Straus and Giroux, LLC.

UNIT 6

Scholastic Inc.: "Apollo's Tree," from *Favorite Greek Myths* by Mary Pope Osborne. Copyright © 1989 by Mary Pope Osborne. Reprinted by permission of Scholastic Inc.

Houghton Mifflin Harcourt: "Arachne" by Olivia Coolidge, from *Greek Myths.* Copyright © 1949 by Olivia E. Coolidge, copyright renewed 1977 by Olivia E. Coolidge. Used by permission of Houghton Mifflin Harcourt Publishing Company. All rights reserved.

BioKids Project: Excerpt from "Spider Webs" by BioKids Project (http://www.biokids.umich.edu) of the Animal Diversity Web (http://animaldiversity.org). Reprinted by permission of the BioKids Project.

Walker & Co.: "The Chenoo," by Joseph and James Bruchac, from *When the Chenoo Howls: Native American Tales of Terror.* Copyright © 1998 by Jospeh and James Bruchac. Reprinted by permission of Walker & Co.

UNIT 7

Kathy Haskins: Excerpt from "Matthew Henson at the Top of the World," from *Against All Opposition: Black Explorers in America* by James Haskins. Copyright © 1992 by James Haskins. Reprinted by permission of Kathy Haskins.

Scholastic, Inc.: Excerpt from *Over the Top of the World: Explorer Will Steger's Trek Across the Arctic* by Will Steger and Jon Bowermaster, published by Scholastic Press/Scholastic Inc. Copyright © 1997 by Expeditions Unlimited Inc. Used by permission.

William Morris Agency: "Up and Over the Top," from *Relating Magazine.* Copyright © by William H. Cosby, Jr. Reprinted by permission of William Morris Agency, LLC on behalf of the author.

How Stuff Works: Excerpt from "How Sign Language Works" by Jonathan Strickland, from www.howstuffworks.com. Copyright © by How Stuff Works. Reprinted by permission of How Stuff Works.

UNIT 8

National Geographic Society: Excerpt from "Super Croc" by Peter Winkler, from *National Geographic for Kids,* March 2002. Copyright © 2002 by National Geographic. Reprinted by permission of National Geographic Society.

Henry Morrison, Inc.: Excerpt from *The Tomb Robbers* by Daniel Cohen. Copyright © 1980 by Daniel Cohen. Reprinted by permission of the author and his agents, Henry Morrison, Inc.

Carus Publishing Company: Excerpt from "Digging Up the Past: Discovery and Excavation of Shi-Huangdi's Tomb" by Helen Wieman Bledsoe, adapted from *Calliope,* October 1997. Copyright © 1997 by Cobblestone Publishing, 30 Grove Street, suite C, Peterborough, NH 03458. All rights reserved. Used by permission of Carus Publishing Company.

RESOURCES

McGraw-Hill Companies, Inc.: From *Elementary Reading Instruction* by Edward Fry. Copyright © 1977 by McGraw-Hill Companies, Inc. All rights reserved. Reprinted by permission of the publisher.

The editors have made every effort to trace the ownership of all copyrighted material found in this book and to make full acknowledgment for its use. Omissions brought to our attention will be corrected in a subsequent edition.

COVER

Oystercatcher Point, Texas © Tim Fitzharris; *two boys walking a dog* © UpperCut Images/PunchStock; *background* © Kevin Schafer/Alamy Ltd.

How to Use This Book

xiii *top* © Pippa West/Shutterstock; *bottom* © Comstock Images/Jupiterimages Corporation; **xiv** © Pipa West/Shutterstock.

UNIT 1

2 © Sirko Hartmann/istockphoto.com; **6–14** © zimmytws/ShutterStock; **6** *center* © AndreyTTL/ShutterStock; **20–28** © Pippa West/ShutterStock; **20** *center* © Comstock Images/Jupiterimages Corporation; **33** NASA; **35** © Corbis; **39** NASA; **44–64** © Comstock Images/Jupiterimages Corporation; **44** *center* © James Steidl/ShutterStock; **69** © Albert L. Ortega/ WireImage/Getty Images.

UNIT 2

74 © MIXA/PunchStock; **78–82** top © istockphoto.com; **78** *center* © Jack Puccio/istockphoto.com; **82** *bottom* © Jack Puccio/istockphoto.com; **88–98** *top* © Bonnie Schupp/istockphoto.com; **88** *center* © Skip Hunt/istockphoto.com; **104–105** *top* © AbleStock.com/Jupiterimages Corporation; **104** *center* © Mia U/ShutterStock; *bottom* The Granger Collection, New York; **105** *center* The Granger Collection, New York; *bottom* © Bettmann/Corbis;**106–108** *top* © Sascha Burkard/istockphoto.com; **106** *bottom* Illustration by Dan Page; **108** *center* © GeoNova LLC.

UNIT 3

112 © David McNew/Getty Images; **116–128** © istockphoto.com; **116, 128** *center* "Cave Canem." Roman dog mosaic from the threshold of a house in Pompeii. Museo Archeologico Nazionale, Naples, Italy. © Erich Lessing/Art Resource, New York; **133** © O. Louis Mazzatenta/National Geographic Image Collection; **134–135** Illustration by Albert Lorenz/ Wilkinson Studios; **136–137** Illustration by Garry Hincks; **137** *Pliny the Younger,* Annunzio da Lurago. Facade sculpture. South Abbondio, Como, Italy. © Alinari/Art Resource, New York; **138** © Scala/Art Resource, New York; **144–156** © Donald R. Swartz/ShutterStock; **144** *center* © ALXR/ShutterStock; **147** *bottom* © Tom Schierlitz/Stone/Getty Images; **161** © Co Rentmeester Inc./Getty Images; **162** Photo by Scott B. Rosen/Bill Smith Studio; **163** *top* Photo by Scott B. Rosen/Bill Smith Studio; *bottom* © Al Franklin/Corbis.

UNIT 4

166 © Eugene Ivanov/ShutterStock; **170–182** *top* © BananaStock/Jupiterimages Corporation; **170** *center* © Sergey Dolgikh/ShutterStock; **181** *bottom* © BananaStock/Jupiterimages Corporation; **187** © James Yang; **194–198** *top* © Stephen Aaron Rees/ShutterStock; **194** *center* © Pablo Eder/ShutterStock.

UNIT 5

202 © Matthew Hertel/istockphoto.com; **206–210** *top* © Comstock/Jupiterimages Corporation; **206** *center* © James Steidl/ istockphoto.com; **208** *center* © KennStilger47/ShutterStock; **216–218** *top* © Photos.com/Jupiterimages Corporation; **216** *center* © Robin Arnold/istockphoto.com; **217** *center* © Photos.com/Jupiterimages Corporation; **218** *center* © Laurin Rinder/ShutterStock; **224–227** *top* © Alexander Sysolyatin/ShutterStock; **224** *center* © Ernesto Lopez Albert/ShutterStock; **225** *center* © Michiel de Boer/ShutterStock; **226** *center* © Mats/ShutterStock.

UNIT 6

230 © 20th Century Fox/Photofest; **234–242** *top* © dabjola/ShutterStock; **234** *center* © Rusiana Stovner/ShutterStock; **238** *center* © Andy Crawford/Dorling Kindersley/Getty Images; **239** *center* © Alistair Dove/Alamy Ltd.; **247** © Anselm Spring/Stone/Getty Images; **248** *top* © Lothar Lenz/zefa/Corbis; *center* © Jerry Young/Dorling Kindersley; *bottom* © Adam Jones/Photo Researchers, Inc.; **249** © Theo Allofs/Stone/Getty Images; **250** *top* © Nancy Rotenberg/Animals Animals. All rights reserved; *bottom* © Hans Pfletschinger/Peter Arnold, Inc.; **251** © Kim Taylor/naturepl.com; **256–262** © Fotocrisis/ ShutterStock; **256** *center* © VEER Antonino Barbagallo/Photonica/Getty Images; **267** © GeoNova LLC.

UNIT 7

272 © Brian Bahr/Getty Images; **276–286** *top* © Armin Rose/ShutterStock; **276** *center* © Bettmann/Corbis; **283** *bottom* © Stockbyte/Getty Images; **291** © The Will Steger Foundation/willsteger.com; **296** © Lynn Goldsmith/Corbis; **306** *center* © Bettmann/Corbis; **309** *bottom* Library of Congress, Prints and Photographs Division [LC-USZ62-13123]; **315–316** Illustrations by Eric Larsen, Portland, Oregon.

UNIT 8

320 © Martin Ray Philbert/Stone/Getty Images; **324** © GeoNova LLC; **326** *left* © Reuters/Corbis; *right* © Scott Rothstein/ShutterStock; **327** Illustration by Precision Graphics; **335** © GeoNova LLC; **340** *left* © akg-images, London; *right* Illustration by Precision Graphics; **342, 344** © O. Louis Mazzatenta/National Geographic Image Collection; **349–351** Illustrations by Anne Kobayashi; **355** © Allana Wesley White/Corbis; **361–365** Illustrations by Boris Zlotsky.